THE BIRTH OF CAPITALISM

The Future of World Capitalism
Series editors: Radhika Desai and Alan Freeman

The world is undergoing a major realignment. The 2008 financial crash and ensuing recession, China's unremitting economic advance, and the uprisings in the Middle East, are laying to rest all dreams of an 'American Century'. This key moment in history makes weighty intellectual demands on all who wish to understand and shape the future.

Theoretical debate has been derailed, and critical thinking stifled, by apologetic and superficial ideas with almost no explanatory value, 'globalization' being only the best known. Academic political economy has failed to anticipate the key events now shaping the world, and offers few useful insights on how to react to them.

The Future of World Capitalism series will foster intellectual renewal, restoring the radical heritage that gave us the international labour movement, the women's movement, classical Marxism, and the great revolutions of the twentieth century. It will unite them with new thinking inspired by modern struggles for civil rights, social justice, sustainability, and peace, giving theoretical expression to the voices of change of the twenty-first century.

Drawing on an international set of authors, and a world-wide readership, combining rigour with accessibility and relevance, this series will set a reference standard for critical publishing.

Also available:

Remaking Scarcity:
From Capitalist Inefficiency to Economic Democracy
Costas Panayotakis

The Birth of Capitalism

A Twenty-First-Century Perspective

Henry Heller

PlutoPress
www.plutobooks.com

Fernwood Publishing
HALIFAX & WINNIPEG
www.fernwoodpublishing.ca

First published 2011 by Pluto Press
345 Archway Road, London N6 5AA
www.plutobooks.com

Distributed in the United States of America exclusively by
Palgrave Macmillan, a division of St. Martin's Press LLC,
175 Fifth Avenue, New York, NY 10010

Published in Canada by Fernwood Publishing
32 Oceanvista Lane, Black Point, Nova Scotia, B0J 1B0
and 748 Broadway Avenue, Winnipeg, MB R3G 0X3
www.fernwoodpublishing.ca

Fernwood Publishing Company Limited gratefully acknowledges the financial support of
the Government of Canada through the Canada Book Fund, the Canada Council for the
Arts, the Nova Scotia Department of Tourism and Culture and the Province of Manitoba,
through the Book Publishing Tax Credit, for our publishing program.

Library and Archives Canada Cataloguing in Publication
 Heller, Henry, 1938-
      The birth of capitalism : a twenty-first century perspective / Henry Heller.
 (The future of world capitalism)
 ISBN 978-1-55266-452-0
      1. Capitalism--History. I. Title. II. Series: Future of world capitalism
 (Winnipeg, Man.)
 HB501.H439 2011   330.12'2   C2011-902371-7

British Library Cataloguing in Publication Data
A catalogue record for this book is available from the British Library

ISBN   978 0 7453 2960 4 Hardback
ISBN   978 0 7453 2959 8 Paperback (Pluto Press)
ISBN   978 1 55266 452 0 Paperback (Fernwood)

Library of Congress Cataloging in Publication Data applied for

This book is printed on paper suitable for recycling and made from fully managed and
sustained forest sources. Logging, pulping and manufacturing processes are expected to
conform to the environmental standards of the country of origin.

10 9 8 7 6 5 4 3 2 1

Designed and produced for Pluto Press by Curran Publishing Services, Norwich, UK
Simultaneously printed digitally by CPI Antony Rowe, Chippenham, UK and
Edwards Bros in the United States of America

For Rebecca and David

CONTENTS

PREFACE AND ACKNOWLEDGEMENTS

The current crisis affects a system which today is approximately 500 years old. The forward motion of the capitalist system is founded on the continued prospect of future profits and economic growth. Yet the way ahead is obstructed by many difficulties: low rates of profit and over-accumulation of capital; under-consumption and insufficient demand; the breakdown of the system of global finance; the prospect of energy shortage and acute symptoms of environmental crisis; and a crisis of world governability. Weighed down by these serious problems, the production of profits and growth in the future within the existing system has been thrown into doubt. The multiplicity and depth of the difficulties burdening contemporary capitalism poses the question of whether the system can stabilize and continue to reproduce itself, whether humanity is on the threshold of a momentous transition to socialism, or whether we face an unending stagnation and even a descent into ruin.

If we want to understand the present, and act effectively within it, knowledge of the past is more necessary than ever. The fall into the credit crunch and deep economic crisis was not only completely unexpected by most politicians but unpredicted by most economists. Events of this nature have not been seen for over 80 years – longer than the memory of nearly everyone alive today. Commentator after commentator has noted that the narrow focus of today's economists left most of them intellectually floundering in the face of such momentous developments. A historical perspective is not, therefore something of interest only to academic researchers and antiquarians. To understand what is happening now, we have to understand how we got here. For this reason, this book returns to a discussion that has been going on for some time among historians, but which the general public at this point needs to know more about – the birth of capitalism, or as it is generally posed, the transition from feudalism to capitalism.

The aim of this book is to explain the background and terms of this vigorous debate, to reassess and shed more light on it, and bring it to the attention of a more general readership. This book is suitable for a general reader who wishes to understand both where capitalism came from, and the key historical debates about its origins. But it is also designed to ensure that a new generation of students and scholars – beset with crisis – look upon this controversy with fresh eyes and a new sense of its significance.

The Future of Capitalism series calls for a fresh look at the fundamental issues and phenomena of world history. It seeks a reconsideration of the concepts and theories required to comprehend the present stage of world development. This work contributes to the effort by re-examining the debate on the transition from feudalism to capitalism in a way that throws fresh light on capitalism's contribution to world development, its current crisis and future prospects. As the greatest crisis of capitalism since the Great Depression unfolds, and the power of emerging capitalist states challenges the centuries-old dominance of the West, a fresh and critical examination of this often Eurocentric debate is necessary to understand the current historic conjuncture.

Two things have inspired the writing of this work. In the first place I have been studying early modern history for nearly 50 years. It is a field of scholarship which is interesting from a great variety of perspectives, including the history of art, music and science. Examining and analyzing the transition question offers the opportunity of summing up the scholarship of this period from a particularly important and challenging perspective. Indeed, the concrete understanding of the period that I bring to bear represents an important qualification for this task.

Politics has likewise motivated my undertaking this book. I have been passionately interested in politics since I was a boy, and I still regard political awareness as essential to the full development of a human personality. In my view history as a discipline can only be a dialogue between the political present and the past. My commitment to politics only became deeper as a result of my engagement with Marxism and the national liberation struggles in the underdeveloped world dating from the anti-war movement of the 1960s and 1970s. Indeed, the latter helped me to overcome the Eurocentric bias of much of my primary research and published scholarship. It was at that time that I began to read the classic works on the transition by Maurice Dobb and Rodney Hilton, as well as the seminal new works of Immanuel Wallerstein, Robert Brenner and Perry Anderson, which were products of the political turmoil of the period. Indeed, my sense of the primacy of politics colours my understanding of capitalism's beginnings. Capitalism is certainly a mode of production, but it should not be looked upon in merely economic terms. One of the motivations behind this work is to advance the idea that capitalism must be understood as a political as well as an economic entity. Therefore this book takes issue with what I regard as the excessively economistic approach of Robert Brenner and his followers, who ironically go by the name of Political Marxists.

From its inception 65 years ago, the debate on the transition was motivated by the sense that the capitalist system is in crisis, and that gaining a historic perspective on its origins and trajectory was important. In the early years of the twenty-first century the sense of capitalism in crisis has deepened. At the same time the debate on the capitalist transition has been illuminated by a growing understanding of world history. Given my knowledge of the early modern period in both Europe and the rest of the world and my growing comprehension of the Marxist view of history, it seemed appropriate for me to undertake the demanding task of carefully tying together the relationship between the concrete facts of history and Marxist theory in a way that does both justice.

In writing this work I owe special thanks to Radhika Desai, whose many theoretical and editorial suggestions have proved invaluable. I would also like to express my appreciation for the cultural theory and post-colonial groups at the University of Manitoba. My discussions with them have forced me to understand the theoretical foundations of my own Marxism more deeply. I am indebted to the patience and careful copy-editing of Susan Curran and proofreading of Chris Carr. Thanks also to my wife, Joanne Inglis, for help with the editorial preparation of the manuscript.

INTRODUCTION: PROBLEMS AND METHODS

The focus of this work is the long evolution from feudalism to capitalism, the most debated and best known among transitions from one mode of production to another. It took 500 years for this transition to unfold in Europe, and it is still taking place in Asia, Africa and Latin America. This transformation began in Europe with the crisis of the feudal system in the fourteenth century and continued until the Industrial Revolution (1780–1850). In this book, I consider this European-centred transition, but do not limit the discussion to Europe. As Marx emphasized, the birth of capitalist relations of production witnessed the simultaneous genesis of the world market. Moreover, from the perspective of the twenty-first century in which capitalist relations of production have spread everywhere and in which multiple centres of accumulation exist, a perspective limited to Europe, or worse, only to England (as it is in the work of some writers on the transition), would simply be parochial.

Bringing this debate up to date is not merely an academic matter. Positions taken on the chief issues in debate will inform responses to the current crisis of capitalism. At the same time all the protagonists in the controversy have agreed that capitalism cannot be understood without understanding its history. Capitalism may be a forward-looking system which functions on the basis of the continuing expectation of profit. But it is also a system based in a historically evolving set of relations – including sale of wage labour and production and circulation of commodities in markets. These operate within a network of financial, legal-political and cultural institutions which are indispensable to their function. Profits emerge out of the particular way in which this system channels the forces of production.

The articulated relationship between the forces of production and the social relations of production of a given stage of world history is called by Marxists a 'mode of production'. In the Marxist conception, there are five or six modes of production: hunting and gathering, slavery, feudalism, capitalism and socialism. While the historical relationship of these different modes and the existence of the sixth or Asian mode of production are in dispute, it is generally accepted that capitalism organized around profit-making must be understood as a system in terms of the relationship between its various parts

– economic, political and cultural. It must also be understood temporally. These parts come together into a profit-generating system or mode of production through a concrete historical process.

As I have noted capitalism is dynamic, fundamentally oriented toward the future, and the fact that today its intellectual apologists are having difficulty envisaging its future is symptomatically quite important. The profits that continue to drive it forward have depended on the existence of private property, the exploitation of what is not private property as a free good, the availability of an intellectually as well as materially alienated work force and the existence of the sovereign territorial state. The territorial state provided an essential political framework within which private capitals sustained by capitalist relations of production emerged and were integrated into a system. In other words markets were created politically as well as economically. It is a central thesis of this book that markets, too, have a real history. In any case it is important that the continued existence of such preconditions for profit-making are today imperilled, and this requires that we try to understand how the elements that compose capitalism came into existence, and how they came to constitute a system.

The scope of this study may seem daunting at first. However, my task here is concerned not primarily with the concrete details of this great historical transformation but with assessing the critical debates that it prompted between Marxist luminaries such as Maurice Dobb, Paul Sweezy, Rodney Hilton, Eric Hobsbawm, Robert Brenner, Immanuel Wallerstein, Perry Anderson, Terence J. Byres and Giovanni Arrighi. While their works are indeed great historical labours in their own right, the topics and issues highlighted by them have helped to organize the historical content of the present narrative. In particular, Brenner's own enormous, wide-ranging and controversial scholarship, extending from late medieval Europe to early modern England, Holland and China, and that of his followers – Ellen Wood, Benno Teschke and George Comninel – bound together loosely in the school of Political Marxism, is one of the most important threads connecting this work.

When I say that that these elements of profit-making were historically constituted I mean that they were neither determined in advance nor did they occur by chance. From the beginning I insist that the initial encounter between the owners of money and proletarians was not predetermined and might not have happened at all. On the other hand, I argue that this historical conjuncture did not come about at a throw of the dice. History is not determined but it is not entirely the result of chance either. The responsibility of the historian is to elicit as well as possible what concrete and determinate lines of causation contributed to the emergence of capitalism. Understanding the balance between determinacy and indeterminacy is critical to gaining a perspective on the important factors at play in the past as well as in the current crisis.

This introduction begins by briefly recalling the history of the largely Marxist scholarship on the origins of capitalism, noting its close connection to contemporary politics and crises. It goes on to give an overview of the book and its argument. It concludes with a consideration of Eurocentrism, a position which, while always problematic both morally and intellectually, has simply been rendered obsolete by the strength of capitalist development far beyond the shores of Europe and its offshoots, and even beyond Japan. Capitalism undoubtedly broke through in Europe. But we assert the existence of a non-European proto-capitalism, and accordingly reject an exclusive Anglocentric or Western European approach to capitalist origins, and insist on the historically late appearance of European economic superiority based on capitalism.

CAPITALIST ORIGINS AND CRISES

My discussion focuses initially on the rich and contentious literature on the transition to capitalism that emerged in the wake of Maurice Dobb's *Studies in the Development of Capitalism*, published soon after the Second World War ended.[1] For all the writers involved in this discussion, understanding capitalism's origins was always a political undertaking, and for most scholars engaged in the enterprise it was an endeavour which sought to look beyond capitalism toward the establishment of a humane, equal and freer order – in other words, socialism. The catastrophe of the two great wars and the Great Depression focused the attention of Dobb on the transition question because of his sense that the capitalist system had entered into deep, possibly terminal, crisis. The result was an outline of a history of capitalism as a unified system with a beginning, middle and possible end. For him, the transition from feudalism to capitalism became the only clear and well-documented example of a passage from one mode of production to another.[2] And understanding it could help to illuminate possibilities beyond capitalism.

Though Dobb's immediate expectations of the imminent end of capitalism were disappointed as capitalism stabilized after the war, the publication of his work provoked considerable debate in the 1950s, and a second and revised edition of *Studies in the Development of Capitalism* appeared in 1963.[3] The political upheavals of the 1960s and economic crises of the 1970s produced a second round of debate on the transition, whose fruits included Hilton's review of the initial debate and influential new works by Immanuel Wallerstein, Perry Anderson and Robert Brenner.[4]

Today, 65 years after Dobb wrote, Marxist scholarship stands at a particularly interesting conjuncture. On the one hand the historic hegemony of Western capitalism over the rest of the world is in serious doubt as rival centres of capitalist accumulation appear in China, India and other 'emerging economies' and link up with one another.[5] On the other, scepticism about the future of capitalism is more widespread than in Dobb's time, its links to economic growth are questioned, and ecological and energy crises loom. A fresh round of scholarly re-examination of capitalism's origins and of the transition from the feudal to the capitalist mode of production is taking place.[6] The French medieval historian Guy Bois, for example, has explicitly compared the deeper causes of the crisis with those that lay behind the crisis of feudalism. He points out that the current crisis, like that of feudalism, is marked by ongoing large-scale unemployment, growing insecurity, violence, social marginalization and outbursts of irrationality egged on by the upper classes.[7]

ECONOMISM AND EUROCENTRISM

Rich though it was, the literature on the transition from Dobb onwards took both an economistic and a Eurocentric view of capitalism's origins, conceiving capitalism as a purely economic system and either assuming it to be a quintessentially European phenomenon or defining it in ways that left the distinctiveness of capitalism outside Europe out of account. These views are historically incorrect and impede a political and suitably universal understanding of capitalism. Both mar the otherwise brilliant contributions of Brenner.

While Brenner broke new ground in stressing the importance of class struggle and the significance of agrarian capitalism in the transition, we argue that he disregarded the importance of the state as the ultimate linchpin of capitalism. For him, the extraction of relative surplus value – increases in investment increasing labour's productivity and therefore surplus value and reducing the value of labour power by lowering of the value of goods consumed by workers – and the competitive markets that made it an imperative were capitalism's defining features. However, as we show, they emerged only as the result of a long process which involved the state as much as markets. Brenner's economism also leads to an anachronistic understanding of the capitalist market and downplays the significance of primitive accumulation and absolute exploitation on a world scale. The undeniable rising productivity of social labour highlighted by Brenner leads him to devalue and ignore the indispensable accumulation of capital that precedes it. Such economism cannot understand capitalism's historic power and its vulnerabilities, which are political.

Economism also leads Brenner and his school to wrongly dismiss the importance of state-backed colonialism and to assume the West's economic superiority *ab initio*. This school also downplays the role of the early modern revolutions in the progress of capitalism, regarding them at best as icing on the cake of an already established capitalism, or at worst as non-capitalist events. As we show, the revolutionary transformation of the state was the critical step in the transition to capitalism.

Brenner's Eurocentrism is related to this minimizing of the importance of revolution in the past and future. He argues that while rural petty producers played a revolutionary role in undermining feudalism in the fourteenth century, thereafter they became economically timid or defensive. The initiative in starting capitalism was taken instead by landlords. We argue, however, that once the constraints of feudalism were removed, an upper layer of petty producers played an aggressive social and economic role in the inception of agrarian as well as early industrial capitalism. Petty producers also played a critical role as the mass base of revolutionary change. It is important to recognize this because it relates to the possibilities of peasant and worker resistance to imperialism in the under-developed world, and the historical importance of the political mobilization of the mass of humanity in the transition not only from feudalism to capitalism, but potentially from capitalism to socialism.

AN ALTERNATIVE READING

This book provides a more complex and nuanced understanding of capitalism's origins. At the birth of capitalism the West was geographically, economically and culturally marginal in the world. In the Middle East, China, Japan and India, the forces of production were equally or more developed. The breakthrough toward capitalism in Europe was a result of a prolonged period of class conflict between the feudal ruling classes and peasants and artisans, during which the balance swung sufficiently away from the former to permit capitalism to emerge. In similar conflicts in China, Japan, India and the Middle East, however, the balance of power remained, at this time, sufficiently in favour of the ruling classes to prevent rupture. And though capitalism's productive superiority over the labour-intensive economy of, say, China was visible by the late seventeenth century, it did not become globally significant until after 1800.

Within Western countries, dispossession of producers from the means of production and the increase and intensification of work – in other words, primitive accumulation and absolute surplus value, both backed by the state – played their part in capitalism's development as much as markets and technical improvements. Abroad, the growing divergence in the economic fortunes of the West and the rest was compounded by aggressive state-sponsored Western conquest, pillage and appropriation of the wealth, land, labour and techniques of non-Western societies as well as the resulting foreclosure of the possibility of an early capitalist breakthrough through Western political domination.

The decline of feudalism in Western Europe began with the series of late medieval revolts of peasants and craftspeople prompted by economic crisis. The royal territorial states which initially emerged to guarantee the continued class rule of the landlords against the upsurge of producers formed a critical political bridge between feudalism and capitalism. By the sixteenth century the balance of class forces forced these states to provide an arena for the generalization and integration of capitalist relations of production, while the breakdown of the feudal order allowed the differentiation of producers into capitalists and wage workers, a process which was greatly aided by the state in England, and to a lesser degree on the Continent. Expansion of production within this new economic order necessitated the creation of home and world markets in which commodities, which was the form products took, could be exchanged. Once again, the state backed the process. Thus, from its beginnings, capitalist development was not merely market-driven. Rather, markets emerged at the national level only as a result of prolonged political and class conflicts, and were established by the coercive, legal and political machinery of the early modern absolutist states which gradually cleared obstacles to them. The bourgeois political and social revolutions in Holland, England and France overthrew the feudal ruling classes of these territorial states and then harnessed them to complete the development of markets and the full entry of capital into agriculture and manufacturing. The revolutionaries, like the protagonists of the late medieval revolts, were petty producers led by the capitalist class that had emerged from their ranks. The resulting development of export-oriented manufacturing combined with colonialism, the slave trade and the plantation-slave system guided by the mercantilist state proved crucial not only to facilitating ongoing capital accumulation but also to overcoming Europe's backward and peripheral global position by establishing first military/political and later economic superiority over the non-European world.

It is now acknowledged that capitalism's development cannot be understood without comprehending the intrinsic importance of the state.[8] It is only by denying the centrality of the state's role in the development of capitalism in Western Europe that a false contrast is set up between this allegedly 'classic' European route, conceived in a largely economistic fashion, and the ways in which capitalism developed elsewhere. The fact is that once under way, capitalism and imperialism threatened other political and social formations. Many places – initially in the immediate periphery of the core Western states, for example in Scotland, Prussia and Russia, but later farther afield, for example in Japan, South Korea and Taiwan – eventually witnessed capitalisms imposed from above, by the state. In these processes, still ongoing in the early twenty-first century, capitalist landlords and/or the state undoubtedly assumed the initiative to combat the adverse consequences of uneven development by engaging in forms of combined development. Combined and uneven development entailed a simultaneous struggle to overcome the barriers to development posed by the capitalism of more advanced states and the backwardness of the traditional economic sectors by far-reaching state intervention. This meant that rather than repeating the stages of previous capitalist development, latecomers sought to absorb earlier advances and used them to emerge in the forefront of capitalist development and profit-making. The role of politics and the state – already large in the development of early capitalism – loomed even larger in these later instances.

PLAN OF THE BOOK

Chapter 1 addresses the decline of feudalism in the West and its resilience elsewhere. Chapters 2 and 3 stress the historical significance of relative surplus value and capitalist markets. All three stress the decisive importance of the state in the processes they discuss. Chapter 2 discusses early modern capitalism in Italy – where, after all, capitalist accumulation, albeit focused on commerce and finance, began – and in Germany and France, where it has been denied or ignored.

Capitalist activity, we argue, sprouted in the late medieval and early modern periods across Western Europe in Italy, Germany, the Netherlands, France and even Spain. Understanding where capitalism developed further, and where such early development was interrupted, also demonstrates the existence of a specifically French route to capitalism which led to the revolution of 1789. Chapter 3 is devoted to a discussion of the origins of English capitalism but moves away from an exclusive preoccupation with England.

Chapter 4 treats the capitalist revolutions in Holland, England and France. It explains why bourgeois revolutions were critical to the further development of capitalism in Europe. They transformed the early modern state into an explicitly capitalist entity. Contrary to the view that the merchant capitalism of early modern Holland remained dependent on the feudal mode of production, we argue that not only did Holland develop an authentic agricultural capitalism, it also experienced a capitalist revolution.

Too much of the necessarily comparative historical analysis of the origins of capitalism has led to insufficiently grounded and too hasty generalization from particular historical situations, usually European. Being at least roughly chronological, the early chapters of this book are necessarily focused on European history. However, the later discussions of capitalist transitions beyond the West European core – in Scotland, the United States, Prussia, Japan, Russia, Japan, Korea, Taiwan and beyond – are anticipated in the non-economistic and non-Eurocentric emphasis of the early chapters. In this wider framework, comparative historical analysis is indispensable. As Terence Byres, who has done so much to make the comparative method in studying capitalism more authentically universal, suggests, 'it is in a comparative perspective that one may reach for possible lines of causality. Comparison has the power to widen the range of possible hypotheses. Comparison can ... prevent analytical closure ... by keeping one alive to ... diversity and historical contingency ....'[9]

The transitions considered in the first four chapters, as well as that in the United States, are regarded as instances of 'capitalism from below', originating among small-scale producers. The fifth chapter focuses particularly on the role of the state where the uneven development of capitalism elicited a response in the form of combined or state-directed capitalisms. It also discusses the role of the state in the fostering of colonialism and slavery, which were critical to overcoming the global marginality of the capitalist West and enabling it to impose itself politically, and eventually economically, over so much of the world, inhibiting capitalist development there. The final two chapters complete the narrative by discussing capital's entry into manufacturing during the Industrial Revolution and by looking at the significance of capitalism in the context of world history. Though vulgar technological determinism regards the Industrial Revolution as decisive to the rise of the West, it was much less so than the birth of capitalism in the sixteenth century. Its full productive power could only reveal itself thanks to the slow accumulation of capital which began three centuries earlier. The final chapter completes the widening of the focus away from Western Europe and England to the broader context of Eurasian and global history, returning to the question of Eurocentrism as well as considering the future prospects of capitalism.

THE ARGUMENT

The overall argument of the work is a fourfold one: that capitalist development was drawn out over a long period, three centuries and counting; that class struggle and changes in the relations of production were historically decisive in their emergence and evolution; that home and world markets developed simultaneously; and that the territorial state was, and remains, an integral component of capitalism.

In the first place, the emergence of capitalism as an apparently self-sustaining 'economic' system, separated from politics, was the consequence of a centuries-long process in which, *pace* Brenner, political coercion played a major role. Autonomous competitive markets only emerged after a long apprenticeship under the protection of the state. Second, the class struggle between feudal landlords and urban and rural producers in the late Middle Ages was crucial to the decline of the feudal mode of production in the West in contrast to the fate of feudalism in states located elsewhere. Socially and economically ambitious, the upper stratum of this group of small-scale producers played the key role in the development of capitalism from the late fifteenth century. It was this proto-capitalist element which was critically important to the emergence of agrarian capitalism and the initial revolutionizing of the means of production in manufacture in a capitalist direction. But class struggle did not cease in the aftermath of the late medieval uprisings, as Brenner would have it. Rather it proved critical to the further development of the capitalist mode of production in the early modern period. The small producers challenged landlord power when necessary and formed the shock troops of the early bourgeois revolutions against feudal absolutism in Holland, England and France. It was from their midst that the bourgeoisie emerged. It was from the bottom layers of these same petty producers that the wage-earning class slowly formed, pushed downward by the more successful small producers.

The development of productive means to enhance the extraction of relative surplus value and the ultimate emergence of the law of value in the competitive market were what distinguished capitalism from feudal systems in Europe and elsewhere. But an overarching theme in this work is that the emergence of these distinctive features of capitalism was a slow process involving force as much as the market. Capitalism's economic superiority did not register economically before the late seventeenth century, and did not become decisive in terms of its global economic and political impact until the beginning of the nineteenth century. It was only at that time that technologically advanced weapons of war deployed against India and China, and machine-made and chemically finished textiles, made possible the historic reversal of the longstanding European balance of payments deficit with Asia. Accordingly, we see the significance of the extraction of relative surplus value as making itself felt only little by little, and as such only amplifying the effects of primitive accumulation and the generation of absolute surplus value in the early phases of capitalism.

The importance of competitive markets and the extraction of relative surplus value in the early development of capitalism have been exaggerated, while the significance of force and the assertion of state power have largely been overlooked. In other words, the way for the extraction of relative surplus value and competitive markets was opened by political processes. This makes it possible to agree with those scholars who argue against a too Eurocentric view of early modern history, which assumes an immediate and manifest economic triumph of the new capitalist mode of production from its first appearance. It is a basic contention of this account that its emergence took centuries and its victory came late. It was not until the Industrial Revolution that Western capitalism forged ahead of the economies of the rest of the world. The Great Divergence between the capitalist West and the rest of the world came after 1800, not in 1500.

Aside from the emergence of capitalist relations of production, this work argues that the simultaneous emergence of the world market triggered processes of uneven and combined development which became an independent factor in capitalism's emergence. They came into play in an effort to counter the relative backwardness of

Western Europe in relation to Asia. Even within Europe, capitalism was not only not a uniquely English phenomenon, it was based on uneven and combined development across different countries. This led to the emergence of a hierarchy of territorial states and rival colonialisms in the early modern period.

The reduced role of competitive markets in driving the early development of capitalism in our account goes with a fourth major argument: that the territorial state was an intrinsic part of the process. Capitalism was not simply about the development of capitalist relations of production or competitive markets. Capitalism arose dialectically within the cradle of a still feudal state. Nations like Italy and Germany that failed to become unified states saw their nascent capitalist development arrested, while capitalism was consolidated in Holland, France and England by the constitution of a territorial state. The gradual emergence of capitalist markets and capitalist relations of production was made possible by the state. The critically important process of primitive accumulation was assisted by the political and legal force of the state at the local and eventually at the national level. The emergence of overseas markets and colonialism were based on the support of the state. The important role of the state in early capitalism is reflected in the importance of mercantilism, the phenomenon of state-driven combined and uneven development, and in the modern period the role of the developmental capitalist state in Prussia, Russia, Japan, Korea, Taiwan, Brazil, India and China. Given the critical role of the state, its class nature and the importance of political and social revolution are highlighted.

THE UNITY OF THE MARXIST METHOD

The Marxist methodology and categories of analysis of the key protagonists in the debate help to unify the discussion despite great differences of argument and emphasis between them. Classically Marxist themes like the nature of a mode of production, of capitalism as a world system, the relative importance of internal and external prime movers in the fall of feudalism and rise of capitalism, the relation between the social relations of production and exchange relations, the tie between the forces of production and the development of classes, the relationship between financial, merchant, agricultural and manufacturing capital and the role of the state, have been the chief axes of debate. The crises of feudalism in fourteenth-century Europe, early nineteenth-century Prussia and Japan during the Meiji Restoration may not appear to have much in common at first glance. But they raise theoretical questions like the relationship between the capitalist mode of production and earlier productive modes, the importance of class relations as against the significance of access to global markets, and the role of the level of development of the forces of production in the transition, which help to tie together these disparate concrete instances.

In particular, Marxism's dialectical method is essential in grasping the transition from the feudal mode of production to the capitalist mode. In terms of this work the development of the new capitalist mode must be understood to have taken place dialectically within the bowels of the old feudal mode. How the new mode of production arose out of the old and then eventually replaced it is the critical question of this inquiry.

The essence of feudalism was the antagonistic relationship between a ruling class of noble landlords who controlled access to land, and a dominated class of subservient peasant farmers. As such, the overall setting of feudalism was a largely agrarian society with limited productive potential. The producers in such a society were largely peasant families interested primarily in producing their own subsistence. Most of the limited surplus they produced was directly or indirectly coerced from them in the form of rent. Capital existed under feudalism as it did in the slave mode of production. It operated in the form of merchant and financial capital facilitating the exchange of commodities and the provision of credit. In other words, it made itself felt at the level of exchange relations. But it did not enter into the sphere of production.

Like feudalism, capitalism is a system that is founded on an antagonistic class relationship. In the capitalist case the opposition is between wage workers and capitalists. The workers who are the producers under capitalism have limited or no control over the means or processes of production, and therefore have restricted or no means of producing their own subsistence. They have no or inadequate means of independently producing their own livelihood. As a result, they are compelled to sell their labour power to employers in return for a wage that enables them to buy food and other necessities. The wage then is essentially the value of the commodity labour power. While the existence of wage labour is necessary to capitalism, it is not sufficient to it. The existence of capitalism also requires the entry of capital into the productive process. Indeed, capital's entry into production is a distinguishing mark of capitalism. Capitalism, in contrast to feudalism, is a system in which capital, combined with technological innovation, progressively introduces ever more sophisticated and productive means into production. Simple tools are replaced with more complex ones, and they, rather than labour, dominate the productive process, with ever more massive machinery and 'fixed capital'. Using these increasingly efficient means of production with which they are provided, workers are able, during their hours of work, to produce increasingly more value than the value of their own labour power. This surplus value – unpaid labour – is the fundamental source of surplus under capitalism, in contrast to the primacy of rent under feudalism. Transformed by the productive process into commodities for sale in the marketplace, surplus value is realized by capitalists as profit. Such profit is then available as surplus capital for further investment in the productive process.

In studying the transition from feudalism to capitalism we are trying to explain both theoretically and concretely the transition from the feudal mode to the capitalist. But to put it in more concrete terms, how, over the course of centuries, did the majority of people come to live in towns and cities rather than the countryside? How was it that whereas under feudalism most people were legally defined as serfs tied to a manor while paying a rent in kind or cash to a landlord, many if not all producers in capitalism became economically and legally free producers working for wages and were conceived of as such? How, finally, did it come about that whereas the object of economic activity under feudalism was consumption, under capitalism it came to be the accumulation of profit? Understanding the means by which this transformation came about is the focus of the transition debate and of our study.

ALTERNATIVES TO MARXISM

However, Marxism does not exhaust this study: non-Marxist historical scholarship is also introduced and assessed as relevant. Marxists have not been alone in interesting themselves in the origins of capitalism. Although there is no shortage of doubters, there are many who believe that Adam Smith's *Wealth of Nations* offers a plausible account of capitalist origins. In his quest to understand the genesis of the market, Smith assumed an innate desire on the part of individuals to improve their material circumstances. According to Smith, they attempted to do this through resort to exchange or commerce. It is through such trade that life gradually improved, and society itself slowly evolved from hunting and fishing to pasturage, then to agriculture, and eventually toward commercialism. The growth of exchange develops as a result of an increasing division of labour and economic specialization. Such diversification requires a growth of capital which comes about through individual saving.[10]

Douglas North and Robert Thomas have recently attempted to improve on Smith while retaining his emphasis on market exchange.[11] For them history was a struggle to overcome Malthusian demographic pressures by creating institutional mechanisms which allow relatively inefficient production on the feudal manor to be replaced by more efficient market methods. It was the successful establishment of private property rights in the sixteenth and seventeenth century which, above all, made this transformation possible.[12]

From the perspective of Marxism, the problem with these views is that, focusing on the market and institutional change as they do, they remain at a superficial level of analysis. Smith's and North and Thomas's outlooks undoubtedly have some merit, but fail to penetrate deeply enough beneath the surface of economic relationships. For Marxists the key changes and the ones that require explanation in terms of the transition problem are changes in the social relations of production: that is, the development of the relationship between wage labourers forced into selling their labour for subsistence, and capitalists in control of the means of production who purchase such labour power and transform it into value and eventually profit.

Another influential theory of the transition has been that of the early twentieth-century sociologist Max Weber. In *The Protestant Ethic and the Spirit of Capitalism* (1904–5), Weber stressed the importance of the development and internalization of a capitalist ideology or spirit of economic accumulation. This spirit values thrift, diligence and the rational and calculated pursuit of profit. Weber found the source of this capitalist ideology in the ethics of Calvinism that crystallized during the Protestant Reformation. Weber acknowledged that the development of the market and wage labour were important to the development of capitalism, but he insisted that there was an elective affinity between this Protestant ethic and such capitalist activity.[13] In other words, Weber argued that the Protestant faith was an important independent variable in the development of capitalism.

Anticipating Weber by 50 years, in the *Grundrisse*, Marx has this to say about the relationship between Protestantism and the accumulation of money: 'the cult of money has its asceticism, its self-denial, its self-sacrifice-economy and frugality, contempt for mundane, temporal and fleeting pleasures; the chase after the eternal treasure. Hence the connection between English Puritanism or Dutch Protestantism and money-making.'[14] Marx saw the connection between the so-called spirit of capitalism and the Protestant ethic. As such the Protestant ethic had a certain historical importance as an ideology of an emerging capitalism. But clearly it existed not simply in an elective affinity with capitalism but in a dialectical relationship with it. This was a more direct level of interdependence than Weber would have allowed. Friedrich Engels, who also took note of the so-called Calvinist predestinarian ethic years before Weber, particularly underscored Calvinism's force as an ideology that served the interests of the bourgeoisie better than the passivity of Lutheranism.[15] As is well known, it was the English economic historian Richard Tawney who in response to Weber, demonstrated that the development of sixteenth-century capitalism drove the spread of English Calvinist Puritanism, not, as Weber's reasoning implied, vice versa.[16]

MARXISM AND HISTORY

As a result of what we regard as their superficial approach we eschew treatment of the transition problem from a Smithian or Weberian perspective and adhere to a Marxist one. Indeed, we have found that the writings of Marx and Engels, though they date from the nineteenth century, nonetheless contain many enduring insights on the transition. They are, of course, inadequate, especially in the light of the enormous progress made in historical research. Marx, for example, had only the vaguest conception of the factors behind the decline of feudalism: that is, the class struggles of the late Middle Ages. In Engels's account of the German Peasant War, to take another instance, the author has little sense of the extraordinary development of manufacturing in Germany prior to the Reformation. On the other hand, the works of Marx and Engels, surprisingly to a present-day professional historian, continue to offer many important insights into the historical and especially the theoretical basis of the transition. Moreover, as it turns out the subsequent Marxist debate on the transition is the one that offers the richest insights into the problem.

In taking a Marxist approach to the transition we should make clear that we are not trying to write a history of the decline of feudalism and development of capitalism. An actual history of capitalism would preoccupy itself above all with eliciting the varied, complex and contradictory routes that societies took as they moved

from feudal or tributary societies to capitalism. This account is
rather a *histoire raisonée* or critical history. This is a type of historical writing that originated in the early modern epoch in which as
much or more emphasis was placed on reflection and commentary
on the meaning of history as on the facts themselves. It focuses on
reviewing the different ways that Marxist scholars have attempted
to explain and theorize the transition. As such it has as much to do
with theory or political economy as it does with history. But such a
history, although preoccupied with theory and comparison, must be
written with ongoing reference to the concrete particulars of history,
and especially the findings of contemporary historical research.

Marx's approach to the relationship between the abstractions
of theory and the concrete particulars of history is outlined in
an important passage in the third volume of *Capital* in which he
delineates the relationship between the mode of production as
the independent variable and the dependent variables of class and
the realm of politics. Despite the apparent determinate role of the
mode of production, Marx insists on the role of specific historic
circumstances which theory must take into account:

> It is always the direct relationship of the owners of the condi-
> tions of production to the direct producers – a relation always
> naturally corresponding to a definite stage in the development
> of the methods of labour and thereby its social productivity –
> which reveals the innermost secret, the hidden basis of the entire
> social structure, and with it the political form of the relation of
> sovereignty and dependence, in short, the corresponding specific
> form of the state. This does not prevent the same economic basis
> – the same from the standpoint of its main conditions – due to
> innumerable different empirical circumstances, natural environ-
> ment, racial relations, external historical influences, etc., from
> showing infinite variations and gradations in appearance, which
> can be ascertained only by analysis of the empirically given
> circumstances.[17]

Concrete historical references were an intrinsic feature even of Marx's
most theoretical works of economic analysis. The abstractions of
theory could only prove themselves by being tested and applied to the
concrete details of history. Engels described Marx's approach in the
following way:

> The critique of economics could ... be exercised in two ways:

historically or logically. ... History moves often in leaps and bounds and in a zigzag line, and as this would have to be followed throughout, it would mean not only that a considerable amount of material of slight importance would have to be included, but also that the train of thought would frequently have to be interrupted; it would, moreover, be impossible to write the history of economy without that of bourgeois society, and the task would thus become immense, because of the absence of all preliminary studies. The logical method of approach was therefore the only suitable one. This, however, is indeed nothing but the historical method, only stripped of the historical form and diverting chance occurrences. ... [W]ith this method the logical exposition need by no means be confined to the purely abstract sphere. On the contrary, it requires historical illustration and continuous contact with reality.[18]

Marx's conception of capitalism and its chief elements was rooted or immanent in historical development and cannot be understood apart from it. Thus the categories that constitute capitalist commodities – use value, competitive markets, money, exchange value and value, private property, capital and abstract and concrete labour – not only have a history, they emerge in it, from it. Moreover, such concepts as value or abstract labour have a real social existence. On the other hand, writing in the middle of the nineteenth century, Marx was preoccupied with analyzing these concepts in order to reveal the logic of capitalist accumulation. Of necessity, the historic origins of such concepts were of secondary concern to him, if only because of a want of sufficient time or available scholarly material. For us, who look forward to the unravelling of these capitalist commodity categories and the beginning of a new historical epoch, the development of these notions out of the concrete circumstances of early modern history is of central interest.[19]

Given that we are concerned not with an established mode of production but with the transition from one to another, we must be even more mindful of history's concreteness. On the other hand, it is also important to not let that overwhelm the need for theorizing about history. Students of Marxism will recall the famous debate between the celebrated English historian Edward P. Thompson and the Marxist theoretician and historian Perry Anderson in the late 1970s. While Anderson defended the need to bring theory to bear on history, Thompson denounced this as overly schematic, as forcing a structure on the past based on the arbitrary imposition of ill-fitting

Marxist concepts.[20] Such concepts seemed to Thompson to contradict the historian's commitment to the concrete as revealed in the primary sources, to a respect for narrative and to the contingency of historical outcomes, none of which ought to be surrendered lightly. Thompson's admonitions in this regard are worth bearing in mind. Indeed, it is essential to admit from the beginning that theory can never completely grasp the complexity of the past. On the other hand, it is important to try to do so, as Anderson suggests, if only to better comprehend the facts of the past, and particularly those which are pertinent to the historical problem at hand. The concrete facts of historical narrative ought properly to be illuminated by a sense of the theory that stands behind them, and vice versa.

Thompson and Anderson also had another disagreement relevant for us. In producing what is perhaps the masterpiece of Marxist historiography, *The Making of the English Working Class*, Thompson may be excused for perhaps paying too much attention to historical agents, men and women and their class consciousness, as against the objective realities of the mode of production and the social relations of production. As Ellen Wood has shown, he had his reasons for doing so: namely, to combat those who would deny the agency and even the existence of such a class.[21] On the other hand, Thompson's emphasis on consciousness and preoccupation with the complex tissue of working-class experience undoubtedly gave license to others to abandon notions of class, mode of production and surplus value altogether, and to take the 'cultural turn' into a fetishized world of discourse and idealist mystification.[22] Thompson cannot be blamed for the deviations of epigones who abandoned Marxism in the age of neoliberalism, and it is for us to reaffirm our commitment to the historical force of consciousness and ideology. But from a Marxist perspective the social and economic aspects of history remain fundamental.

Historical explanation certainly depends on the degree to which the political and cultural is convincingly linked to the social and economic, and the extent to which immediate events are tied to more enduring long-term factors. Revolutions, for example, need to be understood in political and cultural terms which enjoy a certain autonomy and cannot be reduced to the social and economic. Yet the challenge for historians is to try to grasp the ties between these different levels of social existence. In any case our project demands that we take our distance from an overly cultural approach to history which, moreover, shies away from comparison, abstraction, generalization and sense of structure, by invoking the overriding importance of subjective experience, which is necessarily various.

Thompson likewise cannot be faulted for the sins of social history defined as history from below, another academically fashionable approach to history. Nonetheless he, like other British Marxist historians, gave license to an approach privileging the study of workers, plebeians and peasants. This was understandable given the previous neglect of the role of the people in history. But this opened the way to an approach which ignored the study of the political and economic opposition between workers and peasants on the one hand, and landlords and capitalists on the other, in favour of a one-sided preoccupation with the lower orders. The relationship between opposed classes must be the focus of serious study of the origins and dynamics of capitalism. Moreover, class conflict is always resolved at the level of political struggle and the control of the state. Indeed, the doings of the upper class must always be borne in mind when studying history or practicing politics. It is the dynamic of class struggle which must be the focal point of a Marxist approach to history, and especially the study of the origins and development of capitalism.

The structural Marxism of Louis Althusser was Thompson's particular *bête noire*. It was the epitome of what Thompson regarded as a schematic, a priori and overly theoretical approach to history based on the concept of the mode of production, which was the special target of his ire. Yet Althusser himself had insisted on the distinction between a mode of production and a social formation as a way of getting away from an overly mechanical and dogmatic understanding of historical process. According to the latter, the mode of production could not be found in the real world but was rather an abstraction from it. What did exist historically were social formations. While one mode of production might predominate, such a social formation might contain several coexisting modes of production, or fragments of such modes which might be out of phase with one another.[23] This formulation makes sense in terms of apprehending the transition from feudalism to capitalism.

Contrary to the views of non-Marxists, and even some Marxists, historical analysis requires a dialectical or relational understanding of the historical process. Methodological individualism and notions of causation based on the isolation of independent and dependent variables were not incorrect methods. They were merely insufficient. Competitive markets, for example, may determine the success or failure of individual entrepreneurs. But the historical constitution of markets is not only an economic process but also a political, social and cultural one. Explaining their emergence requires understanding the capitalist mode of production as a totality whose constituent parts and overall development cannot be grasped except through an appreciation of their dynamic tension and ongoing interaction with one another. This is obvious with regard to class relations but is also necessary with respect to understanding the relationship between value and capital, markets and class struggle, the concrete and the abstract and the base and superstructure.

CAPITALISM AND WORLD HISTORY

Studying capitalism's origins invariably must lead to differentiating European from non-European societies. No one can deny that capitalism took permanent root first in Western Europe in the sixteenth century, and where it took root – England, Holland, northern France, northwest Germany – it accelerated economic growth. Translated into political and military power, capitalism made it possible for the European states to dominate the rest of the world from the end of the eighteenth century onward. As such it endowed Europe with a deep sense of superiority over other cultures and civilizations. It is this Eurocentric perspective which has increasingly been challenged in recent decades. Eurocentrism and the cultural arrogance that goes with it certainly need to be confronted, and we shall do that. Attention has already been drawn to how the economic superiority of Europe's capitalism became evident much later than most historians think it did. But in contesting Eurocentrism some scholars, including Jack Goody and John Hobson have tried to make light of the historical significance of this eventual economic superiority of the capitalist mode of production as compared to the performance of other non-capitalist societies like traditional China and Japan.[24] In my view such a denial is quixotic. We can no more dispute the higher productivity of capitalist relations of production than we can repudiate the historic facts of European conquest of the rest of the world.

One of the most convincing attempts to contextualize the rise of capitalism within the context of world history was made by the late British revolutionary Marxist Chris Harman.[25] Harman insisted that capitalism was not the result of some special Western European quality or development. The forces of production have been cumulatively developing in Europe, Asia and Africa for centuries, and tendencies toward capitalism emerged in many places. For contingent historical reasons such tendencies culminated earlier in Western Europe than elsewhere, and once they did, further movement toward capitalism outside Europe was frustrated after capitalism triggered European imperialism. From the perspective of the twenty-first century in which non-European poles of development have emerged, the development of capitalism first in Europe is part of a much longer and yet unconcluded historical process. During the Middle Ages and the early modern period there was considerable progress in agricultural and manufacturing techniques in India and especially China. The Middle East, too, saw improvement. In the case of all three regions merchants and craftspeople played an important role. But in the case of China and the Middle East the entrenched power of landed elites, reinforced sooner or later by state bureaucracies, discouraged merchants and craftspeople from investing in the cumulative development of the means of production. This was ultimately the case in India too. In a noteworthy if controversial break from stereotypical Western views of an unchanging India, Harman underlines the recurrent possibilities for the breakthrough of capitalist tendencies in India in the face of the repeated breakdowns of its dynastic state system.

In the Middle Ages Western Europe also saw the adoption of new methods of farming and manufacture, many of which were in fact imported from China, India and the Middle East. Harman concludes that in that epoch Western Europe was an economic backwater compared with much of the rest of Eurasia. In any event in terms of the development of the forces of production the whole of Eurasia shared a common experience. It can parenthetically be added that if we compare the most productive areas of Europe and Asia, as late as the eighteenth century the growth of fixed capital and levels of productivity and gross domestic product per capita were approximately similar.

What ultimately distinguished Western Europe from the rest of the Eurasian continent, according to Harman, was its distinctive political and social evolution. The relative economic backwardness of northwest Europe gave it a weak and fragmented superstructure which favored the flowering of capitalist tendencies more than in the rest of Eurasia. In the context of this political decentralization what became notable was the relative strength of the producer classes. Serfs may have been tied to the land but they largely controlled the processes of production. Merchants and craftspeople were able to achieve a greater degree of autonomy from kings and feudal lords through the development of town charters and liberties. More than the peasants, urban merchants and craftspeople developed an independent productive base and an interest in its expansion and improvement.

The end of the Middle Ages saw a re-consolidation of political authority throughout Eurasia. But in the case of Western Europe the centralized states that did emerge were able to exercise less control than their counterparts elsewhere in protecting the class rule of the landed elites. Indeed, the fourteenth- and fifteenth-century economic and social crisis in Western Europe had enhanced the social freedom of the productive classes. In particular the transformations of that period opened the way for the increasing employment of wage labour by merchants and rich peasants on a scale which distinguished Western Europe from the rest of the world. Ultimately Western Europeans used the increasing economic power which accrued from the development of capitalism to block whatever indigenous capitalist tendencies existed in the rest of the world.

In this light, Eurasia as a whole shared a common development of the forces of production in the pre-capitalist period. Capitalist tendencies were present not only in Western Europe but in China, India and the Middle East. Historic contingencies – political and social – determined that capitalism emerged first in Europe and not Asia. Among those contingencies we would underscore the strength of the state in Asia, and later the effects of foreign intrusion including Western colonialism and imperialism in blocking capitalist development. The restructuring of social and political relations through war and revolution in the twentieth century has produced a model of capitalist accumulation in China and East Asia which is now out-competing that of the West.[26] The same historic contingency, some argue, could lead in the twenty-first century to the overshadowing of European and American capitalism by a still more successful version in the East. Presumably there are some in Asia who look forward at long last to the day when the capitalist East will trump the capitalist West. There is no reason to believe that such an Asian capitalism would benefit humanity as a whole any more than that of the West. In fact the aspiration to replace Eurocentrism with some kind of Asian hegemony will likely run up against the same multiple contradictions of intensifying class conflict, crisis of peak oil, ecological crisis and insufficient demand in the world economy.[27]

1

THE DECLINE OF FEUDALISM

This chapter reviews the debates on the decline of feudalism and origins of capitalism, beginning with the foundational exchange between Maurice Dobb and Paul Sweezy. The two differed primarily over whether an external prime mover, namely the development of commerce with the Mediterranean and the Middle East, or factors internal to feudalism caused the decline of this mode of production. Sweezy argued that commerce overseas served as an external prime mover which undermined feudalism. Dobb and others, including the medievalist Rodney Hilton and the Japanese historian Kohachiro Takahashi, argued that an internal prime mover – the crisis of the feudal mode of production – caused the decline. Meanwhile Eric Hobsbawm, another participant in the debate, insisted that changes in Europe had to be seen in terms of uneven development on a global scale. The decline of feudalism and advance toward capitalism came about through a series of crises that saw previously developed areas of Europe and the rest of the world regress while other regions forged ahead. England emerged at the forefront of this movement.

In the original debate class struggles were recognized as important in feudalism's decline. Subsequent argument centred on Brenner's contention that these class struggles determined not only the decline of feudalism, but the genesis of capitalism. In England, according to Brenner, such conflicts paradoxically led to serfdom's decline but also the landlords' ongoing grip on the land. In the sixteenth century the latter initiated agrarian capitalism by forcing the better-off among the cautious peasantry to take up competitive leases. Based on the work of Guy Bois, Terence Byres and Chris Harman, we reject Brenner's argument. Far from being conservative, petty producers and not landlords took the lead in not only dismantling feudalism, but initiating capitalism through their ongoing political and social struggles and their economic enterprise. In accord with a forces of production approach, furthermore, we insist that the economic and political capacity of this class of proto-capitalists has to be understood in terms of the previous development of the forces of production during the Middle Ages.

Perry Anderson's account of the role of the state shapes our view as well. He points out that faced with revolt from below, the only way that class society survived was through the building-up of the territorial state. Despite its feudal framework the early modern state provided an essential container for the emergence of capitalism. Dobb and Brenner's views of the transition are the focal points of this chapter. Yet their viewpoint is marred by an unfortunate economism and in the latter's case a class determinism. In response we use the work of Hobsbawm, Anderson and Harman to provide a more dialectical view of the transition from feudalism. Hobsbawm's sense of unequal development, Anderson's view of the dual class character of the emerging territorial state and Harman's notion of social class as defined economically but also culturally and politically help to provide this more dialectical sense. These debates cover the chief issues relating to the transition from feudalism, and form the essential basis for understanding debates discussed later in the text.

DOBB'S OPENING GAMBIT

Maurice Dobb was a don at Cambridge throughout his career. He was an economist by training, and founded the discipline of Marxist political economy in Britain. He also helped to mentor a strong left-wing student movement during the 1930s. As a communist he was more or less isolated from other academics especially in his own discipline, though the development economist and Nobel Prize winner Amartya Sen has recently written that 'he was undoubtedly one of the outstanding political economists of this [twentieth] century.'[1]

Dobb justified his intrusion into history by suggesting that economists could put interesting questions to historical data; that the facts of concrete history could be illuminated by economic theory. At the same time he argued that economic analysis makes sense and is fruitful only if tied to the study of historical development.[2] His *Studies in the Development of Capitalism*, published immediately after the Second World War, was based on thorough knowledge of the then existing historiography on the decline of English feudalism and emergence of capitalism.

Dobb based his approach to the transition from feudalism to capitalism on Marx's notion of the mode of production.[3] While he recognized that one mode of production dominated a given epoch, he also accepted that elements of other modes of production could coexist with the dominant mode.[4] In the passage from the feudal mode of production to the capitalist mode, Dobb singled out three decisive moments – the crisis of feudalism in the fourteenth century, the beginning of capitalism in the late sixteenth and seventeenth centuries, and the eighteenth and early nineteenth-century Industrial Revolution.[5] The decline of feudalism and start of capitalism are separated by at least two centuries. The capitalist mode proper dates from the latter half of the sixteenth century and the early seventeenth century, when capital began to penetrate production to a considerable degree.[6]

Modern discussions of feudalism have been plagued by long-drawn-out controversies over its conceptualization. These disputes have centred on whether feudalism should be thought of in essentially political and legal or socio-economic terms.[7] As a Marxist Dobb adopted the third perspective while trying not to not lose sight of the political. According to him, the feudal mode is defined as the extra-economic extraction by overlords of rents or services from a class of subsistence producers. The peasant producers largely control the process of production but are not legally free. Feudalism and serfdom are synonymous.[8] The rise of the political and economic autonomy of the corporate towns, followed immediately by the economic decline of the fourteenth century, marked the crisis of the feudal mode, which was deeply shaken and thereafter continued to weaken. According to Dobb, towns had some part in the decline of feudalism, playing a role in the late medieval revolts, providing refuges to runaway serfs and serving as oases of freedom.[9] But the confrontation between peasants and landlords in the countryside was the main arena of struggle. At the end of the Middle Ages serfdom had vanished while medieval forms of government and the class power of landlords lingered on in a kind of historical twilight.

Though the peasantry as a class had grown stronger, they remained subject to manorial authority. The emerging class of hired labourers was subject to a good deal of coercion as a stratum which resorted to wage labour as a supplement to a livelihood still mainly drawn from subsistence farming.[10] The merchant bourgeoisie became more powerful but cooperated for the most part with the landlords. The novel element lay among urban craftspeople and well-to-do and middling peasants, whose particular mode of production had become independent of feudalism. They were petty producers who were not yet capitalists, but certainly contained a potential to become so, or who began to come under the external influence of capital.[11] In Dobb's conception it was this petty mode of production which predominated economically in the two hundred or so years between the beginning of the feudal crisis and the advent of the capitalist mode in the mid-sixteenth century.

Until Dobb it was generally assumed that the intensification of market exchange and the growing role of money brought about the decline of feudalism. On the contrary, Dobb demonstrated that money and exchange actually strengthened serfdom and feudalism.[12] The emergence of merchant capital was fully compatible with feudalism. Rather it was the economic weakness of the feudal mode of production, coupled with the growing need of the ruling class for revenue, which was responsible for the system's crisis.[13] The lack of incentive to toil and the low level of technique placed a limit on peasant productivity. The further development of productive forces was fettered by upper-class exploitation.

Upper-class demands on peasants expanded inordinately due to the expansion of its numbers, the stimulus of luxury consumption and the exigencies of war and brigandage. This 'parasitic' ruling class expanded through natural increase as well as the growth in the size of great lords' retinues in competition with one another. The rivalry between leading nobles increased spending on feasts, luxury commodities and pageants. Competition extended to warmaking, the nobility's *raison d'être* and its most important form of conspicuous consumption. All this increased economic demands on producers.[14]

The result was economic exhaustion, flight from the land and peasant rebellion.[15] Over-exploitation and stagnant productivity resulted in a decline in population after 1300. Subsequent labour shortages, peasant resistance or threat of flight led to widespread commutation of labour to money rent. The manorial system was further weakened by the thinning of the ranks of the nobility through war, the growing practice of leasing demesne, the emergence of a stratum of rich and middling peasants differentiated from the mass of peasant poor, and the growing use of wage labour. By the end of the fifteenth century the economic basis of the feudal system had disintegrated.[16]

The late medieval social differentiation of the peasantry, a key theme of Dobb's work, prepared the way for the later dispossession of the mass of peasants. The subsequent spread of vagabondage across England and the rest of Europe at the beginning of the sixteenth century was widely commented upon by anxious contemporaries. The appearance of this rootless population heralded the arrival of capitalism, setting the stage for the emergence of capitalist wage labour. The role of the towns was above all to act as a magnet attracting the unfree rural population and forcing further concessions from the landed class.[17]

Dobb's perspective on the role of the towns was later to be contested. What proved enduring was his view of the feudal crisis on the land. Dobb explained that the collapse of feudalism was the result of its own internal contradictions, stemming from the over-exploitation of the peasant producers: 'it was the inefficiency of Feudalism as a system of production, coupled with the growing needs of the ruling class for revenue, that was primarily responsible for its decline; since this need for additional revenue prompted an increase in the pressure on the producer to a point where this pressure became literally unendurable'.[18]

Dobb's interpretation of the decline of feudalism set off the celebrated transition debate. As the repressive machinery of the Cold War closed in, leading Marxist scholars mainly from England and the United States calmly undertook an analysis of the historical foundations of the capitalist system. The subsequent debate unfolded largely in the pages of the well-known journal *Science and Society* during the early 1950s. It then appeared as a booklet whose publication was arranged by Dobb in London in 1954.[19] Widely ignored in the English-speaking countries, the debate was chiefly followed in countries where strong currents of Marxism persisted.[20] The contributions to the discussion were eventually collected, expanded and published in 1976 by one of the participants, Rodney Hilton.[21]

DOBB VERSUS SWEEZY

Paul Sweezy, another celebrated Marxist economist and co-founder with Paul Baran of the *Monthly Review*, was first into the fray.[22] Sweezy agreed with Dobb that serfdom was the dominant relation of production in Western feudalism. But organized around the economically autarchic manor feudalism was a mode of production for use, and as such tended to stagnation.[23] An external force, the growth of trade and increase in production for exchange, was what was necessary to destabilize the system: 'he [Dobb] mistakes for immanent trends certain historical developments which in fact can only be explained as arising from causes external to the system.'[24] Dobb failed to acknowledge sufficiently that the over-exploitation of peasants by the nobles arose from their increasing appetite for eastern luxury commodities. Sweezy's view of an external prime mover was to prove untenable, as the ensuing debate demonstrated that the prime mover was internal to the feudal system. On the other hand, his view forced the participants in the controversy to address the fundamental question of the historic dynamic behind the evolution of the feudal mode of production.

Dobb for one rejected Sweezy's view that feudalism tended toward stagnation, and insisted that it had its own momentum based on its internal – especially class – contradictions.[25] Class conflict between peasants and lords did not directly lead to capitalism. What it did was to lessen the dependence of the petty mode of production upon feudal overlordship, eventually freeing the petty producer from feudal exploitation. Sweezy's trade-driven external prime mover did not hold up in the face of Dobb's historically and theoretically better informed view of feudalism as an internally dynamic system driven by economic growth and class conflict.

While placing greater emphasis on internal factors, Dobb also considered the growth of trade a factor:

> I am by no means denying that the growth of market towns and trade played an important role in accelerating the disintegration of the old mode of production. What I am asserting is that trade exercised its influence to the extent that it accentuated the internal conflicts within the old mode of production.[26]

It was not a case of having to choose one factor to the exclusion of the other but rather consideration of their dialectical interaction.[27] Moreover, Dobb made more explicit than earlier that towns and therefore trade must be understood as internal rather than external to the feudal system.[28]

Sweezy criticized Dobb for not signalling the existence of a system of pre-capitalist commodity production which was neither feudal nor capitalist in the wake of feudalism's demise.[29] This was simply not the case. Dobb had sketched out a prolonged period at the end of the Middle Ages in which the petty mode of production dominated the economy. At the same time he more strongly asserted his earlier stated view that the ruling class remained feudal and that the state continued to be its instrument in the sixteenth century.[30]

TAKAHASHI AND HILTON

The debate on the transition was then taken up by the distinguished Japanese Marxist economic historian Kohachiro Takahashi.[31] Economic history and Marxism having been banned from Japan during the war, Takahashi's intervention represented the renewal of the ties between the re-emergent tradition of Marxist thought in Japan and that of Europe and the United States. Takahashi insisted in the first place that the debate be widened beyond the English case to include Continental Europe. Presciently he held out the prospect that such a wider debate might then illuminate the transition question in Asia.[32]

Takahashi rejected Sweezy's conception of feudalism as a mode of production for use rather than exchange. Commodities are produced and circulate in different modes of production including the feudal. In a definition of the feudal or other modes stress should be placed above all on how products are produced.[33] As such Takahashi strongly supported Dobb's view that the decline of feudalism was due to an internal rather than an external prime mover. But according to Takahashi, Dobb's definition of feudalism was inadequate in that he immediately started from the abstractions of feudal landed property and serfdom. But just as Marx began his analysis of capital from the commodity, so likewise the analysis of feudalism had to begin from the fundamental social units of Western feudalism: the virgate (cottage, small plot, collective rights), the village community and the manor (*seigneurie*). It was the manor which dominated the other two and became the basis for the extraction of feudal rent and the mobilization of labour. The weakening or dissolution of these medieval categories entailed the decline of feudalism in the fourteenth and fifteenth centuries.[34] Further empirical studies of the late medieval crisis only confirm Takahashi's observations.[35]

Takahashi's deeply concrete analysis of the decline of feudalism was theorized by Rodney Hilton. This move toward theory appeared the more warranted as Hilton, of all the participants, was most versed in the concrete details of history. Throughout his career at Birmingham University he dedicated himself to rigorous empirical research in the archives. He became thoroughly familiar with Continental historiography on the Middle Ages and used it in a comparative way to illuminate his research work on England. Hilton was one of a quartet of British Marxist historians – including Christopher Hill, Edward Thompson and Eric Hobsbawm – who were initially close to the Communist Party of Great Britain and who re-founded the study of history in the English-speaking world during the 1950s and 1960s.[36] As such Hilton had a thorough grounding in Marxist theory and was passionately interested in the transition question.

Hilton began by questioning Sweezy's prime mover, long-distance trade. Sweezy's view was based on the so-called Pirenne thesis.

Henri Pirenne, the celebrated Belgian medievalist, claimed that the economic decline of the West coincided not with the fall of the Western Roman Empire but with the closure of the Mediterranean as a result of the Muslim occupation of the Eastern Mediterranean coast in the eighth century. Contrariwise the economic revival of Western Europe began with the reopening of the Mediterranean during the crusades of the eleventh century.

Arguing against Pirenne, Hilton maintained that the decline of the Roman Empire in the West was the result not of the interruption of trade but of internal factors. The decline of commodity production in the Empire began as a consequence of internal economic and demographic regression as early as the third century, hundreds of years before the collapse of Roman political authority, let alone the Arab intrusion into the Mediterranean. Likewise internal factors within Western Europe led to the revival of commodity production and markets before the onset of the crusades.[37] Hilton concluded that the evolution of feudalism was the result of internal factors rather than an external prime mover.

CLASS STRUGGLE

Hilton, like Dobb, produced a theory of the decline of feudalism which stressed class struggle above all.[38] It was the prime mover, and the growth of the forces of production was its dependent variable.[39] As its dynamic element, class struggle between overlords and peasants led to the flourishing of the feudal mode of production and then to its decline. The nobility and princes also engaged in political competition with one another while striving to maximize their rental income. The resultant quest for increased rent at first stimulated technological innovation, the development of towns and commerce, and increases in productivity, only later contributing to feudalism's decline. Among contributors to the debate, Hilton was the first to fully underscore the growth of the forces of production at feudalism's zenith.[40]

The interplay of these factors, including growing production for the market, led to increased social differentiation among the peasants. The richer peasants took more land into their holdings and employed more and more wage labour, which was increasingly that of the completely landless rather than that of smallholders. The better-off peasants resented the demands of lords for rent, and their resentment was reinforced by that of the rest of the peasants, for whom such demands were not merely a restriction on economic expansion but an attack on their subsistence. The struggle over rent sharpened and reached a crisis in the fourteenth century.[41]

Income from rent declined and was only partly compensated for by increases in state taxation, warfare and plunder, and commutation of rents to money payments. Feudal rent was no longer a stimulus to production, and those dependent on it for income eventually had to look to the emerging power of the state for survival.[42] The number of tenants obliged to labour on their lord's demesne and the value of rent, now paid predominantly in money, declined. Overall the legal claims of the lords over the persons of their tenants weakened.[43] Money rent favoured the social stratification of the population of the manor into rich and poor as well as the beginnings of a land market.[44] The holdings of the rich peasants in the manor expanded at the expense of the rest.[45] More peasants were forced to resort to wage labour.[46] Rich peasants and lesser nobles were the most efficient producers in an increasingly market-oriented economy, which began to take capitalist forms. With Hilton's vivid demonstration of the role of class struggle both in developing the forces of production under feudalism and in its decline, this became, along with peasant social differentiation, the fundamental pivot around which debate on the transition would now revolve.

THE ROLE OF TOWNS

Indeed, in Hilton's argument, the role of towns and trade, seen by others such as Sweezy as an independent variable and prime mover, was itself the outcome of class struggle. For Hilton argued that the commutation of rents to money furthered the development of merchant capital and the growth of larger towns within the context of the feudal mode of production.[47] Hilton's view of the towns as part of the feudal system rather than as an external springboard to capitalism was greatly deepened by an article by John Merrington which appeared originally in *New Left Review* and was republished as the final contribution to the debate over *The Transition from Feudalism to Capitalism,* edited by Hilton in 1976.[48] Merrington argued that town-based commerce facilitated the expansion of the feudal mode of production. The urban corporate form, although at times in opposition to local feudal landlords, actually functioned as a 'collective seigneur' within the cellular structure of parcellized sovereignty under feudalism, strengthening its economic foundation as an intrinsic element of it. Feudalism was the first mode to accord an autonomous structural place to urban production and exchange.

Merrington completed his argument about towns and trade being intrinsic components of feudalism rather than external capitalist forces working to undermine it by denying them any role in the emergence of capitalism. For merchant capital did not create surplus value, it only redistributed it. While it played a key role in primitive accumulation, it could not be a source of a permanent self-reproducing accumulation.[49] For that to occur the extension of the market in the territorial state and the emergence of agrarian capitalism were necessary, and when they did emerge, urban merchant capital was reduced to a declining sphere of operations.[50]

Merrington's arguments were a powerful reinforcement of the role of class struggle and the internal logic of feudalism's decline, but they may have overstated the imbrication of towns in feudalism. He overlooked three aspects of their role in its decline. First, the towns served as a potential or actual refuge for the subject rural population, as Dobb pointed out. Second, urban markets strengthened social and political links between rural producers. Finally, as Merrington himself noted, merchant capital played a role in primitive accumulation which was a necessary if not sufficient condition for the development of the capitalist mode of production: that is, the eventual entry of capital into the productive process itself. These aspects of the role of towns and trade could not be so easily dismissed, and as we shall see below, later accounts came to see class struggle and trade as joint factors in the rise of capitalism. Indeed, we shall argue that while exchange helps to maintain feudal relations of production, once capitalist relations are in place it is indispensable to the realization process.

UNEVEN DEVELOPMENT

Takahashi had pointed to the need to broaden the discussion on feudalism to include Continental Europe and Japan. This was part of a general trend in Marxism to extend the concept of feudalism in analyzing non-European pre-capitalist societies, rather than employing the problematical and Eurocentric concepts of communal and Asiatic modes of production. Feudalism, at least after Hilton's intervention, was seen as a progressive mode capable of evolving toward capitalism, whereas the other two categories were seen as stagnant.

In a deceptively simple contribution, Eric Hobsbawm helped to free Marxist understandings from the problems associated with

notions of Asiatic and communal modes of production, and recon-
nected them with ideas about uneven and combined development.
Hobsbawm unreservedly admitted that the forces making for
economic development in Europe were also present elsewhere in the
world. Japanese feudalism, in particular, resembled the European
variant closely, and it was conceivable that capitalism could have
emerged there independently of European influence. In his view the
intrusion of European imperialism ruptured an authentically endogenous process. Having raised the possibility of non-European forms
of capitalism, Hobsbawm nonetheless insisted that the triumph of
capitalism in Europe was unique: 'there is no getting round the fact
that the transition from feudalism is, on a world scale, a case of
highly uneven development'.[51]

We should note that the conception of uneven development dates
back at least to Marx's *Grundrisse* (1857–58), where unevenness
represents the condition for a transition from one declining mode of
production to another rising and more progressive mode. Moreover
uneven development is a fundamental feature of the capitalist form
of development. Its importance throughout the process of capitalist
development cannot be overstated, and is key to understanding the
contemporary capitalist crisis.[52]

With respect to uneven development in Western Europe,
according to Hobsbawm the crisis of feudalism involved the most
advanced sectors of bourgeois development within Western Europe
as well: 'the interesting thing about the 14th century crisis ... is
not only the collapse of large-scale feudal demesne agriculture, but
also that of the Italian and Flemish textile industries. ... England
advances; but the much greater Italy and Flanders never recover.'[53]
Unevenness characterized not only the crisis of feudalism but also
the emergence of capitalism itself. Overall European development
from the fourteenth through the seventeenth centuries was marked
by repeated crises in which regression in one place allowed progress
elsewhere. West European advance came directly at the expense of
Eastern Europe and Asia, Africa and Latin America. The process of
West European transition entailed turning other areas into dependent
economies and colonies. Seizing resources from advanced areas or
later on from colonized regions became an intrinsic feature of West
European development. In other words, the emergence of capitalism
in Europe has to be understood in terms of an ongoing world-wide
process of appropriation based on uneven development both within
and outside Europe. Hobsbawm concludes that 'the net effect of
European capitalism was to divide the world ever more sharply into

two sectors: the "developed" and the "under-developed" countries, in other words the exploiting and the exploited.'[54] Hobsbawm's conception of the transition is one in which unevenness plays a central part. Gain in one place is invariably at the expense of other places, even those that were initially more developed.[55] Hobsbawm's sense of the dialectical quality and the unevenness of the process of transition is a dazzling insight, representing a significant contribution to the transition debate whose importance has even now been insufficiently acknowledged.

THE NEW LEFT TAKES OVER

Hilton's editing and republication of the 1950s transition debate (in 1976) was the consequence of the revival of the dispute in the 1960s. But the political context was quite different. Whereas the earlier dispute had unfolded during the darkest days of the Cold War, its republication took place during the revolutionary ferment of the 1960s and 1970s. Capitalism was deeply challenged by the Vietnam War, which sparked global revolt including revolutionary upheavals in France and Italy. Anti-imperialist revolution reached its zenith in the under-developed countries in the 1970s. In these years Marxist historical writing, especially as a result of the influence of the British Marxist historians, Thompson, Hill, Hobsbawm and Hilton, enjoyed a considerable vogue. Against this background Brenner, Anderson and Wallerstein published their important contributions to the transition debate.

Both Brenner and Anderson assumed a Eurocentric posture. While Brenner was adamantly Eurocentric, Anderson at least made an attempt to widen the discussion of feudalism beyond Europe by including Japan, as we shall see. But Anderson's contention that the inheritance of Rome was essential to the existence of feudalism in the first place and to the eventual crystallization of the capitalist notion of private property definitively placed him in the Eurocentric camp.[56] Meanwhile Wallerstein adopted what he called a world-systems approach, which attempted to view the development of European capitalism from a perspective which included the under-developed countries. With the exception of Takahashi's brief plea for a perspective beyond Europe, endorsed and elaborated through his invocation of uneven and combined development by Hobsbawm, the earlier phase of discussion of the transition question had scarcely touched on the non-European world. The fact that Anderson, and especially Wallerstein, found it incumbent on them to discuss capitalist origins in a non-European context undoubtedly reflects the growing impact of Asia, Africa and Latin America on Western scholarship in the radical 1960s and 1970s.

JAPANESE FEUDALISM

Hilton's republication of the original transition debate itself inspired a broadening of the discussion. A French translation of the English text was published by the radical publisher François Maspero (1977) alongside a companion volume which included an extensive discussion of the transition in Japan by Takahashi.[57] Like many other scholars, Takahashi believed that Japanese feudalism closely approximated that of the West, and that like the Western version, its transition to capitalism was a matter of internal evolution, not, as was usually assumed of non-European cases, due to an external prime mover, in this case Western imperialism. The Meiji Restoration, or so-called capitalist revolution from above, may have been inspired by the threat from the West. However, Takahashi argued, its possibility and form were determined by the internal evolution of Japanese feudalism. The historical priority of Western capitalism could not be gainsaid, argued Takahashi, but its uniqueness, as argued by Hobsbawm, could.

Takahashi notably attributed the top-down nature of Japanese capitalism to the resilience of its feudalism. While capitalism was breaking through in the West, the feudal regime consolidated or reconsolidated itself as the Tokugawa Shogunate in the seventeenth century on the basis of extremely heavy rents-in-kind and personal serfdom. The aspirations of the petty producers in Japan were crushed by the weight of feudal rent and the development of usury. On the other hand, these burdens on the peasants stimulated increased commercialization of the surplus. As a result, proto-capitalist manufacturing and agriculture, including some wage labour directed by small manufacturers and middle peasants, emerged in the countryside prior to the opening of Japan to the West. On the other hand, Takahashi stressed the dominant economic power of the urban merchants and financiers, who operated on the basis of their close dependency on the feudal state and great landlord magnates. Centralized collection of revenue made possible a high degree of commercialization and urbanization as well as an extreme level of peasant exploitation. On the eve of the Meiji Restoration, middle peasants and small manu-facturers began to enter into opposition to the merchant and financial monopolists tied to feudal magnates in a way reminiscent of the

revolutions in England and France. Over-exploitation by landlords led
to increasing misery and ultimately population decline. The country fell
into an increasingly severe demographic and economic crisis which set
the stage for the overthrow of the Tokugawa Shogunate. Yet Japanese
feudalism proved much more durable than that of the states of the
West, and its resilience fundamentally determined the nature of the
capitalism that did emerge.

Takahashi's insistence on the profundity of the economic and
demographic crisis and the polarization of Japanese society between
the proto-capitalist and peasant opposition, on the one hand, and
the resistance of its feudal and big merchant supporters on the other,
has been confirmed overall by subsequent research. Legal serfdom
in the sense of personal dependence appears to have been less
prevalent than in medieval Europe, although economic exploitation
was at least as severe. In fact, though initial advances made early
Tokugawa Japan compare favourably with France under the *Ancien
Régime*, over-exploitation created food shortages, peasant revolts
and population decline. They engulfed the Shogunate in the last
decades of its existence. Popular and proto-capitalist revolt proved
essential to catalyzing a modernizing political elite to dismantle the
institutions of the feudal regime while preserving the essence of
landlord power over the peasantry. But revolt from below fundamentally failed to transform the feudal Japanese social and political
order.[58] Decentralized military power was broken but landlords
continued to control their tenants socially and economically. The
political and economic freedom of the bulk of producers remained
fundamentally constrained. As a consequence it was the state rather
than the petty producers that was to take the lead in capitalist
development. For Takahashi, contrary to Eurocentric prejudice, the
intrusion of the West was merely a catalyst which set off what
was already the internal evolution of Japan toward capitalism.
But despite Takahashi's analysis Eurocentrism reasserted itself in a
sophisticated and nuanced way through the intervention of Perry
Anderson. Anderson dealt with Japanese feudalism in a long note or
appendix added to his *Lineages of the Absolutist State*.[59] He agreed
with Takahashi that feudalism set the stage for a capitalist take-off
and that the parallels between Japanese and Western feudalism
were striking. Anderson underscored the gains in the productivity
of Japanese feudal agriculture in the seventeenth century. The eighteenth century, while less dynamic, was still marked by increased
commercialization, including the spread of cash crops like sugar,
cotton, tea, indigo and tobacco. The urban merchant class expanded

and became more influential while the cities grew prodigiously. Educational and literacy levels were as high as or higher than in the West. Indeed, the potential for capitalist development once a breakthrough occurred was enormous. However, Anderson rejects Takahashi's suggestion that Japan could have liquidated feudalism through the power of its own internal contradictions. An external prime mover was required, which arrived with the abrupt intrusion of American imperialism.

For, Anderson argues, although the conspicuous consumption of the elites set the stage for a major fiscal and economic crisis by the beginning of the nineteenth century, the Shogunate was not in danger of being overthrown from within. The isolation of Japan from the world market fundamentally blocked its evolution from feudalism toward capitalism. Citing Lenin, Anderson stressed that no country became capitalist without linking itself to the global market, a fundamental theme in Anderson's broader narrative of the absolutist state mediating the historical transitional phase between the crisis of feudalism and the rise of capitalism. It was the intrusion of Western trade following the Commodore Perry's expedition that destabilized the feudal regime and led to the Meiji Restoration.

Though this is hardly definitive proof of Anderson's Eurocentric arguments, late Tokugawa Japan, though racked by internal contradictions, did not explode of itself. Eurocentrism aside, however, Anderson's view of Japan has wider theoretical resonances. They suggest that between Dobb's internal prime mover and Sweezy's external prime mover, Anderson favours the latter. Or better, he is arguing that for capitalism to develop, connections to the world market and an appropriate set of social relations of production are both necessary. Anderson's is a fundamentally dialectical view of capitalist origins. This Marxist methodology is manifest likewise in his overall view of the relationship between the relations of production and trade, and above all in his discussion of the origins of the state. As we shall see below, the latter is seen simultaneously as the last redoubt of feudalism and the indispensable framework for the development of capitalism.

As for the Japanese example, it makes evident that the commercial and economic potential of the feudal mode of production in general needs to be taken into account more than it has been.[60] On the other hand, it also suggests that feudal territorial division, lack of secure property rights, and above all, isolation from world trade may block the further evolution of merchant capitalism and a transition to capitalism.

THE LAST RAMPART OF FEUDALISM

Anderson's *Lineages of the Absolutist State* reflected extraordinary mastery of the historiography of the transition. Anderson was, of course, the editor of the *New Left Review*, the influential journal of the English-speaking left intelligentsia. His interest in the transition question is but one of an incredible range of political and cultural interests, and his theoretical insight and erudition have arguably made him the leading Marxist intellectual of this generation.

As we have noted, Anderson conceded the homology between European and Japanese feudalism. Once opened to the global market Japan rapidly made the transition to capitalism. But, for Anderson, only Western European feudalism could have created capitalism. Anderson's view of feudalism and its demise combines an emphasis on class struggle with recognition of the importance of exchange relations. The emergence of the territorial state and the global market both provided indispensable foundations for capitalism. In feudalism the peasant producer was tied to the land by being legally bound to the soil as a serf. Agrarian property was privately controlled by a class of feudal lords who extracted a surplus in the form of rent from peasants by political-legal or extra-economic coercion.[61] These social relations provided the setting for a dramatic increase in productivity during the High Middle Ages.[62] In contrast to Dobb and Hilton, however, Anderson stresses the objective exhaustion of the possibility of further advances in the forces of production as the source of the feudal crisis, rather than over-exploitation of the producers. Population increased, forcing the clearing of increasingly marginal land, while necessary investments in improving the productivity of existing tillage were not undertaken.[63] The subsequent economic crisis provoked widespread peasant revolts which were everywhere defeated in the short term. In the longer run the income and wages of the peasantry improved and serfdom declined.[64]

Anderson also insisted, more than any other previous participant in the debate save Sweezy, on the important role of the towns to this outcome. Urban commercial networks tended to destabilize feudal social relations. Towns served as potential refuges for runaway serfs as well as allies in peasant revolts. Indeed, the most significant rural revolts were located close to towns.[65] In the long term the noble lords' need for commodities produced in the towns led them to commute labour services into money rents and to lease out demesne to peasant tenants. In England in the fifteenth century serfdom

virtually disappeared and peasant incomes rose. Social differentiation increased in the villages, as a stratum of rich peasants emerged
at the top and wage labour spread in the countryside. Anderson
directly addressed the Dobb–Sweezy debate in a long footnote in the
opening chapter of his *Lineages of the Absolutist State*.[66] For him it
was not a case of choosing between rural social relations of production and commercial-trade relations but of their relative weight and
dialectical inter-relationship. Indeed, based on Merrington, Anderson
acknowledged that trade was intrinsic to the feudal mode.[67]

Dobb had already suggested that the early modern state was above
all designed to defend the nobility, and Anderson provided a conclusive demonstration of this thesis. The end of serfdom did not bring
feudalism to an end. The consolidation of the territorial monarchies
at the end of the Middle Ages in fact represented 'a redeployed and
recharged apparatus of feudal domination, designed to clamp the
peasant masses back into their traditional social position'.[68] The
class power of the nobility, which was put in question as a result of
the disappearance of serfdom, was displaced upwards and centralized into the hands of the new territorial monarchies, which became
the principal instruments for the maintenance of noble domination over the peasantry. Moreover, in so far as nobles blocked the
emergence of a free market in land and peasants retained access to
their means of subsistence, feudal relations persisted.[69] Nonetheless,
in England and elsewhere in Western Europe the emergence of the
territorial state created a space essential for the further progression
of the urban-based bourgeoisie. In the medieval period political and
economic control had been combined. With the appearance of the
territorial state in the early modern period, political power began
to be separated from immediate control over the economy, allowing
capitalist forces to emerge. The political order remained feudal while
society under its aegis became more bourgeois.[70]

Anderson sees the emerging territorial state as having a dual
determination:

> the threat of peasant unrest, unspokenly constitutive of the
> Absolutist State, was thus always conjoined with the pressure
> of mercantile or manufacturing capital within the Western
> economies as a whole, in moulding the contours of aristocratic
> class power in the new age.[71]

For all that the development of the territorial state bolstered feudalism,
it also provided an enlarged political space within which capitalism

could develop. In such a space lay the market. Just as Merrington saw the medieval market as intrinsic to the seigneurial regime, Anderson insists that the capitalist market was a creation of the territorial state and almost as much a political as an economic institution.

Anderson's insight into the role of the state is critical to understanding the transition. Moreover, like his formulation of the relationship between relations of production and those of exchange, one must underline the importance of the fact that he grasps the nature of the state in a dialectical way. He demonstrates that the state both saved feudalism and incubated capitalism within itself. It is within the state that the transition is possible in the first place.

BRENNER AND THE LATE MEDIEVAL CRISIS

Beginning with Dobb, scholars separated the period of the decline of feudalism from the period of the rise of capitalism. Dobb and Sweezy, chief protagonists in the initial debate, both acknowledged the existence of an intermediate period prior to the emergence of capitalism, in which a weakened feudalism gave greater freedom to petty producers prior to the emergence of capitalism. Moreover, most of the participants in the debate, while stressing one or another factor leading to the transition, nonetheless tended to acknowledge a multiplicity of causes. Dobb, Hilton and Anderson stressed the vital importance of class struggle in the decline of feudalism. But Brenner took the importance of agrarian class struggle a step further, arguing that as it unfolded in England in the late Middle Ages, it not only destroyed feudalism but created a path leading directly to the emergence of capitalism. In taking this view Brenner largely abolished the conceptual and chronological divide between the decline of feudalism and the origins of capitalism.[72]

Brenner is a historian at UCLA who began his scholarly career as a student of early modern England. With roots in a radical family, he became politically active in the 1960s in the Trotskyist movement in the United States and is currently an editor of a leading Marxist journal, *Against the Current*. While maintaining his interest in the transition problem, he has become recognized as a leading analyst of the current capitalist crisis through the publication of *The Boom and the Bubble: The U.S. in the World Economy* (2002).[73] For his PhD he produced a magisterial thesis, *Merchants and Revolution: Commercial Change, Political Conflict, and London's Overseas Traders, 1550–1653*, which while not bearing on the end of feudalism debate, proved important to the controversy on the English Revolution.[74] It is a work founded on deep primary research. His conception of the transition, like that of most of those involved in the transition debate, is simply based on a close reading of the current historiography.

His view of the transition question is informed theoretically by the influence of analytical Marxism, a school of thought which was prominent in the 1980s and to which Brenner subscribed. It has recently been shown that analytical philosophy as a whole was a product of the 1950s Cold War, which saw Anglo-American philosophy sever all ties with Continental philosophy, transforming itself into a politically disengaged professional discipline preoccupied with constituting a formal model of knowledge.[75] Born in the midst of the waning of Marxism in the 1980s, analytical Marxism purported to salvage whatever could be saved by applying the same techniques of formal logic to Marxism. Committed to a positivist logic, this approach rejected a dialectical sense of totality, movement and contradiction to its own cost.[76] Brenner's view of the transition is fundamentally weakened by this constraining methodology.

THE EAST–WEST DIVIDE

Dobb and Hilton had already made the late medieval population collapse and ensuing class conflicts central to their conception of the crisis in England and elsewhere in Europe. In Brenner's view such conflicts arose from a crisis of peasant accumulation, productivity and ultimately subsistence provoked by over-exploitation. Excessive landlord exploitation and the inherent conservatism of the peasant mode of production placed definite limits on the productivity of peasant agriculture. As Dobb and Hilton had argued, Brenner stressed that landlords used extra-economic coercion to extract more and more surplus from the producers. More originally he demonstrated the inherent economic limitations of the peasant economic mode within the constraints of the medieval manor. The economic objectives of peasants within the bounds of the manor were not to improve their holdings, maximize output or deepen their relation to the market, but rather to ensure the reproduction of the family unit. As a result a definite limit was imposed on economic growth. In the ensuing crisis the survival of the mass of producers was put into question. Following the demographic collapse of the fourteenth century, intense class struggles revolved around the issue of serfdom and the control of land. The outcome of these struggles in the different parts of Europe depended on varying historical and social circumstances.[77]

Brenner denied that trade or towns were important in the transition. Indeed, he rejected the idea that the towns in any way contributed to the dissolution of feudalism.[78] On the contrary, it was the development of rural networks of solidarity and cooperation that was important to the varying outcomes of the late medieval class struggles, notably between West and East Europe.[79] For some reason the relation of such networks to the existence or not of urban-based trade is not considered by Brenner as it had been by Hilton and Anderson. In Eastern Europe the weakness of the peasantries faced with landlord power led to the imposition of serfdom. In the class struggles in France, in contrast, the peasantry not only consolidated its free status but was able to hold onto land and rights into the early modern period. Surplus extraction sufficient to maintain the nobility transferred itself from the local to a higher level through the crystallization of the territorial state.[80] Whereas local rents withered, royal taxes were employed to benefit the warrior and court nobility, amounting to a new system of centralized rent. The feudal system was perpetuated as a result.

THE LOGIC OF ACCUMULATION

England represented a third way that led to agrarian capitalism. Peasants were able to win personal freedom but were less successful in the class struggle than their French counterparts. As a result English nobles were able to hold onto most of the cultivable land, and from the late fifteenth century onward, they began to rent this land to rich farmers on terms which favoured enhanced rents based on growing profits. According to Brenner, 'with the peasants' failure to establish essentially freehold control over the land, the landlords were able to engross, consolidate and enclose, to create large farms and to lease them to capitalist tenants who could afford to make capital investments'.[81] Unlike medieval peasants, capitalist tenants needed to improve productivity in order to meet landlords' demands for higher rents, and in turn, to obtain higher rents landlords found themselves advancing capital to tenants in order to improve output. An economic logic of accumulation was initiated. On this basis there emerged the classic tripartite division of landlord/capitalist tenants/ wage labourers which transformed English agriculture in a capitalist direction.[82]

Brenner underlined the rupture between the logic of this new order and the old feudal order. In feudalism both the exploiting landlords and peasant producers had direct access to the means of reproducing their existence: that is, land for the peasants, rent for the landlords. In pursuit of their subsistence, the goal of the peasants was to produce as much of their needs from the land as they could without resort to the market. In the heyday of feudalism labour rents or rents-in-kind provided for the maintenance of the landlords. Consequently both classes were spared the necessity of buying what they needed to reproduce themselves on the market, and therefore the need to produce for exchange or to sell competitively. They were not required to cut costs and therefore to improve production through innovation, specialization and accumulation. Whatever innovations there might have been were absorbed into the way of life of the peasant class, which was based largely on economic subsistence. The new relationships between landlords and proto-capitalist tenants at the end of the Middle Ages broke this traditional logic of social reproduction and imposed another based on cumulative economic growth.[83]

One can only applaud Brenner's insistence that class struggles in the countryside were decisive to the fall of feudalism and transition to capitalism. It lent rigor to a perspective previously taken by Dobb and Hilton. In conformity with the views of the latter, Brenner's relations of production or social property relations approach especially targeted Sweezy and what Brenner dubbed his 'neo-Smithian' insistence on the importance of trade.[84] It also took aim at the neo-Malthusian historical school exemplified in the work of Michael Postan and Emmanuel Le Roy Ladurie. They argued that the decline of population accounted for the disintegration of feudalism. However, subsequent exchanges published in the *Brenner Debate* (1985) amply confirmed the strength of Brenner's endogenous perspective on population. He conceded that in the absence of technological change, the ratio of land to labour determined the upswings and downswings of the population. But for him this argument reinforced the centrality of class relations. They set the parameters of demographic cycles and ultimately helped to burst through their limits.[85]

BOIS OBJECTS

Critics of Brenner attacked on the one hand his over-emphasis on class, and on the other his misunderstanding of late medieval class relations. As against his one-sided insistence on the determining influence of class struggle, they insisted on the importance of a forces of production approach which understood the dialectical relationship between class capacity and the forces of production (material as well as non-material) at the command of a class. Class struggle remains at the focal point of their view of the decline of feudalism. But their conception of class is broader and more deeply situated in material reality than Brenner's.

The French medieval historian Guy Bois was the first to voice such objections to Brenner's view of feudalism's demise. In *The Brenner Debate* Bois expressed scepticism over Brenner's rather schematic emphasis on economic class while insisting on the importance of the forces of production perspective, understood as the material and non-material resources at the disposition of a class. Bois calls Brenner's perspective a kind of 'political Marxism' which reacts against economistic tendencies in historiography by stressing political and social agency. Bois acknowledged that Brenner's injection of strong doses of class struggle into his account was commendable, and that it had been ignored in the past. However, he objected to the sketchy and overly ideological manner in which Brenner introduced such conceptions. He called it a voluntarist view of history divorced from all other objective contingencies and from laws of development specific to a particular mode of production.[86] In other words, Bois complained that Brenner's view is based on too superficial a view of the economic history of the medieval period and of the dynamics of its mode of production.

Bois insisted, for example, that the medieval hierarchical network of markets based on small and large towns could not be separated from the development of the *seigneurie* or manor, as Brenner would have it. The market, according to Bois, developed coincidentally with and was dependent on the system of manors or *seigneuries*:

> the market is in no way an entity which is foreign to feudal society: its introduction, or rather its development, is linked with the introduction of new seigneurial structures and ... the market played a central role in the development of medieval society.[87]

Indeed, the medieval market was not simply an autonomous economic mechanism which peasants entered or withdrew from at will, as pictured by Brenner. It was in part a coercive institution through which peasant surplus was extracted and commercialized by landlords using merchants as intermediaries.[88] This insight of Bois's that markets were not strictly economic entities but also had a coercive or political aspect is of critical importance to an understanding of both the feudal and capitalist modes of production.

With regard to the decline of feudalism, furthermore, Bois asserts that feudalism declined because of the tendency of rents to fall, which resulted from the structural contradiction of large-scale property and small-scale production. The dominant class was unable to maintain the economic base of its hegemony because there was an erosion of the productivity of family labour on the increasingly small patches of arable land as a result of population growth.[89] Bois emphasizes the importance of the blockage of the forces of production in setting off the late feudal crisis. At the same time, beyond the realm of economy which preoccupies Brenner, Bois stresses the many-sided nature of the late medieval crisis – political, religious, cultural – reflected as a crisis of values but also of class conflict. Writing in 2000, he insisted on and indeed demonstrated the similarities between the crisis of feudalism and the current crisis of the capitalist system.[90]

HARMAN'S RIPOSTE

Brenner's view has become dominant at least in the world of English-speaking Marxist academics, and some of Brenner's followers have proudly accepted the label 'Political Marxism' and constituted themselves into a veritable school based on his approach.[91] More recently, Chris Harman has engaged with Brenner and his followers by insisting, like Bois, on the importance of the forces of production, in opposition to Brenner's emphasis on class.[92] The recently deceased Harman, a Trotskyist militant since the upheavals of the 1960s, was long the political and intellectual leader of the influential British Socialist Workers Party. Harman was an acknowledged authority on Marxist crisis theory, played a leading role in transforming the *International Socialism Journal* into an authoritative intellectual and political journal, and authored the monumental and enduring *A People's History of the World*.[93]

Harman insisted that the social capacity of a class depends on the productive forces that undergird it. Such forces include the material, intellectual and political resources at its disposition. The capacity of a class to change the social relations of production depends on its ability to mobilize such resources. Historic change occurs when the existing social relations block the further development of the forces of production. In Harman's view Brenner turns these relationships upside down, subordinating the forces of production to the determination of class relations. At the same time Brenner's rejection of the dialectic makes him take an excessively economistic view of class.

Harman insists on the increases in the productivity of agriculture in the High Middle Ages both in England and on the European Continent. Agricultural surpluses were marketed in the towns, manufactures were consumed not merely by nobles but also by peasants and townspeople, and commercial ties between producers in town and country were strengthened. Wage labour began to be employed on a limited basis by incipient capitalists. Social differentiation among the peasantry strengthened these tendencies.

The late medieval crisis affirmed rather than annulled these economic and social advances of the twelfth and thirteenth centuries. During that period of difficulty the lead in opposition to the nobles was taken by those peasants and craftspeople who were most in command of the forces of production that had developed in the previous period of prosperity. In other words, Harman considers the social upheavals of the fourteenth century throughout Western Europe to be a proto-capitalist revolution brought on by the development of the forces of production in the High Middle Ages and their fettering by the persistence of feudal relations. According to Harman, the religious heresies, new cultural movements and revolutionary social movements of the late Middle Ages were important factors in the decline of feudalism, but find no place in Brenner's economistic and point of production perspective.[94] Harman concludes that Brenner's approach 'may be "class struggle" Marxism, but it is class struggle without any element of class consciousness determining its outcome. Its focus is not really on politics at all, but on purely economic struggles confined to the countryside.'[95] We might add that whereas Brenner's notion of the intrinsically conservative peasant behaviour might appertain under conditions where feudalism was a stable system, he fails to address changes in peasant behaviour under conditions where feudalism was in the process of disintegrating. In point of fact the late medieval disintegration of the economic and social controls of the feudal manor helped to create more opportunistic economic attitudes among prosperous peasants.

Brenner denies Harman's view that either the expansion of the forces of production or commercialization led to the emergence of an incipient class of enterprising agricultural and urban proto-capitalists. While the peasants won their personal freedom, late medieval class struggle allowed the English landlords to retain and extend their control of the major part of the arable sector. Capitalism and a new class of rural capitalists emerged from above, with the establishment by landlords of commercial leases let out to prosperous tenant farmers. At stake in this disagreement is whether capitalism was an economic project emerging from the feudal ruling class, as Brenner would have it, or was rather an initiative which emerged from below as a result of an across-the-board struggle against feudalism, as Harman argues. If we are to believe Brenner, late medieval changes in social-property relations determined the onset of capitalism in the sixteenth century. But there is no historical warrant for seeing the development of the capitalist mode in merely socio-economic terms, and especially not those outlined by Brenner, in which continued landlord domination remains key. The establishment of capitalist leases by landlords, rather than being the driving force behind rural capitalism, appears to have been a belated response to the emergence of a class of capitalist farmers in a long-term process which cannot be comprehended in terms of the persistence of landlord power in a market economy. The transformation of a whole society and culture cannot be reduced to such a presumed single first cause. Brenner nonetheless insists on the emergence of capitalist social property relations which determined the development of capitalism from the fourteenth century.

THE ROLE OF SOCIAL DIFFERENTIATION

A recent article published by Terence J. Byres powerfully reinforces Harman's viewpoint.[96] Byres himself is a scholar of Indian history and Marxist political economy. Long an influential figure at that focal point of third world Marxism, the University of London's School of Oriental and African Studies, he was the major force behind the creation of both the *Journal of Peasant Studies* in the 1970s and the new periodical, the *Journal of Agrarian Change*. As he proudly declares, he was heavily influenced by Hilton in studying Indian agriculture. Indeed, his article attacking Brenner is based on the closest possible scrutiny of Hilton's works. Prior to invoking Hilton against Brenner, Byres produced *Capitalism from Above and Capitalism from Below* (1996), a great work of comparative history heavily focused on peasant social differentiation and based on Lenin's *Development of Capitalism in Russia* (1899).[97] We will examine Byres's tome later. Hilton we have seen is celebrated as a historian of the medieval English peasantry whose publications were at one and the same time steeped in archival research and informed by Marxist theory. It is this body of work that Byres has carefully analyzed and brought to bear especially against Brenner's view of the roots of capitalist origins. Whereas Brenner minimized social differentiation within the medieval peasantry, stressing its homogeneity as a class, Byres makes the differentiation of the peasant class the linchpin of his notion of capitalist development:

> So, rather than suggesting that it was the leases that brought about the necessary class formation ... which is what Brenner appears to argue (that it was the lords who were the essential agents – that the causality ran from the lords), might one not suggest a causality running in quite the opposite direction: that it was the rich peasantry that forced the pace, rather than the landlords: that, indeed, one cannot grasp the nature of the eventual transition without reference to the differentiation of the peasantry?[98]

In the thirteenth century, if not before, the peasantry were internally divided between rich, middle and poor elements. Rich peasants had more livestock and land, and often worked for the lords as bailiffs, stewards and rent collectors, helping the lords maintain control of the bulk of the peasants. Contrary to Brenner's notion of an essential equality among medieval peasants, the better-off peasants' enforcement of legal-political control over the remainder of the peasantry on behalf of the nobility amounted to economic control over them. The power of the rich peasants increased during the thirteenth century as they were able to market part of their agricultural surplus and purchase the labour of poor peasants and incipient wage earners. Their ability to produce surpluses had been enhanced by previous gains in productivity or improvements in the forces of production. In the late medieval crisis their power grew alongside that of the rest of the peasantry in relation to the nobles, as rents and personal servitude declined and more land became available for purchase.

The crisis reduced the numbers of poor peasants and wage earners, limiting the ability of better-off peasants at this stage to hire labour. It was the middle peasants whose numbers and incomes rose most notably during this period. But from the late fifteenth century onward it was rich peasants who came to the fore, benefiting in particular from the cheap labour increasingly available as a result of the demographic recovery. This was a process which occurred across the face of Western Europe but assumed decisive significance in England. As we have noted, Brenner stressed the offering of economic leases by landlords to prosperous farmers as integral to capitalist beginnings. But he said nothing about where the farmers able to take up such leases came from. According to Byres, such farmers were the product of previous social differentiation and especially the period of feudal disintegration. They then became the prime movers of sixteenth-century capitalism, which was based on the dispossession of a growing mass of peasants and their subjection to the emerging power of rural capital. This account seems to be consonant with Harman's notion of the emergence of a class of rural proto-capitalists in the late medieval crisis in a position to command new forces of production.

Byres, Harman and Bois do not underestimate the importance of class struggle to the decline of feudalism. They stress rather that the outcome of such struggles must be related to the level of development of the forces of production. In its turn, the level reached by the forces of production under the command of a given class determines the capacity of that class for leadership in class conflict.[99] Brenner had seen the peasantry as more than willing to engage in class struggle against landlords in the late medieval crisis but also, being essentially peasants, unwilling thereafter to seize new economic possibilities opened by the decline of feudalism. Peasants engaged in market activity, but only in so far as did not endanger the subsistence family household. Only an upper stratum of this class was forced out of passivity by the imposition of competitive rents by the landlords at the beginning of the sixteenth century. It is the logic of accumulation imposed from the outside in the form of these competitive rents which initiates capitalism. Byres, expanding on Hilton's view and opposing Brenner, sees the peasantry as socially combative and its upper stratum as the active base of an emerging capitalist class eager to seek opportunity in the market. Opportunity presented itself in the late medieval crisis with the disintegration of the restrictions of feudalism. Increasingly freed from the constraints of the decaying manor, rich peasants sought economic opportunity by acquiring access to more land, marketing increasing amounts of livestock and grain, and employing increasing amounts of wage labour. The enclosures of the sixteenth century transformed this impulse into capitalist accumulation.

As a parenthesis to the above discussion we should note that the question of the role of the petty producers in capitalism has implications beyond their destiny in the late Middle Ages or sixteenth century in Europe. Peasant farmers and craftspeople did not disappear with the full emergence of capitalism, as is suggested by the above discussion. They have continued to be an important social group within Europe and in the rest of the world, constituting and reconstituting themselves right up to the present. Indeed, the present crisis of capitalist agriculture has led to the re-emergence of movements in many countries attempting to revive the peasantry as the basis for a sustainable agriculture. Hence the class nature of this group continues to be a matter of some political moment.

Earlier analyses tended to view the peasantry from the perspective of capitalist or socialist modernization, in which they were regarded as a dated social anomaly. Ernesto Laclau argued in the 1970s, for example, that they form part of an archaic set of social relations which blocked the emergence of a fully developed capitalism in the under-developed countries and facilitated the export of surplus within global imperialism.[100] On the other hand, Jairus Banaji, who was more sympathetic, argued that rural petty producers were really disguised proletarians even in the absence of a real accumulation of capital.[101] In other words Banaji tries to rehabilitate the peasantry by reclassifying them as part of the proletarian class. Neither Laclau nor Banaji are able to perceive the peasantry in terms of the future viability of an enhanced subsistence economy. In any case in the light of our view of capitalism, which sees both wage labour and the ongoing entry of capital into production as indispensable components of the capitalist mode, Banaji's view appears dubious under the constraints of imperialism. The role of such rural petty producers might be quite different in a socialist economy. In such circumstances a revived peasant economy could help to absorb the constantly expanding global *lumpenproletariat* and constitute one essential part of a sustainable agriculture.

DIALECTICS OF SOCIAL RELATIONS

As we have seen, the initial debate on the transition focused on whether the prime mover in the long decline of feudalism was long-range trade or factors internal to the feudal system. The outcome of the dispute was a nearly unanimous consensus that the exhaustion of feudalism from within, especially as the result of class struggle, was critical to its decline. The subsequent debate centred on Brenner's view that class struggle alone was critical not only to feudalism's decline but also to setting the stage for the beginning of capitalism. According to him, changes in the social relations of production unique to England, giving control of the land to the landlords but depriving them of control of persons, determined that they would attempt to gain control of future surplus by instituting competitive leases and encouraging primitive accumulation.

In contrast to Brenner's economistic and class-determinist method we have insisted that the importance of the economic and social must be understood in the light of a dialectical perspective. Economic and social factors have their part as elements of a contradictory totality in which culture and politics have a role. Of course we accept the notion that changes in the social relations of production were critical to the demise of feudalism. But when it comes to the origins of capitalism, I reject Brenner's notion that it was English landlords who played the major role in the origins of capitalism in the face of the economic passivity of the peasant producers. Rather than landlords being decisive to the inception of capitalism, I have made the importance of the late medieval social differentiation of the producers a central theme of my conception. In the new economic circumstances of the sixteenth century, the petty producers would increasingly divide into rural capitalist producers and wage workers. The revolts of the rural and urban petty producers against feudalism reflected not merely their social combativeness but their economic and even religious aspirations as well. They were neither socially nor economically passive as pictured by Brenner. The class capacity of these producers must not be taken for granted but be seen as a product of the previous medieval development of the forces of production.

The early emergence of capitalism, furthermore, cannot be understood as an exclusively English affair, but must be seen in terms of Western Europe as a whole. The struggle against feudalism and the development of capitalist relations appeared across Western Europe at the end of the Middle Ages. In order to fully grasp the specific conditions which allowed capitalism fully to crystallize in England, its development in Italy and elsewhere on the European Continent should be traced and brought into comparison with the English example.

2

EXPERIMENTS IN CAPITALISM: ITALY, GERMANY, FRANCE

The purpose of this chapter is to demonstrate that capitalism's beginnings cannot be understood by looking at the isolated case of England. Capitalism – from the start a single system – actually began in Italy, spread to Germany and then to Holland and France. England was the last stop in this progress. Using the examples of Italy, Germany and France, which have been largely ignored in the transition debate, this chapter shows that many of the factors leading to the development of capitalism in England and Holland were also present in these countries. The key difference between these countries, where the development of capitalism was arrested or limited, and England and Holland lay in the balance of power between capital, the state and feudal power. Italy failed to consolidate a territorial state because of the too great strength of merchant capital, while in Germany and France feudalism proved too strong. Our study of these cases will demonstrate that, in addition to the economic conditions stressed by Brenner, two political conditions were critical to the successful development of capitalism: the existence of a territorial state, and the influence of capitalist or incipiently capitalist classes over the state. The faltering of capitalism in Italy, Germany and France sheds light on the importance of the more propitious political conditions which obtained in Holland as well as in England. And capitalism, being a single system which developed in an uneven fashion, meant that its eventual consolidation in Holland and England came at the expense of its further development elsewhere in Europe. The proper way of conceiving of capitalism's origins is thus through a series of experiments which finally had their successful *dénouement* in these two states.

Brenner's insistence in his early work that capitalism developed more or less exclusively in England is certainly contrary to Marx's views. He saw capitalism as a global or globalizing system of which Continental Europe was a part. The earliest process of capitalism, the expropriation of the peasantry, took place across Western Europe. Marx described it in Volume One of *Capital*:

the proletariat created by the breaking up of the bands of the feudal retainers and by the forcible expropriation of the people from the soil, this 'free' proletariat could not possibly be absorbed by the nascent manufactures as fast as it was thrown upon the world. … They were turned en masse into beggars, robbers, vagabonds, partly from inclination, in most cases from stress of circumstances. Hence at the end of the 15th and during the whole of the 16th century, throughout West Europe, there was a bloody legislation against vagabondage.[1]

Such primitive accumulation was necessary to clear the ground for capitalism. England was only the classic instance of this process of expropriation, which Marx makes clear took different forms and followed different paths in different countries.[2]

Far from believing that capitalism originated in England, Marx explicitly recognized that capitalism developed first in the city-states of Renaissance Italy.[3] Engels saw the revolution that shook Germany in 1524–25 as an early bourgeois revolution that arose from the development of capitalism there. Marx characterized the early processes of the emergent capitalism, what he called the different moments of primitive accumulation, as distributing themselves:

now, more or less in chronological order, particularly over Spain, Portugal, Holland, France and England. In England at the end of the 17th century, they arrive at a systematical combination, embracing the colonies, the national debt, the modern mode of taxation, and the protectionist system.[4]

England became the final station in a movement across the face of Western Europe, which as it developed came to involve more than the mere expropriation of the peasantry from the soil.

In the light of this more global conception, Perry Anderson recently criticized Brenner's Anglocentric view for what he describes as a 'capitalism in one country' approach. It makes only slightly more sense, according to him, than the notion of socialism in one country.[5] While the latter makes nonsense of socialism as a transcendence of the limits of capitalism based on the territorial state, the former not only ignored the sequencing of primitive accumulation across Western Europe that Marx traced, but also forgot Lenin's insistence that no state has ever become capitalist without connection to the world market.

There is an unfortunate parochialism in Brenner's viewpoint, and its negative consequences are many. It allowed Brenner to make exaggerated claims about the role of competitive markets in the early development of capitalism. It led him to fail to take proper account of politics – in particular the centrality of a unified territorial state and the influence of capitalist merchants and manufacturers over its policies. This chapter will begin to remedy this by viewing the origins of capitalism from a Europe-wide perspective. Accordingly, we will examine the development of capitalism in Italy and Germany in the first place. Failing to take permanent root in these places, these capitalisms must be understood as prologues to the development of capitalism in England. These failed or partially successful transitions on the Continent help to illuminate the reasons for England's ultimate success. They also show that the development of capitalism is uneven – that success in one place comes at the expense of failure elsewhere. Finally it shows how historically contingent its full development was. This chapter also discusses the case of capitalism in France, whose development did not miscarry so much as retreated into hibernation under the seventeenth-century Bourbon monarchy. The great influence of Brenner's Anglocentricism has meant that the origins of capitalism in that country in the early modern period have been denied, helping to foster the serious misconception that the French Revolution was not a capitalist revolution. The discussion of Holland is left to the next chapter, where its history better fits in the sequence of early modern bourgeois revolutions.

RENAISSANCE ITALY

Marx noted that capitalism first developed in Italy, and it dominated the European economy of the late Middle Ages. Yet Italy was scarcely mentioned in the original Dobb–Sweezy debate. The first attempt to take Italy into account was made at an inter-university conference held in Montreal in 1975.[6] Giuliano Procacci, a participant in the original debate, insisted first that there was no one Marxist theory, only Marx's hypotheses of the transition and differing interpretations of them. Second, he pointed out that the transition had been Europe-wide. An important implication of this was that it was naïve to assume an exact similarity and symmetry in comparing various national transitions. This is even more the case when it is understood that the development of an international market and the concomitant economic and geographic disequilibria were conditions of the transition itself.[7] Here Procacci echoed Hobsbawm, who stressed world-wide uneven development as an essential characteristic of capitalist development. From this we conclude that comparison may be essential and insightful, but has inherent limits. For the transition is not repeated in the same sequence (with or without interesting variations) by every country. It can be radically, qualitatively, different because capitalist development is a single global historical process.

Third, Procacci introduced specifically Italian concerns into the discussion. Marxists in that country stressed that despite political division, the late medieval period saw the emergence of an internal market for labour and goods in the peninsula and, as a consequence, the appearance of agrarian capitalism in the fertile Po valley. Capital there entered and transformed agricultural production, and producers were transformed into wage labourers. Industrial development was likewise strongest there, especially in Lombardy. Elsewhere, by contrast, historians found the development of capitalist agriculture to have been weak.

Procacci's insistence on the importance of markets was followed by the comprehensive and profound analysis of the origins and failure of early Italian capitalism in the light of the Dobb–Sweezy debate by the distinguished *Annales* scholar and Marxist historian Maurice Aymard.[8] Following closely in the footsteps of the master of the *Annales* School, Fernand Braudel, Aymard acquired a deep understanding of Italian Renaissance history based on primary research.[9] Beginning his analysis of capitalist origins by surveying the vestiges of feudalism in late medieval Italy, Aymard observed that by the mid-fifteenth century the remains of serfdom had disappeared throughout the Italian peninsula. A stage had been reached in which people could sell their labour freely. Indeed, the expropriation of the peasantry through enclosures – taken as a hallmark of capitalism in sixteenth-century England – had already begun in Italy in the thirteenth and fourteenth centuries.

In the wide plains of the Po valley – the most productive land in Italy – capitalist farming became prevalent. Throughout the rest of the peninsula, but especially in the centre, share-cropping was the most widespread form of tenure. Meanwhile in Naples and Sicily large arable estates continued to dominate. But over time the presence of the old ruling groups and the vestiges of feudalism there weakened. The landlords who owned or who were able to buy, sell and exploit these large estates came to be mainly urban merchants and notables. This change was manifest in a more intense and systematic exploitation of labour rather than enhanced capital investment. Hence the historic backwardness of southern Italian agriculture.

Alongside the large estates of the south a system of compact homogenous farmsteads of up to several hundred hectares emerged elsewhere by the fifteenth century, in conjunction with a more urbanized and commercialized economy. Such allotments produced a great variety of crops based on extensive and intensive methods of cultivation. Modern or rational economic attitudes and accounting methods appeared, and in contrast to the large estates, these smaller holdings also displayed the tendency to invest large amounts of fixed as well as variable capital. The employment of wage labour paid in money was used more than elsewhere in Europe.

The consolidation of five large states on the peninsula by the fifteenth century enlarged markets. Inter-regional and maritime trade between north and south also grew. Compared with the rest of Europe, markets and the commodification of agriculture were highly developed. Italian agriculture of the fifteenth and sixteenth centuries possessed all the elements of high farming that later emerged in England.

Large amounts of urban or commercial capital flowed into agri-culture not simply to buy but to improve land. Aside from landlord proprietors there was a class of farmer-owners who utilized capitalist methods of land management and in particular employed wage labour. It was during this Renaissance that northern and central Italy took on the aspect of the celebrated *bel paesaggio*, or beautiful landscape, with its characteristic sculpted and terraced hillsides and valleys.[10]

These developments not only raised the net agricultural product, and provisioned a particularly dense urban network in the north, but by doing so allowed a very early expansion of the manufac-turing sector.[11] In the fourteenth and fifteenth centuries the whole peninsula including the south was commercially linked in inter-regional and maritime networks dominated by the northern cities of Milan, Genoa, Venice and Florence. The integration of the primary, secondary and tertiary sectors allowed a high degree of urbanization and the emergence of new political structures, social relations and cultural values which are associated with the Italian Renaissance.

The merchants of northern Italy (along with those of Flanders, on whom more below) dominated European wholesale commerce from the thirteenth through the fifteenth centuries. They controlled the markets for raw materials and the outlets for manufactured goods. Long-distance trade in both precious and bulk goods lay in their hands. As needed, they developed new commercial and financial techniques while creating a financial network which covered Europe and the Mediterranean. Their dominance over international trade in wool cloth, silk, armaments, paper and glass set off the first systematic processes of capital accumulation, and resulted in the reorganization of the countryside, especially in the Po valley.[12]

THE DOMINANCE OF MERCHANT CAPITAL

Aymard holds that it was the northern Italian cities which were responsible for the economic transformation of the countryside. Looking at their role specifically from the perspective of the Dobb–Sweezy debate, Aymard contends that Sweezy was right to see trade as a decisive factor in the transition, though he was wrong to see it as an exogenous force in causing the decline of feudalism and development of capitalism.

According to Aymard the very merchant base of this capitalism – which was authentic enough – defined its limits. Unlike agriculture, no transformation of the means of production occurred in manufacturing, including in the all-important cloth industry dominated by merchants and guilds. Italian merchant capitalists proved to be uninterested in transforming the means of production in manufacture:

> we find once again the 'structural' character of merchant capital and its indifference to the mode of production of those commodities that enter into circulation which led to its continued preference for simple financial control over producers rather than real control of the processes of production.[13]

Rural capitalists were blocked from developing industry by the influence of urban merchants. Furthermore, the urban merchants who dominated this economy failed to develop a truly national market, which was critical to the further development of Italian capitalism. Only the creation of a wide and deep national market, especially one protected by a centralized territorial state, could have maintained the competitiveness of Italian manufacturing in the long term.

THE FAILURE OF ITALIAN CAPITALISM

According to Aymard there are three major interpretations of Italian capitalism's failure to advance further. The first, epitomized in the work of Ruggiero Romano, insists that despite the appearance of modernity the Italian economy failed to achieve real breakthroughs in productivity. Not only did agriculture and industry remain technologically inert, this stagnation was compounded by an urban–rural conflict which lacked any dialectical 'virtue': that is, did not issue in any positive economic outcome.[14]

The second position, reflected in the view of Renato Zangheri, is a more nuanced version of the first.[15] It acknowledges that real transformations in the direction of capitalism occurred in the late medieval period. But this modern sector remained too weak and local. No national market or national unification took place. Surpluses generated were not reinvested in agriculture or industry but in churches, country villas and palaces. As the sixteenth century waned, rent and interest came to dominate a process of refeudalization which included the north. These two interpretations stressing the internal evolution of Italy should be placed in a third, more international interpretative context. From this perspective Italian merchant capitalism, such as it was, could not fully transcend its links to a Europe-wide feudal framework and so merged back into it.

This wider view is provided by Immanuel Wallerstein – like Aymard a follower of Braudel.[16] For Wallerstein the decisive factor in the evolution of Italy was the emergence of the capitalist world economy after 1450. Whereas late medieval Italy had shared the dominant role in the European economy with the Netherlands, the new economic hierarchy that emerged following the European voyages of discovery saw Italy's decline. It lost its core position to Holland, which in turn lost out to England. With the emergence of the world market, the timing of capitalist development was critical to determining a country's eventual position in the magic circle at the capitalist core or outside of it. As it turned out, Italy's capitalism was too early while England's was timed just right.

But, Aymard complained, despite Wallerstein's references to the rural sector, he prioritized trade and industry at the expense of the social realities of Italian agriculture in explaining the failure of Italian capitalism. As a result of his bias toward exchange he was unable to get at the root of the failure of the Italian transition. This lay in excessively exploitative social relations of production. Aymard's own explanation of the falling-back of Italian capitalism focuses on the character of the merchant capitalism of the towns.[17] In a way which was unique to Europe at the time, the merchant capital of the cities dominated and transformed the whole Italian countryside and most radically the north. Despite the wars of the first part of the sixteenth century, Italy fully participated in the positive West European conjuncture of that period. All the conditions for further accumulation and expansion were present including buoyant profits, expanding demand, good prices, and increased production and consumption, amid stable or increasing productivity in industry and agriculture.

It was the flow of Italian merchant capital into the countryside above all that made this surge of growth possible, but also determined its limits. The expansion of the Italian economy continued until about 1600. But from the 1570s agriculture was unable to sustain the commercial and industrial sectors, with food prices leaping ahead of those in trade and manufacturing. Signs of over-exploitation, deforestation, erosion and ecological devastation of the land began to appear.[18] The links between the north and south of the peninsula weakened, as northern cities tended to abandon the import of southern wheat and raw silk, while liquidating previous investments in southern land or municipal bonds. Instead the political and merchant elites of the northern towns came to favour urban self-reliance, based on the exploitation of their own countrysides and through investment in local municipal bonds. From 1600 a long inertia set in. Even the ruralization of industry did not allow a reconquest of foreign, let alone domestic, markets, which contracted.

THE PREDATORY CITY-STATE

According to Aymard, it was the contradiction between the interests of urban elites and the rural dwellers which blocked further growth. The towns began to restrict freedom of markets, or permitted only those that were regarded as serving their interests, imposing controls on grain prices, production, marketing and exports in order to ensure supplies to their expanding populations, especially the urban poor. Rents rose, and the profit levels of capitalist farmers stagnated or declined. Between 1480 and 1680 grain prices rose twice as fast as prices for manufactures or raw materials, and wages declined. Once urban populations began to stagnate, imports of grain from the south as well as exports of textiles to southern Italy fell. By the seventeenth century the Italian economy was reduced to local urban economies exploiting an immediate hinterland through rents and taxes.

As Aymard suggests, the Italian city-state and the merchant capitalism it spawned appeared to have had a built-in limitation. This was not unlike the view of Braudel, who spoke of the city-state and the countryside dominated by it as the basis for its expansion and power, and at the same time the cause of its ultimate weakness.[19]

Anderson's perspective also comes close to Aymard's. As Anderson saw it, the Italian city-states usurped rather than transformed feudal power, and in this respect suggest Merrington's concept of the medieval town as a component part of the feudal system or as being unable to transcend it. But, according to Anderson, it must also be acknowledged that the Italian city-state was at fundamental odds with its countryside.[20] The latter was considered and treated as a conquered territory. The peasants had no rights of citizenship and little sense of loyalty to the city, to which they were subject politically and economically.

Aymard also argued that the Italian city-states had no chance of conquering and unifying Italy – an indispensable step in the creation of a unified territorial state and national market. Divided between themselves, they could not translate their urban-based economic power into mobilizing their rural populations toward such a project.[21] This argument reinforces Bois's point that markets were not neutral economic entities, but depended on the political power of one or another jurisdiction.

While Aymard's arguments, and those of other historians who stress the limitations of Italian merchant capital, are well founded, I wonder whether Aymard's discussion of the transition debate does that debate full justice. Though he chastises Sweezy for wrongly thinking of trade as an exogenous rather than endogenous force in capitalist development, he largely ignores the emphasis of Dobb and other debaters on the positive economic role of the petty producers. Yet it could be argued that the extraordinary development or over-development of Italian overseas or exogenous trade from the Middle Ages onward warped the development of Italy's internal economy by giving too much power to exporters and overseas merchants at the expense of small-scale rural and urban producers who, I would argue, took the lead in developing English capitalism.

Ultimately Anderson's suggestion that the failure of Italian capitalism was political seems conclusive.[22] The inability of Italy to unify itself into an early modern territorial state set the limits to the development of its capitalism. No doubt this failure was connected to the entrenched localized power of these same merchant capitalists. Successive attempts to carry out such a unifying revolution from above by emperors or despots during the late medieval period were defeated. Failure blocked the emergence of a national market and of a national political entity that could defend Italy militarily and economically against foreign invasion. Unable to launch overseas exploration on their own, Florentine and Genoese captains and merchants ended up taking the lead in Spanish, French and English overseas ventures. The lack of a national state not only made it impossible for capitalism to emerge in Italy until the nineteenth century, it led to a divided Italy becoming the plaything of foreign powers. In the sixteenth and early seventeenth centuries it was Spain that dominated the Italian peninsula. Subsequently the French and Austrian Hapsburgs vied with Spain for influence. These great power rivalries ensured that the peninsula would remain split into a multitude of small states and principalities. Within these political entities clerical and noble elites were able to maintain themselves at the expense of a weak bourgeoisie.

GERMAN CAPITALISM

Northern Italy continued to be the dominant actor in emerging European capitalism until the rise of Antwerp and the North Atlantic from the 1520s onward.[23] But between the 1470s and the 1520s the most advanced pole of up-and-coming capitalism in Europe was Germany, or the so-called Holy Roman Empire. Its geographical position between still-dominant Italy and the emerging Netherlands helps to explain its dynamism. But more significant was the extraordinary expansion of its mining and metallurgical industries. Especially important were the gold and silver mines of the Tyrol, Erzgebirge (Saxony/West Bohemia) and Hungary/ Eastern Slovakia. Organized and controlled on a capitalist basis, these mines, which employed tens of thousands of wage workers, provided the liquid capital in the form of precious metals which was critical to the spectacular early expansion of the capitalist economy in Europe (1470–1530). Silver and gold from Central Europe also supplied virtually the only commodities Europeans could exchange for Chinese, Malay and Indian silks, spices and porcelains. Control of precious metals facilitated the opening of new trans-oceanic sea lanes, circumventing in part the Mediterranean and allowing Europeans for the first time to trade directly with Asia. After 1530 American silver allowed this initial direct commercial link to expand into an enormous world market.[24]

Like Italy, Germany emerged from the Middle Ages divided into many territories. Indeed, its very decentralization facilitated the initial emergence of markets and manufacturing based on hundreds of economically interconnected free or imperial cities operating within the web of late medieval feudal relations. In this respect, Germany differed fundamentally from late medieval Italy, where only vestiges of medieval feudalism remained. But in Germany the feudal nobility, territorial princes and the Holy Roman Emperor not only survived, but were becoming stronger. In this respect Germany also differed from England, where we have seen that serfdom and lordship declined in the fourteenth and fifteenth centuries. This initial process of feudal decline then set the stage for the emergence of English capitalism in the sixteenth century. In Germany, by contrast, serfdom and lordship grew stronger at the end of the fifteenth and beginning of the sixteenth century, and the new economic dynamism in fact made possible the simultaneous strengthening of not only capitalism but also feudal reaction. The result of this volatile contradiction was the famous social and political explosion known as the German Peasant War (1524–25), characterized by Friedrich Engels as an early bourgeois revolution.

ENGELS AND EARLY BOURGEOIS REVOLUTION

As a still young professional revolutionary, Engels was not inspired by an interest in historical research or mere intellectual curiosity to investigate the German Peasant War. Basing himself on the historical work of William Zimmerman, a German historian, Engels wrote his *Peasant War in Germany* in the immediate wake of the revolution of 1848, to teach political and historical lessons and to inspire fellow revolutionaries in Germany.[25] Engels's analysis of the conditions in which the revolution took place stressed the lack of German political unity and social cohesion and the progress of its mining, manufacture, trade and agriculture. At the same time he acknowledged the relative economic weakness of Germany compared with Italy, the Netherlands and England at the beginning of the sixteenth century.[26]

But the political failure of Germany was uppermost. Its failure to achieve national unity guaranteed both that the bourgeois revolution would be aborted and that Germany would remain excluded from world commerce:

> while in England and France the rise of commerce and industry had the effect of intertwining the interests of the entire country and thereby brought about political centralization, Germany had not got any further than grouping interests by provinces, around merely local centres, which led to political division, a division

that was soon made all the more final by Germany's exclusion from world commerce.[27]

Here Engels confirms my stress on the importance of the creation of the territorial state and access to the world market to the development of capitalism.

As their power grew, Germany's territorial princes levied heavier taxes and servile obligations on the peasants.[28] The patrician rulers of the towns were allied to the feudal lords, and oppressed the rest of the urban population, including the rich and not-so-rich burghers, whom Engels pointedly compared to the middle-class liberals of his own time. The burghers emerge as a moderate opposition, aspiring to share in the town governments from which they were excluded and attacking the privileges and property of the clergy. Beneath them came the plebeians – ruined burghers, small-scale craftspeople, journeymen, day labourers and the numerous forerunners of the *lumpenproletariat*, some of whom became part of a radical opposition.[29] No better, perhaps even inferior to them, were the peasants, who earlier had engaged in numerous local revolts, but who had never come together in a general national revolt.

Though Germany was politically and economically divided on the eve of the Peasant War, the Reformation created a crisis during which revolutionary political and social ideas spread deeply and broadly in the population. During this crisis three large camps coalesced: Catholic or reactionary, Lutheran bourgeois reformist, and revolutionary.[30] The religious conflicts of the sixteenth century were class conflicts fought out on the basis of the shibboleths of religion. This was the result of the ongoing powerful influence of the Church, as a consequence of which all questions – political, juridical, social and economic – were still posed largely in religious terms:

> this supremacy of theology in the entire realm of intellectual activity was ... an inevitable consequence of the fact that the church was the all-embracing synthesis and the most general sanction of the existing feudal order. It is clear that under the circumstances all the generally-voiced attacks against feudalism, above all the attacks against the church, and all revolutionary social and political doctrines were necessarily also mostly theological heresies.[31]

With roots deep in the Middle Ages, the heretical ideology of the

burghers, to which some of the nobility also subscribed, called for
the material dispossession of the wealth and privileges of the ecclesiastical order. Agreeing with such notions, peasant and plebeian
radicals took things a step further by calling for political, social and
even economic equality.[32] The propertyless, of whom there were
increasingly large numbers, challenged the notion of a class-based
society by espousing in utopian fashion the idea of all things in
common.[33]

The Catholic conservative camp included the imperial authorities, the ecclesiastical and some lay princes, the richer nobles, the
prelates and urban patricians. The Lutheran camp attracted to itself
all the propertied members of the opposition, including the mass of
the nobility, the burghers, and even some lay princes who wished
to seize the property of the Church and increase their independence
from the Holy Roman Empire. The peasants and plebeians constituted the radical party.[34] The most important leader of the latter
group was Thomas Münzer, who vainly advocated communism and
a pantheism which, according to Engels, approached atheism.[35]

While the aspirations of the radical party were doomed to fail, so
too were those of the more moderate reformers. No effective alliance
between elements of the nobility and the bourgeoisie of the English
sort emerged. In England serfdom had largely disappeared by the
end of the Middle Ages and the old nobility was virtually wiped out
in the Wars of the Roses, replaced by a new nobility of bourgeois
origin. In contrast serfdom was still rampant in Germany, and the
nobles drew their income largely from feudal sources. Political
power lay overwhelmingly at the local and regional level.[36]

The nearest approximation to a bourgeois revolutionary program
was articulated by Wendel Hipler in the so-called Heilbronn
Manifesto, issued at the height of the Peasant War. Engels is careful
not to claim that Hipler's program was an expression of the bourgeoisie: it was rather an expression of 'what may be described as
the cross-section of the nation's progressive elements, [which] anticipated modern bourgeois society.' While nominally written on behalf
of the peasantry, the Heilbronn program called for a standardized
currency, standard weights and measures, abolition of internal
customs duties and so on: demands which were more in the interests
of the townsmen than the peasantry. In order to reach out to the
nobility, concessions were made that substantially approached the
modern system of redemption and would have transformed feudal
into bourgeois landlordship.[37]

Engels at one point compares the German Peasant War to the

French Revolution from a political point of view. In the case of the eighteenth-century revolution in a politically unified France, the whole country was split into two clearly opposed camps. In a deeply divided sixteenth-century Germany, this was a rank impossibility.[38] On the other hand, Engels saw the Peasant War not simply as a German event but as an international one, based on the prospects for the further development of capitalism. As he reiterated on returning to the theme many decades later, 'Reformation – Lutheran and Calvinist – is the No. 1 bourgeois revolution, the Peasant War being its critical episode. ... Revolution No. 1, which was more European than the English and spread in Europe much more rapidly than the French.'[39] Indeed, the Reformation spread throughout Western and Central Europe.

HISTORY IN THE DEUTSCHE DEMOKRATISCHE REPUBLIK (DDR)

Rejected by bourgeois historiography, Engels's materialist interpretation of the Peasant War and the Reformation became the foundation of the viewpoint of the historians of the now defunct German Democratic Republic (DDR). But respect for this view was more than mere state and party orthodoxy. Though much historiographical water has flown under the bridge, Engels's interpretation holds up remarkably well.

It should be pointed out that East German Marxists historians were still inclined to take Luther's and Münzer's religiosity more seriously than did Engels. This stress on the historical importance of religious consciousness was in accord with the growing intellectual and economic rapprochement between the two states of divided Germany from the 1980s. Intellectuals in the DDR made efforts to conciliate Western German opinion while remaining faithful to their own materialist outlook. Their research also confirmed Engels's view of the under-developed nature of the German bourgeoisie as a class. Finally, and perhaps most importantly from our perspective, the scholarship of both communist and Western historians revealed that contrary to Engels's idea of a Germany economically lagging behind other countries, it was in the vanguard of an emerging European capitalism in the period 1470–1530.

Between the 1950s and the 1970s East German historians produced a rich historiography on early modern German capitalism, the Reformation and the Peasant War. The results of this research were summarized in a magnificent collective history of the German early bourgeois revolution published in 1974.[40] This work argued that the early bourgeois revolution in Germany must be understood in the international context of the full flowering of the humanist culture of the Renaissance, the consolidation of the territorial state in France and England, the overseas discoveries and the beginning of the primitive accumulation of capital. This Europe-wide epoch saw the decline of feudalism, and the origin and development of merchant and manufacturing capitalism. The outbreak of the early bourgeois revolution in Germany represented the zenith of this emerging capitalism.[41]

Population growth and overseas expansion led to an expansion of demand for commodities from the last third of the fifteenth century. The gold and silver mining sector expanded prodigiously – in the Tyrol and Styria, the Erzgebirge and in the border region between Western Hungary and Slovakia – facilitating exchange and accumulation in the first phase of capitalist expansion down to 1530. Capitalist relations of production were established throughout this key sector, with technical progress and substantial capital investment by capitalists from Nuremberg and other south German cities.[42] Moreover, the influence of financial and merchant capital was also apparent to a greater or lesser degree in the grain and woad trade and the extensive metallurgical, wool, silk, linen, fustian, grain, salt, glass-making and printing industries that spread across the face of Germany. As the Reformation crisis approached, increasing sectors of the German economy came under the control of the powerful Függer family and other powerful merchant and banking firms.[43]

In Italy and England feudalism declined and capitalism took its place, but in Germany a powerful feudal reaction consolidated itself as the capitalist economy and financial and merchant capital advanced. Capitalism exacerbated class conflict at every level of German society, prompting noble violence, increased feudal dues and growing attempts to impose or reimpose serfdom on the peasantry, especially in southern and southwest Germany and the Rhineland in the late fifteenth and early sixteenth centuries. The imposition of serfdom even served as a tool by which territorial princes exerted their authority.[44] On the other hand, though they lacked leadership and common objectives the resistance of the common people became equally fierce, leading to the plebeian, worker and peasant protests that characterized the period leading to the Reformation crisis.[45]

The further development of capitalism was also hemmed in by the imperial and feudal order. The Hapsburg emperor sought to rule a universal European state, not a unified and centralized Germany. The emperor, as well as the territorial princes, blocked a national political project. At the same time, serfdom and feudalism fundamentally barred the route to the development of capitalism in agriculture.[46] Such a route might have been opened by the demands of the peasants during the Peasant War to abolish serfdom, sweep away both feudalism and the nobility, and consolidate government under the emperor. The peasants also demanded an end to the established Church with its landed wealth and feudal privileges, and the installation of a democratic church based on a revolutionary interpretation of the Gospel.[47] The latter demand would have dissolved the ideological foundation of the feudal order. The end of feudalism and serfdom would have eased the burden on the peasantry, helped to improve output and furthered the primitive accumulation of capital.[48]

This account, like Engels's, minimizes the role of the bourgeoisie in the Peasants' War. Indeed, in so far as the financiers, merchants, burghers and skilled craftspeople participated in these events they generally sided with the Catholic or moderate Lutheran party, which opposed rural and urban radicalism. Faced with popular revolution, merchant capital was prepared to make its peace with feudalism. It was the peasants and plebeians rather than the still-nascent bourgeoisie who led the way in this unsuccessful attempt to further the development of capitalism in Germany.[49] The failure of this democratic revolt, the eclipse of the German mining industry by the increasing flow of New World bullion into Europe, and competition from the Dutch and the English sealed the fate of this early upsurge of German capitalism. The trade of the numerically larger, but impotent, merchant class of Germany came to be subordinated to 'the bourgeoisie of little Holland'.[50] As in the case of Japan, lack of direct access to the world market helped to stifle German capitalism.

REVOLUTION OF THE COMMON PEOPLE

Developed in the DDR at the height of the Cold War, this view of the Peasant War became part of the ideological struggle between East and West. With some exceptions West German historians rejected this Marxist interpretation. However, historians in the West were unable to produce a more convincing account. Their critique of the East German view, it must be said, was too often marked by misconception, logic-chopping and misrepresentation,[51] and the East German interpretation remains the most convincing.

How convincing can be seen from the reception of Peter Blickle's *Die Revolution von 1525*, published in West Germany in 1975. Its

substantial endorsement of the East German position prompted a
dramatic shift in the West German perspective on this crucial event
in Germany's history. Moreover on the one main point of difference between Blickle and the East German school, later criticism
vindicated the latter.

Originally published in the mid-1970s and republished in an
expanded and revised fourth edition in 2004,[52] Blickle's work
undoubtedly reflected the influence of the radicalism of the 1960s
in West Germany. Not only was Blickle respectful of the Marxist
position, he agreed that the Peasant War represented a profound
crisis that threatened to overthrow the whole feudal order. The
authoritative nature of Blickle's account cast a pall over the earlier
Cold War historiography of the Reformation, produced so zealously
in the West. On the other hand, Blickle differed from the East
German interpretation on the key argument that the revolt was an
early bourgeois revolution. Rather, he portrayed it as an urban and
rural communal movement of common people, based on a radical
and egalitarian interpretation of the Gospel of the Reformation. In
Marxist terms, Blickle's view of the Peasant War is one of a conflict
between feudal lords and urban and rural petty producers.

TOM SCOTT'S STRUCTURAL ADJUSTMENT

This was challenged by the British academic Tom Scott, one of the
most prolific and erudite contemporary scholars of the Peasant War.
His text on German history between 1300 and 1600 is an extraordinary synthesis of recent scholarship on this exceedingly complicated
period, and its axis is precisely the Peasant War. Scott provides an
astonishingly clear and detailed analysis of the underlying forces
leading up to and away from the uprising. Scott summarized his
differences with Blickle on the Peasant War in a 2002 article.[53]
He counters Blickle's view of a unified rural communal society
challenging feudalism by portraying the advanced development of
commercial agriculture, urban trade, mining and manufacturing, and
finance capital in considerable detail. The growth of rural industry,
including putting-out systems operated by merchant capital and the
high degree of social differentiation in the villages between well-
to-do peasants, cottagers, the landless and servants, throws doubt on
the notion of a unified rural communal revolution.[54] Extraordinary
advances in research into the economic history of the period allow
Scott to refute Blickle's notion of the Peasants' War as a communal
revolution or of a revolt of petty commodity producers.[55]

However, while Scott's views broadly confirm and amplify those of the Marxist historians of the DDR on the extensive develop-ment of merchant and finance capitalism in Germany prior to the Reformation, he does not agree with them that the resultant crisis constitutes an early bourgeois revolution. He insists that the relations of production on the land determine capitalist develop-ment, and that the mere existence of markets or manufacturing does not, in itself, demonstrate it. Invoking Brenner, he notes that there is a difference between involvement in the market and dependence on it. The former, in fact, could help sustain feudal agriculture.[56] The preconditions for a genuine transformation of the agricultural economy to capitalism – the commodification of landlordship and of labour – were, Scott argues, entirely absent in Germany in the late fifteenth and early sixteenth centuries.[57] The commercialization of agriculture that did occur was fully compatible with feudalism. There was no crisis of feudalism, but rather only a structural transformation of it. According to Scott, it is difficult to speak of a crisis of feudalism when in fact landlords were improving their position rather than in decline.[58] As for German history overall between 1300 and 1600, Scott sees continuity rather than rupture. The three centuries under consider-ation 'witnessed the consolidation of a society of estates within a fragmented constitutional polity'.[59]

Scott's structural-functionalist analysis of the meaning of the Peasant War in German history must be taken seriously, informed as it is by an extraordinary mastery of the subject. Moreover, his insistence on the decisive importance of rural capitalism to the development of capitalism is something with which Marxists including those of the former DDR would have concurred. Having said that, we cannot ignore the significance of the massive entry of capital into, and the development of, capitalist relations of production in the very large mining industry in this period for the development of German and indeed European capitalism. Nor can we neglect the extraordinary influence of merchant capital on virtually every aspect of the extensive German manufacturing sector. Indeed, Scott himself admits, even as he denies a crisis of feudalism, that the Peasant War was:

a crisis in the sense that the assertion of seigneurial power produced a reaction on the part of those pushed down into a uniform category of subjection, of those, who, in the context of the 1520s, were able to invoke 'biblicism' against 'feudalism'.[60]

But this admission is of greater moment than Scott realizes. The Marxist view, and indeed the view of Blickle, is that the Peasant War was not merely a structural rearrangement of the feudal order but a fundamental or revolutionary challenge to it. The overthrow of feudalism in these circumstances would have meant the initiation of the process of primitive accumulation on the land. While citing Brenner on markets, Scott ignores Brenner's argument that the fourteenth-century crisis was critical to both the decline of feudalism and the inauguration of capitalism in England through class struggle. While Brenner's notion of a simultaneous death of feudalism and birth of capitalism in the fourteenth century has been contested by Byres in particular, who continues a line of interpretation shared by Dobb, Hilton and even Sweezy, it was precisely in Germany at the beginning of the sixteenth century that there really was both a crisis of feudalism and an attempted breakthrough of capitalism. In England the Peasant Wars of the fourteenth century spelled the liberation of the peasant producers and corresponding decline of feudalism. In Germany, on the other hand, the late medieval class struggles of the peasant producers against feudalism only reached their climax in the sixteenth century. Capitalism was born in the midst of a dramatic class conflict between the rural producers struggling to liberate themselves and a strong feudal reaction. The attempt to overthrow feudalism and install capitalism occurred simultaneously. This is what made the crisis there so acute and the Peasant War so significant.

Finally, Scott's contextualization of the Peasant War must be criticized. He views it in the framework of German history. From this perspective, he insists on the continuity of German history, signalled by the failure of the popular uprising and triumph of feudal absolutism. Having weathered the crisis the feudal system reconsolidated itself in the modern period on the basis of the princely states of a divided Germany. Throughout the early modern period the rulers of these aristocratic states centralized and bureaucratized their principalities in imitation of the absolute governments of their more powerful Hapsburg and Bourbon neighbours. But for Engels and the historians of the German Democratic Republic, the context of that event was certainly Germany, but more importantly, the wider global history of capitalism. In that sense, the Peasant War was an experience of rupture and change – Revolution No. 1 in the chain of early bourgeois revolutions furthering the advance of the capitalist mode of production, as Engels's revolutionary perspective led him to conclude.

FRANCE

Having dealt with the failed development of capitalism in Italy and Germany, we turn finally to the case of France. It is important because of its role in the transition debate, especially as it unfolded under the influence of Brenner. Marx and Engels saw France as part of an emerging world-wide system of capitalist accumulation whose focal point was northwest Europe. As we saw, Marx includes it among the West European states undergoing diverse moments of primitive accumulation. Although he did not consider the matter in detail, Engels noted that capitalism in France developed within the contours of the emerging absolutist state. According to him, this early modern French monarchy reflected a balance between the emerging bourgeoisie and the feudal nobility.[61] Anderson slightly modified this conception. He regarded the monarchy as above all reflecting the interests of the nobility, while recognizing that the absolute state fostered the influence of a commercial and manufacturing bourgeoisie moving toward capitalism.[62]

BRENNER'S OTHER

Brenner, however, flatly denied that capitalism developed in France. The origins of capitalist accumulation lay in England alone. The notion that both feudalism and a subordinated capitalism could dialectically coexist within the absolute state is excluded by Brenner's monocausal logic. Indeed, in Brenner's hands France reinforces the uniqueness of English capitalism by becoming the perfect foil for the latter, experiencing the same upsurge of class struggle as England in the late Middle Ages with a quite different outcome. In France, peasants came to control roughly 45 or 50 percent of the land as against only 25 or 30 percent in England.[63] As a result of the greater share of property retained by the French peasantry, whatever tendency there was towards capitalism in sixteenth-century France was arrested. It is, then, the differing allocation of property and the contrasting relations of production that determined the divergent evolution of the two countries in the early modern period. In the eyes of Brenner, England is the model and norm of capitalist origins. France is the feudal *other*. Brenner has recently muted his initial thesis of English uniqueness by acknowledging that Holland, like England, also made the transition to capitalist agriculture. But France remains the preeminent example of failed transition.[64]

As the most important Marxist authority on the transition

question today, Brenner's view matters a great deal. His treatment of France has provided grist for the mill of the revisionist trend in historiography which has sought to sever the relationship between the French Revolution and the development of capitalism. Since Marx it has been the view of Marxists that, like the English Revolution, the French Revolution was a bourgeois and capitalist revolution. Such a view was a fundamental feature of the Marxist view of history. The Brenner thesis could suggest that given the non-capitalist evolution of France under the *Ancien Régime*, such a bourgeois and capitalist revolution was, to say the least, doubtful. In a curious way Brenner's view based in Marxism dovetailed with a developing scholarly and political trend against the Marxist view of the French Revolution known as revisionism.[65] This undeniably conservative historiographical current, ascendant since the 1980s, attacked the idea that the revolution in France could be understood as a bourgeois and capitalist revolution.

Among Marxists who denied the capitalist basis of the revolution was George Comninel.[66] According to him, the bourgeoisie in France prior to the Revolution did not base itself on profit but on rent. Moreover, wage workers were dependent, not on wages, but on their own sources of subsistence.[67] This view coincided with Brenner's notion of the ongoing hold of the French peasantry on the land, and certainly Comninel's teacher Ellen Meiskins Wood was deeply influenced by Brenner on questions of capitalist origins. She agreed with Brenner's insistence on the origins of capitalism lying exclusively in the social relations of production of the English countryside. Under French absolutism feudal rent dominated to the point that there was no capitalist bourgeoisie. The French Revolution was a bourgeois, but not a capitalist, revolution.[68] What was an argument in Brenner's work turned into a dogmatic certainty in the hands of Comninel and Wood.

CAPITALISM IN FRANCE

As I have argued elsewhere, Brenner, Comninel and Wood are gravely mistaken on France.[69] As in England, the sixteenth century saw an ongoing advance of the capitalist bourgeoisie. The religious civil wars (1562–94) were undoubtedly a period of economic regression and confused conflict of all against all – the bourgeoisie divided against itself, peasants against peasants, as well as against nobles and townspeople and, to top it all, nobles against nobles, and all sides in revolt against the state. On the other hand, there can be no doubt that class conflict between bourgeoisie and nobles was the critical element. And it is reflected in what we know of the subjective experience of these conflicts. For example, one of the French King's representatives in the Midi, the Baron Raymond de Fourquevaux, reported in 1573 that the source of the violence lay in the fact that the nobility were confronted by an increasingly aggressive bourgeoisie.

The essential arena of conflict was a struggle over the land, in which the peasantry were being drawn in on the side of the bourgeoisie. The response of the nobles was to abandon the peasants to violence.[70] As in the German Peasant War, the nobility responded to the threat from below by carrying on a class war from above. But the pugnacious French bourgeoisie were prepared to challenge the nobility in a way that the German bourgeoisie did not. Far from exhausting itself in the long war, the bourgeoisie, in league with the urban plebeians and an increasingly aroused peasantry, was prepared to confront noble power more and more as the conflict unfolded.[71] The concept of noble status itself came under ideological attack.[72] In the end, the Catholic and Protestant nobles who had revolted were forced back into obedience to the king in order to protect themselves from the growing menace of the Third Estate. This was the basis on which the Bourbon Henri IV (1594–1610) was able to begin to reconsolidate the monarchical state.

The increasing political and social assertiveness of the bourgeoisie was based on its growing economic strength. The civil wars were hideously destructive, and resulted in a considerable economic and demographic regression. In the south of France, the capitalism that had developed in the first part of the sixteenth century faltered. On the other hand, things were very different in the richer grain lands of the north. The violence and heavy taxation of the civil wars may have forced many subsistence peasants off the land, but the bourgeoisie benefited from what amounted to primitive accumulation. A class of rural bourgeoisie in pursuit of profit was able to consolidate itself.[73] The increased dependence of the expropriated peasantry on wages ensured the availability of abundant supplies of cheap labour for agricultural work. A wave of interest in agricultural improvement, new mechanical inventions and new manufactures developed during the religious wars, which continued through the reign of Henri IV.[74] Indeed, the Bourbon monarchy sought to support and control these initiatives through its mercantilist policies.

The seventeenth-century French state tried to contain this bourgeoisie while favouring the reconsolidation of the power of the nobility and church. That it was successful in the short run was signified by the decline of the so-called sixteenth-century offensive of profit in favour of an offensive of rent. On the other hand, the rural and urban bourgeoisie that had emerged in the sixteenth century, though hard-pressed, survived and persevered in the seventeenth century.[75] It re-emerged with new vigour in the age of Enlightenment. Capitalism expanded prodigiously in the last century of the *Ancien Régime. Pace* Brenner et al., the revolution that came at the end of that century was undoubtedly not merely bourgeois, but as we shall see in Chapter 4, also capitalist.

CONCLUSION

If, nevertheless, capitalism failed to blossom on the European Continent as fully as it did in England, surely its most glaring deficiency was the absence of unified territorial states in Italy and Germany. At the beginning of modern times Germany and Italy were as much nations as were France and England, and both witnessed the development of capitalist classes. But the failure to construct national territorial states in the former countries aborted for the time being their capitalist futures. The lack of such a state deprived merchants and entrepreneurs of the protection necessary to gain control of foreign markets and territories, blocked the further development of national markets and arrested the maturation of their bourgeoisies. The case of France is more contradictory. There the state did foster the development of a bourgeoisie to a certain extent. This is especially evident in the reign of Henri IV at the end of the sixteenth century, when the monarchy explicitly committed itself to a mercantilist policy. Especially important was its resolve to expand French access to the world market through a commitment to colonialism. Indeed, the continued construction by the monarchy of a strong national state by economic and other means strengthened French capitalism when it did emerge.

On the other hand, the still divided and weak bourgeoisie was in no position to overthrow the nobility or to take control of the state during the religious-civil wars. The rather disorganized attempts by bourgeois elements to gain political, fiscal or religious concessions were rebuffed by a state increasingly committed to unrestricted royal sovereignty and to protecting the interests of the feudal aristocracy and established Church. Under such circumstances the capitalism that developed in the sixteenth century continued to exist but under severe constraints. In the latter part of the sixteenth century capitalism did establish itself on the great open fields of northern France, and there was an intense interest in agricultural improvement. But under the Bourbon kings' heavy rents and taxes, ongoing economic difficulties and political control of the grain trade hampered further capitalist development. Capitalism was forced onto the defensive until the eighteenth century.

Aside from the lack of political unity, the other great handicap of capitalism in Italy and Germany was failure in the agricultural sector. In the case of Italy, capitalist agriculture emerged in the Po valley. There the work force was fully proletarianized and capitalist farmers, urban merchants and the state made major capital investments in agriculture. On the other hand, earlier tendencies toward a national market in agricultural commodities weakened toward the end of the sixteenth century. Rural investment flagged, erosion and deforestation became more pronounced, and city-states increasingly adopted protectionist agricultural policies. The ongoing dominance of urban merchant capital smothered the initiatives of rural petty producers. Increasing grain prices tended to make wages in the industrial sector higher than in England, France and Holland, undermining the competitiveness of Italian manufactures. In the case of Germany and France, the importance of class struggles to the containment of capitalism should be underscored. The resilience of the feudal nobility in these instances was noteworthy. While the outcome of such struggles was not predetermined, the balance of class forces was important to the outcome.

As we have noted capitalism began in Italy, and spread across the Alps to Germany and into France and the Netherlands. England was the last and most successful way-station in its early emergence. It was in the wake of this succession of more or less successful experiments that capitalism flowered successfully in England. This in itself has important implications for understanding a possible transition to socialism. While nothing is certain or predetermined, we can suggest at least that socialism is developing historically through a succession of trials and errors based on an analogous underlying and general tendency. But having examined the birth of capitalism and its limits on the Continent, we turn to England, where it emerged for the first time in a complete form. In doing so we shall remain conscious of its antecedents on the Continent. Moreover we shall examine English capitalism while always bearing in mind its global context.

3

ENGLISH CAPITALISM

In the last chapter I insisted, against the Anglocentric view, that the development of capitalism must be seen as the birth of a global system which included Western Europe as well as much of the world beyond it. Its early seeds were found not merely in England, but in Italy, Germany and France as well as in Holland. We concentrated on the fortunes of capitalism on the European Continent to substantiate this point. This chapter deals with the early development of English capitalism, but in a way that underlines the need to see it in a global and European context, rather than as a development unique to England.

The most important scholars we deal with in arriving at this view are Dobb, Wallerstein and Brenner. According to Dobb, capitalism began in England with the entry of capital into production, which he dated from the late sixteenth and early seventeenth centuries. Its origins were diverse but Dobb, as we know, stressed the importance of the transformation of the social relations of production through primitive accumulation, and through their subsequent transformation in what he described as the 'really revolutionary way'. In opposition to merchant capital, which typically imposes an economically stifling control over still largely traditional methods of manufacture, the really revolutionary way is one in which petty producers in certain lines of industry become capitalists by undertaking to bring these sectors under their control while reorganizing production and introducing new manufacturing methods and techniques. This path, championed by petty producers, is really revolutionary not only economically but also socially and politically, in a way that merchant capital is not.

As in the chapter on the decline of feudalism, the main theme of this chapter is the debate on the relative importance of social relations of production championed by Dobb and Brenner or the influence of the market as argued by Wallerstein. I believe this to be a false dichotomy. It is based on a failure to understand that capitalism is a circular totality in which capital as self-expanding value always originates in production and its relations, but must realize itself again and again through market exchange which eventually universalizes itself. The resultant realization of capital in money form allows rein-vestment in production and the renewal of the accumulation cycle. The production of value is the decisive moment in this circuit, but exchange and a return to the money form are also indispensable to the self-expansion of value. Indeed, the renewal of production cannot take place without it. As Brenner and his followers would have it, the development of competition and the extraction of relative surplus value from the beginning play the key role in the development of capitalism. But it is my view that the emergence of these autono-mous economic mechanisms itself has a history which is to be found in the coercive effects of primitive accumulation, the extraction of absolute surplus, colonialism and state policies rather than through innovations which were exclusively economic.

DOBB VERSUS SWEEZY

The English case is critical to the debates between those, like Dobb and Brenner, who stressed the importance of social relations of production in capitalism, and those, like Sweezy, who also stressed the importance of the market, and especially the development of the world market. Sweezy's views were aligned with those of the world system analyst Wallerstein, who relied on a Braudelian interpretation of capitalist history. Along with Sweezy, Wallerstein saw capitalist relations of production in the core capitalist states as significant, but only as part of a world-wide system of exchange in which profits were generated not simply in capitalist agriculture or manufacture in the system's core, but also at the periphery. According to Wallerstein, Polish landlord magnates or Jamaican plantation owners were as much capitalists as English wool-cloth manufacturers. However, the bulk of profits generated at the periphery of the system were remitted to the capitalist core through a system of politically enforced unequal exchange. According to Wallerstein, states and political control were also critical to understanding capitalism as a world system.

Brenner attacked Sweezy's and Wallerstein's views which stressed the centrality of markets as 'neo-Smithian'. He insisted that the essence of capitalism lay not in exchange, which generates no new wealth, but in changes in the social relations of production at the centre of the system. The dynamism of capitalism was to be found not in the extraction of absolute surplus value dependent on the labour of slaves or serfs on the system's periphery, but as a result of the extraction of relative surplus value based on wage labour found at its core. It was in English agriculture of the sixteenth century, based on the issuing of competitive leases by landlords, that the first impulses toward capitalism manifested themselves. The ensuing necessity on the part of capitalist farmers to compete economically unleashed the unprecedented productive capacity of capitalism. While Brenner put his finger on the core of capitalism's productive power, something which was more or less ignored by Wallerstein, he failed for his part to take account of the lead role of capitalist farmers and the ongoing importance of primitive accumulation and the extraction of absolute surplus value both in England and in the under-developed world. He also appeared to believe, incorrectly, that capitalism could exist in a single country. Finally, while rightly stressing capitalism's prodigious and unprecedented productivity, he ended up focusing on the predominant role of landlords, economic leases and competitive markets, to the exclusion of the critical role of the state and its coercive power in the development of capitalism.

Earlier we noted that both Dobb and Sweezy had postulated the existence of an intermediate phase between the decline of feudalism and the beginning of capitalism.[1] In this phase petty commodity production and exchange appeared to predominate economically. This would accord with Marx's celebrated formula C–M–C for exchange relations during which merchants did not occupy a dominant place in the market. Sweezy referred to this transitional phase as pre-commodity petty production, in which there were no really predominant relations of production to put a stamp on the whole economy and society. According to Sweezy, this phase, although real, nevertheless could not be thought of as crystallizing into a social system like feudalism or capitalism.[2] Much evidence exists that small-scale producers – peasants and craftspeople – prospered during the late Middle Ages and the first decades of the sixteenth century on the basis of such petty production. While acknowledging this, Dobb cautioned against seeing this phase as a stage in the development of society in its own right. Rather, he insisted, it had to be seen from a revolutionary perspective on world history. From this point of view the critical question is which class is the ruling class, and, for this period, the answer is that while the early modern English state more and more accommodated capitalism and capitalists within its ambit, the ruling class remained feudal and the emerging territorial state was the political instrument of its rule,[3] a position which was later endorsed by Anderson in his account of the absolutist state in Europe.[4]

Dobb took an eclectic position on the actual beginnings of capitalism. He singled out the importance of the entry of capital into manufacturing in England, which he dated from the late sixteenth and early seventeenth centuries. This took the form either of the complete subordination of hired wage workers to an entrepreneur, as in the coalfields, or the partial subordination of craftspeople to an entrepreneur through the putting-out system.[5] Dobb also underlined the importance of the rise in prices in the sixteenth century, which saw a dramatic decline in real wages and a surge of profit for the emergent capitalist class.[6] As in his discussion of the decline of feudalism, Dobb recognized the significance of the process of economic differentiation of the peasantry to the origins of capitalism.[7] And, if this multiplicity of factors was not enough, Dobb also underlined the importance of foreign trade. Although it absorbed a relatively small percentage of total economic output, foreign trade, Dobb argued, played an important role in stimulating the expansion of English manufacturing.[8] While taking these different factors into account Dobb nonetheless singled out two for special emphasis in a way which accorded closely with Marx's own account of capitalism's origin.

PRIMITIVE ACCUMULATION

The first of these was primitive accumulation. Dobb understood primitive accumulation to be an accumulation of capital claims or titles to existing assets, whether in England or overseas, for speculative purposes. As such it was a source of profits. But he also assumed that the class undertaking such primitive accumulation was capable of transforming such capital claims into means of production capable of generating profits.[9] In other words such titles could sooner or later become capital, which could hire alienated labour, from whose unpaid labour value could be extracted and then profits realized. Following Marx, however, Dobb laid particular emphasis on the primitive accumulation of land in England. According to Dobb, the essence of primitive accumulation of land was the transfer of property from subsistence peasant producers into the hands of an ascendant bourgeoisie, and the consequent pauperization of the former as a result of their divorce from the means of production.[10] The basis of accumulation lay in this divorce of the peasant producers from the means of production, with their consequent need to sell their labour power to capitalists in return for a wage forming the foundation of ongoing accumulation.[11] The enclosure movement between the sixteenth and eighteenth centuries was the primary means of primitive accumulation in England.[12] But we should reiterate that the English case had counterparts elsewhere in

Continental Europe at the time, and it remained a world-wide and ongoing phenomenon important to the subsequent development of capitalism, as we will discuss.

THE REALLY REVOLUTIONARY WAY

The other factor in capitalist development singled out by Dobb and stressed by Marx was what they called 'the really revolutionary way'. According to Marx and Dobb, production was historically reorganized under the capitalist mode of production in two possible ways.[13] In one, merchant capital took control of the steps in the process of production from the outside, as it were, translating surplus labour into profits and reaching wider markets but doing little to revolutionize the means of production. This was typical of Italian merchant capitalism. Only the second way was 'really revolutionary', with small producers engaged in the actual production process undertaking to reorganize production in their branch of manufacture. It is considered really revolutionary because it was more likely to lead to the acceleration of economic innovation and technological change that we consider characteristic of capitalism. In contrast to this, as Dobb notes, merchant capital may restrict and smother attempts at economic innovation by those producers who come under its domination. Indeed, Dobb noted that capitalists emerging from the ranks of petty producers tended to oppose monopolies and ultimately absolutist governments, while the former group of merchant capitalists tended to be complicit with the established order.[14] Complementing this development in manufacture was the emergence in the countryside of a class of increasingly well-off small producers who employed wage labour and were transforming themselves into capitalist farmers.[15]

While Sweezy expressed scepticism over Dobb's reading of Marx, and dismissed the notion of a 'revolutionary way' altogether,[16] other contributors to the transition debate accepted Dobb's view with few reservations. As we have seen, Dobb noted that the role of such emergent capitalists entailed not only opposition to merchant capital but, sooner or later, opposition to feudalism and absolutist government.[17] In a piece published in *Science and Society* in 1990, I suggested that this was key to understanding revolutionary politics in the early modern period.[18] At the same time the alliance between feudalism and merchant capital is important in explaining the failed transition to capitalism in Italy and Germany, which was discussed in Chapter 2.[19]

WALLERSTEIN'S WORLD SYSTEM

A new stage in the debate was reached in 1974 with the publication of the first volume of Wallerstein's *The Modern World System*.[20] An American sociologist and Marxist specializing in Africa, Wallerstein was much influenced by third world dependency theory and the protest movements of the 1960s. Wallerstein had also been influenced by the thought of Braudel, the leader of the *Annales* in France. Braudel conceived of the history of global capitalism from the perspective of someone who regretted the decline of European and especially French power. Braudel, who considered himself a socialist, may perhaps be described as a sentimental imperialist. He rejected the upheavals of the 1960s, while his acolyte Wallerstein embraced them. Wallerstein's interest in developing world systems theory arose from his awareness that contemporary capitalism based on American hegemony was in trouble, yet rooted in a system of unequal relations which was both tenacious and of long standing.

At Binghampton University he created the Fernand Braudel Centre which published *Review*, a Marxist academic journal based on his notion of world systems. Wallerstein may be said to have revived and developed the position of Sweezy. He took from the latter the need to move from a single nation or parochial unit of analysis to a wider perspective on capitalism based on global commercial and political interchange.[21] In common with Dobb and Brenner, he acknowledged that the class struggles of the fourteenth century marked the crisis of feudalism. But in contrast to their stress on changes in the relations of production as key to capitalist origins, Wallerstein emphasized overseas expansion which, in the first instance, was a way out of the impasse of class conflict from the perspective of the ruling class. It led towards the beginning of capitalism.[22] The expansion of the world market is an exit from class conflict.

Marx had noted that the sixteenth century saw the emergence of both proletarian labour and the world market. For him these two developments, tied together dialectically, marked the beginning of the capitalist epoch. But Wallerstein acknowledged the importance of the proletarianization of labour only in passing, emphasizing instead the emergence of the world market or a trade-based division of labour as the starting point for accumulation.[23] On the basis of such a commercial development the early modern European political order might have evolved in the direction of a world empire, as had the ancient civilizations of China, Greece and Rome. In the first part of the sixteenth century the Spanish-Hapsburg Empire under

Emperor Charles V (1516–58) made a serious bid to establish such a political dominion. If the Emperor Charles had succeeded, expanding markets and capital accumulation would have been permanently constrained by the fiscal and bureaucratic limitations of an overarching world state or political empire. But Charles's failure to consolidate an imperial state allowed Europe to evolve in the direction of a world economy, or a capitalist world system characterized by a single division of labour or capitalist market, but multiple states and cultures.[24] The failure of political empire favoured the proliferation of wage labour on the basis of a world market but also increased non-wage labour. Geographically, this 'world economy' of the sixteenth century expanded to western, southern and east-central Europe, and included the Mediterranean, Latin America and the coast of West Africa.[25]

Wallerstein may have decentred proletarian or wage labour, but only to place it in his more widely conceived capitalist world system. Its three main sectors were distinguished on the basis of the forms of labour each featured, the forms favoured by ruling classes in each sector based on the economic constraints and possibilities for profit within the emerging world market. At the core of the system in northwest Europe, wage labour became the dominant form of exploitation in agriculture and manufacture. In the semi-periphery which embraced the rest of western and central Europe, tenant farming, sharecropping and petty commodity craft production prevailed. In the peripheral zones of Eastern Europe, Africa and Latin America which produced mainly grain and sugar, serfdom and slavery or coerced cash crop labour became the rule.[26] The existence of free or wage labour specified or defined the emerging capitalist economy, Wallerstein acknowledged, as 'the "relations of production" that define a system are the "relations of production" of the whole system, and the system at this point in time is the European world-economy'.[27] But free wage labour could not be found throughout the world system, Wallerstein insisted. Free labour was the form of labour control used for skilled work in core countries. Coerced labour was used for less skilled work in peripheral areas. The combination of free and unfree labour was the essence of capitalism.[28] This was a radical redefinition of capitalism, motivated by Wallerstein's belief that accumulation at the centre was based not merely on the exploitation of wage workers in Europe, but also on the exploitation of producers on the capitalist periphery.

In the core the market became the principal means of the control of labour. But such capitalist states also tended to be strong with regard to other strong states and with respect to weaker political entities in the semi-periphery and the periphery. In the periphery states were weak or even non-existent.[29] In the semi-periphery and the periphery political or physical coercion of the labour force persisted, and was even intensified, as they were absorbed into the capitalist world system. The development of classes was a function of, or depended on, its international division of labour.[30] In this system of uneven development and of strong states dominating and coercing weaker ones, economic surpluses tended to move from the periphery and semi-periphery toward the core.[31] Over the long term under-development in the periphery developed in tandem with development in the core based on unequal exchange. The initial advantages of higher skill levels and more fixed capital reinforced by greater political power provide the core countries with a cumulative advantage over states located toward the periphery. 'Hence,' concludes Wallerstein, 'the ongoing process of a world-economy tends to expand the economic and social gaps among its varying areas in the very process of its development.' [32]

BRENNER'S ATTACK ON 'NEO-SMITHIAN MARXISM'

In launching his attack on Wallerstein, Brenner insisted that what essentially differentiated capitalism from prior modes of production was its systematic tendency toward economic growth. The continual advances in labour productivity characteristic of capitalism had been facilitated by changes in the relations of production or property relations in the late Middle Ages that we have noted. Based on these changes, the onset of capitalism in the late fifteenth century increased productivity, reduced the price of goods and obtained a greater total output from the producers. This made it possible for the capitalist class to increase surplus without necessarily having to resort to increasing work time, intensifying work or reducing the standard of living of producers. The distinctiveness of capitalism lay in the extraction of relative surplus value through the development of the forces of production, which gave rise to a process of accumulation by means of cumulative innovation or, in other words, increasing productivity rather than depressing the workers' wages or increasing their work time. This also laid the basis for an expanded reproduction of capital. Brenner insisted on this distinction because he wanted to argue that Wallerstein failed to take seriously enough the significance of the enhanced productivity of labour which is possible through the unique relations of production characteristic of the capitalist mode.

According to Brenner, Wallerstein is unable to do so in part because of his commitment to dependency theory. Wallerstein insists on the essential role of the under-development of the periphery to the development of the core through the transfer of surplus. Thus, for Wallerstein the mere extension of production for profit based on market opportunities brings about accumulation. For Brenner, in contrast, production for profit based on exchange will only engender systematic accumulation when it expresses certain specific social relations, namely, a system of free wage labour where labour is a commodity:

> only where labour has been separated from the means of production, and where labourers have been emancipated from any direct relation of domination (such as slavery or serfdom), are both capital and labour power 'free' to make possible their combination at the highest possible level of technology.[33]

Only when both labour and capital are commodities freely exchangeable in the market will the resulting competition between productive units force them to produce at the socially necessary labour time necessary to survival, and entice them to surpass this level of productivity to reap the super-profit which, for a time, is the prize of the innovator. It is only under the pressure of such market constraints that capital accumulation develops. Brenner ties Wallerstein's market-based view to a line of thought running from Adam Smith to Sweezy and the dependency theorist André Gunder Frank. Wallerstein, Sweezy and Frank share Smith's view that the specialization induced by a market-based division of labour will in itself produce gains in productivity.

According to Brenner, Wallerstein and Sweezy appear to take a class perspective but in reality their analysis is tied to an atomistic or individualist approach to economic behaviour which is rooted in Smith. In contrast, Brenner insists that it is only under changed social relations of production where it is possible to employ free social labour that accumulation based on the extraction of increasing amounts of relative surplus value takes place. Under capitalist relations of production innovation, productivity increase and cost reduction become systemic economic imperatives; they are no longer choices. According to Brenner, attempts to increase surplus where the relations of production or class relations necessitate employing serf or slave labour take place where there is ongoing political control of labour, and therefore there is no systemic compulsion toward economic innovation. The innovation that does occur is based on the vagaries of chance.

Brenner allows that Wallerstein does interest himself in class relations. But he argues that for him the transformation of class relations of production are merely the consequence or effect of commercialization. The early modern capitalist class in England – merchants, bankers, manufactures, gentry, capitalist farmers – was merely the heterogeneous expression of the expansion of markets at home and overseas. So was the incorporation of peripheral regions like Eastern Europe into the world capitalist market: it compelled the owners of feudal states to act increasingly as capitalist entrepreneurs. Wallerstein does not distinguish between the development of capitalism in the sense Brenner conceived it and the regressive transformation toward serfdom in the relations of production that took place under the impact of world market integration in Eastern Europe. For Wallerstein, serfdom, slavery and wage labour are all equally capitalist forms of labour control, differing only according to their place in the division of labour or the forms of economic specialization that develop in the world market. The distinctive role of wage labour in producing systemic imperatives towards accumulation through innovation and increases in labour productivity is ignored. Indeed, Wallerstein cannot see that the bias of the modern world toward technological innovation is based on the existence of distinctively capitalist relations of production founded on wage labour.

According to Brenner, Wallerstein discounts social relations of production because he shares dependency theorists' idea that capitalist development and under-development are two sides of the same coin. The development of capitalism in the core states led to, and came at the expense of, under-development in the periphery. Such a view is incompatible with Brenner's view of capitalism's historical distinctiveness: accumulation via innovation rooted in the historical development of a class system based on wage labour.

In Wallerstein's perspective, surplus is steadily transferred over centuries from the periphery toward the core. Higher levels of skill and greater accessibility to capital reinforced by the coercive power of the strong core states ensure such a historic transfer of wealth. As Brenner puts it, in dependency theory under-development is the result of a primitive accumulation of capital extracted from the periphery by the centre and the resultant lack of capital in the periphery.

For Brenner the primitive accumulation of capital in the periphery has nothing to do with the origin of capitalism. Quoting Marx,

Brenner insists that 'the so called primitive accumulation is nothing else than the historical process of divorcing the producer from the means of production.'[34] In other words, primitive accumulation was the process of forcing subsistence producers from the land, forcing them to sell their labour power for a wage, and in so doing, turning the land into capitalist means of production. This occurred not in the periphery but in England.

Brenner does not 'deny there was a long-term transfer of surplus away from the periphery'.[35] But he locates its cause elsewhere. Surplus was extracted by pumping out absolute surplus value through reducing wages and keeping workers' subsistence at minimal levels. This limited the internal market for capital or consumer goods in peripheral countries. The upper classes were only interested in importing luxuries in return for the locally produced surplus. And the development of free wage labour was inhibited by the predominance of forced labour coexisting with peasant subsistence producers. But the flow of surplus out of peripheral countries was not determined by the unequal economic and political relationship with the centre as Wallerstein or the dependency theorists argued. Rather, it was the class-structured lack of investment opportunities that determined this outflow. Other than the restricted market for luxuries, there was no market to make investment profitable. Driving the point home, Brenner uses the example of early modern Poland. He shows that not only could it not initiate capital accumulation because of its class structure based on serfdom, it could not even adequately respond to market opportunities for its grain stemming from Western Europe. As a counter-example, Brenner points to the English eighteenth-century colony of Pennsylvania. In contrast to most colonies and regions in the periphery where forced labour predominated, the population of Pennsylvania was mainly composed of free small-scale farmers, allowing the slow development of a process of capital accumulation.

Brenner recognized that his challenge to Wallerstein represented another round in the transition debate which had earlier seen the defeat of Sweezy's notion of capitalist origins based on the development of long-distance trade as the prime mover. Certainly Brenner's critique was a conceptual *tour de force*. Steeped as it was in a deep understanding of both Marxism and the historical process, Brenner's arguments decisively reassert the primacy of the development of capitalist relations of production to the origins of capitalism. In particular it points to the development of capitalism in agriculture as critical to the inception and consolidation of the new mode of production in England and elsewhere.

THE PROBLEMS WITH BRENNER

At the same time, Brenner's position was not without its problems, all of them concerned with the privileged position England enjoyed in his account of the origins of capitalism. Brenner was absolutely correct to insist that the extraction of relative surplus value or increases in labour productivity is only made possible by the proletarianization of labour. Yet Brenner tended to exaggerate the actual increase in agricultural productivity that occurred in the early phases of capitalism. Robert C. Allen has shown that over the period 1500 to 1800 overall output of grain in England rose by 150 per cent.[36] Over the same period output per worker increased by 43 per cent. But most of this gain came in the eighteenth century in the period of the so-called agricultural revolution. In the sixteenth century, which is the period when the extraction of relative surplus value and productivity increases are supposed to have begun working their magic according to Brenner, output per worker actually declined, if we follow Allen. Productivity experienced a modest if steady rise in the seventeenth century. This seventeenth-century growth was enough to overcome the Malthusian crises to which other states in Europe were still subject. It is real growth, but of a moderate, rather than spectacular, kind. It is only towards the end of the whole period that competitive markets began perhaps to drive increases in productivity. Indeed, it ought to be kept in mind that it is not a certainty that competitive markets actually were responsible for the increases in productivity of the eighteenth-century agricultural revolution. The most that we can say is that they were then in place in a way that was not the case earlier.

Brenner's tendency is to associate the generation of relative surplus value based on free labour with the core, and the production of absolute surplus value with the unfree labour of the periphery. England, whose economy was increasingly based on the extraction of relative surplus value, advanced rapidly. The rest of Europe, where economies lacked this feature, lagged behind, retarded rather than bolstered by its connection with the periphery:

> But surely *to the extent* that the early modern 'European world economy' … was defined by the interconnected systems of production based on coerced cash crop labour in the periphery and based on free labour in the core – it remained fundamentally 'pre-capitalist:' a sort of renewed feudalism, with a somewhat wider scope. The lack of a real breakthrough was indeed reflected

in the inability of the 'modern world economy' to provide the material underpinnings for continuing economic-industrial growth in most of Europe through the early modern period decisively better than had the serf-based economy of Europe during the mediaeval period.[37]

This analysis invites some scepticism. While he is right to insist that the capitalism is characterized by a systematic imperative towards producing relative surplus value, Brenner forgets that Marx saw these two forms of surplus extraction as working in tandem in the development of capitalism in England as well as the rest of Western Europe. According to Marx, increases in the working day, reductions in wages, increases in the intensity of work were all methods of increasing surplus value, *alongside* introducing new methods and technologies and reorganizing work or increasing labour productivity. The historical evidence suggests that the extraction of absolute surplus value remained important to the accumulation of capital in England and northwest Europe from the sixteenth until the middle of the nineteenth century.[38] Indeed, the revisionist view of the Industrial Revolution which has become predominant among economic historians since the 1980s strengthens an emphasis on the importance of the extraction of absolute surplus value to the history of accumulation. Such revisionism does not deny the importance of the new technological and organizational achievements of the Industrial Revolution, whose contributions to the economic growth of the period were taken for granted by most earlier historians. But this revisionism does diminish their weight in the overall English economy until the later nineteenth century. As such it dramatically reduces the earlier overly optimistic estimates of economic growth in the late eighteenth and early nineteenth centuries. While there was some economic growth, labour productivity throughout the economy scarcely rose during the Industrial Revolution. Per capita income prior to the onset of the Industrial Revolution was a lot closer to the level of the period of Industrial Revolution than previously believed.[39]

More generally Brenner over-emphasizes the extraction of relative surplus value at the expense of the overall accumulation process, whereas it is necessary to keep in sight the dialectical historical and economic relationship between capital accumulation and the development of relative surplus value. As capitalism advances the growth of the productivity of social labour leads to the devaluation of all existing capital, as the value of commodities is determined not by the labour time taken by their production originally but by the labour time taken for their production currently. This labour time steadily diminishes as the productivity of social labour grows. Therefore existing capital, instead of appearing as the result of a long process of previous accumulation involving primitive accumulation and the absolute as well as relative exploitation of labour, appears in an illusory fashion the result of a relatively short reproduction period. The previous long and painful accumulation of capital necessary to the further increase in the productivity of social labour is lost sight of by Brenner.[40]

The most we can say about the period 1500–1800 from this perspective is that technological innovation and the reorganization of production facilitated a gradual if uneven rise in the extraction of relative surplus value in agriculture and manufacturing in England, and to a lesser extent on the Continent. Progress in this respect gradually increased from the seventeenth century onward. Sparked by previous advances in Flanders, innovations like enclosure, mechanization, three-field crop rotation, water meadows and selective breeding made headway in England and northern France in the eighteenth century. The same century saw the emergence especially in England of increasingly capitalized and concentrated industries based on technological breakthroughs like the spinning jenny, flying shuttle, power loom, puddling of iron and the steam engine. But it should be stressed that most of these innovations came late in this 300-year period. Over the whole early period the development of dispersed rural industries and large numbers of large-scale handicraft workshops or so-called manufactures – the characteristic forms of industrial growth – saw longer hours and greater intensity of work at subsistence or near-subsistence wages as much or more than it did increases in relative surplus extraction through technological innovation. At the very least both methods of surplus extraction went hand in hand with the extraction of relative surplus value, gradually amplifying the extraction of surplus through continued or intensified absolute exploitation.

THE NON-EUROPEAN CONTRIBUTION TO EUROPEAN CAPITALISM

Brenner's acknowledgement that the extraction of absolute surplus value from the periphery did happen was acompanied by his discounting the importance of such non-European surpluses to capitalist accumulation in Europe. This is no mere academic matter. It stems from his fundamental political and theoretical disagreement with dependency theory. Brenner, of course, is a distinguished professor, but like Wallerstein he was caught up in the events of the 1960s and has ever since been close to the theoretical positions of the Fourth International. Reflecting this perspective, Brenner attacked dependency theory as promoting the overcoming of under-development by delinking politically and economically from global capitalism, rather than pursuing international class struggle. According to Brenner, this is to move toward the utopia of trying to achieve socialism in one country.[41] The alternative is a politics which understands that capitalism is a globally interdependent system based on raising the productivity of labour, in which the only real choices are to join the capitalist system, or better, to overthrow it. Accordingly, a revolutionary politics strives for international revolution in which the working class assumes revolutionary leadership in both developed and under-developed countries. The transformation of the relations of production or of class relations by revolutionary means must be the primary objective in the under-developed as well as the developed world.

Such a politics has a certain validity in that it insists on the necessity of the working class remaining in the driver's seat in carrying forward a revolution which is both socialist and global. The force of this position has been demonstrated time and again by the failed attempts to institute national and democratic revolutions based on compromises with the bourgeoisies of different countries. On the other hand, the weakness of this perspective, aside from its tendency to political inflexibility and dogmatism, is its overly optimistic view of the possibility of positive historical change in the face of imperialism and under-development. At the same time it has made the serious mistake of over-valuing the political importance of the first world proletariat and thereby failing to take the political and economic potential of the under-developed world seriously enough.

It led Brenner himself to under-rate the contribution of the under-developed world to capitalist development, and ironically for someone committed to the international class struggle, to fail to take a sufficiently global view of such development. Indeed, Brenner's view is frankly too Anglocentric, let alone Eurocentric. For in our view the Continental European and non-European contribution was indispensable to the development of capitalism. We have already noted how important the development of silver and gold mining in Central Europe was to the earliest phase of capitalism in the late fifteenth and sixteenth centuries. It was critical in providing a means of exchange and store of value, making possible the initial upsurge of capitalism in Europe and the establishment of the capitalist world market based on trade with Asia. This flow of bullion was greatly amplified by the mines of Mexico and Peru, which began to deliver their riches to Europe from about 1530. By 1640 at least 180 tons of gold and 17,000 tons of silver had reached Europe from America. In the course of the sixteenth century the circulation of metal coins in Europe increased eight or ten times. A certain percentage of this precious metal made possible the expansion of the Asian trade. In Asia in the same period the stock of silver originating from the Americas (as well as Japan) may have tripled.[42] This accretion of precious metal, it should be realized, is not a matter of heaping up treasure or even setting masses of goods into circulation, but of using money capital to set alienated labour to wage work, and extracting unpaid labour as surplus value.

THE CAUSES OF UNDER-DEVELOPMENT

Brenner was certainly correct to insist that the fundamental reason for the failure of accumulation to take hold in peripheral countries was the class structure in such countries. But he discounts the effects of external political and economic pressures in creating and shaping that class structure. Spanish and English political and economic control of Latin America helped to maintain an upper class which blocked a possible social and political evolution or revolution that could have made capital accumulation possible. Whole strata of Latin America's class structure served colonial and imperialist masters as *compradores*. Serfdom, imposed by an increasingly assertive Polish aristocracy, was powerfully reinforced by the demand for grain on the West European market. In turn the American Revolution, which facilitated the evolution of Pennsylvania and the other colonies of the northeast of North America towards capitalism, involved overthrowing the power of a local merchant oligarchy. But it also required breaking links with and dependence on a powerful political and economic empire, which was standing in the way of such an evolution. In other words, colonialism and imperialism internalize themselves in the class structure of dependent societies, reinforcing elements that are essentially *comprador*. They oppose capitalist development, and delay and inhibit the onset of capitalist accumulation. In turn limiting the intrusion of foreign political and economic influence proved critical to the process of capital accumulation. The creation of a strong territorial state under whose protection an indigenous capitalist bourgeoisie could develop was essential to the development of strong capitalist states like the United States.

PRIMITIVE ACCUMULATION IN THE PERIPHERY

Brenner has summarized his own view of the origins of capitalist development in England in an article on the origins of the English Revolution
in a *festschrift* in honour of his teacher Lawrence Stone.[43] Here, he
makes much of Marx's concept of primitive accumulation as it bears on
the English countryside.[44] In the formulation offered by Marx, subsistence peasants were dispossessed and had to turn to wage work or were
forced to sell their labour in return for wages. The land – the basic means
of production – became capital in so far as it produced value based on
the work of wage workers and became part of a system of exchange in
which surplus value was realized as profit. But this does not exhaust
Marx's understanding of primitive accumulation. As he goes on to say in
his famous discussion in the last part of the first volume of *Capital*:

> the discovery of gold and silver in America, the extirpation, the
> enslavement and entombment in mines of the aboriginal popula-
> tion, the beginning of the conquest and looting of the East Indies,
> the turning of Africa into a warren for the commercial hunting
> of blackskins, signalled the rosy dawn of the era of capitalist
> production. These idyllic proceedings are the chief momenta of
> primitive accumulation.[45]

Marx especially singles out as an instance of primitive accumulation
the massive transfer of surplus from South Asia to England at the
time of the conquest of the Indian subcontinent which clearly helped
England finance its Industrial Revolution and its global wars against
revolutionary France (1792–1815).[46]

Rosa Luxemburg saw primitive accumulation in the early modern
and modern period as being closely linked to colonialism. It was
militarism or the use of force that constituted the essential link
between the two:

> It [militarism] fulfils a quite definite function in the history of capital,
> accompanying as it does every historical phase of accumulation. It
> plays a decisive part in the first stages of European capitalism, in
> the period of the so-called 'primitive accumulation', as a means of
> conquering the New World and the spice-producing countries of
> India. Later, it is employed to subject the modern colonies, to destroy
> the social organizations of primitive societies so that their means of
> production may be appropriated, forcibly to introduce commodity
> trade in countries where the social structure had been unfavourable

to it, and to turn the natives into a proletariat by compelling them
to work for wages in the colonies.[47]

Luxemburg glimpsed the historical relationship between the inception
of capitalism in Europe and the invasion of the rest of the world by
the Europeans from the sixteenth century onwards. Especially noteworthy is her sense of the importance of the primitive appropriation
of the land from the indigenous population. Indeed, according to
Massimo De Angelis, Luxemburg already understood that primitive
accumulation is an inherent and continuous process throughout the
global history of capitalism.[48]

More recently David Harvey has elaborated on primitive accumulation, or as he calls it 'accumulation by dispossession', in order to
remove any implication that it is a phenomenon characteristic only
of capitalism's origins and not its maturity. He sees it as a process
going on both in the heart of capitalism and at its periphery from
the sixteenth century right down to the present. In its latest forms
it includes such phenomena as the privatization of public water
systems, expropriation of homes, farms or small businesses for the
sake of large-scale private development, corporate theft of workers'
pension funds, and last but not least, the invasion of oil-rich
countries. Land, gold, silver, petroleum and other tangibles in Europe
or overseas were not in themselves capital, Harvey explains.[49]
Whether of European or non-European origin, they became and are
still becoming capital in so far as they are included in an economic
circuit in which surplus value is produced from the work of wage
workers and as part of a system of exchange in which surplus value
is realized as profit. It can be concluded that primitive accumulation
outside Europe in the early modern period was as important to the
development of capitalism as it was within Europe, and that the
extraction of absolute surplus value as well as relative surplus value
characterizes capitalism. This strongly suggests that colonial control
over the periphery, and politically controlled labour in general, was
more important to accumulation than Brenner allows.

Brenner's conception of primitive accumulation in relation to
the market is also historically problematic. He appreciatively cites
Marx's assertion with respect to primitive accumulation that 'the
expropriation of the agricultural producer, from the soil, is the basis
of the whole process'.[50] According to Brenner, Marx noted that
England is the classic case of primitive accumulation:

for Marx, this classic form involved a series of processes by which the English lords used coercion, law and taxation to reduce the former peasant possessors to market dependence; by which a class of capitalist tenant farmers emerged to take up the lords' commercial farms on economic leases, and by which, through force and the market, a proletariat devoid of the means of subsistence and production arose to hire themselves out to the capitalist farmers as agricultural labourers.[51]

Brenner tends to mistake the reason for Marx's emphasis on primitive accumulation in England. Marx did not underscore it because it produced any specific class pattern, he stressed it because he wanted to underline the role of force in creating the capital relation – with accumulated means of production on the one hand and a proletariat devoid of any on the other – and because he wanted to emphasize that even in England, especially in England, this was the basis of the apparently peaceful and bourgeois pursuit of accumulation. Brenner conflates this with his own insistence on the importance of the imposition of economic leases by landlords on capitalist farmers as if they were part of a single process.

It is true that Marx notes the leasing of the land by noble landlords following enclosure, but he does not indicate that these leases were competitive or economic. As we shall see, there are some scholars who doubt the importance of these so-called economic leases to the process of accumulation, or indeed whether they existed at all in the prolonged initial period of agricultural capitalism. More fundamentally, fully formed markets or rational and competitive markets in land and labour were more the result of a historical process of primitive accumulation and growing opportunities for profit for capitalists than the driving force behind them. Capitalist rent and property emerged out of the development of wage labour, rather than capitalist rent and property producing wage labour. It should be emphasized that capitalist property rights established themselves gradually, and that it was only in the aftermath of the English Revolution that landlords obtained absolute legal control of their property rather than holding them on the basis of feudal tenure.

MARKETS AND HISTORY

In Brenner's account most peasants are reduced to market dependence, and a small number of others emerge as capitalist tenant farmers to take up the lords' commercial farms on economic leases. Higher prices for grain and wool in the first part of the sixteenth century encouraged these trends by opening up opportunities for profit. But it is a mistake to assume, as Brenner apparently does, that an already rational and competitive market imposed a strict market rationality on the emerging rural capitalists. As we have seen, increased opportunities for profit failed to reflect themselves in increases in agricultural productivity in the short run during the sixteenth century. In the longer term, a more rational and competitive market favouring innovation was the consequence of the growing possibility for profits realized through the coercive effects of primitive accumulation and the gradual progress of exchange relations. In other words capital – born of primitive accumulation and pursuing its repeated cyclical movement in the course of realization – eventually removed, by economic but also political means, the barriers to exchange inherited from the old mode of production, and imposed a more rational and competitive market. The initial profitable windfalls of the sixteenth century, reinforced by unprecedented inflationary pressures, cannot be thought of as the way 'normal' or established markets based on competition operate, but rather describe a process of market formation. Competitive markets did not fully emerge until the seventeenth century under the shock of straitened economic conditions which encouraged greater discipline in the market.[52] Overall it is the circular movement of capital which undermines the obstacles in its way that leads to market competition rather than vice versa. The emergence of capital as a circular totality has a history that Brenner does not grasp but rather takes for granted.

The ongoing barriers to fully rational markets in the first two centuries of capitalism based on the political practices inherited from the feudal mode of production need to be emphasized. C. G. A. Clay's study of social and economic change in early modern England takes note of ongoing government interference in the market to ensure social stability.[53] Dobb emphasizes the degree to which markets in England were controlled and regulated by formal and informal commercial monopolies.[54] Such monopolies increased in the late Elizabethan and early Stuart period. The Stuarts even tried to restore the decayed guild system. An end to monopolies at home and abroad was to be one of the fundamental demands of the revolutionaries of the Civil War. All this is just another way of saying that until the English Revolution helped to sweep away many of these restrictions, there was nothing approaching a competitive market.

Gregory Clark, a neoclassical economic historian, complains that determining the rental value of farmland in the first part of the sixteenth century is not easy, since in early years much farmland was not rented for its (hypothetical) current rental value. Instead land was held on a bewildering variety of tenures or customary leases, which were well below supposed or estimated market values. At the beginning of the sixteenth century one can hardly speak of a real market in land.[55] Keith Wrightson confirms Clark's view, describing how over the next century a rational land market only gradually emerged out of a process that involved enclosure and class struggles including struggles over rents.[56] Brenner speaks about capitalist farmers taking up economic leases. Yet having stressed class struggle in the fourteenth century, Brenner seems content to ignore it in the sixteenth century. In contrast Mark Overton points out that the establishment of rental terms between landlords and capitalist farmers was fraught with conflict, which frequently led to lawsuits and violence.[57] We have already spoken of the role of force in constituting both national and international markets. It is important to understand the creation of the markets in land at the local and regional levels in a like way.

The creation of a labour market, like the creation of a land market, was a prolonged and highly coercive process which was more political and ideological than based on the market. The process of primitive accumulation already reflects this. Dispossessing producers moreover did not automatically lead them to take wage work. The imposition of humiliating and punitive poor laws was required to deal with recalcitrants and vagabonds. Indeed, one aspect of the new Puritan Calvinist religion that especially appealed to the emerging class of rural and urban capitalists was that as a form of ideological coercion it helped employers to enforce and implant a ferocious and paternalistic work discipline on their workers.

In sixteenth and seventeenth-century England, furthermore, labour was not viewed as an unfettered commodity whose disposition could be left to the play of the market. Rather those who worked for wages were seen as a common resource to which the powerful in the community had rights. Labourers and artificers had legal obligations to make that resource available, not on the basis of terms set by the wage worker or the market, but on terms imposed by the local community. While for the most part they were not members of an employer's household and under his control, wage workers were governed paternalistically in an analogous way.[58] Wage labour remained under strict local government control. Employers used these paternalistic regulations to continue to block labour mobility and to suppress workers' demands for improved working conditions into the modern period. It is only in the nineteenth century that there emerged a labour market and labour as a free commodity, as it were. Moreover it only did so after prolonged struggle by the emerging trade union movement.[59] *Pace* Brenner, these developments were pointed out in Marx's *Grundrisse*.[60]

I should underscore that I agree with Brenner that in the history of capital the appearance and spread of wage labour and a market for it must be regarded as decisive. They are the basis on which value emerges, as we see below. Yet it is important to appreciate that the development of wage labour itself has a history. It emerged as the gradually predominant element in a complex set of hierarchical forms of economic exploitation and domination in the early modern period which included apprenticeship, craft workshops, domestic service, indentured labour, female employment both in and outside the family, child labour and slavery. The successful abolition of capitalism, I might add, will involve the settling of accounts with this complicated historical legacy of exploitation, in which labour is not really free.[61] The abolition of capitalism is not simply a matter of doing away with the capitalist economy and state through social and political revolution. It entails a prolonged struggle to democratize the centuries-old social and economic hierarchies of the existing division of labour. In any event it does not help to speak, as Brenner does, of the free play of labour in the market from the sixteenth century.

THE CAPITALIST FARMER

The class of capitalist tenant farmers who took up the so-called economic leases offered by landlords is central in Brenner's arguments. But whereas for Dobb, Hilton and Byres the appearance of this class was critical to the eventual flowering of rural capitalism, Brenner minimizes their role. As in his account of the decline of feudalism, it is the landlords who retain the initiative. In the struggles of the late Middle Ages the latter succeeded in holding onto the major part of the arable land. Then in the sixteenth and early seventeenth centuries the nobility, including the high aristocracy, are pictured by Brenner as innovative capitalist landlords. Responsive to the competitive pressures of the marketplace, they assume leadership in leasing their lands on competitive terms to tenants who are also compelled to innovate in order to meet their rents. As both landlords and capitalist farmers were forced to encourage innovation, a process of capital accumulation developed in the countryside. As described by Brenner, it is the landlords who force the pace in this movement toward capitalist agriculture. They overshadow their tenants, who are forced to accept and accommodate themselves to changes in their leases imposed upon them by their landlords. Such a top-down view of capitalist origins, if true, would tend to clinch Brenner's argument that the landlord-dominated social property relations that emerged out of the class struggles of the late Middle Ages inexorably determined the capitalist development that followed.

Brenner's evidence on the ongoing control of the bulk of the land by landlords, and the emergence of capitalist farms organized on the tripartite classic division between landlord, tenant farmer and wage labourers, is incontestable. On the other hand, he offers little evidence that landlords took the lead in the consolidation of capitalist farms. On the basis of intensive archival research, Jane Wittle questions Brenner's notion that short-term leases by landlords helped to spark the engrossing, or the reorganizing of the land in England into larger units.[62] Rather, she argues that enterprising peasant producers took the initiative in creating such farms. While Whittle's argument is based on evidence from Norfolk, and would have to be extended to be conclusive, she does show that, in this area at least, landlord interference in the market for customary land was minimal in the period up to 1580. The value of rents to landlords fell in the fifteenth century, and they were diminished further in the sixteenth century by inflation. Tenants, not landlords, benefited from rising land values, and it was tenants, not landlords, who brought about engrossment. Far from the market being imposed upon peasants from above as Brenner would have it, the emerging land market was integral to strategies of peasant acquisition and landholding.[63] It was the advancing class of capitalist farmers rather than the landlords who, seeing opportunity in the market, took the economic initiative.

Brenner's view of a landlord-led agrarian capitalism in England is also contested on other grounds. Mark Overton, who has an impressive mastery of the concrete details of contemporary research, argues that tenants were not at the mercy of landlords with respect to the terms of their leases.[64] Leases often protected tenants, and these protections were frequently upheld in the courts. Economic differentiation was a process which occurred between tenants. Landlords did not frequently take the initiative in innovation; it was tenants and freeholders who did. Large farms were not a prerequisite for higher land productivity. Crop yields were independent of farm size from the seventeenth century onwards.[65] Finally, on Brenner's view which minimizes the significance of the independent peasant producer in England, we would expect that agrarian capitalism developed in areas where landlord control was strong and peasant property rights were weak. In fact the reverse is the case, according to Overton. The most striking advances in output and land productivity occurred in areas where lordship was relatively weak. All this argues for the decisive importance of the small producer in control of the means of the production, rather than the landlord.

Overton's critique appears to be derived from the views advanced earlier by the distinguished historian of English agriculture H. J. Habakkuk.[66] Habakkuk denied that landlords were an active economic class involving themselves in the improvement of agricultural methods. He even questioned the idea that, as late as the end of the eighteenth century, they were prepared to impose economic leases on their tenants. Rather than creating the new agriculture, Habakkuk concluded that they were the passive beneficiaries of it. Habakkuk's view of economic leases is echoed by that of P. K. O'Brien and D. Heath on the actual evolution of so-called economic rents as late as the eighteenth century:

> In any case, the turnover of established in favour of more efficient farms probably changed rather slowly, if only because such 'commercial' behaviour alienated other families on the estate and reduced their confidence to invest in land and improvements that gestated slowly through the seasons. Co-operation between landlords and tenants continued to depend far more upon tradition than upon contractual obligations. The eviction of families that had resided upon an estate for generations may have become more common in the eighteenth century but was still regarded as bad form. Tenancies-at-will worked best wherever owners and their stewards operated in a rather close working partnership with tenants and provided them with well-maintained farms, sound advice, and above all adequate rewards or compensation for investments in the long-term productivity of farm land.[67]

According to these authors, the time of economic rents arrived not in the sixteenth, seventeenth or eighteenth centuries but only in the wake of the French and Industrial Revolutions.

SALVAGING BRENNER?

Brenner's stress on the importance of agrarian class struggle to the decline of feudalism and setting the stage for the emergence of capitalism is fundamentally important. So too is his emphasis on the accumulation of capital through the extraction of relative surplus value made possible by capitalist relations of production, in contrast to the 'Smithian' approach of Frank and Wallerstein. On the other hand, his dismissal of the importance of absolute surplus value and primitive accumulation, especially in the periphery, is unfortunate. His assumption of the sixteenth-century market as rational and competitive appears anachronistic. His privileging of the landlords over the rural bourgeoisie as the prime agent of capitalist develop-ment is doubtful. It is also problematic with regard to the English Revolution, as we shall see.

Brenner's problems are only magnified by his epigones. When Ellen Wood recently restated Brenner's views on the origins of capitalism,[68] she emphasized the importance of the development of wage labour to the onset of accumulation even more than him, and connected the growing dependence of wage earners on the market for items of household consumption to the development of the home market for manufactures.[69] She may even have understated the extent of wage dependence, and of the self-exploitation of farmers and craftspeople employing no wage labour under the compulsion of the market on which they had become dependent.[70] The statistics assembled by Gregory King, writing toward the end of the seven-teenth century, testify to as much as 40 per cent of the population in England being dependent on wages for a livelihood.[71] Jan De Vries found that wage labour was already in the seventeenth century the single most important source of income throughout much of northwest Europe.[72] That being said, in the social relationships in sixteenth and seventeenth-century rural England the growing influence of wage labour did not amount to a free market in labour, as we have already seen, nor did it imply the extent of market dependence assumed by Wood. The persistence of apprenticeships, master–servant relationships, indenture and the constraints of the Poor Law inhibited the full development of an unconstrained labour market.

In explaining the emergence of capitalism, Brenner laid emphasis on the role of capitalist landlords imposing economic rents on more affluent tenant farmers. According to him, this forced the latter to innovate in order to meet the terms of their leases. It was the new system, based on market compulsion, which was forced on landlords and tenants that sparked accumulation. Wood helps us to understand Brenner's logic further. She notes that certain of Brenner's critics have questioned his emphasis on landlords rather than better-off peasants in the genesis of capitalism. Wood responds that it was less a question of which class took the lead than of understanding the process of market compulsion imposed on both. Indeed, she argues that those who take the view of the above critics do not fully understand the difference between market involvement and market compulsion. The latter was key. In so far as they think that mere involvement in the market automatically leads rich peasants to become capitalist farmers, Dobb, Hilton and Byres fall back into a Smithian or commercial model of capitalism.[73]

But Wood only changes the subject. As we shall see, whether we place the emphasis on capitalist farmers or nobles has everything to do with our understanding of the social and political history of capitalism. Since this is so, we would do well to examine Wood's arguments further. Do we really have to choose between market coercion and market opportunity? Hilton's and Whittle's researches suggest that market opportunities drew rich peasants more and more into the market. Such involvement would eventually have made them subject to the competitive pressures or the coercive effects of the market. Moreover, Wood's position has a dogmatic quality which is not only belied by the concrete historical circumstances, but also contradicted by the very authorities she invokes. In *The Origins of Capitalism* she harks back to the work of Karl Polanyi, praising him for understanding that markets were historically evolved institutions.[74] But Polanyi insisted that markets in England were embedded in society until the end of the eighteenth century, and indeed even afterward, and as such were deeply regulated. How Polanyi's conception can be reconciled with Wood's notion that markets in England operated on the basis of competition, freedom and rationality from the beginning of the sixteenth century is unclear.

I conclude that Wood's, and indeed Brenner's, conception of the operation of the market is anachronistic. While both chastised Wallerstein for his Smithian notion of capitalism based on individual choices and the division of labour in the market, and both insisted that primacy be given to relations of production or social property relations, they too place enormous stress on the market, albeit a market conceived as perfect or perfectly competitive in the economist's sense. In a manner of speaking they have thrown the market out the front door but only to smuggle an even more dogmatic conception of it through the back. There is a lesson in this. Forms of commercial or financial capitalism based on markets to the exclusion of production can be regressive. Hilton, Takashi and Dobb saw them as reinforcing feudalism. They helped to smother the shoots of capitalism in Italy and Germany. Their intrusion into industry tended to stifle innovation in manufacturing, as Marx and Dobb stressed. Brenner and Wood rightly emphasize that the market can never initiate accumulation. On the other hand, as Brenner and Wood suggest, where capitalist relations of production become fully entrenched, the market including its commercial and financial aspects can, once matured, foster economic competition and capital accumulation. I would go further, insisting that the realization process made possible by markets is indispensable to the further expansion of capitalism, understood as a totality based on an expanding spiral of value.

THE BIRTH OF VALUE

It should be noted that Wood is deservedly celebrated as a political theorist. She is at her best in describing the connection between the emergence of agrarian capitalism and the tentative emergence of a labour theory of value in the work of John Locke, in particular in his ideas about property rights. For such rights were, in his view, labour-based. Only the investment of labour to improve land, to increase its productivity, could justify the dispossession of indigenous populations, first in Ireland and later in the American colonies.[75] Such ideas, Wood argues, distinguished England's distinctively capitalist colonialism from Spain's or other European countries'. And they arose from an agrarian capitalism driven, by the late seventeenth century, by the dynamic of relative surplus value.[76] As Wood notes, Locke was not alone in adumbrating the notion of labour as the source of value. In fact, there were frequent assertions among Locke's contemporaries of the view that labour was the source of value.[77] While they did not articulate a full-fledged labour theory of value (that would only come with Marx), it is significant that the late seventeenth century saw a cluster of thinkers prepared to assert that labour was the source of value. It reflects the growing role of labour power in England's emerging capitalist economy. In other words, the recognition by late seventeenth-century students of economy that labour is the measure of value signals for the first time the definitive supersession of earlier pre-capitalist forms of economic exploitation by capitalist relations of production and exchange.[78]

How profound a social transformation this represented was suggested by Marx where he noted that Aristotle had already discovered that there must be a relation of equality between the values of commodities. But to identify such a relation one must acknowledge that all labour is equal. Living in a profoundly unequal society, Aristotle could not articulate the notion of the equality of labour. Founded on slavery, Greek society had as its basis the notion of the inequality of human beings and their labour. The idea of value, or that all labour in general is equal, cannot be comprehended until the notion of human equality has established itself in consciousness as a popular prejudice.[79] Such an idea did emerge in the course of the levelling social and political transformations in England in the seventeenth century.

CONCLUSION

In this chapter our discussion has underscored the ongoing force of Dobb's account of capitalist origins, in particular his views on the importance of primitive accumulation and of the really revolutionary way led by petty producers. These views were challenged by Wallerstein, who revived, modified, and expanded Sweezy's original stress on the importance of exchange. His view of capitalism as a world-wide system of economic and political relations has ongoing if incomplete explanatory power, but Brenner's critique and reiteration of the decisive significance of the wealth-creating potential of the new capitalist relations of production in the capitalist core remains critical to any understanding of the capitalist accumulation process. On the other hand, I believe that Brenner's conception of the history of capitalism is parochial and economistic. Brenner has gotten ahead of himself in insisting on the overwhelming influence of the extraction of relative surplus value as a factor driving accumulation prior to the Industrial Revolution. His ideas about the effect of competitive markets in which landlords are leading actors appear historically anachronistic. Uncomfortable with dialectics, Brenner fails to see capitalism as an expanding totality in which production and realization are each indispensable, and in which each has a history. He pays little or no attention to the role of the state as an intrinsic feature of capitalism. The state played a critical role from the very beginnings of capitalism, and capitalism cannot really consolidate itself as a mode of production without control of the state. It is the state that helps capitalism to generalize and organize itself. Beyond a certain point capitalism cannot develop further without control of the state. Accordingly, it is the question of the consolidation of the capitalist state through revolution that we must now address.

4

BOURGEOIS REVOLUTION

This chapter reasserts the classic Marxist view of the English and French Revolutions as bourgeois and capitalist. These revolutions proved critical to the consolidation of the new mode of production. The revolution in Holland was likewise bourgeois and capitalist. Economistic readings of the origin of capitalism tend to discount the importance of all three revolutions, and Brenner, though he recently conceded that early modern Holland was capitalist, ignored its revolution. Contrariwise I argue that from the beginning the state was intrinsic to capitalism as a result of its generalizing and integrating functions. Its revolutionary transformation at a certain point was essential to capitalism's development.

With regard to England Brenner and Wood argue, improbably, that the necessary and sufficient conditions for the development of capitalism were established by changes in the social relations of production during the late medieval period. The English revolution was neither capitalist nor bourgeois. At best it confirmed an already functioning capitalism politically. In the case of France Comninel, supported by Wood, asserts that its revolution was somehow bourgeois but not capitalist. I shall demonstrate that such views are in conflict with existing scholarship. The views of Brenner and his followers represent an unwarranted revision of the Marxist view of history in which the revolutionary mobilization of the people and notably its most organized elements are central elements to the transition from feudalism to capitalism. In my view the roots of this pessimism are to be found in the failure of the revolutionary politics of the 1960s.

Revolution plays a central role in Marx's and Engels's theory of history. Capitalism developed within the pores of feudalism. As it matured feudalism was transformed into the absolutizing royal state in both England and France. In an initial phase the emerging bourgeoisie and the royal state acted in partnership, especially to curb the private and anarchic violence of the nobility. But beyond a certain point, the state began to interfere with the further development of capitalism, and restricted the growing power and ambition of the bourgeoisie while protecting the interests of the nobles. The Dutch, English and French revolutions represented the moment

when the bourgeoisie took things into their hands politically and put
an end to both feudalism and absolutizing or absolute government.
In the transition from feudalism to capitalism we see revolution as
the moment in which the fetters inhibiting the full development of
capitalism were finally cast aside. As a consequence of these revolutions, existing class relations and the superstructure of society were
transformed so as to clear the way for the blossoming of a fully
mature capitalism.[1]

The English and French revolutions, as well as the revolution
in Holland, are the classic Marxist examples of bourgeois and
capitalist revolutions. In recent years there has arisen a substantial
literature questioning this view. Much of this work is anti-Marxist,
committed to undermining the Marxist view of history. However
an important strand of this revisionist history is associated with
Brenner's ideas. To what degree Brenner endorses them is unclear.
In any case, this revisionist viewpoint has crystallized into a school
of thought known as Political Marxism. This chapter will test the
claims of this school.

By capitalist revolution we understand the sweeping away of
feudal obstacles to the further development of the capitalist forces
of production by a violent and more or less rapid transformation of
the state and social relations. Masses of workers, craftspeople and
peasants were necessarily involved in such great transformations.
In these three revolutions the petty producers and especially the
emerging capitalist element among them played a key role. But these
revolutions are considered bourgeois as well as capitalist because
the bourgeoisie – profit-seeking merchants, manufacturers and rich
peasants, but also lawyers, state functionaries, scholars, physicians
and even a minority of enlightened nobles – assumed political and
social leadership over the revolutions and became their principal
directors and beneficiaries. In the wake of such upheavals the
state acted purposely to spread and integrate capitalist relations of
production throughout society. Contrary to the views of the Political
Marxists, bourgeois revolutions were also capitalist revolutions.

HOLLAND

At this point it is important to remind ourselves that Engels judged
the Peasant War in Germany in the light of the notion of bourgeois
revolution. He saw it as a revolution ahead of its time, or as an early
bourgeois revolution. Capitalism, if not a mature bourgeoisie or a
national state, had come into being. But the absence of the latter

two elements caused this Revolution No. 1, or early bourgeois revolution, to fail. Germany reverted to feudalism. Meanwhile in Italy the absence of a political revolution from above which might have created a territorial state guaranteed the decline of its precocious capitalism. The vanguard role in the advance toward capitalism was taken by Holland and England.

Although they did not explicitly say so, scholars infer that Marx and Engels saw the revolution in Holland as a second early bourgeois revolution. They look upon this second and successful revolution as a prologue to the English and French revolutions.[2] In the first part of the sixteenth century the 17 provinces of the Low Countries became part of the Hapsburg Empire of Charles V (1516–56). Already a focal point of northern European trade and manufacture, the economy of the Netherlands grew spectacularly during the first part of the sixteenth century. Led by Antwerp, which became the epicentre of global commerce, the leading towns and the 17 provinces paid heavy taxes to the emperor, but enjoyed special privileges and gained access to the expanding trade of the Hapsburg Empire in Europe and in the New World. During this period the influence of Protestantism – Lutheran, Anabaptist and Calvinist – rose, as did that of a reform-minded and humanist Catholicism.

Circumstances deteriorated following the accession of Philip II of Spain (1556–98). The latter imposed bureaucratic control over the provinces, harshly attacked the Protestants and raised taxes at a time of growing economic difficulties. At first, the local nobility took the lead in opposing these measures. But in 1566 an iconoclastic fury on the part of the middle sort of people and the popular classes swept the major cities. Philip responded by sending the Duke of Alba at the head of the Spanish army into the Netherlands. Over the next four years Alba succeeded in suppressing the uprising by means of a campaign of terror. But in 1572 revolt broke out anew. Some rebels in exile ('sea beggars') seized the port of Brill, which allowed the insurgents to pursue the war against Spain from the sea.

The focal point of the rebellion became the northern provinces of Holland, Zeeland and Friesland, with power shared between the estates of Holland and the aristocratic military commander and stadtholder William of Orange. In response to the Spanish sack of Antwerp (1576), the northern and southern provinces agreed to a policy of religious toleration and a common fight against the Spanish army (the Pacification of Ghent). The growth of Calvinist radicalism led the elites of the southern provinces to reassert their loyalty to Phillip at the beginning of 1579 (Union of Arras). A few weeks later five northern provinces, including Holland and Zeeland, and major cities like Antwerp, Bruges, Ghent and Brussels, joined together in the Calvinist Union of Utrecht. The provinces of the Netherlands at this point permanently divided, as the new Spanish commander, the Duke of Parma, recaptured Flanders and Brabant. The city of Antwerp was again sacked (1585) by the Spanish army, causing tens of thousands of Calvinist merchants and craftspeople to move to Amsterdam. Dug in behind the rivers and canals of Holland, the Dutch army held off the Spanish while the insurgent navy raided Spanish merchant shipping in the Atlantic and the Caribbean. Indeed, in the midst of this protracted and revolutionary war of liberation, the Dutch republic with its focal point at Amsterdam emerged at the forefront of the European economy. By 1609 a truce with an exhausted Spain was arranged. The independence of the Dutch Republic was affirmed in the Peace of Westphalia (1648).

Once established the Dutch republic was dominated by merchant capitalism. Its vast merchant marine, highly specialized and productive agriculture, export-oriented industry and control of not merely the European bulk trade (fish, grain, wood, wheat), but also the more remunerative trades in spices, sugar, furs, silk and wool cloth made Holland the centre of the world market in the seventeenth century. A powerful merchant elite lay at the core of this system of commercially based capital formation, whose operations were facilitated by the development of banking, insurance and joint-stock companies.[3]

In the early years of the last century Dutch Marxist historians developed the view of the revolt against Spain as a bourgeois revolution. According to them, in the first part of the sixteenth century the interests of merchant capitalists were strongly tied to the Hapsburg monarchy. But the policy of absolutism brought in by Philip II reflected a growing antagonism between the nobility and the bourgeoisie. The iconoclastic fury marked the beginning of the first successful bourgeois revolution. Merchant discontent awakened the working class, especially in the Flemish textile cities. The ensuing revolt was fuelled by high grain prices and commercial crisis. The revolution was stymied in its early years by the ambivalence of the property-owning class, which was fearful of lower-class radicalism. The unity of the bourgeoisie of the emerging Dutch republic was further inhibited by its lack of cohesion as a result of the play of special interests and parochialism.[4]

The communist historian J. A. N. Knuttel, who published in the 1920s, saw the significance of the war of liberation as clearing the way for capitalism, and specifically merchant capitalism, in accord with Marx's concept of bourgeois revolution. According to Knuttel, this breakthrough occurred as a result of the initial unity of class forces, which included the lesser nobility, merchants, craftspeople and workers. Opposition to the established order combined economic motives with hostility to the Catholic Church, which was bound up with the old order. Following the iconoclastic fury, these revolutionary elements turned on one another, leading to the decline of the movement in the southern Netherlands. In the north neither the working class nor the nobility were very strong, ensuring the dominance of the bourgeois element. On the other hand, the influence of merchant capital inhibited the development of manufacturing, and ultimately led to rule by a corrupt commercial oligarchy.[5] Although modified by more recent research, this view of the origins of the Dutch revolt as the first successful bourgeois revolution has remained essentially intact.[6]

Beyond the historians of Holland it is perhaps Giovanni Arrighi among recent Marxist scholars who has done most to advance the idea of a successful early modern Dutch capitalism. Arrighi founded his own view on Wallerstein's world-systems and trade-based approach, asserting that Holland occupied a key role in the emerging cycles of global capitalist accumulation. He stresses its innovations in land warfare in defeating the Spanish/Genoese empire, the first capitalist world power. At the same time he points out how it learned how to internalize the cost of war into the structure of private trading corporations like the East India Company in a creative way, acquiring an unprecedented capacity to carry on naval war, assuring its commercial dominance overseas. Arrighi then points to the importance of Holland's financial strength in besting commercial rivals and using its overall economic strength to secure its hegemony, based on promoting the balance of power while reinforcing proto-nationalist ideas in the monarchical states. In Arrighi's view these accomplishments allowed Holland to become the second of the great imperial systems of historic capitalism.[7]

DUTCH MERCHANT CAPITALISM

Dutch Marxist historiography clearly viewed the revolution as capitalist. Yet it was challenged by a more sophisticated perspective coming from outside Holland. However enduring their account of the revolution has proved to be, Dutch scholars failed to pay much attention to Marx's theoretical analysis of merchant capitalism: capital accumulated on the basis of social forms of production –

feudalism, slavery – that were foreign to it and not subject to it. According to Marx, this is clear:

> in the history of the carrying trade, as conducted by the Venetians, Genoans, Dutch, etc., where the major profit was made not by supplying a specific national product, but rather by mediating exchange of products between commercially – and generally economically – undeveloped communities and by exploiting both the producing countries. Here we have commercial capital in its pure form, quite separate from the extremes, the spheres of production, between which it mediates. This is one of the main sources from which it is formed.[8]

Accumulation of capital occurs but without entering into the sphere of production. Commercial capital can act as a solvent of pre-capitalist social relations. But if feudal or slave relations are strong enough in the producing countries, it can also strengthen them. According to Marx, in Holland manufactures developed, but in industries especially related to exports, and notably in shipping and ship building. Manufacturing and colonialism were closely tied, as colonies served as an outlet for manufactures as well as facilitating accumulation through market monopoly. And in a passage referring to overseas primitive accumulation, Marx notes that 'the treasures captured outside Europe by undisguised looting, enslavement and murder flowed back to the mother-country and were turned into capital there'.[9] *Pace* Brenner, Marx believed that Dutch and other merchant capitalisms contributed significantly to European primitive accumulation, and quite clearly at the expense of the economies in the peripheral countries.

Despite the viewpoint of Arrighi and the Marxist historians in Holland, recent historians have had a hard time accepting the notion of Holland as a fully fledged capitalist state. Hobsbawm did acknowledge that Holland allowed the capitalist world economy to overcome the instability of the so-called seventeenth-century crisis. The conception of such a seventeenth-century crisis was brilliantly articulated by him to describe the widespread political and economic difficulties that marked that period in the wake of the initial take-off of capitalism.[10] The economy of capitalist Holland (and England) proved most successful in overcoming this economic shakeout. Hobsbawm's conception of the seventeenth-century crisis stirred argument but remains convincing.[11] But based on Marx's view of the limits of merchant capitalism, Hobsbawm judged Holland to be 'in many respects a feudal business economy, a Florence, Antwerp or Augsburg on a semi-national scale'.[12] In the face of what Hobsbawm described as the crisis of the seventeenth-century economy, Holland 'survived and flourished by cornering the supply of certain scarce goods and much of the world's business as a commercial and financial intermediary. Dutch profits did not depend greatly on capitalist manufacture.'[13]

It is Ellen Wood who most forcefully makes the case for thinking of the Dutch economy as pre-capitalist. According to her, its large cities and productive agriculture were sustained not by capitalist production, but essentially by international trade. Dutch producers including farmers were apparently not subject to the competitive pressures associated with capitalism. The influence of low-cost grain from Eastern Europe reduced the demands of competition by lowering the cost of basic inputs. In effect Dutch farmers were subsidized, allowing them to produce higher-cost and more profitable farm commodities like cheese and meat. Likewise in the international marketplace, the Dutch did not so much compete as rely on direct and indirect coercion to maintain their privileged commercial position.[14] Harking back to the previous chapter, we recall Wood's purist view of the capitalist market, which operates on the basis of perfect competition rather than on the basis of subsidization, protection and violence.

Proclaiming himself a follower of the Political Marxism of Brenner and Wood, Benno Teschke echoes this purist view of the market in his treatment of Holland in his recent study of early modern international relations. Teschke directs his fire particularly at Arrighi's view of Holland. In the first place, he denies that the Dutch republic, even in its heyday, ever had the capacity to impose hegemony over the international state system. Moreover, Holland's rise was based less on internal productive innovations than on commercial profit taking. Its military innovations, which were hailed by Arrighi, reflected not so much its rise as a capitalist power as its ability to turn trading profits into military innovations, protecting its trade. Such steps did not alter the age-old logic of unequal exchange sustained by military power.[15] Furthermore, 'trade in no way generated aggregate economic wealth; it merely redistributed surpluses. Merchant wealth is therefore not capital.'[16]

But Teschke confuses the existence of capital with the existence of the capitalist mode of production. The goal of merchant capital, which according to Marx certainly exists in both the feudal and capitalist modes of production, is profit. It may only incidentally create

growth and can also be economically regressive, as we have repeatedly noted. But it can also play a progressive role. It helps to dissolve
feudal relations, and is a necessary if not sufficient precondition
for the establishment of the capitalist mode of production, which
leads to accumulation or economic growth. Indeed, as Brenner and
Wood have stressed, once the relations of production have changed,
the competitive pressures induced by the market may be key to the
enhancement of labour productivity and capitalist accumulation.

AGRARIAN CAPITALISM

Basing themselves on Marx's conception of merchant capitalism,
Hobsbawm, Wood and Teschke reject the existence of early modern
Dutch capitalism. Yet there is in Marx a view of Holland which
leads one to be less certain of such a cursory dismissal of Dutch
capitalism. In Volume One of *Capital* Marx discusses the origin
of the so-called national debt. He explains that it first took root
in Holland as a way of financing Dutch colonial expansion. As he
explains, public debt became one of the most powerful levers of
primitive accumulation. Such debt provided almost risk-free returns
to financiers and merchants who invested in it. At the same time,
it was financed by taxing the mass of the population. This system
was first introduced in Holland. According to Marx the great
seventeenth-century Dutch patriot Hans De Witt extolled it:

> as the best system for making the wage-labourer submissive,
> frugal, industrious and over-burdened with labour. The destruc-
> tive influence that it exercises on the condition of the wage
> labourer concerns us less however, here, than the forcible expro-
> priation, resulting from it, of peasants , artisans, and in a word,
> all elements of the lower middle class.[17]

This passage from *Capital* must lead to an understanding of Marx's
notion of primitive accumulation to include more than the expropriation of English peasants from the land and the pillaging and
dispossession of non-European populations. Rather it anticipates
Harvey's recent conception of accumulation by dispossession in
which, for instance, employee pension funds are willy-nilly confiscated by private corporations, or the unemployment funds of
workers are appropriated by governments. Clearly such practices
are not merely a phenomenon of recent times but date back to the
early history of capitalism.

Marx's observations suggest the emergence in seventeenth-century Holland of an expanding pool of wage earners whose labour was generating profits that derived from more than exchange relations. Indeed, recent research reveals the existence in seventeenth-century Holland of an extremely large, if segmented, proletariat.[18] Elsewhere in *Capital* Marx notes that in Holland commercial credit and dealing in money developed along with trade and manufacture. Indeed, financial capital became subordinate to industrial and commercial capital. According to Marx, 'in the seventeenth century … Holland served as the model country of economic development, just as England does today.'[19] Such a view is hardly compatible with the view of Holland as a 'feudal business economy'. Holland, in fact, had a substantial manufacturing base with the most advanced technological infrastructure in Europe. The annual number of patents issued in Holland between 1590 and 1680, for example, slightly exceeded the number issued in England between 1660 and 1740.[20]

It is in this context that Brenner launched a major new intervention in the 1990s. Invited to a conference of experts on the economy of the early modern Netherlands to discuss his views, Brenner tossed off a paper which not only defended his notion of capitalist origins, but asserted, contrary to his earlier Anglocentric perspective, that early modern Holland was a fully capitalist economy.[21] Unlike in most of the rest of Europe, landlords were not a significant factor in the evolution of the agrarian economy of the northern Netherlands in the late Middle Ages. Instead, an ecological crisis precipitated a transformation of the peasant economy in the direction of capitalism. The subjugation of these agricultural producers to dependence on the market, and the rise of a large market-dependent population involved in trade and industry, occurred as part of a single process of agricultural transformation.

The progressive conversion of the low-lying peat soils of the northern Netherlands to grain agriculture in the late Middle Ages led to a settling of the peat and a rise in the moisture content of the soil. The land became unfit for the production of bread grains like winter wheat. Producers were forced to turn toward cattle farming, dairying and the extensive cultivation of summer grains. Farmers retained possession of the land, but lost the option of subsistence farming. As a result, they were forced into dependence on the market for their inputs. They became subject to competitive pressure, and obliged as a result to enter sectors of production that maximized return. In short, they were transformed into market-dependent *capitalist farmers*:

the peasants of the maritime Northern Low Countries had had no intention of bringing about a transition from pre-capitalism to capitalism. But as an unintended consequence of the acts of reclamation ... they ended up undercutting the ability of the soil to support production for subsistence and transforming themselves into market-dependent capitalist farmers.[22]

Instead of producing bread grains, they had to buy them, and were able to do so by producing in an increasingly efficient way specialized food products (cheese, butter, meat, barley, hops) for sale in the burgeoning markets found in the towns and cities of the southern Netherlands. Growing imports of grain from Eastern Europe lowered the cost of food and increased the farmers' discretionary purchasing power as well as that of the expanding urban populations. In addition, many farmers supplemented their income by finding employment in ship-building, fishing, tanning leather, brick-making and so on.

Cheap food and low wages favoured urbanization and the emergence of competitive industries like beer-making and wool cloth manufacture. By 1500 half the population lived in towns, and the level of full-fledged proletarianization in the northern maritime provinces likely stood at 50 percent. If ultimately Holland had to cede pride of place to England, it was because, unlike the latter, it remained too dependent on international markets. These were still based on feudal relations of production, and were overcome by the economic downturn of the seventeenth century. Relative to England, Holland was dragged down by the crisis.

Brenner's account is in itself a *tour de force*: all the more so, as it is punctuated by a systematic critique of the objections offered by the distinguished Dutch economic historians at the conference. In the course of making his case for Dutch capitalism, Brenner takes account, for the first time, of the insistence of some Marxist scholars of the importance of peasant differentiation to the development of capitalism. He acknowledges that this occurred in the northern Netherlands, albeit as a consequence of market competition rather than through such competition and deliberately regressive taxation. Brenner also touches on the Dutch revolt, but sees its consequences largely in economic terms. Immigration of skilled craftspeople from the south allowed the Dutch wool cloth industry to become internationally competitive. The abandonment by many merchants and financiers of Antwerp for Amsterdam made the latter city the focal point of world trade and finance.

In Brenner's account there is no recognition of the importance of the revolutionary struggle against Hapsburg political absolutism and the Counter-Reformation, or of the long war of national liberation. Nonetheless, Brenner's analysis greatly strengthens the view of the Dutch Revolt not simply as a bourgeois but as an authentically capitalist revolution. Earlier we have seen that Dutch Marxist historians regarded the triumph of the middle class in the northern Netherlands as the result of the fortuitous weakness of both the nobility and the proletariat compared with the southern Netherlands. But clearly from Brenner's analysis it can be inferred that the Dutch revolution triumphed because the northern economy was strongly capitalist, having a capitalist agriculture as its foundation. Moreover, contrary to his view of England, where the initiative lay in the hands of the landlords, according to Brenner, it was the rural and urban middle class who held the initiative both economically and politically in Holland. Finally, Brenner's view of Dutch capitalism tends to undercut his earlier insistence on the exclusive importance of the increase in the extraction of relative surplus value or gains in labour productivity to capitalist development. As he clearly acknowledges, the advance towards capitalism in Holland was heavily dependent on the availability of cheap grain from the periphery of Wallerstein's world economy lying east of the Elbe – grain which was the product of a serf economy based on a regime of absolute exploitation.

Brenner's view of Holland as a capitalist country was unacceptable to Wood, who, we can recall, had previously dismissed the notion that seventeenth-century Holland was capitalist. For her, grain from east of the Elbe represented a subsidy to Dutch farmers, reducing competitive pressures on them. According to her, unrelenting competition for all inputs was a *sine qua non* for capitalist accumulation based on the extraction of relative surplus value. Moreover, the Dutch resorted to direct and indirect violence to retain their commercial dominance. In Holland producers, including farmers, were apparently not fully subject to the competitive pressures associated with capitalism because it was the subsidy provided by low-cost Eastern grain that allowed them to produce higher-cost farm commodities like cheese and meat. Likewise, in the international marketplace the Dutch did not so much compete in the market as relied on direct and indirect coercion to maintain their privileged commercial position.

More in sorrow than anger, Wood responded to Brenner.[23] The main thrust of her reply was to fully elaborate her understanding of what a completely competitive market consists of, and to reiterate that England is the only early modern instance of such an economy. In particular, she insisted that cheap grain from Eastern Europe belied the notion that Holland was a capitalist economy: 'the influence of low-cost grain producing regions, which benefited the Dutch even more than other economies, if anything reduced competitive pressures by lowering the costs of basic inputs'.[24] But in my view this is tantamount to arguing that low prices for oil from the under-developed world based on imperialist relations meant that the Western European and American economies in the twentieth century were not fully capitalist. Wood is loath to accept the obvious truth that extra-economic factors have always been at work in the history of capitalism. She goes so far as to argue that the Republic's power was enhanced in large part by devoting much of its tax revenues to military ventures that gave it advantages in international trade that were not based on strictly market criteria. Therefore, according to her, Holland was not capitalist. The economism and ahistoricity of such a view is remarkable. As we have seen, Marx singled out the relationship between military spending and the national debt, which he considered important to understanding the way that capitalist primitive accumulation worked in Holland and elsewhere. Like Arrighi, furthermore, recent Dutch scholarship has linked heavy military spending with state policies of consciously stimulating economic demand.[25]

THE POLITICAL MARXISTS

In the case of Holland, Brenner clearly kept a distance from Wood. Wood, Teschke and Comninel all based their views on Brenner's original conception of the genesis of capitalism. They especially took to heart his view of the distinctiveness of capitalist markets as not merely encouraging, but necessitating increases in labour productivity.[26] Bois described Brenner's view rather dismissively as a type of political Marxism which ignored the material foundation of class capacities. Nonetheless, the scholars who followed in the footsteps of Brenner adopted the designation Political Marxism as a badge of honour. Coming to prominence in the wake of the collapse of Soviet Marxism and the triumph of neoliberalism, these researchers made it a point to question commonly accepted orthodoxies on the left, including the notion of bourgeois revolution.[27]

Despite breaking with the consensus of Political Marxism over the question of capitalism in Holland, Brenner's perfunctory treatment of the political and social dimension of the Dutch Revolution conformed to this group's overall dismissal of the importance of the notion of bourgeois revolution. According to Marx and Engels, early capitalist development in England and France climaxed in bourgeois revolution. In Teschke's view this conception assumed a self-conscious and united class, the bourgeoisie, as the main agent of the revolution. Teschke's conception that Marx thought of the bourgeoisie as self-aware and unified at the moment of revolution requires immediate correction. As Marx described the revolutionaries of seventeenth-century England and eighteenth-century France in *The Eighteenth Brumaire of Louis Napoleon*, they did not understand their projects explicitly in class terms, but rather in terms of the Bible or the Roman Republic.[28] That the ideology of these revolutionaries was to be found in the political ambiguities of evangelical Protestantism or Roman republicanism suggests not full class consciousness but a consciousness which reflects a class in the making, or one seeking to bridge differences between classes, or perhaps both. That Marx pointed this out reflects a more sophisticated understanding of class and its relation to concrete history than Teschke supposes.

Teschke noted that, as a result of what he termed the revisionist attack on the idea of bourgeois revolution, the Political Marxists, in contrast to other Marxist currents, had jettisoned the concept of bourgeois revolution.[29] The nexus between capitalism and the bourgeoisie in the case of the English and French revolutions or other bourgeois revolutions had to be severed.[30] In other words, the tide of scholarship which put into question the reality of a so-called bourgeoisie and of a bourgeois revolution was such that Marxists had no real choice but to abandon the idea of a bourgeois revolution. The fact that much of this revisionist scholarship in both English-speaking and French academia emanated from liberal or conservative sources that might have reasons other than academic for arguing against the concept of bourgeois revolution did not trouble Teschke.

Teschke was not bothered either that the notion of jettisoning the idea of bourgeois revolution meant throwing out the most revolutionary component of the Marxist theory of history, or the element most intimately linked with the expectation of future proletarian revolution. The conception of bourgeois as well as proletarian revolution assumes that underclasses can acquire sufficient economic and political power to overthrow the ruling class. Political Marxism suggests that the economic and political initiative in the advance of history always remains with the ruling class. Indeed, in the eyes of

Political Marxists, in the case of late medieval France, the one case in which the lower class was most successful in class war, success in holding onto the land condemned it to an interminable economic stagnation and tyranny under the *Ancien Régime*. Nonetheless, Teschke is certain that the weight of historical evidence and the theoretical arguments of the Political Marxists have shown that 'while the English revolution was not bourgeois, it was capitalist; and while the French Revolution was bourgeois, it was not capitalist. This re-interpretation presents a fundamental breakthrough for Marxism.'[31]

It might be a breakthrough for academic Marxism, and if it were historically correct we would be obliged to respect it. But it can hardly be counted a triumph for revolutionary Marxism, or for what Dobb referred to as the revolutionary view of world history. Rather the position of the Political Marxists on revolution appears to be what the French refer to as a *fuite en avant*, or headlong retreat in the face not of historical facts but of neoliberalism. What is the link between neoliberalism and Political Marxism? There undoubtedly is one, although it is indirect. I would argue that neoliberalism shaped the overall intellectual *zeitgeist* of the last decades. Neoliberalism itself is profoundly antihistorical, being a set of policies that seek to deny the profoundly unstable economic history of capitalism and especially unfettered capitalism. Postmodernism proved a major collaborator, and it too was deeply antihistorical, as Ellen Wood helped to show.[32] It was in this atmosphere that not coincidentally historical revisionism came to the fore in both England and France. In the milieu of professional historians there could be no thought of repudiating history itself. But what postmodernism was to the literary disciplines, revisionism was to academic history. Occupying strategic places in academic and cultural life, historical revisionists gained enormous influence by exploiting certain lacunae in the Marxist accounts of the English and French revolutions. Indeed we must admit that this way of looking at things produced a significant body of real scholarship on the English and French Revolutions through the creation of a veritable school of history on both sides of the Atlantic. A Marxist view of the English and French Revolutions became a laughing stock in such quarters. Given the power of such an institutionalized academic viewpoint, it is not surprising that some who abided by Marxism capitulated to revisionism. Yet at its core revisionism, including Political Marxism, is a rejection of the significance of revolution. Above all it is a repudiation of the revolutionary aspirations of the 1960s, the more so as a Marxist view of the bourgeois revolutions is still vibrant, as we shall see.

ENGLAND

Teschke's notion of the English Revolution is based on Brenner's account. The latter begins by delineating in much greater detail than Teschke the development of Marx's theory of bourgeois revolution. After describing its early permutations, Brenner claims that in *The Communist Manifesto* – following the liberal French historians of the nineteenth century, François Mignet, Augustin Thierry and François Guizot – Marx reached his mature conception of the bourgeois revolution. It was based on the development of the forces of production under the command of an emergent bourgeoisie. At first allying with the monarchy to curb the feudal nobility, the maturing bourgeoisie ultimately entered into opposition to the monarchy – the latter counterposing itself to their increasing economic and social demands, and falling back on the support of the nobles: 'Marx has the bourgeoisie and absolute monarchy entering into alliance in the early modern period in order to destroy their common enemy, the parasitic feudal nobility. Then, as the bourgeoisie grew in strength the absolute monarchy gravitated back toward the old nobility.'[33] By overthrowing both monarchy and nobility, the bourgeois revolution cleared away the remaining obstacles to its progress, as well as that of the capitalist economy.

Brenner takes an entirely different tack, based on a class determinism which stresses the initiative of the landlords. Basing himself on a reading of the *Grundrisse* and *Capital*, he claims that that far from production governing property or class relations, the character of production was itself conditioned by the established structure of property relations.[34] In accord with his theory of the predominant role of landlords dating from the outcome of the class struggles of the late Middle Ages, Brenner insists that they took the lead in the process by which peasant producers were reduced to market dependence in the sixteenth century. The landlords assumed the initiative in instituting primitive accumulation and creating a class of capitalist tenant farmers who took up competitive leases, while most subsistence peasants were driven off the land and were forced into selling their labour for wages. In the process the conditions were created for further capitalist accumulation.[35]

Brenner then concludes that Marx's account of landlord-inspired primitive accumulation undermines the foundations of his theory of bourgeois revolution, as the landlords themselves removed the remaining fetters on capitalist development. The logic of his account of Marx's conception of primitive accumulation was to render bourgeois revolution superfluous: 'Marx's idea of the so-called primitive accumulation ... appeared to undermine the historical and theoretical foundations of the theory of bourgeois revolution.'[36]

It is against this background that Brenner undertook a review of the historiography of the English Revolution. As he explains, the traditional social interpretation of the revolution was developed by R. H. Tawney, Christopher Hill and Lawrence Stone in the 1940s and 1950s.[37] It roughly follows Marx's forces of production approach, with the addition of Tawney's notion of the rise of the gentry, or emergence of an agrarian capitalist class headed by the lesser nobility or gentry. This social interpretation collapsed because its supporters could not prove that in the seventeenth century the landed class divided between capitalist and feudal landlords, or that these two groups split along political lines during the crisis of the English Revolution.

According to Brenner, Stone's *Crisis of the Aristocracy* played a key role in discrediting the social interpretation.[38] In particular Stone took issue with Tawney's rise of the gentry thesis, arguing that the rise of the lesser nobles and eclipse of the aristocracy was only a transitory phenomenon. He argued that it was not a question of the aristocracy in crisis, but of the aristocracy in the process of successful political and economic transformation. By the beginning of the seventeenth century almost all of the greater nobles had abandoned the lordly or feudal mode of reproduction, and in consequence were improving their economic prospects. Unable to collect rent any longer by means of extra-economic coercion, as under feudalism, the aristocracy took the lead in the process of primitive accumulation and the imposition of economic rents on their land.[39] In describing this process of aristocratic renewal, Stone helped to undermine the traditional social interpretation of the English Civil War as a revolt by a new bourgeoisie which had arisen in the interstices of the feudal order against a still largely feudal ruling aristocracy.[40]

Based on Stone, Brenner rejects the traditional social interpretation of the English Revolution. On the other hand, in his justly acclaimed *Merchants and Revolution* Brenner also refuses to accept the conclusion that the revolution had no social and economic basis, as claimed by the revisionists.[41] Rather he sees the conflict as having been between what he calls the patrimonial monarchy and its diverse group of supporters, including merchants and nobles, and an opposition which also included merchants and nobles. Like its counterpart in France, the patrimonial English monarchy sought to establish control over the country by, among other measures, being able to directly extract surplus from the rural population. An alliance of capitalist landlords, merchants and others ranged them-selves in opposition to this project. It was this group rather than a class that triumphed through the revolution.[42]

In speaking about the monarchy, Brenner uses the term 'patri-monial'. This usage, stemming from Max Weber, allows him to distance himself from Dobb's and Anderson's view that the early modern monarchy in England was still feudal, or if you like the last rampart of feudalism. To admit this would be to undercut his view that England was already a capitalist country in the sixteenth century. The term patrimonial is meant to suggest the gap between the monarchy and the landlords, who in Brenner's view are capital-ists.[43] Yet, in seeming contradiction, he is also forced to admit that like the French monarchy, his so-called English patrimonial state was the negation of capitalism – its project constituting a funda-mental barrier to the further development of capitalism. Hence the issue in the English Revolution was removing the remaining barriers to the future of capitalism. In other words, we can say that, far from the English Revolution being, at best, icing on the capitalist cake, its outcome was critical to its future development. Brenner's view seems quite contradictory. But overall it puts him in the camp of revisionism, rejecting the idea that the English Revolution was a bourgeois revolution as understood by Marx.

As one would expect, Wood follows Brenner closely. Calling the English Revolution 'bourgeois', she claims, requires a definition so vague and general as to empty it of meaning. In passing we might note that 'noble' is likewise a rather vague, broad and historically disputed term, which nonetheless, like the term 'bourgeoisie', refers to the fundamental Marxist notion of class. According to Wood, if the revolution advanced the development of capitalism it was by consolidating the position of the already capitalist landlords, who in any case were already dominant in society and the state. It was a case of pushing on an open door. The revolution was not a class struggle that gave victory to a capitalist bourgeoisie against a ruling class that was thwarting its progress. The class struggle that did occur in the revolution was between the ruling class and subordinate popular forces. The latter's class interest had as much to do with opposing as promoting the progress of those capitalist landlords or their bourgeois allies. Yet Wood notes that this view does not deny the role of capitalist tenant farmers in the development of capitalism. What it does deny is the connection between this reality and the revolution.[44] Whatever Wood may say on this latter point, the fact is that in Brenner's version of the development of agrarian capitalism, stress is overwhelmingly laid on the role of the landlords as increasingly the recipients of capitalist rents, rather than on the economic initiative of capitalist farmers.

As to the role of the landlords during the revolution, Stone had claimed that no correlation has emerged between noble political alignments during the revolution and their degree of economic enterprise.[45] Yet Norah Carlin considers the actual statistical evidence offered by Stone in support of this sweeping claim – so important to Brenner – to be surprisingly unimpressive.[46] Moreover, if we focus on the nobility of the northwest of England, the most substantial base of royalist support during the Civil War, they turn out to be less enterprising, less wealthy and less well educated than their brethren in the south.[47] Indeed, Andrew Bell Appleby has shown that whereas in the south landlords were encouraging the development of agricultural capitalism, those in the royalist heartland of the northwest took the lead in a seigneurial reaction against the peasantry.[48] Roger Manning does not deny that many landlords across England encouraged their tenants to make improvements in order to meet their so-called economic rents. On the other hand, as part of the same process many others practised what he describes as a fiscal seigneurialism which had nothing to do with positive economic initiatives. As such they inspired ongoing popular protest.[49] But the important point surely is that, contrary to Brenner's and Stone's view, not all landlords in England, and especially not in the royalist bastion of the northwest, can be considered capitalist landlords. As such this region must be seen as constituting a crucial economic and social base of royalist political support.

THE CAPITALIST FARMERS IN MARX

As we have noted, in Brenner's version of the development of agrarian capitalism it is the passive role he assigns to capitalist farmers, in contrast to the aristocratic class, that is notable. On the contrary, in chapter 29 of Volume One of *Capital*, entitled 'Genesis of the capitalist farmer', Marx places most of the emphasis on the appearance of rural capitalists as the principal agents of emerging capitalism, with the landlords playing a secondary role.[50] Prior to the sixteenth century the circumstances and size of their farms were still limited. Both farmers and wage labourers who still maintained little plots improved themselves by their own labour. In other words, the economic circumstances and the scale of the farms of these petty producers were still limited. It was the agricultural take-off which began in the last third of the fifteenth and continued almost until the end of the sixteenth century that enriched these emerging agrarian entrepreneurs, while impoverishing most of the rest of the rural population. In a historically evocative image Marx notes that the striking thing about these farmers was that they made their capital breed by employing wage labour, while paying part of the surplus value to the landlords as rent. Enclosure of the commons permitted them to expand their holdings of livestock, while increasing the manuring of their expanding leaseholds. Meanwhile, inflation allowed them to lower real wages and increase prices, reaping rich profits as a result. Marx's view, which is scarcely disputable, is that a class of increasingly powerful and ambitious capitalist farmers arose in the sixteenth century and seized the economic initiative.

For Marx it is the capitalist farmers who become the decisive figure because from now on they exploit and control the labour of the wage-earning producers:

> When the capitalist tenant farmer steps in between landlord and actual tiller of the soil, all relations which arose out of the old rural mode of production are torn asunder. The farmer becomes the actual commander of these agricultural labourers and the actual exploiter of their surplus labour, whereas the landlord maintains a direct relationship, and indeed simply a money and contractual relationship, solely with this capitalist tenant.[51]

It is the command of wage labour that makes the capitalist farmer pivotal to the new mode of production. The landlord recedes into the background.

As we saw in Chapter 3, Dobb built on Marx's insight, underlining the key role of small producers as the decisive agents in the development of not only capitalist agriculture, but also manufacture. In the case of agriculture, substantial peasants rented land, relying on wage labour that became available in increasing quantities as a result of the process of enclosure. It was from this rising element of farmers that most of the innovations in agricultural technique emanated.[52] As we have seen in the previous chapters, Overton and Byres argue that tenant farmers and other rural capitalists were the dynamic element in the capitalist transformation of the English countryside. They often successfully resisted the economic demands of landlords. In fact, agricultural capitalism developed in areas where lordship was weak and peasant property rights were strong. The most striking advances in output and land productivity occurred in areas where lordship was relatively weak. It was rural capitalists rather than landlords who took the initiative in agricultural innovation.

THE MIDDLE SORT

In this generation it is Brian Manning who has built his interpretation of the English Revolution on Marx's and Dobb's view of capitalist development.[53] A student of Christopher Hill, Manning's reputation was overshadowed, as was Hill's, by the tide of revisionist history from the 1970s. Such revisionism includes the Political Marxism of Brenner and Wood. Nonetheless, in a series of works Manning sketched a view of the English Revolution based on the rise of an emergent middle class, or of the so-called 'middle sort of people', which has gained increasing if grudging scholarly acceptance. While in agreement with Brenner and Wood that capitalism implanted itself in England in the sixteenth century, Manning argues that the monarchy, and the ruling class of aristocrats and greater gentry who supported the monarchy, constituted a continuing barrier to further capitalist progress. On the contrary, Brenner denies that elements of the aristocracy and greater gentry constituted such a barrier. Rather, they led the way toward capitalism. Furthermore, Manning argues that it was the mobilization of the middle sort, or rather of a revolutionary element from within this middle sort, that provided the social base of the parliamentary cause and enabled it to triumph. The monarchy and aristocracy were eventually restored, but not before the monarchy was transformed into a constitutional regime and feudal tenure became private property.[54]

Manning identified the largest landowners, made up of the aristocracy and greater gentry, as the ruling class. They wielded political power at the local and national level prior to the revolution. The remaining middle and lesser gentry, according to him, were a status group. It was a political and religious split in the ruling class that made the revolution possible. The largest class was the independent small producers, made up of peasants and small craftspeople. In the course of the sixteenth century a growing social differentiation of this group took place. This division tended toward the emergence of capitalist farmers and small manufacturers employing wage labour, on the one hand, and those producers with no or little means of production, selling more and more of their labour in return for wages, on the other. Manning shows how the rising economic power of the former group reflected itself in their greater influence on local religious and social life. In contrast to Brenner's and Wood's over-emphasis on agrarian capitalism, Manning points out the importance of the emergence of industry in both country and town, and the interaction between farming and manufacturing activity in certain regions of the country. In Manning's view the development of capitalism is not merely about agriculture, but about the interpenetration of capitalist industry and agriculture.

By the seventeenth century the term 'middling' or 'middle sort' was used to differentiate the better-off commoners from the gentry and from the wage-dependent poor. In the 1630s these middle sort – not a class but a class in the making – became more and more alienated from the monarchy as a result of the imposition of non-parliamentary taxation and what were regarded as Popish religious policies. Deeply imbued with Protestantism, which was existentially understood as the national religion, this middle group was deeply offended by royalist religious policies, which included the restoration of railed-off altars and the wearing of surplices by the clergy – practices with deeply conservative social meaning. In Manning's account, it is this proto-capitalist element emerging from below and in command of labour power, and not the capitalist landlords, that was the dynamic political and social component in English society, and which seized the initiative in the revolution.

Both contemporary accounts and modern historical scholarship confirm that the bulk of support for the parliamentary side in the Civil War came from the middle sort, both in town and country: lesser gentry, independent freeholders, enterprising small landholders and industrial craftspeople. It is notable that landlords were unable to control the political allegiance of these elements, including their own tenants. Remarkable was the mobilization for Parliament from industrial regions and towns, especially where Puritanism and hostility to government economic regulations were strong.[55] The bulk of the aristocracy and gentry – capitalist landlords or not – were frightened by popular disorders at the beginning of the revolution and the political mobilization of the middle and lesser sort, and consequently supported the monarchy. Some workers and less-well-off peasants sided with the king. As Dobb had argued, the majority of big merchants who were tied to the monarchy and aristocracy were royalist when forced to choose sides.

Manning underlines the importance of Brenner's *Merchants and Revolution* in illuminating the difference between the established merchants who supported the monarchy, as against the new merchants connected to colonial endeavours and linked to the parliamentary cause. While old merchants tended to limit their activities to trade, the newer element involved themselves in the processing of colonial products like sugar and tobacco. Overwhelmingly favourable to Parliament, they supported and profited from the Cromwellian conquest of Ireland. Many of these merchants were younger sons of minor gentry, provincial merchants or prosperous farmers. They backed a more democratic London government and the abolition of episcopacy in favour of Presbyterianism or Congregationalism. Brenner's colonial merchants were clearly in the forefront of an emergent revolutionary bourgeoisie according to Manning. Brenner is silent about the revolutionary political role of this merchant vanguard, despite the fact that his research revealed their critical function. The reason, of course, is his rejection of the idea of bourgeois revolution.

Manning demonstrates that the mobilization of the middle sort of people played a critical role in the triumph of the parliamentary side. On the basis of their support, the ruling class of magnates and upper gentry were politically marginalized, and power at the local level devolved on those who held lesser gentry status or even on those from the middling group. At the national level the republican regimes of the 1650s went a considerable distance in constituting a strong centralized state organized to enhance English commercial, naval and colonial power, to the satisfaction of leading elements among the middling sort.

Indeed, Brenner's failure to take seriously the importance of control of the state to the development of capitalism seriously vitiates his theory of capitalist origins. The state provides the public space within which the reproduction of capitalist relations of production is possible. In effect such a state develops policies which totalize such a space in favour of capitalism. As such, a state that favours rather than obstructs the development of capitalism is indispensable, and cannot be thought of as external to its development. Tony Smith considers it crucial, insisting that the state is 'no mere epiphenomenon of capital'.[56] Reconciling opposed class interests and inter-class rivalries, the state provides the public context necessary for continuing capital accumulation. As such the state cannot be thought of as apart from the social relations of capital. Rather it is an intrinsic part of such relations. Smith writes about the contemporary state, but his observations apply even more forcefully to the early modern state. In that connection, it is noteworthy that the revolution did away with the Star Chamber, High

Commission, Court of Wards and feudal tenure – those institutions
and legal arrangements that most impeded capitalist development.
The monarchy was brought under the control of the men of property
in the Parliament, while it lost its control of the judiciary as well.[57]
The subsequent creation by the state of the Bank of England and
stock exchange established a nation-wide system of money and
credit.

The aristocracy was eventually restored to power because the
widespread popular unrest during the revolution did not lead to the
dispossession of the aristocracy as a whole or as a class. Meanwhile,
the unrest and political and religious radicalism unleashed by the
revolution frightened many among the better-off middle sort. But the
old ruling class returned on the basis of closer collaboration with the
middle sort, and with most of the remaining obstacles to capitalism
removed. Manning notes that:

> the fundamental fact is that the aristocracy was not expropri-
> ated by the revolution: it retained its estates and its status,
> though deprived temporarily of its political power. In essence
> the Restoration was the re-establishment of the aristocracy in
> political power, but under new terms of relationship to a state
> evolving into a great naval, commercial, colonial and industrial
> power, and to increasing interdependence with the 'middle sort
> of people'.[58]

Manning carefully and cautiously concludes that the English
Revolution was a class struggle. According to him, whether or not
a struggle was a class conflict depends on the degree to which issues
of class were involved. Despite the social diversity on both sides,
it is none the less the case that an aristocratic ethos dominated the
royalist cause, however many plebeians fought for it. An egalitarian
ethos emanating from the middle sort helped to mobilize the parliamentary party, even though it contained some aristocrats and some
of the latter even led it nationally. Indeed, the parliamentary party
was suffused with anti-aristocratic sentiments. Such antagonistic
feelings toward the aristocracy marked off those of the middle sort
who followed the parliamentary party as opposed to those who
remained neutral or who supported the royal side. Moreover, the
committed supporters of Parliament among the middle sort had
greater influence over events.

The middle sort of people was based in the class of independent
small producers. Some of these were rising to become capitalist

employers, and others were declining into wage-earning employees. Classes are constantly being shaped and reshaped, a process out of which history is made. A whole class does not become radicalized or class conscious at once, and the middle sort lacked the coherence to assume a common class position. Groups become conscious of themselves as classes in opposition to other classes. As a result of such collision, elements of the middle sort became aware of the conflict between their economic and social interests and those of the party of the aristocracy.

As we have seen, in the name of Political Marxism Teschke asserted that the English Revolution was not bourgeois, but was capitalist. I beg to differ. In accord with Manning, I accept the view that the revolution was made by a bourgeoisie in formation rather than a fully fledged bourgeoisie in the style of the Victorian age. Indeed, I accept the view that a bourgeois revolution does not require the bourgeoisie as a necessary agent, provided that it clears the way for the further advance of capitalism.[59] On the other hand, the role of new merchants of London in making the revolution, the social make-up of the republican governments and the outcome of the revolution justify us in continuing to refer to the English Revolution, like the Dutch Revolution, as a bourgeois revolution. Moreover, such a revolution did not entail the complete destruction of the aristocracy. That did not happen even in the French Revolution. What was required was that it cease interfering in the further development of capitalism.

FRANCE

Teschke speaks of the French Revolution as a bourgeois revolution, but not a capitalist one. This follows from Brenner's notion that in contrast to England, capitalism failed to develop in France at the end of the Middle Ages owing to its different property relations.[60] It is George Comninel who developed this notion into a revisionist view of the French Revolution. Comninel, like Brenner, believes that Marx mistakenly accepted the categories of liberal nineteenth-century French historiography which supposed a basic conflict between the nobility and the bourgeoisie. In consequence, he misconstrued the nature of the revolution of 1789 as a bourgeois and capitalist revolution. The following discussion is designed to confute this Political Marxist view of the French Revolution. Its purpose is to show that both capitalism and a capitalist bourgeoisie were intrinsic to the revolution.

According to Comninel, a class that based itself on profit did not exist in France prior to 1789. Appropriation of surplus value by a bourgeoisie did not occur. Both the nobility and the bourgeoisie based themselves on rent and income from state offices. As a result, Comninel believes that the two groups must be regarded as members of a single class. Hence, the conflict that did break out between the bourgeoisie and the nobility in 1789 was essentially an inter-elite struggle rather than a class conflict.[61] On this point Comninel is in complete accord with leading conservative revisionists of the French Revolution. Comninel rejects the idea that capitalist farming existed on the large tenant farms of northern France that operated on the basis of wage labour and profit. He disallows the idea that such operations were capitalist because the labour force was kept dependent on its own subsistence production rather than being fully proletarianized. Furthermore, the process of production was blocked from expansion and improvement of the means of production by a whole body of traditional practices, rights and obligations.[62] Wood, Comninel's thesis supervisor, found these arguments persuasive. The French Revolution may have been bourgeois but it was not capitalist. Prior to the French Revolution capitalist conditions did not exist.[63]

RURAL CAPITALISM

Like Brenner, Comninel and Wood rightly emphasize the existence of an agrarian capitalism and a rural bourgeoisie as a *sine qua non* for the existence of capitalism. But in Chapter 2 we saw that such a capitalism did consolidate itself in France at the end of the sixteenth century. Moreover, despite the triumph of the absolute state and a heavy burden of rent and taxes, this bourgeoisie persisted in the seventeenth century alongside a commercial and even manufacturing bourgeoisie. It re-emerged with new vigour in the eighteenth century.[64]

We have seen that Comninel denied that the tenant farmers of the rich grain lands of northern France were capitalists. Yet in the eighteenth century the Physiocrat Anne-Robert-Jacques Turgot described them as 'agricultural capitalist entrepreneurs'. These rich peasants who rented large farms favoured a free market in grain, as espoused by Turgot. They organized production using their own tools and equipment. At the same time, they employed a workforce paid in wages. Based on their operations, they derived a profit and as a result paid the landlords what amounted to a capitalist rent.[65] Indeed, the farmers of such enterprises had to pay not only these rents, but usually also seigneurial dues, taxes and tithes. But since their farms were on fertile lands that were close to good roads and towns, they were able to take advantage of high prices and to enjoy profitable returns. Yet they often enhanced their revenues by farming ecclesiastical tithes and seigneurial obligations. As such, the incomes of such farmers were made up of both capitalist profits and feudal rents. They also earned money from taking interest on loans to poorer peasants. Through their business and social connections and their lifestyle, these farmers constituted part of the bourgeoisie alongside those of the middle class who lived in the surrounding bourgs and towns. Jean-Marc Moriceau describes these wealthy farmers in the Ile de France as attaining the level of a kind of gentry in the eighteenth century.[66]

In northern France this elite of wealthy farmers constituted a minority among the more numerous and broader group of prosperous peasant ploughmen or *labourers*. On a lesser scale than the wealthy farmers, they too hired wage labour and loaned grain, ploughs, wagons and money to their less well-off neighbours. As such, they too were part of an emergent class of rural capitalists. More generally, we can say that the French countryside even in the south and west saw a halting and tentative progress toward capitalist relations in agriculture and the development of an agrarian bourgeoisie.[67]

Moriceau notes that in the Ile de France and over much of the rest of the north of France, genuine agricultural improvement took place. Especially in regions close to cities that were affected by new agronomic ideas and by the growing availability of manure, productivity significantly increased in the second half of the eighteenth century.[68] The idea of introducing agronomic improvements spread to the better-off peasants through the increasing influence of country postmasters, who often were themselves successful farmers. The intrusion of capitalism played an important role in destabilizing the countryside and mobilizing the rural population on the eve of the revolution. Capitalist farmers emerged as the leaders of the rural revolution.

THE RISE OF POLITICAL ECONOMY

In the years leading up to the revolution, capitalism emerged rapidly not only in agriculture, but also in industry, as we shall see.[69] These dramatic economic changes and the incipient financial and economic crisis of this period produced a remarkable outpouring of economic literature. Between 1750 and 1789 some 2,200 books on political economy were published in France, with 804 appearing in 1789 alone.[70] These numbers testify to the reality of profound economic change. Led by François Quesnay and Turgot, the leading economists of the time organized themselves into the so-called Physiocratic School. The Physiocrats based themselves on the theory that value, or as they put it net product, derived from the land. At the same time they were fervently committed to laissez-faire within the framework of a so-called legal despotism – an idealized version of the *Ancien Régime.*

Marx had high praise for the Physiocratic School, seeing them as the first economists to sketch a theory of surplus value.[71] According to a recent study of the school by Gianni Vaggi, profit was a systematic feature of the Physiocratic understanding of the so-called net product or surplus.[72] Indeed, the decades leading up to the revolution saw the evolution of Physiocratic teaching in the direction of explicitly capitalist conceptions. Following Quesnay, Nicole Baudeau, a popularizer of Physiocratic doctrine, demonstrated the productive potential of free or wage labour and of the capitalist entrepreneur in both farming and manufacture.[73] As is well known, another Quesnay disciple, Turgot, actually attempted to introduce a free market in grain and labour during his tenure as controller-general and minister of finance. Indeed, it is in Turgot's writings that we witness the transformation of Physiocratic teaching from an economic theory based on agriculture into a theory of capitalism proper. This was simply a reaction on the part of a sophisticated economic thinker, on the one hand, to the increasing pervasiveness of capitalist farming based on wage labour, and on the other hand, to the growth of manufacturing.[74]

In his principal work, *Réflexions sur la formation et la distribution des richesses* (1766), Turgot repeatedly underlines his fealty to the basic principles of Physiocratic theory. Nonetheless, in a backwards and forwards manner, Turgot moves toward a recognition of the value-creating potential of both industry and agriculture, of the essential role of capital to the activity of farmers and manufacturers, and to the common condition of agricultural and farm workers, both of whom were competing to sell their labour to employers in return for a wage.[75] In Turgot's work the primary focus becomes not land as a material entity that produces wealth, but capital as a value which attempts to expand and realize itself whether in farming or manufacture.[76] At the same time, Turgot explicitly acknowledges the more productive and advanced form of capitalist agriculture based on capitalism, prevalent throughout the north of France where competitive leases were the rule.[77] While Turgot harked back to the notion of the net product at various points in the *Réflections*, he increasingly acknowledged the role of profit in capitalist activity.[78] Turgot's economic principles, like those of other French theorists of the time, were a reflection and theorization of what had already emerged in French society, and which he hoped would develop further.

The Physiocrats were not without their critics. Jean-Joseph-Louis Graslin and Emmanuel-Joseph Sieyès rejected altogether the idea that land was the source of wealth. On the contrary, they asserted that it was labour which was the true source of wealth. Labour in both agriculture and industry produced value.[79] The position of Sieyès in this respect had important political implications. In the Physiocratic scheme elaborated under the *Ancien Régime* the landed proprietors enjoyed a special place as receivers of the net product. But in the social order described in Sieyès's justly famous revolutionary pamphle*t Qu'est-ce que le tiers etat?* this group simply vanishes.

WAGE LABOUR IN FRANCE

The growing prominence of a labour theory of value was directly tied to the increasing dependence of most of the population on wages. But, according to Comninel, no true proletariat existed because the wage-earning class, which Comninel acknowledges existed, was required to live off its own subsistence. An authentic proletariat must be dependent on the market for its means of subsistence as well as be wage-based. As a matter of fact, Comninel's concept of a wage-earning class living off its own subsistence appears to be a bit of a contradiction in terms. If wage workers in eighteenth-century France could sustain themselves through their own subsistence, why did they turn to wage work in increasing numbers? As we have already seen, the rural wage-earning class in eighteenth-century France in fact did not, and could not, live off its own subsistence. That is why it turned more and more to wage work.

It is true that many rural workers had gardens and were able to glean and forage for a certain portion of their subsistence. It is this possibility that Comninel points out. Nonetheless, a substantial part of the food, and eventually even the clothing and household articles of rural workers, had to be obtained by spending money in the market. Money – indispensable to subsistence – was only available to the labouring classes through the sale of their labour power in the market in return for wages. Consequently, the sale of labour in return for wages was an intrinsic feature of the eighteenth-century economy. Moreover, dependence on wages seems to have increased among the rural population throughout the century. Following from this growing importance of wage labour, the role of surplus value or capitalist profit produced by wage workers composed an expanding element in the eighteenth-century French economy.

Comninel's view is perhaps based on the purist idea that a true proletarian is one who not only must sell all their labour power in the market, but also one who must buy all their means of subsistence in the market as well. Comninel apparently would have us believe that the rural labouring population prior to the revolution was not proletarianized because it did not obtain all means of subsistence from the market.

While the degree of wage dependency varies depending on time and place, it is also true historically that growing dependency on wages entails a progressive loss of control over the means of production on the part of producers as capitalism develops. From Comninel's quite unhistorical and mechanistic perspective, proletarians, and hence capitalism, either do or do not exist. From this standpoint it is impossible to distinguish, over time, degrees of wage dependence as the capitalist economy evolves. In Comninel's view the working class comes into being fully developed *ex nihilo* or it does not exist at all. There is no making of the working class through the vicissitudes and contradictions of concrete history. Indeed, Comninel contrasts eighteenth-century French peasant producers with what he represents as a truly proletarianized English rural workforce who are consequently utterly dependent on the market. Eighteenth-century England is pictured, in contrast to France, as a place where a fully rational agrarian capitalism existed.[80] That this was far from having been the case has recently been shown, for example, by J. M. Nesson. Not only did commons rights largely survive in England into the nineteenth century, even a peasantry continued to exist, according to Nesson.[81]

In the decade prior to the outbreak of the revolution, the influence of the Physiocrats waned. Turgot continued to be read, but now alongside the work of Adam Smith, whose reputation grew larger and larger on the eve of the revolution.[82] Successive editions of his work appeared, and his ideas became an important part of the ideological context in which the National Legislative Assembly swept away feudalism and imposed a legal framework of liberal capitalism based on the principles of constitutional government.[83] The growing popularity of Smith in France was not simply a reflection of the popularity of British liberal ideas. It was a response to the fact that in the four decades prior to the revolution, capitalism, which had been weak and underground, suddenly surged powerfully to the surface. It is precisely the rapidity of such change that engendered revolution.

THE REVOLUTIONARY CRISIS

There can be no question about the existence of agrarian capitalism on the eve of the revolution of 1789. On this basis there occurred a tremendous expansion of commerce, especially foreign and overseas commerce. Manufacture also grew spectacularly. The investment of capital and the reorganization of manufacture in the direction of concentration and centralization of production were especially notable in mining and cotton and chemical manufacturing. As a consequence in the last decades prior to the revolution there took place an enormous growth of the role of profit in the economy, and the power and influence of the economic bourgeoisie.[84] In the actual revolution the regime of aristocratic privilege and feudalism was swept away, and the legal and political superstructure of society was reorganized in order to facilitate capital accumulation. The continued entrenchment of feudalism under the absolute monarchy and the overwhelming popular revolution against it made the revolution an event of epochal scale.[85] On the basis of this tremendous upheaval the bourgeoisie assumed power. Moreover, there was a clear consciousness that the bourgeoisie had taken power. Ongoing industrialization and the experience of the Revolution helped to create the beginnings of working-class consciousness as well.[86]

CONCLUSION

In summary I have reasserted the classic Marxist view of the Dutch, English and French revolutions as capitalist and bourgeois revolutions. The emergence of the territorial state after 1500 in France and England was critical to the initial development of capitalism in these two places. In Holland such a state was produced by its prolonged revolutionary struggle. Few would deny the growing strength of capitalism in England. We have likewise established its growing presence in Holland and France prior to their revolutions. Sixteenth-century monarchies had based themselves on the support of landlord nobles in the first instance, but also drew support from merchants and an emerging layer of manufacturers and rural capitalists. But at a certain point the growing power of these embryonic capitalists came into conflict with the increasingly absolutist rule of the Hapsburg, Stuart and Bourbon monarchies. The latter hemmed in the further development of capitalism and the social and political aspirations of a still young and emergent bourgeoisie. Increasingly these monarchies fell back on the landlords and more conservative elements of the merchant class for support. In the revolutionary crises, in each instance the lead was taken not by the established merchants, who tended to support the existing regime or sit on the fence, but by lesser merchants and better-off petty producers, urban but also rural. As a result of revolution, the state was restructured in each case to enhance the further accumulation of capital at home and abroad, and to advance the social and political ambitions of the bourgeoisie. By transforming the state from a feudal to a capitalist institution, the revolutions in Holland, England and France helped to consolidate capitalism as a system. In taking this view we have challenged the view of Brenner and the Political Marxists, who would deny the significance and even the existence of these bourgeois and capitalist revolutions.

These early modern revolutions exemplify the formation of a capitalism from below, which was likewise seen in the United States following its revolution. These were classic bourgeois and capitalist revolutions, which we would argue were indispensable to the full flowering of capitalism. But even in the case of Holland, England and France capitalism was facilitated by state support in the form of mercantilism, colonialism and colonial slavery. Indeed, their revolutions intensified such state support. Beyond this are cases like Scotland and Prussia in the eighteenth century, where another possible passage to capitalism occurred, based on a type of revolution from above instituted by the state and the landlord class. It is to a consideration of the role of the state in supporting or instituting capitalism that we turn in the next chapter.

5

POLITICAL CAPITALISM

The Dutch, English and French Revolutions were both popular and bourgeois-capitalist revolutions. The petty producers, especially the emergent or proto-capitalist element, were paramount in these capitalist revolutions from below. In this chapter we take up Lenin's contrast between such 'capitalisms from below' and 'capitalisms from above'. The outlines of these contrasting historical paths derive from Lenin's conceptual elaboration of Marx's contrast between the revolutionary petty-producer-led transition and the non-revolutionary merchant-led transition to capitalism. In fact Lenin's stress on the rural petty producers as key to the emergence of capitalism from below echoes across the previously discussed original transition debate, influencing the views of Dobb and Hilton on the transition in England.

England has been my prime example of the installation of capitalism largely from below. While gentry, landlords and merchants had their part, I have insisted that the main dynamic of the transition came from the grassroots. But it will be one of this chapter's main purposes to break from an Anglocentric view of capitalist origins and to extend our understanding of such beginnings by introducing a comparative perspective. I have already shown that the revolutionary path of capitalism from below applies to Holland and France as well as England. Following Lenin, I shall show how the phenomenon of capitalism from below extended across the Atlantic to nineteenth-century America in the wake of its revolution. Discussion of the Prussian example as well as the instances of Scotland and Japan allows us to contrast the notion of capitalism from below with that of capitalism from above: that is, capitalism imposed by landlords and the state.

Capitalism from above features landlords in control of a state, or a state acting independently, responding to capitalism's uneven development by consciously producing 'combined development', a form of accelerated, conscious and planned development of capitalism. But even capitalisms developing from below were hardly immune to this logic of state intervention. Early modern Holland, England and France adopted policies like mercantilism and colonialism in the service of capitalist development. Recognizing this is important in opposing Eurocentric and economistic views, which assert that capitalism was an economic system which in its 'classic' forms at least did not require fostering by the state, and in particular that colonialism and slavery had little or nothing to do with its development. I argue, on the contrary, that the state played a key role in the development of capitalism, whether from above or below, and that the overseas initiatives of the state represented a crucial step in strengthening European capitalism and vaulting it from economic marginality to world primacy.

Throughout the chapter Lenin's conception of the origin of capitalism based either on the American path from below or the Prussian path from above serves as a key. Following the history of these paths enables me to show that control over the state by bourgeoisie supported by small producers or by landlords helped to determine the character of the capitalism that developed in each instance. A revolution which creates a state like the United States which rests on small producers opens the way to the free play of the market. Under such conditions capitalist relations and forces of production develop most rapidly. But it will be shown that even so the state intervened heavily to support this process. The Prussian instance demonstrates in turn how the state not only intervened to ensure the survival of its nobility, but aided them in making the transition to capitalism at the expense of the peasant producers. As their historical development has recently been fruitfully explored from the point of view of capitalism from above, the examples of Scotland and Japan are discussed with an eye to developing a comparative understanding of alternative routes to capitalism. The decisive role of the state is illustrated by applying Trotsky's conception of combined and uneven development to the Scottish path to capitalism. It illustrates the speed and contradictory nature of capitalist development in states with archaic social relations.

Mercantilism is commonly thought of as an economic policy and doctrine based on state intervention in the economy which was characteristic of the early modern period. I argue that it is as characteristic of modern capitalism as it was of the early modern form. Moreover it exemplifies one of the ways that the coercive role of the state has been used to accelerate the accumulation of capital. Anderson, Wallerstein and Teschke argue that mercantilism reflected the views of a state directed by the nobility. On the contrary, mercantilism was among other things an expression of the interests of a rising bourgeoisie within the absolutist state. Indeed, its most successful practitioner was capitalist England. Following the seventeenth-century revolution from below, bourgeois economic interests predominated in that state. Colonialism and slavery were two of the most successful features of mercantilism backed and protected by the state. The role of colonialism and slavery in the development of capitalism has been greatly disputed. Discussion of these disputes will open the way for the next chapter, which deals with the Industrial Revolution.

LORDS IN THE MAKING OF THE MODERN WORLD

In my argument so far, I have made clear that the bourgeois and capitalist revolutions in Holland, England and France opposed absolutist regimes based on the landlord class. This was true even of the Spanish monarchy's intervention in the Low Countries in light of the European-wide aristocratic social and political base of the Hapsburgs. The foundation of the royalist cause in England, likewise, was the landed class. While there were capitalist landlords in England, most landlords supported the monarchy, and only a minority supported Parliament. The main social base of the revolutionary party was rural and urban petty producers as well as merchants and manufacturers. Moreover, it was principally from this same social element that agrarian and manufacturing capitalism emerged.

In emphasizing the bourgeois and capitalist character of these early revolutions, I have opposed the arguments of Brenner and his followers that it was landlords who played the main role in ushering in capitalism in England, for Brenner the first and classic path of capitalist development. Now I aim to put the role landlords did play in the development of capitalism in perspective. While it was not central in the English case, it was in other places. And this difference in the social character of the regimes that opened the way for capitalism made a lasting political difference: they contributed to the emergence of modern democratic political orders or to twentieth-century fascisms, or determined that modern class struggle would assume the form of Gramscian wars of position or of movement.

The origins of modern dictatorship or democracy are the central problematic of Barrington Moore's famous *Social Origins of Dictatorship and Democracy: Lord and Peasant in the Making of the Modern World*.[1] Though urban merchant and industrial capitalists were involved, the political destiny of modern states was determined by agrarian social relations, according to Moore. In the early modern revolutions discussed by Moore, including England,

France and the United States, it was an emergent agrarian capitalist class which included capitalist farmers, rather than a dominant landlord class, that played the key role in the transition to capitalism. This was true also in heavily urbanized Holland, as Brenner has shown. Where the early modern transitions to capitalism were based on the grassroots of society as in the above cases they proved critically important to the emergence of a democratic political order. On the other hand, Moore argued that the continued dominance of landlords over peasants in Germany and Japan in the process of capitalist development led to a politically reactionary outcome in the form of modern fascism. It eventually could lead, as in the case of twentieth-century China and Russia, to the elimination of the landlords altogether and the installation of communist regimes.

Successful early modern political revolution made it possible to pursue modern class struggle within the limits of a liberal democratic political order. Contrariwise the failure of such early modern struggles ensured that modern class struggles in Germany, Japan, Russia and China would take the form of violent counter-revolutionary or revolutionary conflict. Moore's formulation has the virtue of linking the development of capitalism to class struggle and the nature of the state. Its indebtedness to Lenin's distinction between capitalism from above and below is patent. But in terms of its modern outcome it is also reminiscent of Antonio Gramsci's distinction between the conditions which allow class wars of position (parties, unions, strikes, legislation) as against those of movement (insurrectionary politics).[2] Moreover, Moore's analysis suggests that revolutionary or non-revolutionary transitions to capitalism mark significant historical differences. It is a world away from the indifference to the question of political revolution in the approach to the transition problem of the school of Political Marxism.

Engels was the first to note that a transition from feudal society to capitalism had arisen on the basis of the institution of capitalism from above, in the form of Prussian landlords taking the lead in using the state to initiate and institute capitalism.[3] Moreover, for him the character of such a transition was no mere academic question. It bore on the political and economic future of capitalism and the prospects for socialism in Germany and elsewhere. In *The Peasant Question in France and Germany* (1894) he tried to deal with the fact that the peasants in these two countries remained an influential political element that had to be dealt with by astute socialist policies. On the other hand, he noted that as a result of the development of landlord capitalism the peasants were no longer a factor in the important German state of Prussia: 'east of the Elbe the same process has been going on for centuries; here too the peasant is being increasingly "put down" or at least economically and politically forced into the background'. They were no longer a significant element. Big landed estates in Prussia present a simple political case: 'we are dealing with undisguised capitalist production'.[4] It was not necessary to temper socialist measures in Prussia, as it was elsewhere in Germany where peasants remained politically influential.

The agrarian question was of urgent concern for the most important successors of Marx and Engels, particularly for Karl Kautsky, the acknowledged leader of German Social Democracy until the First World War, and Vladimir Ilyich Lenin, the leader of Russian Bolshevism. In *The Agrarian Question* (1899) Kautsky sought to deepen Engels's analysis by assembling and examining data from Germany, France, Britain and the United States with an eye on their political implications. He was particularly interested in the different pace and character of capitalist accumulation in industry and agriculture. His study included the extent of rural capitalist development, its emergence in different national contexts and the barriers that impeded its further progress. Kautsky analyzed both the nature of class relations and the forms of the productive forces, including the level of mechanization. The penetration of capitalism in agriculture was more complex than in industry, but was no less inexorable. It would be wrong for Marxists to either retard or accelerate the disappearance of the peasant producer, Kautsky concluded.[5]

But while Lenin fulsomely praised Kautsky's work and its political conclusions, he was above all concerned with the possibility of revolution in Russia. It was in this context that he elaborated Engels's conception of capitalism from above into one of two contrasting paths to capitalism. In the second edition of *The Development of Capitalism in Russia* (1907), Lenin outlined the alternative routes to capitalism:

Either the old landlord economy, bound as it is by thousands of threads to serfdom, is retained and turns slowly into purely capitalist, 'Junker' economy. The basis of the final transition from labour-service to capitalism is the internal metamorphosis of feudalist landlord economy. The entire agrarian system of the state becomes capitalist and for a long time retains feudalist features. Or the old landlord economy is broken up by revolution, which destroys all the relics of serfdom, and large landownership in the first place. The basis of the final transition from labour-service to capitalism is the free development of small peasant farming.[6]

Under the Prussian path the state assumes a capitalist form but retains feudal characteristics. As Lenin puts it in *The Agrarian Programme of Social-Democracy in the First Russian Revolution*, composed the same year, the Prussian route assumes the political form of a 'landlord monarchy'. The American path leads to what he describes as a 'farmers' republic'.[7] In the same work he names the alternative paths as Prussian and American:

> These two paths of objectively possible bourgeois development we would call the Prussian path and the American path, respectively. In the first case feudal landlord economy slowly evolves into bourgeois, Junker landlord economy, which condemns the peasants to decades of most harrowing expropriation and bondage, while at the same time a small minority of *Grossbauern* ('big peasants') arises. In the second case there is no landlord economy, or else it is broken up by revolution. In this case the peasant predominates, becomes the sole agent of agriculture, and evolves into a capitalist farmer.[8]

In this passage Lenin points out the terrible economic consequences of Prussian-style capitalism on the mass of producers. Elsewhere in the same work he contrasts this outcome with what is possible for such producers under the American route:

> A mass of free farmers may serve as a basis for the development of capitalism without any landlord economy whatsoever since, taken as a whole, the latter form of economy is economically reactionary, whereas the elements of free farming have been created among the peasantry by the preceding economic history of the country. Capitalist development along such a path should proceed far more broadly, freely, and swiftly owing to the tremendous growth of the home market, and of the rise in the standard of living, the energy, initiative, and culture of the entire population.[9]

In these few lines Lenin captures not only the economic but also the political difference a capitalism from below made to the political and social evolution of England, France and the United States as suggested by Moore. At the same time we are able to appreciate better why Gramscian class wars of position have characterized these countries, compared with the class wars of socialist revolution and fascist counter-revolution in places like Russia, Germany and Japan where capitalism came to predominate.

At the same time as he outlined these contrasting paths Lenin moved from a Eurocentric to a global understanding of capitalist development. Initially preoccupied with the development of capitalism in Russia in order to contest *narodnik* claims that it was not developing and could not develop there, and to lay down an understanding of how socialism could arrive there that was more sophisticated than their naïve conception of 'skipping' capitalism, he aimed, in *The Development of Capitalism in Russia* (1899), to show that despite economic backwardness, capitalism was emerging in Russia in the late nineteenth century. Indeed, Lenin's text is path-breaking in dealing with the emergence of capitalism in a non-Western country. Later, during the First World War, which he and other Marxists recognized clearly as an imperialist war first and foremost, his attention turned to backward and colonized countries in general in *Imperialism, The Highest Stage of Capitalism* (1916). Together these two works shifted the focus from capitalism in the West to its development on the capitalist periphery. It need hardly be added that, following in the footsteps of Marx's discussion of the prospects of socialism in Russia, this reorientation raised the spectre not simply of further capitalist development, but of the breakthrough of socialism on the periphery.[10] Indeed, it needs to be underlined that Lenin's discussion of both imperialism and the development of capitalism in Russia is preoccupied not with the historic development of capitalism, but with learning from the past in order to make socialist revolution in the future. In Lenin we find a deeply politicized understanding of the transition in which the state plays a fundamental role.

THE AMERICAN AND PRUSSIAN PATHS

Lenin's distinction between the Prussian and American paths formed the starting point for an extended historical and comparative analysis of American and Prussian capitalism by Terence Byres.[11] We encountered Byres earlier in the debate on the decline of feudalism. He criticized Brenner's stress on the importance of social property relations and the initiatives of landlords in the development of capitalism, emphasizing instead the differentiation of the peasantry through market mechanisms.

Lenin's account of the American path toward capitalism highlighted the absence of a strong landlord class as a barrier to the

process of the social differentiation of the rural producers. The basis
of the transition was a process of differentiation within the mass of
peasant-farmers – the market-driven evolution of economically well-
positioned producers into capitalist farmers, and the transformation
of disadvantaged petty producers into wage workers. Lenin initially
hoped for such an evolution in Russia. He regarded the failure of
a landlord class to develop in America as a result of the continuing
availability of 'unoccupied free land'. Byres notes that Lenin's
remark unfortunately leaves out the forcible expropriation of the
aboriginal population of North America. In contrast it should be
recalled that Lenin's mentor Marx did not ignore the dispossession
of the aboriginals. We can recall his passing and sarcastic reference
in *Capital* to the fact that 'the extirpation, the enslavement and
entombment in mines of the aboriginal population ... signalised the
rosy dawn of the era of capitalist production'.[12]

Two pages further Marx shifts his glance to the North American
mainland:

> The treatment of the aborigines was, naturally, most frightful in
> plantation colonies destined for export trade only, such as the West
> Indies, and in rich and well-populated countries, such as Mexico
> and India, that were given over to plunder. But even in the colonies
> properly so called, the Christian character of primitive accumula-
> tion did not belie itself. Those sober virtuosi of Protestantism, the
> Puritans of New England, in 1703, by decrees of their assembly
> set a premium of £40 on every Indian scalp and every captured
> red-skin: in 1722 a premium of £100 on every scalp; in 1744, after
> Massachusetts-Bay had proclaimed a certain tribe as rebels, the
> following prices: for a male scalp of 12 years and upwards £100
> (new currency), for a male prisoner £105, for women and children
> prisoners £55, for scalps of women and children £50.[13]

Such passages indicate that Marx fully understood that the growth
of capitalist forces of production came at the expense of non-
European peoples. Rosa Luxemburg in *The Accumulation of Capital*
(1912) pointed out how 'in the wake of the railways, financed by
European and in particular British capital, the American farmer
crossed the Union from East to West and in his progress over vast
areas killed off the Red Indians with fire-arms and bloodhounds,
liquor and venereal disease'.[14]

Nonetheless, when it came to evaluating capitalism in its own terms,

Lenin like Marx thought of the United States as the most advanced capitalist country, unleashing extraordinary productive forces while promoting social and political progress. In the case of the productive forces, not only did agricultural output increase, there also developed an expansion of demand for manufactures including agricultural means of production as well as consumer items.[15]

Lenin's other path to capitalism, as we have noted, was 'capitalism from above' or the Prussian route to capitalism. There, the late eighteenth and early nineteenth-century feudal class gradually transformed itself into a class of capitalist farmers in a way that stifled the development of the peasant economy. As Lenin described it, the Prussian landlord dependence on serfdom of the early modern period continued, while being slowly transformed in the direction of capitalism. Byres concludes that Prussian agriculture became capitalist while retaining many feudal aspects, and was reactionary in its effects on the population: 'this was a far more reactionary solution for the agrarian question than the English or the North American .... It was politically and socially reactionary. It was also "economically reactionary".'[16] Prussian landlordism became Junker-controlled capitalist farming, the new basis for the social and political domination of this class. The peasants were reduced to wage workers while still bearing the degrading stigma of serf status, and the development of the home market and the forces of production were retarded because of the impoverishment of the mass of the population.[17]

Byres's scholarly study, which includes economic and historical sources that have appeared since Lenin wrote, finds the latter's account of the Prussian path still convincing and scarcely departs from it. His investigations enable him to deepen Lenin's notion of the Prussian path's economically reactionary nature. He acknowledges that Prussian capitalism did release labour for industry. On the other hand, it did not provide a market for producer or consumer industries, and did not supply capital or food to the industrialization process. Industrialization progressed in spite of, rather than because of, the contribution of capitalist agriculture in Prussia.[18]

In contrast Byres's account of the American path differs substantially from that of Lenin. It features a much greater regional diversity than indicated by Lenin. Though Lenin was aware of the plantation slavery economy in the Southern states of the United States, he underestimated its importance. More importantly, contrary to Lenin's expectations the social differentiation of the agricultural population into capitalist farmers and agricultural workers in the North did not run its course, and the bulk of American agriculture remained based on the family farm or petty commodity production. Not only did the spread of tenant farming and the development of mechanization in agriculture allow the perpetuation of the family farm,[19] according to Byres:

> we also see, in the activities of the American state, powerful inter-vention which served to reinforce significantly the survival of the family farm/petty commodity production. ... That state interven-tion acted to maintain and support agricultural overproduction and so sustain the widespread existence of family farms.[20]

With regard to the intervention of the state, Byres refers to the American government's clearing of the West of its indigenous popu-lation, conversion of the land from state-owned to private property, encouragement of the railways and establishment of state banks. In the longer run he refers to the establishment of permanent farm subsidies by the federal government in the 1930s.[21] The conception of American capitalist development as the result of the free play of the market is completely mythical. Yet Byres's own account of American capitalism from below might be criticized for not making more of the importance of political revolution, with the significance of the American Revolution and Civil War and the role of petty producers in these conflicts. Breaking with the English state and capitalist merchant oligarchy in the initial revolutionary clash and ending slavery in the second conflict made it possible to consoli-date a strong state, allowing the better part of North America to be exploited on a capitalist basis. Farmers, petty merchants and craftspeople provided the rank and file of the victorious armies in these conflicts.

Byres achievement was to criticize and deepen Lenin's conception of the two paths to capitalism, and by doing so show how fertile a political and historical conception it was. He concludes his study of the American and Prussian path in the transition with reflections on the significance of these cases to the study of capitalist origins elsewhere. He argues that such an extension of Lenin's idea requires investigations of the nature, the prerequisites and the class agents of accumulation, which almost invariably will be found to lie in the countryside.[22] As Brenner has suggested, the outcomes of such transitions are determined by class struggle. But, Byres argues, the nature of the landlord class in each instance, as well as the process of peasant social differentiation, must be studied in greater detail than Brenner allows. The intervention of the state is also critical to the transition, and must be investigated carefully. Finally, *pace* Brenner, the form and level of development of the productive forces are crucial to an understanding of the nature and outcome of class conflict.[23] In the Prussian and American cases, the transition was provoked by a crisis in the feudal and slave modes of production respectively. But such a crisis need not have led to the end of the system, whose existence might have been indefinitely prolonged. In both cases a dramatic external political shock – the crushing defeat inflicted by Napoleon in the Prussian case, and defeat of the South in the American Civil War – was the catalyst for the demise of the existing system.[24]

Byres concludes that his study suggests great diversity in the historical circumstances under which a transition can occur. But such diversity does not obviate or preclude the need for theory.[25] In fact Byres's work on the Prussian and American path constitutes a remarkable vindication of a comparative and theoretical approach to the problem of capitalist transition. The main categories with which he works – the traditional Marxist categories of class relations, mode of production and the state – have allowed him to study the problem at a sufficient level of abstraction to be generalized to the problem of transition not only in these two instances but also other cases.[26]

COMBINED AND UNEVEN DEVELOPMENT IN SCOTLAND

Neil Davidson has recently analyzed the transition to capitalism in eighteenth-century Scotland as an example of capitalism from above. As in Prussia, the conversion of the nobility from feudalism to capitalism was essential to the future. Equally important was the fact that the Scottish state had a reactionary character, facilitating the imposition of capitalism. In England the 1688 Glorious Revolution ended the seventeenth-century civil war by thwarting the final attempt to impose Stuart absolutism, and inaugurating a capitalist and constitutional state. In backward Scotland the revolution of 1688 only restored the feudal regime. Centralized government had been imposed on a still-feudal Scottish society by the Stuarts. Their overthrow returned power to a feudal nobility to whom the rural population were personally subject. The Crown ruled through heritable jurisdictions and military tenures controlled by certain great feudal families.[27]

In the decade that followed, the restored Scottish establishment feebly responded to an especially severe subsistence crisis which killed as many as 15 percent of the population of one million.[28] Population catastrophe was followed by the crash of the speculative colonial venture in Panama known as the Darien Project (1698). Much of the nobility as well as the commercial bourgeoisie of the Lowlands bought land sight-unseen in Panama. The Scottish state and civil society proved unequal to the colonial effort, and it collapsed, setting off a nation-wide financial and commercial crisis.[29] The successive disasters convinced the Scottish ruling class that the only way out was to accept union with England (1707).

Over the next half century, though feudalism remained in place, it came under increasing strain as a result of the growing pressure of English commercial and financial influence. A minority of great lords responded positively by moving toward capitalism, while the rest of the nobility sought to deal with their dire economic circumstances by increasing the exploitation of their peasant tenants while participating in a succession of Jacobite political uprisings.[30] The Jacobites were led by the most unreconstructed feudal nobles, and professed loyalty to the Stuart line. With their final defeat at Culloden in 1746, the British Parliament in which pro-unionist Scottish nobles and commoners sat ended Scottish feudalism as a socio-economic system by abolishing military tenures and heritable jurisdictions, albeit leaving intact the economic power of lords over tenants.[31] Enough of the structure of the feudal state was retained to ensure one-party Tory rule in Scotland on the basis of a total rural electorate of less than 3,000 male voters. Under this reactionary political set-up the capital Edinburgh had a mere 33 voters.[32] Meanwhile with no other economic option open to them, the bulk of the Scottish lords made a rapid transition towards capitalist agriculture. In Scotland as in Prussia, capitalist relations of production were imposed by the landlords.

In the wake of this change Scotland experienced an extraordinary economic transformation:

the transformation which took place in Scotland between 1746 and 1820 was unprecedented in European history and would not be seen again on such a scale until the industrialization of Russia after 1929. Indeed, the experience of Scotland was far closer to that of Russia than England in terms of the speed and intensity with which it occurred.[33]

Its rate of economic growth, including industrialization, equalled or even surpassed England's. Citing Wallerstein, Davidson even speaks of a 'Scottish Great Leap Forward'.[34] These dramatic changes were introduced by an emerging capitalist class made up of the now-capitalist nobility, tobacco and sugar merchants, academics and professionals, sustained by a British state which totally excluded popular representation.

We have seen that uneven development is a fundamental if not a founding characteristic of capitalism. In explaining this rapid and deep transition, Davidson makes use of this idea but he enriches it by employing Trotsky's further conception of combined and uneven development. Davidson notes that uneven development is often confused with combined and uneven development. He explains that the notion of uneven development is part of the classical Marxist tradition, and this is the way we have employed it up to now. The notion of combined and uneven development, on the other hand, grew out of the debates on revolution in the international socialist movement at the turn of the twentieth century. According to Trotsky, the notion of uneven development should properly come before that of combined development, because the latter grows out of the former and completes it. It is a conception which arises out of the advance of industrialization and imperialism. According to Trotsky, workers in under-developed countries like Russia can seize the political initiative on the basis of such a theoretical conception.[35]

Under capitalist conditions, the economic advance of some states requires those left behind to try to catch up: 'crucially, the prior development of some states cannot but affect the conditions under which the late developers enter the world system, not least through imperialist domination which prevented the latter from becoming independent centres of capital accumulation'.[36] In the case of Great Britain, not only were English merchants ahead of their Scottish counterparts, they actively blocked their entry into the world market. Yet obstacles put in their path by English capitalists were dramatically surmounted by Scottish entrepreneurs. Davidson concludes, 'a theory of uneven development alone, however, even in a modified form, is inadequate to explain the pattern of development in Scotland, or indeed anywhere else. We also require a theory of combined and unequal development.'[37]

This theory was initially outlined by Trotsky to show how a revolutionary political situation developed in Russian as a result of capitalist development:

When the productive forces of the metropolis, of a country of classical capitalism ... find ingress into more backward countries,

like Germany in the first half of the nineteenth century, and
Russia at the merging of the nineteenth and twentieth centuries,
and in the present day in Asia; when the economic factors burst
in a revolutionary manner, breaking up the old order, when
development is no longer gradual and 'organic' but assumes
the form of terrible convulsions and drastic changes of former
conceptions, then it becomes easier for critical thought to find
revolutionary expression.[38]

From the perspective of global history Trotsky explained that:

> a backward country does not take things in the same order. The
> privilege of historic backwardness – and such a privilege exists
> – permits, or rather compels the adoption of whatever is ready
> in advance of any specified date, skipping a whole series of inter-
> mediate stages. ... The development of historically backward
> nations leads necessarily to a peculiar combination of different
> stages in the historic process.[39]

Often this process of assimilation and modernizing development
proceeds within an overall social and political structure marked by
archaism, as was the case with Russia but also Scotland.[40] Trotsky
concluded that 'without this law ... it is impossible to understand
the history of Russia, and indeed of any country of the second, third
or tenth cultural class.'[41]

It was the sudden and rapid transformation of Scotland into a
capitalist country that provided the catalyst for the dawn of the
Scottish Enlightenment. At the heart of this cultural movement
lay the birth of political economy – a body of thought which
sought to theorize the transition to capitalism and provide a
program for its advance. Its single greatest achievement was
Adam Smith's *Wealth of Nations*, which as Hobsbawm put it,
'is best read – as his contemporaries read it – as a handbook of
development economics'.[42] Davidson insists that the program of
political economy of Smith and the others was bourgeois and
capitalist in its class basis and revolutionary in its intent, which
was to impose capitalism on rural Scotland.[43] Smith, in particular,
aimed to reduce the role of the state, which he identified with the
vestiges of feudalism, while at the same time freeing market forces
within the field of civil society.[44] Along with other members of
the Scottish Enlightenment, he sought to accelerate the removal
of the remaining legal obstacles in the way of the modernization

of Scottish agriculture while dissolving the intellectual barriers to enlightenment by substituting the study of political economy for obscurantist Calvinist or Jacobite ideology. The goal was to enable Scotland to compete in all respects with the English within the British state.[45] In such a politically unified British state the only possible development strategy for a Scotland undergoing combined and uneven development was paradoxically not to further increase state intervention, but to accelerate the introduction of laissez-faire economic policies.

Born at the climax of the Scottish transition from feudalism to capitalism, Smith's work constitutes the first comprehensive theorization of the emergent capitalist system. That Smith could conceptually bring together the various elements of capitalism into a political-economic synthesis reflects the growing maturity of the capitalist system as a whole toward the end of the eighteenth century.

JAPANESE CAPITALISM

In the view of Byres the Japanese case is another example of the imposition of capitalism from above. The Japanese instance, as was noted in Chapter 1, already formed part of the original debate on the capitalist transition during the 1950s. Takahashi had pointed out that proto-capitalist elements were already challenging Japanese feudalism prior to the Meiji Restoration. Nonetheless, he conceded that feudalism remained important throughout the early modern period, and inflected the development of Japanese capitalism into the twentieth century. Hobsbawm and Anderson took account of proto-capitalist tendencies in Japan prior to the intrusion of Admiral Perry, reflecting an internal dynamic in the direction of capitalism. But Anderson insisted that the prime mover was the incursion of the West, which forced Japan to join the world market – an indispensable attribute of capitalism.

The agrarian question or when and how the key capitalist transition in agriculture took place, which preoccupied Byres, also divided two contending schools of Japanese Marxist scholarship in the first part of the twentieth century, and Byres provides a useful account of their debates. The *Kozaha* or feudalist school intellectually supported the Japanese Communist Party's position, which envisaged the revolution in Japan occurring in two stages: a bourgeois democratic revolution against feudalism and then a socialist one. According to interwar *Kozaha* scholars, the Meiji

Restoration had simply reformed the feudal land system, leaving the emperor as an absolutist monarch, albeit one who now relied on the support of bourgeois capitalists as well as feudal landowners. The extreme poverty of the largely tenant farming population, whose payments in kind to the landlords amounted to about 50 percent of gross product, tended to confirm the *Kozaha* analysis that even by the 1930s no agrarian transition to capitalism had occurred. While they did not deny that capitalism existed in Japan, it was based on semi-feudal landownership and semi-serfdom. The Comintern's 1932 thesis concurred: the Japanese situation could not be appraised 'without taking into account and analyzing the peculiarities of the system prevailing in Japan, which combined extraordinarily strong elements of feudalism with a very advanced development of monopoly capitalism'.[46]

By contrast the *Ronoha*, or workers and peasants school, supported the left wing of various socialist parties which rivalled the Communist Party theoretically and politically. It held that a direct advance to socialism was possible because capitalism had penetrated all aspects of Japanese society, including agriculture, since the Meiji Restoration, a bourgeois revolution. The peasantry was undergoing disintegration into a class of wage labourers as capitalism developed in the countryside as well as everywhere else in society. The high level of tenant rent was the result of the extreme competition for land between producers rather than of landlord coercion.[47]

Byres accepted the *Kozaha* emphasis on the persistence of feudalism, in which landlords continued to control the peasantry, whose holdings were minimal. He also emphasized the prevalence of tenancy, the scarcity of wage labour and the very high rate of surplus extraction through a heavy burden of rent. But he departed from this school, emphasizing the central role of the Meiji state in the capitalist transition in dissolving classic Japanese feudalism. These measures fell short, however, of preventing the further development of feudal tenancy. State power was also used to break peasant resistance to high rents, usury and heavy taxation. Indeed, government taxation of the peasantry was vital to the accumulation of capital outside of agriculture.[48]

In these debates it is the *Kozaha* perspective, which stressed the persistence of feudalism, that is the more persuasive. Even the onset of capitalism was conditioned by the continued extraction of surplus by heavy landlord rents. Capitalism was then imposed by the state using these surpluses to initiate capitalist modernization. Such a process represents a variant of the path of capitalism from above, familiar in the case of Prussia and Scotland. But in contrast to the latter cases where the landlords became the agents of capitalist accumulation, it was the state itself that directed this process. Those scholars in the *Kozaha* school who regarded the reforms of the American occupation as decisive to the full flowering of Japanese capitalism were particularly discerning. The post-1945 agrarian reform raised the productivity of Japanese agriculture, released labour into industry, destroyed the political and social grip of the landlords and ensured the triumph of industrial and finance capital.[49]

In the case of Japan a capitalist transition occurred without the presence of capitalist relations in agriculture. Rather, it was the surplus pumped out of the agrarian sector that largely financed capitalist industrialization. In each case the state played an essential role in this process, albeit in Japan the landlords initially played an intermediary role. Such a state-directed transition, which may also be seen in Taiwan and Korea, presents another variant of capitalist transition alongside the Dutch, English, American, French, Scottish and Prussian examples. Byres doubts the likelihood of such a state-directed transition in Pakistan and India, where landlord influence remains considerable.[50] On the other hand, the examples given do not exhaust the diversity of possible passages to capitalism. Based on these examples the following factors have to be taken into consideration in studying capitalist transitions taking place in other parts of the under-developed world: the nature of the landlord class, differentiation of the peasantry, class struggle, labour supply, changes in the productive forces and the role of the state.[51]

This discussion of the role of the state in Asian capitalism points to the fact that the development of capitalism has varied greatly. Whereas late-developing Japan represents a clear case of state-directed development, England seems an instance of a more largely market-driven capitalism. The United States appears as an even more extreme example of the latter. Yet the state loomed large in the early stages of English capitalism, and some regard the United States as an outright neo-mercantilist state. It maintained high tariffs, and forcibly and consciously instituted capitalist agriculture at the expense of slave holders and the hunting and gathering populations. Russia exemplifies the very embodiment of state-directed capitalist development. The case of German capitalism, based on an alliance of capitalist landlords on the one hand, and bankers and industrialists on the other, appears to approximate the Japanese and Russian model. It has been suggested that these cases, as well

as those of, for example, Korea and Taiwan, might all be examined
from the perspective of the so-called developmental state. Even
mercantilist Holland and England could be regarded as instances of
such a state.[52] An understanding of capitalist development requires
a comparative understanding of such historical and geographical
differences and the role of the state in each instance. Likewise we
should be open to comparing these cases with those of the socialist
Soviet Union and Maoist China. In terms of their development
strategies, both socialist states appear to be closest to the example
of Japan, in which the surpluses necessary to industrialization
were squeezed out of the peasantry by the state. The difference
would seem to lie in the Soviet and Chinese attempt to not only
exploit but reorganize peasant production. Indeed, in the latter case
Mao pursued policies of rural industrialization comparable to the
development of rural industrialization in early modern Europe.

THE MERCANTILISM OF FREE TRADE

The deep-seated prejudice that capitalism represented a triumph
of free trade over political imperialism goes back to Adam Smith.
In fact as John Gallagher and Ronald Robinson pointed out long
ago, capitalism has used both overt political imperialism and free
trade to assure global domination depending on the historical and
strategic circumstances.[53] For both political and economic reasons,
Smith was a committed advocate of the free market and a believer
in a minimal state. A determined opponent of Stuart and other
absolutist monarchies' restraints on individual and economy liberty,
he aimed to reduce the role of the state to undertaking public works
and maintaining order. He was at pains to denounce what he called
the mercantile system, or state-regulated overseas trade. According
to Smith, mercantilism was biased in favour of foreign trade and
export-oriented industry to the neglect of the development of the
internal economy, which depended on agriculture and attendant
industries. Smith, to be sure, was to a certain extent a supporter
of overseas commerce, regarding it as favourable to the division of
labour, competitiveness and innovation. However, he was opposed
to protectionism and the conquest and maintenance of colonial
possessions.

Countries that acquired colonies in quest of power in international affairs often benefited less than the countries that were
hindered from acquiring such colonial possessions. The regulations

that were designed to exclude rivals frequently ended up crippling the industry of the colonizing power.[54] Such prohibitions represented a distortion in the efficient employment of capital which might otherwise be used to meet more effectively the demands of the market at home and abroad. Smith here is theorizing based on an amnesia which ignores the history of capitalism which was based on state protectionism. Excluding foreign goods through tariffs and navigation acts allowed local manufacturers to accumulate capital, create a home market, and force open foreign markets. Smith's amnesia in fact is a harbinger of the moment, noted by Gallagher and Robinson, when the politics of early modern capitalist imperialism gave way to the politics of free trade in England, the most advanced of the capitalist states.

In this discussion of capitalist origins, we have seen how the early modern state was at first essential to prolonging the feudal order but in the longer run provided an indispensable framework within which capitalism and national markets developed. Continuing to take the English case as our example, the state's enclosure acts, labour statutes and poor laws, justices of the peace, regulated markets, militias, armies and navies, definition of private property relations, provision of means of exchange and credit, and government contracts were indispensable to early capitalism. Mercantilism has been seen as being concerned with state-directed and supported overseas trade as part of this pattern of state intervention in the economy. But it is important to emphasize that the internal economy of early modern states was another important aspect of the mercantile system, or mercantilism. The creation of national export industries dependent on the state entailed restructuring which enhanced the internal as much as the external power of the state.

In the eyes of early modern governments no real distinction existed between political and economic power. In its latter aspect mercantilism was a theory of international relations viewed from an economic perspective. Such doctrines reflected policies of economic nationalism which characterized European governments between the sixteenth and eighteenth centuries. No one better summed up the mercantilist theory than the late seventeenth-century political economist William Petty. In 1690 Petty described the theory as concerned with 'the Wealth of every nation, consisting chiefly in the share which they have in the Foreign Trade with the Commercial World rather than in the Domestick Trade, of ordinary Meat, Drink, and Cloaths, &c. which bring in little Gold, Silver, Jewels and other Universal Wealth'.[55] As Michael Perelman notes, 'for Petty universal wealth was merely a sign of power which derived from the development of the economic forces of the nation'.[56]

Under the sway of Adam Smith's negative judgement, the assessment of mercantilism on the part of liberal economic theorists and historians has traditionally been hostile. Government interference, the existence of monopolies and the overall search for economic rents have been seen as crippling economic growth. However, strands of a dissenting interpretation remained alive. The nineteenth-century German historical school, influenced by the neo-mercantilist views of Friedrich List, tended to be more favourable to the role of the state in the economy, and in the 1930s when state intervention was on the agenda, the history of mercantilism attracted much interest. It was then that the great works on the history of mercantilism by Eli Heckscher and Jacob Viner were written.[57] The followers of Smith tended to deride the mercantilist belief that money was an essential ingredient in the wealth of a nation. On the contrary, John Maynard Keynes argued that the mercantilist view was an implicit recognition of the tie between the abundance of money and low interest rates which would stimulate trade and investment.[58]

Despite its bias toward laissez-faire, Ronald Findlay and Kevin O'Rourke's recent sweeping history of world trade adopts a historical perspective which eschews passing judgement on whether mercantilism was positive or negative. The authors explain that the mercantilist theoreticians of the seventeenth and eighteenth centuries regarded international trade as a zero-sum game. Colonies were regarded as a market for manufactures and a source of raw materials from which foreigners had to be excluded. Political and military conflict between states was taken for granted. Those states that could garner a sufficiently large amount of financial resources would triumph in war. Such success could then ensure the wealth necessary to maintain and extend the power of the state. The objective of a state's economic policy was to secure monopoly control over a given sector of trade, thereby gaining monopoly profits and providing the means to carry on warfare. Acquiring precious metals was important in this regard. Given the presumed reality of the zero-sum nature of these conflicts, the liberal notion of gains from trade to all parties as a result of peaceful commerce was beside the point.[59]

As our brief discussion of the historiography of mercantilism indicates, non-Marxists have made important contributions to an understanding of mercantilism. Nonetheless, in the course of discussing the transition to capitalism, the Marxist school provides important insights into the theory and practice of mercantilism.

Marx himself regarded mercantilism as part of the apparatus of the early modern state which promoted capitalism. It is a feature of a system of state power, parts of which can be found in the states on the European Continent, but which comes together in England at the beginning of the seventeenth century. It involved a systematic combination of elements which included colonies, a national debt, a modern mechanism of taxation and the protectionist system. Each of these elements makes use of the state, defined as the concentrated and organized force of society, to accelerate the transition from the feudal to the capitalist mode of production. Summing up this process, Marx concludes:

> But they all employ the power of the State, the concentrated and organized force of society, to hasten, hothouse fashion, the process of transformation of the feudal mode of production into the capitalist mode, and to shorten the transition. Force is the midwife of every old society pregnant with a new one. It is itself an economic power.[60]

As Perelman notes, Marx saw mercantilism as an attempt to overcome the slow development of the internal and overseas market by the use of coercion to speed the accumulation of capital.[61] In other words political power was used to create and accelerate the emergence of markets, as we have emphasized. Elsewhere Marx speaks of colonialism, public debts, heavy taxes, protection, commercial wars and such like as 'children of the manufacturing period'.[62]

As a set of economic ideas, mercantilism marked the first attempt to speculate about the emerging capitalist order according to Marx:

> The first theoretical treatment of the modern mode of production – the mercantile system – proceeded necessarily from the superficial phenomena of the circulation process as individualised in the movement of merchant's capital, and therefore grasped only the appearance of matters.[63]

This was partly the result of commercial capital being the first independent mode of the existence of capital in general, but it was also the consequence of the overwhelming influence of commercial capital in the period when feudal production was overthrown and modern production began to develop.[64] Moreover, for Marx mercantilism served the interests of a rising bourgeoisie:

the national character of the mercantile system is not merely a phrase on the lips of its spokesmen. Under the pretext of concern solely for the wealth of the nation and the resources of the state, they, in fact, pronounce the interests of the capitalist class and the amassing of riches in general to be the ultimate aim of the state, and thus proclaim bourgeois society in place of the old divine state. But at the same time they are consciously aware that the development of the interests of capital and of the capitalist class, of capitalist production, forms the foundation of national power and national ascendancy in modern society.[65]

It is under the mercantile system that industrial capital, and consequently wage labour, first develops in antithesis to, and at the expense of, feudal landed property. Indeed under mercantilism, 'one form of wage labour, the industrial, and one form of capital, the industrial, were recognized as sources of wealth, but only in so far as they produced money.'[66]

Dobb perceptively discussed the economic motivations behind the mercantile system. According to him, those who wrote on economic matters, and the merchants themselves, took it for granted that political interference or economic regulation by the state was indispensable to making a profit in trade. The petty mode of production still dominated, and the rent of land still seemed the only natural form of surplus. According to Dobb:

> the productivity of labour was still low, and the number of workers employed by a single capitalist was seldom very numerous. It was accordingly still difficult to imagine any substantial profit being 'naturally' made by investment in production. ... Under such circumstances if merchants or merchant manufacturers were to be subject to unrestrained competition what basis for profit could there be?[67]

More or less unrestricted competition and the extraction of surplus value were seen as incompatible with one another. Without regulation which limited competition and protected price margins, merchant capital might enjoy windfalls but could obtain no enduring source of income. As a result it was believed that trade and industry would languish for lack of an incentive to invest money in such enterprises.[68] Dobb is here speaking of overseas trade, but *pace* Brenner such conditions have to be borne in mind with respect to the evolution of the internal market as well.

Mercantilists of the seventeenth century sought to increase the amount of money circulating in the state. This was part of a drive toward a favourable balance of trade. What was sought was an increase in exports, particularly of manufactures, while permitting as few imports as possible. The French finance minister Jean-Baptiste Colbert (d. 1683) defined commerce abroad as facilitating the import of goods that favoured manufacture while placing an embargo on the import of foreign manufactures. While the import of foreign manufactures was discouraged, the import of raw materials necessary to manufacture at home was sanctioned. A favourable balance of trade which drew money into the country could be expected to increase prices internally. At the same time, it tended to depress the price level of the country from which the gold had been drained. It thereby helped to lower the price of the products which were purchased abroad for import, and to raise the price of exported commodities – the policy of buying cheap and selling dear. These notions particularly applied to captive or colonial markets in which alternative sources of supply could be politically excluded.[69]

According to Dobb, mercantilism simply continued at the national level the exploitative policies of the late medieval towns in relation to the surrounding countryside. As such, the mercantile system played an important role in the nurturing of capitalist industry. From this perspective mercantilist authors sometimes regarded the surplus gained from foreign trade as the only real source of accumulation and state revenue. It was essentially the economic policy of an age of primitive accumulation, Dobb concluded.[70] By this he meant that accumulation took place as a result of trade based on political manipulation and control of exchange.

As we noted, Keynes suggested that mercantilist thinkers associated a plenitude of money with cheap credit or low interest which would stimulate the economy. Dobb demurred, saying that the balance of trade and the profits so derived were uppermost in the minds of theorists and policy makers. From the late seventeenth century onwards proponents of mercantilism made no simple connection between the quantity of money in circulation and interest rates. Emphasis was placed instead on the growth of commerce, a capitalist class and stock or capital as the surest ways to ensure the availability of credit.[71] From the same period dates a preoccupation with using a favourable balance of trade to create employment at home through an expansion of manufacturing industry. At the same time, the mercantilist conception of prosperity was premised on the notion of keeping wages for workers low.[72]

Keynes brought forward more historical evidence than Dobb credits him with for his view of a mercantilist notion of monetary economic stimulation. But the disagreement between the two is about more than just historical facts. Keynes advanced his overall argument about the balance of payments, the level of interest and economic activity to counter the still-prevalent liberal orthodoxy of the 1930s that such relationships were self-adjusting in terms of the international division of labour and should not be tampered with. In his eyes the mercantilist policy which tried to bring money into the country and lower the rate of interest was a laudable attempt to stimulate the economy using the relatively primitive political tools at hand. The Marxist Dobb, like orthodox economic liberals, tended to be sceptical about the feasibility of such short-term and politically inspired fixes.

Dobb clearly sees mercantilism as a policy emanating from the royal court and the ruling state elites. But he also views it as reflecting the interests and outlook of the more privileged merchants and manufacturers. Clearly these two groups were affiliated, the one subordinated to the other. Dobb is sensitive to the fact that that the class basis of the two groups differed. That being the case, he also points out that the system of privileges, monopolies and rents fuelled conflict between the privileged merchants and manufacturers and the newer merchants and manufacturers.[73]

Perry Anderson's view of the class basis of mercantilism follows from his view of the early modern state, which he sees as reflecting the class interest above all of the nobility. As such mercantilism represented the economic outlook of a feudal ruling class that had accommodated to an integrated national market yet retained its fundamental perspective on matters economic and political. It was a theory of the intervention of the political order into the workings of the economy in the interest of both the prosperity of society and the power of the state. Its amalgam of the political and economic represented the antithesis of the later Smithian attempt to separate the political from the economic – a nexus which scandalized the Scottish political economist.

If we follow Anderson, the aristocratic bias of the policy is reflected above all in its attitude toward war. Whereas Smith and his followers were predisposed in favour of peaceful and mutually advantageous commerce, the mercantilists were strongly bellicose. They stressed the necessity and profitability of war. According to them, a successful economy depended on success in war. It was the same zero-sum view applied both to war and economic life, according to Anderson. While this is undoubtedly a brilliant insight, one would have to question whether bellicose attitudes were unique to the nobility. It makes it appear that a policy of war would presumably have to be foisted on a reluctant early modern bourgeoisie. Yet for the most part, the latter group were equally bellicose, although for different reasons. War was an intrinsic part of the history of the emergent bourgeoisie. Indeed, based on his notion of aristocratic control over the early modern state, Anderson insists that mercantilism emanated from an aristocratic perspective on international politics. This runs counter to the more convincing view shared by Marx and Dobb that it emanated from the bourgeoisie within the structure of the state, which absent a bourgeois revolution was still dominated by the nobility. Mercantilism undoubtedly sought the suppression of particularistic obstacles to commerce within the national territory, and strove to create a unified domestic market for commodity production. It characteristic creations were the royal manufactures and regulated guilds in France, and the chartered companies in England. The medieval and corporatist lineage of the former seems evident.[74]

Unlike the above authors, Arrighi focuses on the mature mercantilism of the eighteenth century. He regards mercantilism as a synthesis of capitalism and territorialism, which was perfected by the British and the French in the eighteenth century. According to Arrighi the British instance represents a third stage in the historic cycles of global capitalist development, in which capital was fused with state power as the basis of great imperial power. It challenged the established positions of the Spanish, Portuguese and Dutch empires. Mercantilist policy had three parts: colonialism based on settler colonies, capitalist slavery and economic nationalism. Of the three, settler colonialism was the most important, relying largely on the private initiatives of subjects. French and English colonies were more successful than the earlier colonies of their rivals. Slavery grew out of the colonies' need to supplement their labour force, and reached huge proportions in the eighteenth century. The third element was economic nationalism, which facilitated the open-ended accumulation of economic surpluses and the construction of the domestic or national economy of the mother country. Through private and bureaucratic initiatives the French and British monarchies internalized as much of the inputs necessary to war and state-making as was feasible, enlarging the tax base while strengthening the state. Britain's island geography and transatlantic status gave it an important comparative advantage.[75] Nonetheless, both eighteenth-century British and French mercantilism were quite successful.

Teschke's view of mercantilism arises from his overall view of the evolution of international relations. It is based on an extension into the field of international relations of the premises of Brenner and Political Marxism, with which he strongly identifies. He rejects the dominant paradigm of the discipline of international relations which considers the Treaty of Westphalia of 1648, ending the wars of religion, as the founding moment of the modern state system. Rather, geopolitical modernity began with the Glorious Revolution in 1688, which saw the birth of the first capitalist state in England, and was marked above all by the consolidation of parliamentary rule in that country. The subsequent expansion of English capitalism in the eighteenth century then step-by-step undermined the governments and the state system of the *Ancien Régime*. Modern sovereignty embodied in English politics should not be confused with absolutist sovereignty, which was reflected in the Treaty of Westphalia. The Bourbon monarchy in France was the most perfect exemplar of the latter. French absolutism is regarded by Teschke as standing in complete opposition to English capitalism, in conformity with Brenner's and Wood's view of non-capitalist France. Like Wood, too, Teschke views Holland as an example of merchant capitalism closely tied to feudalism. Indeed, whereas Arrighi regards Holland as the linchpin of seventeenth-century European politics, Teschke downgrades its importance in the operation of the post-Westphalian system.

Mercantilism created a structural nexus between trade and government. Such a structural link between the economic and political is the antithesis of modern capitalism. Commercial capitalism under the mercantile system was not capitalism. According to Teschke, international trade under capitalism is characterized by open and competitive markets. Under dynastic conditions, mercantilism was a geographical strategy of extending the accumulating reach of pre-modern states, not a qualitative change in the logic of the world economic order. Internationally, the redistribution of wealth through unequal exchange was a zero-sum game: total wealth was not increased thereby. The zero-sum conception which conceived of total wealth as finite was elevated into an economic law in mercantilist doctrine. This was because the sphere of production remained outside its theoretical scope: 'profits from trade were not systematically reinvested in the means of production but in the means of violence'.[76] On a national level, economic growth was thought of in terms of absolute population growth, absolute gains from trade and immigration, or absolute territorial gain.[77]

Teschke's account is deficient in its view of the relationship between the state and market on at least three counts. In the first place, he refuses to take account of the fact, already pointed to by Arrighi above, that the most successful mercantile state was not an absolutist state, but the most successful capitalist country: post-revolutionary eighteenth-century England.[78] Robin Blackburn has described the English mercantilism of that period as an inverted one, not with financiers and merchants serving the *raison d'état* any longer, but with the state serving capitalist purposes. For all that, it was still mercantilist in that the state more than ever interfered in the market. The state created a zone of imperial 'free trade' for its merchants and manufacturers, offered them protection and gained favourable terms for their entry into other markets.[79] Eighteenth-century France, too, is an example of a successful mercantile state which willy-nilly was drawn in the same direction. Despite its feudal and absolutist character, competition with England forced it to increasingly preoccupy itself with the well-being of French commerce and industry.[80]

Second, Teschke fails to recognize that as mercantile states both England and France were very interested in the development of new, more productive manufacturing technologies. This is true of virtually all mercantilist regimes in the eighteenth century. Third, and most egregiously, Teschke quite mistakenly twists the story of capitalism into a history of the triumph of the market and the effacement of the state. Nothing could be more in conformity with the opinions of Adam Smith and further from the historical truth. It belies Marx's view that the mercantilist state was used to accelerate the creation of the market. England did not become a truly free-trading state until the mid-nineteenth century, and then only for a generation. Its free-trade ideology amounted to propaganda designed to discourage would-be industrial competitors like the United States and Germany. Statesmen and thinkers like Alexander Hamilton of the United States and Friedrich List of Prussia fully appreciated the importance of state protectionism to the development of industry. The United States, the most dynamic capitalist state of the nineteenth century, may right-fully be considered neo-mercantilist. As against the Smithian view of the history of capitalism, which insists that it is the history of a progressive liberation from the thrall of the state, the existence of a strong state is integral to it. Indeed, I have insisted on this as a basic theme from the late Middle Ages onward.

COLONIALISM

As I have noted, Marx closely connected mercantilism with the development of industry. It was an aspect of the age of early modern manufactures. According to Marx colonialism was a critical feature of the mercantile system:

> Today industrial supremacy implies commercial supremacy. In the period of manufacture properly so called, it is, on the other hand, commercial supremacy that gives industrial predominance. Hence the preponderant role that the colonial system plays at that time.[81]

Marx's judgment of colonialism was an ambivalent, or better a dialectical, one. For while condemning its injustice and ills, he also saw colonialism as advancing the development of capitalism as a world system, and ultimately leading to socialism, which he conceived of as a unified global order based on social and political equality. From the sixteenth century the development of capitalism and colonialism was part of a single process of increasingly global accumulation. Western Europe was undeniably at the centre of capitalism. But socialism would put an end to uneven development and self-evidently would have no political headquarters.

Many historians and postcolonial theorists choose to deny or forget Marx's dialectical approach and universalist and socialist perspective on the ultimate fate of capitalism. Looking at the short or medium term they prefer to see Marx's view as fundamentally Eurocentric. But I cannot go along with those who take offence at Marx for his view of the history of capitalism. For him the extension of European domination over most of the rest of the world while capitalism universalized itself was a historical process that could not be ignored, wished away or merely denounced. Two centuries or even half a millennium under the thrall of capitalism is not long in terms of humankind's long past or socialist future.

Marx's critics accuse him of Eurocentric attitudes. Where such lapses occurred they have been acknowledged and criticized by Kevin Anderson, a recent sympathetic student of Marx's approach to non-Western societies.[82] But Anderson makes clear that Marx's faults in this respect have little to do with his essential point of view. Those who brandish the charge of Eurocentrism against him often do so because they refuse or are unable to appreciate his dialectical sense of the historical process, his mordant sensibility and his tough-mindedness.[83] This dialectical approach was the one he took to the study of capitalism itself. In the *Communist Manifesto* and the *Grundrisse*, for example, we find magnificent paeans in appreciation of the power of capitalism. At the same time such praise is accompanied by denunciation of the intrinsically exploitative and destructive character of the system, which degrades the producers and nature itself. This double-sided perspective helps to reinforce Marx's authoritative and scientific method with an aesthetic and stylistic sense of detachment which helps readers grasp the fact that history proceeds in an ironical fashion. Writing about India, for example, his early accounts viewed the British conquest as positive although violent, because it furthered the progress of capitalism in England through primitive accumulation, while leading to the liquidation of the so-called Asiatic mode of production. This was inescapable as capitalism extended its global reach. Yet reporting the bloody-mindedness and racism of the British in repressing the Indian Mutiny (1857), Marx brought to the surface what he had undoubtedly already understood, namely, the cruelty of the British conquerors. Moreover it was not overly Eurocentric of him correctly to conclude that the British in India were preparing the ground for their own demise, as the Indians would sooner or later develop the capacity to liberate themselves from British domination.[84]

Marx's views on India have been questioned at a deeper level.[85] Based on what is now understood of the economic and manufacturing dynamism of India during the eighteenth century, some critics point out that Marx's notion of India as locked into the Asian mode of production, based on the symbiotic relationship between village peasants and artisans, is open to serious doubt. Yet in a nuanced response Irfan Habib has pointed out that Marx's early view of the Asiatic mode was not set in stone. He was never prepared to go so far as to acknowledge that pre-colonial India could be considered a particular form of feudalism, as some scholars do today. On the other hand, as he studied further, he came to acknowledge that private property, commodity exchange and a class structure did emerge in early modern India, and that it was accordingly far from being a stagnant society. Habib also noted Marx's condemnation of the deliberate destruction of Indian textile manufacturing by the British at the beginning of their rule, and the way they milked India through the siphoning off of tax as the tribute of 'good government'.[86] On the other hand, we should recognize that Marx's approval of the British policy of building railways, introducing Western education and political centralization must be offset by the recognition that the

British systematically crippled Indian manufacturing and inhibited economic development almost up to the end of their rule.[87]

Marx understood that the exploitation of India was made possible by colonialism, which he saw as basically a form of political and military domination. Likewise he understood that it was essentially through military conquest that the English imposed landlordism on Ireland. Furthermore, English political control enabled them to undermine Irish industry at the same time as they were destroying Indian manufacturing.[88]

The English conquest of Ireland was based on what Wood argues was a distinctively English and capitalist landlord-based colonialism. Its distinctiveness from the Spanish, French and Portuguese form of colonial exploitation was rooted in an agrarian capitalism whose dynamic lay in raising the level of relative surplus value.[89] In other words English colonialism was an outgrowth of a unique and superior form of capitalist economy. This judgement perhaps makes sense with respect to some British colonies of North America like New York and Pennsylvania in the short run. In the longer term such English-style landlordism was undermined in North America by access to cheap land.

We can question whether it applies to Ireland at all. Marx noted that under colonialism Irish agriculture was organized along similar lines to English capitalist agriculture. He furthermore recognized the capitalist aspirations of Irish tenant farmers. But, contrary to Wood, he stressed that both the labour and capital of such farmers, rather than going toward the creation of more relative surplus value and further accumulation, were for the most part confiscated by rack-renting and largely absentee English landlords.[90] Political and economic colonialism in Ireland, it should be noted, worked through what has been described as a classic form of racial oppression – the precursor of the racial oppression inflicted on African slaves in the New World.[91] Viewed from this perspective, racism was a form of ideological control that was born in the early modern period and was designed to reinforce colonial domination and exploitative relations of production.

Following the Second World War many theorists in the under-developed countries explained under-development through the notion of unequal exchange. Samir Amin, for example, underscored the transfer of surplus from colonial countries to the developed world as a result of the transfer of surplus value from countries of lower to those of higher productivity.[92] Apparently unbeknownst to Amin this process of unequal exchange had already been pointed out in Marx's *Grundrisse,* in a critique of David Ricardo's theory of comparative advantage entitled 'Two nations may exchange according to the law of profit in such a way that both gain, but one is always defrauded'.[93] As Marx explains:

> nations may continually exchange with one another, may even continually repeat the exchange on an ever-expanding scale, without for the that reason necessarily gaining in equal degrees. One of the nations may continually appropriate for itself a part of the surplus labour of the other, giving back nothing for it in the exchange.[94]

In common with other proponents of the dependency school, Wallerstein views unequal exchange as a characteristic feature of colonialism, facilitating the export of capital from the periphery and its accumulation at the centre of the world system. Responsibility for this state of affairs was due in large degree to the power of the strong states in the core, which politically enforced economic inequality. In direct opposition, Brenner insisted that the failure of capitalism in the periphery and the haemorrhage of capital toward Europe was due not to colonial domination but rather to the class relations within colonized states which stymied the rise of capitalism. As we have noted earlier, Brenner ignores the way that the international relations of dependency shape internal class relations in favour of ongoing colonialism.

Jim Blaut, a Marxist geographer, has been the most outspoken opponent of Brenner's Eurocentrism, regarding it as directed against not only Wallerstein's view, but also other proponents of the dependency school like Amin and André Gunder Frank. Blaut made known his position in different places, but nowhere more cogently than as part of a debate in the journal *Political Geography* (1992).[95] Prior to 1492, according to Blaut:

> Europe was not in any way ahead of Africa and Asia in development or even in the preconditions of development. After 1492, Europeans came to dominate the world, and they did so because 1492 inaugurated a set of world-historical processes which gave to European protocapitalists enough capital and power to dissolve feudalism in their own region and begin the destruction of competing protocapitalist communities everywhere else.[96]

There are four main points to Blaut's argument:

- Europeans had no advantage over Africans or Asians prior to 1492 in respect of an evolution toward capitalism and modernity. Medieval Europe was no more advanced or progressive than Africa or Asia.
- It was colonialism especially in the Americas which made capitalism possible and gave Europe the advantage after 1492.
- The exploitation of the Americas in the sixteenth and seventeenth century produced much more capital than is acknowledged and enabled a major transformation of European society.
- There was no uniquely European transformation of relations of production from feudalism to capitalism, as Brenner and others have insisted. Rather, there was a transition toward capitalism from a range of broadly feudal and feudal-tributary modes of production that was hemisphere-wide prior to 1492. It was European colonialism after that date that arrested the process outside of Europe.

In response to the first point, Chris Harman, who was committed to the idea that Western Europe was the starting place of early capitalism, conceded Blaut's argument to an extent.[97] According to him, the productive forces of humanity were developing across Eurasia and in Africa over a long period prior to 1492. In several places in these regions, tendencies to capitalism were emerging. But Harman underscores that for contingent historical reasons such tendencies emerged more slowly elsewhere than in Western Europe, and this provided Europe with an advantage. On the contrary, Blaut asserts that these proto-capitalist tendencies were developing uniformly everywhere. But even if this is true, the first breakthrough to capitalism turned out to be a zero-sum game, with the Europeans emerging as the winners. Once ahead, the Europeans were able to maintain their advantage by force.

Moreover, the development of European colonialism, which is Blaut's second point, is regarded by him as the key stumbling block in the way of further non-European capitalist development. Indeed, it should be stressed that the essence of colonialism is in the final analysis not economic domination. It is about the use of force and the opportunities that force allows. Political control permits the restructuring of economic relations in favour of those who wield coercive power.

But colonialism has to be understood in dialectical fashion as an outgrowth of the dynamic development of capitalism within Europe. Its development did not come out of the blue, but reflected the expansive drive of capitalism. It arose out of the quest for increasing amounts of bullion necessary to supply the rapidly emerging capitalist marketplace within Europe at the end of the fifteenth and beginning of the sixteenth centuries. The urgency to find fresh sources of gold and silver was admittedly increased by the simultaneous search for profit in the African slave trade and slave plantation economy, as well as the growth of the Asian spice trade. In the course of its subsequent development, colonialism expanded out of the need to find markets for European manufactured products, create settler-colonies and profit further from the slave trade and the slave plantation economy.

It should be reiterated that even so, Europe's early overseas success was as much or more a military and political than an economic one. Yet its martial and administrative superiority already reflected a growing technical and organizational capacity which was an outgrowth of an internally expanding capitalist economy. It then used its martial strength and political power to enhance its internal economic development while expanding its political and economic reach further overseas. In other words, Blaut tends to view colonialism as a contingent, or perhaps political and military, factor ensuring European success, while standing in the way of the economic development of non-Europeans. In fact colonialism sprang from Europe's internal dynamic, which for better or worse included both its emerging political and economic strength.

André Gunder Frank radically challenged Blaut's conception.[98] Contrary to Blaut's view of even global development, Frank insisted on its uneven character. Against the whole pack of Eurocentric historians, he argued that in 1492 and for long afterward it was Asia that was globally in the economic ascendant, not Western Europe. But it should be immediately recalled that it was Hobsbawm who first invoked uneven development as part of the original transition debate conceding the backwardness of Western Europe in relation to much of Eurasia. But instead of seeing this as a disadvantage as Frank would have it, Hobsbawm argued that it turned to Western Europe's advantage. Hobsbawm, we can recall, also harked back to the notion of uneven development, insisting that capitalism developed on the periphery of Eurasia and entailed a process of rapid coming from behind and leaping ahead. In other words, it was the very backwardness of the West which gave it an advantage.

Marx's view of the integral role and significance of overseas conquest and colonialism in the history of capitalism remains intact. From the beginning his view of colonialism was dialectical, destructive of non-European societies while helping to accelerate the development of the capitalist world market and the process of capital accumulation. Blaut's argument that Europe's conquest of the world was not based on capitalism but rather on colonial conquest is unsustainable because the power of colonial expansion depended on the growing strength of capitalism. Frank's point about the economic superiority of Asia over Europe throughout the early modern period confirms that economic progress was far from being a monopoly of Western Europe. On the other hand, the notion of uneven capitalist development in which what had been peripheral emerges as the centre is key to understanding the eventual advance of Western Europe over the rest of the world.

SLAVERY

At the focal point of colonialism were the slave trade and the colonial slave plantations. The relationship between capitalism and slavery has been debated even more fiercely than colonialism. The slave and colonial trades emerged as the most dynamic sectors of the Europe-centred capitalist economy in the seventeenth century. It stoked the flames of European, and especially British, trade and manufacturing-based economic expansion in the eighteenth century. British exports accounted for over 56 percent of all industrial production in the period 1700–1760, and over 46 percent in the period 1780–1800. Overwhelmingly North America, the Caribbean and Latin America were the major markets for these overseas sales.[99] It is estimated that in 1770 this Atlantic trade furnished as much as 55 percent of 'gross fixed capital formation investment' in Great Britain.[100] At the heart of this Atlantic economy, including the North American mainland, lay the slave trade and the plantation economy based on slave labour. Already in the sixteenth century the number of Africans taken from Africa as captives and enslaved amounted to 370,000. By the eighteenth century the total reached no less than 6,130,000. In 1800 there were over 3 million slaves in the Americas despite an enormous mortality.[101]

It was Eric Williams, in his *Capitalism and Slavery* published in 1944, who first made the connection between the profits made in the slave trade and slave plantations and the Industrial Revolution.[102] He argued that the surplus extracted from the sugar-slave planta-tion complex and the associated triangular trades opened the way to industrialization. Williams's thesis was contested by historians uncomfortable with the idea that the breakthrough of European capitalism was based on slavery. They succeeded in throwing some doubt on his statistics regarding the profitability of slavery and the significance of exports, arguing that the capital necessary to industrialization was available within the British economy. Yet Williams for the most part has been vindicated by recent historiography.[103]

Certainly there is little question now that the sale of manufactures in the Caribbean was important to the development of British capitalism in the eighteenth century. The speed-up in the rate of industrial growth based on exports depended in good part on purchasing power generated by the British West Indies. It seems that demand stemming from Africa, the Caribbean and North America ultimately generated by the production of sugar raised the export of manufactures from Britain abroad by a large factor. It may have been responsible for more than half of the growth of English exports in the third quarter of the eighteenth century. The institution of slavery had an important effect in increasing investment in the Empire through the development of the triangular trades with North America and the Caribbean, as well as in the building of maritime and transportation infrastructure. Return on this investment in turn increased income in England. At the same time the re-export of sugar to the Continent brought enormous profits.

How can we understand the relationship between capitalism and slavery? The classic analysis of the slave mode of production is by the Marxist historian of Greek Antiquity, Geoffrey E. M. de Ste Croix.[104] According to him, the free wage labourer has his own labour-power to sell and must be considered variable capital. In contrast, the slave is the property of the master, and as such is a means of production, or is a constituent part of constant or fixed capital, like land, tools and draft animals.[105] In Antiquity slavery was not the only form of unfree labour. But it was the archetypical form of such labour, and the one on which the ruling class depended for its control over society and the state.[106]

What was its relationship to capitalism in the early modern period, when wage labour was gradually becoming the dominant form of exploitation? In attempting to answer this question we find that there are a number of differing positions. Wallerstein, concerned as he is with conceiving capitalism as a single system, considered slavery and serfdom as forms of exploitation alongside wage labour as part of a capitalist world-system which emerged in the sixteenth century. Although wage labour defines the capitalist system, slavery and serfdom are integral parts of the global capitalist division of labour according to Wallerstein. Coming from the completely opposed tack of neoclassical economics, American historians Robert Fogel and Stanley Engerman applied quantitative techniques to economic history and claimed that the American slave plantation operated like an efficient capitalist enterprise. Fogel and Engerman particularly denied that slave labour was any less productive than wage labour or intrinsically incompatible with capitalism.[107] Critical to their argument is a comparison of southern plantation with northern capitalist farming. Critics point out that the two econometricians use questionable data and measurements of productivity in their comparison, so that the results turn out in favour of southern plantation agriculture.[108]

According to Byres, at a time when capitalism was flourishing and developing, slavery had to adapt to the norms of the capitalist world market. But he insists such adaptation does not make slavery capitalist. Planters in the Southern states of the United States sought to accumulate and maximize profits, but that did not transform them into capitalists. Rather they sought to restore and maintain an archaic mode of production.[109] Rakesh Bhandari, contrariwise, argues that so long as capital seeks to valorize labour through profits, it can do so through a variety of forms of exploitation: slavery, labour tenancy, nominally independent petty commodity producers, and formally free wage labour. From the perspective of capital there is no essential difference between a wage worker who is a wage slave and a slave who is an enslaved wage worker.[110] In opposition to Bhandari, I would argue that it is only the labour power stemming from wage labour that allows the ballooning of value and capital accumulation through the extraction of relative as against absolute value, involving systematic and cumulative gains in productivity. For Bhandari to be correct he would have to show that forms of exploitation like slavery could produce such continuing increases in productivity.

In two massive volumes, *The Overthrow of Colonial Slavery, 1776–1848* (1988) and *The Making of New World Slavery* (1997), Robin Blackburn has made a fundamental contribution to understanding the relationship between slavery and capitalism.[111] For many years a stalwart of the *New Left Review*, Blackburn is professor at the New School of Social Research and at Essex University. Both of Blackburn's books are both theoretically informed and deeply rooted in archival research. In discussing early modern slavery, Blackburn seeks to distinguish Eastern European serfdom from New World slavery, and thereby sets himself at a distance from Wallerstein. The latter had insisted that the emergence of the capitalist world system made Eastern Europe the granary of the West. The profits derived from exports encouraged landlords to turn their peasant tenants into serfs while tying the Eastern European economy to the capitalist world system. But, according to Blackburn, serfdom east of the Elbe was not the product of the capitalist mode but the response of landlords to the demographic crisis of the late Middle Ages. The subsequent turn of landlords to grain exports required very few productive imports from the West, and stimulated no reciprocal commercial exchanges. Eastern Europe was barely integrated into capitalism. In contrast the American slave plantations were established to produce cash crops for sale in Europe, which was their sole purpose. They remained intimately tied to imports of European manufactured goods, which included means of production as well as consumer items. At their height Polish grain exports never amounted to more than 15 percent of production, with luxury goods dominating imports. Europe's trade with the slave plantations was more conducive to cumulative and reciprocal expansion. Hence New World slavery was much more closely tied in with West European capitalism than was serfdom in Eastern Europe.[112]

Blackburn agrees with Byres that New World slavery was not intrinsically capitalist in its internal dynamic. Rather, the slave economies of the New World were a form of primitive accumulation. They were primitive because their productive organization relied not on the economic coercion of the sale of labour power, but on non-economic compulsion. The producers were compelled by direct and physical coercion to produce a surplus and a commodity for sale in the market. Britain's formal and informal empire rested on its military, and especially its naval, strength, or in other words on violence or the threat of violence. If primitive accumulation had completed itself within England by 1700, it was reinforced and extended for a century and more overseas through slavery.[113] Summing up his view of the relation between slavery and the emergence of industrial capitalism, Blackburn notes that:

> capital's thirst for surplus-value and the necessarily uneven advance of mechanization has, indeed, repeatedly produced regimes of extended primitive accumulation, in which forced or sweated labour is driven to match the pace of machine industry, and is expected to rely on 'natural economy' or communal resources for their reproduction. New World slavery was the first and least-camouflaged expression of this capitalist logic.[114]

But if Blackburn's view captures the essence of the relationship between early modern slavery and capitalism, the question remains of the extent of its importance to the development of capitalism since the sixteenth century, and more particularly, to the origins of the Industrial Revolution in the late eighteenth and early nineteenth centuries. The early historians of the Industrial Revolution (1880–1945) were nearly unanimous in linking the expansion of British commerce of the eighteenth century, including the slave trade and plantation slavery, with the onset of industrial capitalism.[115] British Marxist historiography, including Hobsbawm's *Industry and Empire* (1964) and Christopher Hill's *From Reformation to Industrial Revolution* (1968), acknowledged the importance of this link.[116] After the Second World War a new trend in academic historiography surfaced, stressing the importance of British internal factors to the Industrial Revolution. It became dominant by the late 1960s and remained so until the 1980s.[117] The turn toward examining the roots of industrialism in Britain was obviously to be welcomed. But we cannot help noticing the connection between this Eurocentric trend and hostility towards the Williams thesis in these years, which coincided with decolonization and national liberation struggles in the third world.[118] Some still bearing the white man's burden were unwilling to acknowledge that there could be a relationship between capitalist development, the Industrial Revolution and slavery that might merit an apology.

Brenner of course cannot be counted as one of these. But among Marxists who have espoused the internalist view, it is he who has been most outspoken. In the first place, Brenner argues that the capital required to build the first factories was actually relatively slight. Accordingly, he questions whether a heaping-up of capital by primitive accumulation was required as a precondition for industrialization. Furthermore, along with others, he argues that it was the growth of the home market that was decisive to the development of the colonial trade. The growth of internal demand in Britain for colonial products was the independent variable that animated the Atlantic trade, which was subordinate to it.[119] Since the 1980s historiography in fact has veered back toward emphasizing the significance of overseas trade to industrialization. In 1982 Engerman and O'Brien wrote in strong support of the leading role of exports in the industrialization process in England between 1688 and 1802. They demonstrated that up to 50 percent of the non-agricultural workforce in England and Wales was employed in production for export. They showed that increases in overseas sales accounted for much of the increase in manufacturing output during the period.[120] Meanwhile Utsa Patnaik has shown the tremendous sums that Britain skimmed from the slave plantations and India through fiscal manipulation and re-export of colonial products. Liberal economists obsessed with computing comparative advantage in weighing up the balance of colonialism take little account of these realities she points out.[121]

It is Blackburn's work on slavery, meanwhile, which is the outstanding Marxist reflection of the trend toward taking the role of slavery and colonialism in industrialization seriously. In answer to Brenner, Blackburn admits that the initial outlays for factory construction tended to be relatively small. But he points out the huge sums invested in the laying down of infrastructure: canals, roads, harbours, docks, warehouses and shipping, all of which required capital. In addition, if manufacturers required relatively little fixed capital, they needed copious amounts of working capital or credit.[122] Much of this capital came from the Atlantic trade. Moreover, the overseas market was the most dynamic sector of the British market in the eighteenth century, and its range included the whole of the Americas. Its growth and volume cannot be accounted for by the growth of demand from the home market. Rather, profits from this sector provided much, if by no means all, of the capital required for industrialization.[123] As I pointed out earlier, dazzled as he is by the rise of the productivity of social labour under capitalism, Brenner loses sight of the source of the capital that made productivity growth possible.

Merchant capitalists were the most important backers of the first generation of industrial manufacturers. The mass-produced goods produced in the latter's factories were in good part aimed at the American market. This is especially true in the all-important cotton industry, where the connection between slave-trading merchants and producers of cotton goods, as well as metal and other manufactured products, was particularly close.[124] Finally, the direct connection between the development of the slave cotton plantation and the rise of cotton manufacture needs to be underlined. Cheap raw cotton from the Caribbean, then from the deep South of the United States, gave Britain its competitive edge, helping to inspire the spread of industrialization. Moreover, that success spurred the spread of slavery based on the cotton plantation.[125]

Overseas trade, the slave trade and the slave plantation clearly reinforced the development of capitalism and the Industrial Revolution. But Blackburn's account insists that capitalism battened on this

older mode of production and exploited it until it had exhausted
its possibilities. While underscoring the importance of slavery to the
emergence of industrial capitalism, Blackburn insists on its ultimate
limits. It is this that Byres explores in his treatment of the economic
development of capitalism from below in the United States. His main
stress is on the transformation of the petty producers of the United
States into capitalist farmers. But Byres emphasizes that this trend
was rivalled by the development of the slave plantation. In accord
with the views of Marx and the well-known historian of American
slavery Eugene Genovese, Byres argues that beyond a certain point,
slavery was incompatible with industrial capitalism. Byres criticizes
Fogel and Engerman's attempt to prove that the slave plantation was
an efficient form of capitalist enterprise. Not only did it have fundamental limitations with respect to making gains in productivity, it
cramped the development of the home market in the southern states.
This is obvious with regard to the impoverished slave population.
Not so evident was its effects on the million of white small rural
producers living in the slave states of the American South. Byres
observes that the Southern master class which politically ruled these
states shielded this class of farmers from the capitalist marketplace.
But in doing so it blocked the process of social differentiation which
was underway in the north and west. As a result, most of these
farmers were unable to serve as a home market for manufactures
in the South. Nor could they acquire the capital necessary for agricultural improvement, as was the case elsewhere in the American
Union.[126]

CONCLUSION

Looking back we can note that the theoretical conceptions of Lenin,
Trotsky and Marx have formed the basis of the argument of this
chapter that the state played a central role in the development of
capitalism. Lenin's idea of capitalism from above and below has
been our central guidepost. The cases of Prussia, Scotland and Japan
have been used to demonstrate that capitalism can develop as a
result of initiatives from the state and the landlord class. Trotsky's
insight into the role of combined and uneven development reinforces
the idea of the key role of the state in a capitalism imposed from
on high. But our account of the role of the American state demonstrates that politics were to the fore even in cases of capitalism from
below. Finally Marx's view of mercantilism as a use of the power
of the state as a means of accelerating the growth of the market

has guided our examination of the mercantile system. Moreover I have abided by his view that mercantilism above all reflected the interests of a rising bourgeoisie, albeit one initially contained within the shell of the absolute state. Furthermore I have insisted that the most successful mercantilisms were practised not by absolutist but by post-revolutionary capitalist regimes like Holland and England. Colonialism and slavery were two vitally important aspects of the mercantile system. Their relationship with the development of capitalism has been much disputed. I have sided with the position that they were critical to its development. Indeed, I have taken the position that colonialism and overseas slavery were vitally important to industrialization. Growing markets, plunder and profits from abroad proved essential to the Industrial Revolution at home. It is to the disputes over the origins and nature of the Industrial Revolution that we next turn.

6

THE INDUSTRIAL REVOLUTION: MARXIST PERSPECTIVES

The Industrial Revolution marked the climax of the long transition from feudalism to capitalism. Capital entered the productive process and transformed the means of production. Its arrival opened up the possibility of ending natural scarcity for the first time in human history. It also led to a vast extension of the West's global power. The West's hegemony over the rest of the world fostered an ongoing sense of European superiority over non-European peoples.

Much history of extremely high quality has been written about the Industrial Revolution by Marxist and non-Marxist scholars on the basis of deep empirical research, rigorous quantitative methodology and novel perspectives.[1] This account engages with some of the most controversial historical questions that have arisen in writing about this momentous event, questions that also turn out to have divided Marxist from non-Marxist scholars. While taking note of the contribution of non-Marxists throughout, it demonstrates the way that Marxist historians have decisively shaped the ongoing debate.

Marxist scholars have maintained, as Marx did, that the Industrial Revolution, although obviously significant, was less so than the inception of capitalism in the sixteenth century. The Industrial Revolution must be understood as capitalism's *dénouement*. Historical research has confirmed this view. In this light I shall demonstrate that although the Industrial Revolution did underwrite a European illusion of cultural superiority over the rest of the world, in fact its triumph arrived late, and proved more transitory and less absolute and unqualified than previously thought.

Marxists have tended to stress the socially and politically disruptive character of the period of the Industrial Revolution, while non-Marxists have emphasized its continuity with the past. The Marxist view would seem to be the more historically plausible. Not only do non-Marxist historians tend to ignore the disruptiveness of the Industrial Revolution, they are prone to downplay the attendant exploitation of the common people, whether the emergent working class or plantation slaves. While Marxists focus on changes in production and relations of production in explaining the Industrial Revolution, non-Marxist scholars of late rather questionably have stressed the importance of consumption. They have also, unfortunately as we shall see, tended to resort to a technological or intellectual determinism in the way they interpret the important relationship between the Scientific and Industrial Revolutions. Indeed, it is our view that non-Marxist historians of the Industrial Revolution tend to be excessively economistic and too dogmatically liberal in their approach.

The term 'Industrial Revolution' was coined in the first decade of the nineteenth century to refer to the mechanization and concentration of manufacturing already in progress. By the 1840s reference to the Industrial Revolution had become part of current English and French usage. Though it referred to major technical transformation, it already carried with it an implicit comparison with the immense impact of the French Revolution. It was in the 1830s that the term was first employed by Peter Gaskell in *The Manufacturing Population of England* (1833) in the decisive sense of a new order of society.[2]

As between Marx and Engels, it was Engels who first made use of the term Industrial Revolution in this more profound sense. In the introduction to his celebrated *The Condition of the Working Class in England* (1844), Engels referred to how:

> the history of the proletariat begins with the second half of the last century, with the invention of the steam-engine and of machinery for working cotton. These inventions gave rise, as is well known, to an industrial revolution, a revolution which altered the whole civil society; one, the historical importance of which is only now beginning to be recognized.[3]

According to Engels, the Industrial Revolution started with the introduction of machinery driven by the steam engine, beginning with the cotton factories. It not only created the proletariat – the revolutionary class of the future – it ushered in the transformation of the whole of society.

From our perspective, there are many senses in which the Industrial Revolution constitutes the climactic moment in the development of capitalism. It is the moment when capital entered and fully transformed industry. It is also the moment when the extraction of relative surplus value as a method of exploiting labour finally triumphed. The extraction of relative surplus value, or increases in productivity due to technological improvements or the redeployment of labour, had already played a part in the history of capitalism. Evident in the reorganization and gradual improvement of agriculture since the sixteenth century, it also was manifest in the restructuring of industry through the increasing division of labour in handicraft manufacture and the spread of the putting-out system. But as I have repeatedly argued, the effects of the extraction of relative surplus value on the capitalist economy were at first comparatively limited. Early capitalism depended mainly on the extraction of absolute surplus value, by extending the working day and year, intensifying work and keeping wages low. In this stage the extraction of increasing relative surplus value manifested itself in gradual and cumulative improvements in agriculture and rural industry. But the extraction of absolute surplus value remained fundamental to capitalist production. With the onset of the Industrial Revolution the extraction of relative surplus value became decisive. The introduction of machinery and the reorganization of production into centralized factories released the full productive potential of social labour organized by capital. The result was a dramatic rise in the share of industry in British national output.

Revisionism in the sense of questioning Marx's view of the Industrial Revolution has marked the ongoing debates on the Industrial Revolution. As we have noted, revisionism has stressed continuity as against the Marxist insistence on rupture. It has been sceptical of the Marxist view of the importance of the world market in favour of an internalist account of the growth of industry. In opposition to Marxist emphasis on changes in the relations of production, it has stressed the importance of consumerist demand as a factor. In this light it has cast doubt on the Marxist notion of the immiseration of the working class. Indeed, it has questioned the very notion of the existence of a working class. It has underscored the importance of ideas, especially scientific ideas, while ignoring their social context.

Challenges to the Marxist view have fuelled a stimulating and constructive historical debate on the Industrial Revolution while forcing Marxists to deepen and refine their analysis. Often made in the light of revisionist arguments, the contributions of Marxists like Steven Marglin and Harry Magdoff on the labour process, E. P. Thompson and Perry Anderson on the nature and culture of the working class, Hobsbawm and Thompson on the standard of living, Ben Fine and Ellen Leopold on consumerism have deepened understanding of the origins and effects of the Industrial Revolution.

It will be seen that contemporary Marxist scholarship like that of Marx and Engels has been focused above all on the effects of the Industrial Revolution on the working class. But debates between Anderson and Thompson have also fundamentally altered understanding of the nature of the capitalist class, while demonstrating that far from imposing a unitary view, Marxism can widen debate. Furthermore as we shall see, it was left-wing historians who made the connection between the English Revolution, the Scientific Revolution and the Industrial Revolution. As a result the Marxist view of the Industrial Revolution has more than held its own in the face of ongoing revisionist challenges. On the other hand, I shall argue that an appreciation of Marx's view of the origins of the Industrial Revolution remains indispensable to an understanding of it. Forming an essential part of Volume One of *Capital,* Marx's theoretical analysis of the changes in the relations of production and the productive process attendant on industrialization are basic to an understanding of his conception of capitalism itself.

HOBSBAWM AND THE OVERSEAS MARKET

As we saw in the Chapter 5, while profits of overseas trade, colonialism and slavery played a critical role in setting off the Industrial Revolution, Marx and most Marxist historians rightly stressed changes in the relations of production as decisive. In short order we will consider these innovations. In this section we follow through Chapter 5's argument by taking a closer look at the perspective of Hobsbawm, that doyen of nineteenth-century history who insisted most strongly of all Marxists on the importance of foreign trade and colonialism to the onset of industrialization. Hobsbawm's arguments, which encompass the long-drawn-out history of pre-industrial capitalism, illuminate the revolutionary nature of the changes wrought by the introduction of modern machine production and the industrial factory. But against the revisionist view which tends to ignore the overseas market and the history of colonialism, he reiterates the importance of the world market to the Industrial Revolution.

One of the celebrated quartet of Marxist historians which included Hilton, Hill and Thompson, we encountered Hobsbawm in the original debate on the transition, where he emphasized the importance of uneven development, then noted his work on the geographical reorganization of capitalism in the economic crisis of the seventeenth century. But while these contributions were important, Hobsbawm's main focus was the nineteenth century, whose primary

documents considered his historiographical home ground. Although
he touches on the Industrial Revolution at many points in his
writings, an early work, *Industry and Empire* (1969) sums up his
overall position.[4] According to Hobsbawm, the overseas market
– supported at every turn by government intervention – expanded
much more, and much more rapidly, than the home market in the
eighteenth century. As he puts it, 'home demand increased – but
foreign demand multiplied'.[5] And this market expansion overseas
decisively influenced the heart of the production process: most innovations of this period occurred in the production of goods which
were demanded by export markets. Cotton manufacture, the first
industry to be mechanized, was fundamentally tied to the export–
import sector. Its raw material had to be entirely imported from the
tropics or sub-tropics, and from the end of the eighteenth century
it sold the greater part of finished goods to colonial and overseas
markets.

British foreign policy focused on securing colonies and opening
up the markets of the rest of the world to British manufactures. The
victories of the British navy and army in the colonial wars of the
eighteenth and early nineteenth centuries meanwhile denied such
markets to French and Dutch competitors.[6] Hobsbawm adds that
that these military ventures further expanded industry and productivity, with major improvements in iron production and in machine
tools being sustained by large-scale orders from the Admiralty.[7]
Hobsbawm's insights on this score have been confirmed by more
recent writing, and it has become a truism that military expenditure
aided the progress of the eighteenth-century British economy.[8]

Hobsbawm's stress on the importance of the non-European
world to the Industrial Revolution in England in part reflected the
climate of opinion of the 1960s, when the anti-colonial movement
of the post-1945 period was at high tide. Hobsbawm repeatedly
compared early British industrialization with the industrialization
drives of the socialist and under-developed countries. His approach
was, of course, Marxist but also reflected an overall concern
with economic development in under-developed countries which
animated much Western historiography of the Industrial Revolution
during the period 1950–75,[9] though it should be admitted that
this historiography remained Eurocentric, with the influence of
the American modernization theorist Walt Rostow being more
noticeable than that of Marx or Lenin.

While putting the emphasis on the leading role of the market
overseas – its importance being as an outlet for most of the

products of leading industries like cotton – Hobsbawm also took into account domestic demand, which still provided the largest vent for manufactured products overall. Increase in population expanded both the labour force and consumer demand, although expanding poverty after 1750 placed clear limits on the latter. The main advantage of the home market was its size and dependability. It afforded a large underpinning for the development of an industrial economy, the stimulus for major and widespread improvements in inland transport, a strong base of demand for the coal industry and the dissemination of certain key technological innovations.[10] Overseas trade, military expenditure, colonial wars, protectionism and internal demand constituted the necessary and sufficient conditions for the Industrial Revolution according to Hobsbawm.

MARX ON MANUFACTURE AND INDUSTRY

In analyzing the reasons behind the Industrial Revolution, Marx put much more stress on developments within England than did Hobsbawm. According to Marx's account in the concluding chapters of Volume One of *Capital*, successive waves of primitive accumulation within England provided a stream of workers for the mechanized factories. The dispossession of the peasants likewise entailed the gradual undermining of rural industry and the eventual separation of agriculture and industry. This in turn widened the market for machine-produced industrial commodities. At the same time, agricultural improvement cheapened the price of wage labour.[11] As Marx depicted them in *Capital*, these changes occurred over a long-drawn-out period and then suddenly culminated in the Industrial Revolution in the late eighteenth and early nineteenth centuries. Of course we recall that elsewhere Marx took up Hobsbawm's point of stressing the importance of the development of the world market, including the development of colonialism under the aegis of the mercantile state. His view of the development of capitalism was that of a dialectical totality which included changes in the relations of production as well as exchange, or in other words realization.

Marx focused particular attention on the development of manufacture, in its original meaning of products of the hand during the long lead-up to the Industrial Revolution. He regarded the manufacture or handicraft workshop as the most advanced form of industrial enterprise prior to the introduction of power and machine-driven factory production. The economic advantage of the handicraft workshop lay in the division of labour within the enterprise.

Manufacture prefigured, and later evolved into, the mechanized factory. Indeed, Marx insisted that manufacture or handicraft workshop production was the characteristic and most advanced form of the capitalist mode of production between the sixteenth century and the last third of the eighteenth century. For Marx the distinguishing feature of the whole earlier phase of capitalism with which we have been preoccupied in this volume was manufacture. True, he placed great emphasis on the development of capitalist agriculture from the sixteenth century onward, but it is noteworthy that he called the whole period between the sixteenth and eighteenth centuries the age of capitalist manufacture not capitalist agriculture. In other words, what was decisive for him were those elements in the early modern period which prepared the ground for the Industrial Revolution: the revolution in the forces of production, or the break-through to centralized manufacture using power-driven machinery.[12] Revolution in this department had the potential to revolutionize all other sectors of the economy.

Rural and domestic handicrafts did not simply disappear in the face of the development of manufacture beginning in the sixteenth century. Rather they coexisted with and were reorganized by manufacture, according to Marx. The stage of manufacture, therefore, always rested on the handicrafts of towns and the domestic subsidiary industries of rural districts, over time destroying these in one form and resurrecting them in another. It produced a new class of small villagers who cultivated the soil as a subsidiary occupation, but found their chief occupation in domestic handicraft manufacture, the products of which they sold to the manufacturers directly, or through the medium of merchants.[13] In Marx's view the so-called putting-out industry of the early modern period constituted what he called the 'formal subsumption of labour to capital', a stage prior to its 'real subsumption'. Town merchants enlisted the services of spinners and weavers, but also tanners and ironsmiths and other artisans, in the rural areas, effectively subordinating them to urban manufacture, by taking over available and established labour processes, rather than transforming them and their technology internally as in the 'real subsumption' that would come later. Under merely formal subsumption, capitalists did however control access to the market, and so they controlled raw materials, means of subsistence and in many cases the instruments of production as well as credit.

Merely formal subsumption was an instance of what Marx described as the non-revolutionary way. Manufacture was the stage of handicraft workshop industry that immediately preceded modern machine production. His detailed and patient examination of manu-facture and its venerable place in capitalism's long early history underscored the tremendous and sudden breakthrough represented by the Industrial Revolution. The essential difference is the change from 'the formal subsumption of labour' to its 'real subsumption'. The latter, achieved by the introduction of machinery and the reor-ganization of production in the industrial factory, brings the worker under the complete or "real control" of the capitalist. This real subsumption of labour is what makes possible the full mobiliza-tion of social labour, which unleashes the enormous increase in the productive power of capital which is the hallmark of the Industrial Revolution.

Marx begins by describing the advance that the stage of early modern manufacturing represented over isolated craft production, which was common in the Middle Ages. He stresses the organiza-tion and technological innovations which set 'manufacture' off from earlier forms of industrial production. As a new form of productive organization, 'manufacture' was centered in a workshop of skilled hand workers under capitalist control, carrying out one or a variety of tasks. As a new process of production, it introduced the division of labour, though operations done by hand were still dependent on the skill of individuals and retained the character of a handicraft. Preoccupied with the eventual arrival of the Industrial Revolution, Marx was more concerned to point out the limitations of the system of manufactures than to detail all its different forms. He noted three basic inadequacies. First, because a hierarchical structure based on the division between skilled and unskilled workers was inserted into the division of labour, the number of unskilled workers could not be extended infinitely. Such a hierarchy among the workers entailed the ongoing power and influence of skilled workers, and prevented the full application of the division of labour.[14] The coming of the Industrial Revolution was to break the power of the skilled workers over production, allowing a full division of labour around machinery. Second, the narrow basis of handicraft itself excluded a really scientific division of the production process into its constituent parts.[15] The division of labour could only go so far, for all parts had to be capable of being done by hand, and each formed a separate handicraft. The Industrial Revolution centralized knowledge of production in the hands of capitalists and their managers. Workers lost their control of the separate stages of production. On the other hand, the centralization of knowledge allowed for a scientific reorganization of the whole production process.

The third and greatest problem, however, was the inability of
capital to seize control of the whole disposable labour time of
the manufacturing workers. Since handicraft skill is the foundation of manufacture, and since within manufacture mechanization
as a whole possesses no objective framework independent of the
workers themselves, capital is constantly compelled to wrestle with
the insubordination of the workers. Quoting Adam Smith, Marx
acknowledges that workers are made stupid and ignorant in the
stage of manufacture because they are forced to produce within
the increasingly narrow limits of their niche within the workshop
division of labour.[16] On the other hand, the refusal of workers
to submit to the discipline of the workplace and to allow capitalists to control their time is also a characteristic of the period of
manufacture: 'capital is constantly compelled to wrestle with the
insubordination of the workmen'.[17] Manufacture is able to give the
capitalist, rather than the workers, control of the product. But the
capitalist cannot equally control the workers. It is the distinguishing
feature of industrial capitalism that the capitalist finally achieves
this control over the production process and over the workers
themselves.[18]

The Industrial Revolution may be seen as arising out of the technical
progress made during the manufacturing period. The division of
labour in manufacture, for all its limitations, represented an advance
over the limited production possible through independent handicraft
production. Manufacturing streamlined, improved and multiplied the
tools and implements of labour, and introduced specialization and a
greater division of labour, setting the stage for the development of
industrial machines by inventors such as Arkwright and Watt, which
were made up of combinations of such instruments.[19] The purpose
of introducing machines into capitalist production was to increase
the rate of surplus value – the volume of surplus value divided by the
total of variable wages or variable capital.[20] But the effect is to greatly
expand the productive power of industry, especially as the introduction of machinery is spurred on by the effects of competition. Early
machines were in reality combinations of simple tools linked to a
motive force. As such Marx noted that the introduction of machinery
in the cotton industry predated the use of the steam engine as the
motive force.[21] The implication of this was that the perfection of the
steam engine was not a precondition of machine production but a
result of it.

It was the increasing accumulation of capital in the hands of
individual capitalists that set the stage for the revolution in the

mode of production. The introduction of machinery into capitalist industry issued, as Marx put it, from a process in which the
productiveness of labour ripened as if in a hothouse.[22] However,
it was only with the development of the modern factory based on
machine production that a sudden and complete transformation of
the conditions of labour took place, deserving the name revolution.
In manufacture the worker made use of a tool. In the industrial
factory the machine made use of the worker. The movement of the
instruments of labour proceeded from the actions of the workers
in manufacture. In the industrial factory it is the movements of the
machine that determined the movements of the workers. The worker
becomes a mere appendage of the machine: 'machinery is put to a
wrong use, with the object of transforming the workman, from his
very childhood, into a part of a detail-machine'.[23] Machine-factory
production thus facilitated the transition from the formal to the real
subsumption of labour to capital.[24] Furthermore in those sectors of
the economy where industrial capitalism became dominant, a new
type of capitalist – the captain of industry – emerged to rival the
traditional merchant capitalist or banker of the age of manufacture.
The new industrial capitalist organized and planned production
while wielding an unprecedented authoritarian discipline over the
workforce as required by machine production.[25]

DOBB AND THE PROLETARIAT

Dobb's views on the decline of feudalism and birth of capitalism
sought to resume and update Marx's own understanding, and in
doing so set off the transition debate. With respect to the Industrial
Revolution, Dobb summarized many of Marx's insights, and refined
them in the light of current historical research. Dobb saw the period
as one in which the productivity of labour increased based on rapid
technical change, the ranks of the proletariat greatly expanded, the
market for consumer goods and the size of capital investment grew
rapidly compared with the past.[26] But the transformation of the
means of production in the direction of mechanization was actually
a long-drawn-out process, with some sectors leading the way at
the end of the eighteenth century, while others clung to the older
methods of manufacture and domestic production until late in the
nineteenth century. The survival of these older methods of production meant that a homogenous factory proletariat did not emerge
until the last quarter of the nineteenth century.[27]
    Dobb argued that the relative scarcity of labour in the first part

of the eighteenth century helped to promote the technical innovation that brought on the Industrial Revolution. Once initiated, such
technical innovation enabled capital to save on labour: 'capitalism
as it expanded was able to economize on the parallel expansion of
its proletarian army'.[28] The subsequent growth of the proletariat
was based on the fact that the death rate fell toward the end of the
eighteenth century while the birth rate remained at a high level. The
death rate, and particularly the infant mortality rate, moved upward
again from 1815 in response to the deterioration in the standard
of living of the increasingly urbanized workers.[29] Meanwhile the
acceleration of enclosure, the ruin of handicraft industries and
the dismantling of the traditional Poor Laws added to the size
and flexibility of the labour market. Returning to a fundamental
theme of his earlier view of capitalist origins, Dobb insisted that
many of the emerging captains of industry were of humble origins.
They came from the ranks of master craftspeople or yeomen with
limited capital, while going into partnership with more substantial
merchant capitalists. As such they were more likely to be technologically and organizationally skilled themselves, and thus more capable
of controlling the productive process than the possessor of capital
alone. On the other hand, Dobb warned against making too much
of this in explaining the Industrial Revolution. Access to substantial
sources of capital was essential to the success of the new industrial
enterprises.[30]

THE LABOUR PROCESS

In the 1970s Stephen Marglin's 'What do bosses do? The origins
and functions of hierarchy in capitalist production'[31] and Harry
Braverman's *Labor and Monopoly Capital*[32] rekindled discussion
of the respective roles of technical and control functions in the
capitalist labour process, setting off a whole new enquiry. The first
challenged conventional ideas on the origins of the division of labour
and the factory system, arguing that both were introduced not for
reasons of efficiency, but because they offered capitalists the means
for greater control of their workforce and an opportunity to claim
a higher proportion of surplus value. Contrary to the accepted view
that the rise of the factory was caused by the introduction of power-
driven machinery, Marglin dismissed the idea of the 'technological
superiority' of the factory, and with it, the idea that labour processes
in capitalism were determined, at least to a significant extent, by
the requirements of technology. Factories existed, Marglin argued,

well before powered machinery, and what was really at stake in the Industrial Revolution was not efficiency, but social power, hierarchy and the discipline of labour. He also pointed out, and has recently emphasized, the way the factory itself became an impetus to technological innovation. Capitalists sought out and developed techniques that were compatible with large-scale factory organization. The adoption of the water frame in textile manufacturing was an example. Originally designed as a small machine turned by hand and capable of being used in the home, it was patented by Arkwright and only thenceforth built as a large-scale piece of machinery driven by water or steam power. Marglin argued that, even though the factory did not actually determine prevailing forms of work organization, capitalist control and machines were nevertheless most highly developed in the factory form of organization.

It was this high degree of capitalist control in the factory that in turn constrained the direction of the future development of technology: 'the key to the success of the factory, as well as its inspiration, was the substitution of capitalists' for workers' control of the production process; discipline and supervision could and did reduce costs without being technologically superior'.[33] The implication of Marglin's analysis was that only those technological innovations that allowed greater capitalist control can develop under capitalism. A new technology, however beneficial to the environment, will not be developed if it contradicts the quest for greater capitalist control. Contrariwise a technological innovation that would capture more surplus value by replacing intractable human labour with energy-hungry machinery is unlikely to benefit the environment. While there is much to Marglin's view, which stresses the role of machinery in ensuring more capitalist control over the social relations of production, contrary to his argument, it is important to stress that such machinery does increase the rate of surplus value as Marglin acknowledges, and under the force of competition must generalize itself. Furthermore, if only as a by-product, such machinery did vastly enlarge the forces of production, and that was a spectacularly important aspect of the Industrial Revolution.

Harry Braverman's *Labor and Monopoly Capital* also formulated connections between changes in technology and work organization. His book went back to the Industrial Revolution to seek the origins of scientific management and Fordism in order ultimately to comment on the implications of the computer revolution of the 1970s. It looked at phases of mechanization in the Industrial Revolution as an aspect of the history of the rise of scientific management. Braverman described the rise of the modern corporation in terms of the growth of automation. He emphasized the essential importance of capital's drive to gain control over the labour process in order to make more predictable the extraction of surplus value from workers. Such a drive leads to the homogenization of work and the reduction of skill required in productive jobs, an ongoing historical process which he claimed has continued into the present. Over time workers lose control over most aspects of the work process in the factory and became more and more deskilled. Such an argument ignores the increasingly common consciousness and economic interdependence produced by such a homogenization process. Moreover, the recent rise of so-called cognitive capitalism based on internet technology raises questions about the inexorable deskilling of work and the growing control of capital over the work process.

Both Marglin's and Braverman's works were published at a time when advanced computing technology and a new microelectronic revolution of the 1970s and 1980s were first becoming apparent. The future implications for employment, job structures and manufacturing organizations were predicted to be unprecedented, and so they have proved to be. But the final political and economic outcome of these developments remains undecided.

TECHNOLOGICAL DETERMINISM

As we have seen, Marx stressed the significance of the machine to the Industrial Revolution. According to Maxine Berg, Marx and his followers overdid this emphasis on the machine while failing to understand the ongoing importance of the division of labour. Berg is a professor at the University of Warwick who began her career researching the social and cultural dimensions of the Industrial Revolution, and has become increasingly interested in exploring its global context. According to her, in some industries it was the division of labour that proved revolutionary. The building industry is a good example. Historians have underlined the traditionalism of the building trades, as little new machinery was introduced in the nineteenth century. But the key to changes in the production process was not machinery, but the rise of general contracting from the 1830s: that is to say, a transformation in the organization of work. Marxists have also attributed far greater success to machinery in compelling the reorganization of the work process than the real history of, and evidence from, workplace struggles actually allows.

Berg also made a number of related criticisms of Marxist understandings of the labour process under capitalism. Though Marxists
argue that technological change is the outcome of struggles between
workers and capitalists, they have been from the start subject to,
and have failed to expunge, a linear framework of technological
determinism. Moreover, she argues, the search by Marxists for
examples of deskilling, divisions of labour and mechanization in
any historical period is inspired by questions and interpretations of
production and work suitable only to England and other modern
Western capitalist economies. Berg also accuses Marxists of seeking
to situate their individual studies in terms of key turning points that
marked out the transition to manufacture, or to modern industry as
the case may be. The result has been a failure to grasp the diversity
of the experience of industrialization. There were many alternatives
to mechanization in improved hand technology, the use of cheap
labour-saving materials, the division of labour and the simplifica-
tion of individual tasks, which were developed in their own right.
Finally, according to Berg, another problem of the Marxist perspective is its narrow focus on the workplace and production process.
The impact of the Industrial Revolution on culture, community and
family was ignored. This is a peculiarly 'male' perspective, and it is
not surprising that most historical studies of labour processes are
focused on a male labour force and male attitudes to work. Happily,
according to Berg, recent social historians have stressed the role of
the world outside of work in shaping the structure and attitudes of
the so-called labour aristocracy.[34]

Marx must be defended against Berg's criticisms because he was
by no means unaware of the impact of the Industrial Revolution
on more traditional industries. As a matter of fact, he noted that
in his own time manufactures still using the old methods like the
potteries, glass-making, baking and nail-making had fallen under
capitalist exploitation as much as the mechanized factories.[35]
Marx furthermore pointed out that the gradual prevalence of the
mechanized industries was important because it tended to force the
pace of capitalist change throughout the economy and to forecast
its future development. Moreover, in the final analysis Marx was
not an academic historian dwelling on the past but a revolutionary
communist. In stressing the importance of the machine and the
factory he was focusing on the most deep-seated and in the end the
most historically influential aspect of the Industrial Revolution. It
was the machine and factory that were the leading edge of a new era
which made possible the vast expansion of production that flowed

from the transformation of the mode of production. It was from the factory that the revolutionary figure of the industrial capitalist emerged, who commanded the industrial work force and would dominate the new age.[36] More important from the socialist perspective, the birth of the organized proletariat within the industrial factory held out the prospect of ultimately overturning the whole capitalist order. Berg's contention that Marx's and Engels's neglected consideration of family, community and family is a point well taken, though Engels's *The Condition of the Working Class in England* is a litany of the horrific effects of the Industrial Revolution on the moral and cultural state and the poor housing, clothing and food of workers and their families in the new industrial cities.

Other Marxists too come out better than Berg's criticisms suggest. Dobb noted the unevenness of the mechanization of industry, while the revered Marxist historian Raphael Samuel, a pioneer of the cultural history of the Industrial Revolution, demonstrated that the struggle over the introduction of machinery remained a crucial aspect of class struggle in many sectors of manufacturing well into the nineteenth century. Moreover, Samuel argues that far from superseding traditional sectors of manufacture, sectors dominated by mechanized industry more often than not incorporated these older methods of production rather than replacing them altogether.[37]

Mention of Samuel reminds us that he was among the chief inspirations of the *History Workshop Journal* founded in 1976. The journal consciously dedicated itself to the recovery of history from below. As such it assumed a deliberately socialist perspective in which feminism and Marxism had an important place. The culture of the Industrial Revolution – gender, family, urban life, entertainment and sports – was among its preoccupations. In this light Berg's insistence on the need to overcome a narrow Marxist economism in the study of the Industrial Revolution, while laudable, appears somewhat misplaced. Inspiring this turn toward understanding the culture of the working class above all was the towering figure of E. P. Thompson, who surpassed all his Marxist predecessors in recovering the origins of the English working class.

THOMPSON AND THE WORKING CLASS MAKING ITS OWN HISTORY …

Marx and Engels viewed the Industrial Revolution as a catastrophe for workers, who lost control of their work and were dispossessed, and whose standard of living was reduced to bare subsistence as a result. While Dobb was fully cognizant of these deleterious effects on workers, he tended to discount the social and political unrest that accompanied the Industrial Revolution, characterizing the period as one in which the working class remained deeply divided. To the contrary, Hobsbawm put stress on the level of social and political discontent during the period. In his study of the Industrial Revolution and in other writings, he underlined the successive waves of Luddite and radical, trade-unionist and utopian-socialist, and finally democratic and Chartist agitation that characterized the period 1815–48. According to Hobsbawm, 'no period of British history has been as tense, as politically and socially disturbed, as the 1830s and early 1840s, when both the working class and the middle class ... demanded what they regarded as fundamental changes'.[38] It was the Industrial Revolution as well as the French Revolution that brought the people, and more especially the proletariat, onto the stage of modern history.

But it was Thompson – another in the quartet of great British Marxist historians – who most deeply and controversially explored the cultural and social meaning of the Industrial Revolution, and his work gave rise to the greatest number of critical controversies. Thompson was motivated by a profound commitment to reconstituting the history of the English working class, rescuing it from its internment in the archives. He began this work by taking up Marx's remarks, which we have already noted, about the lack or refusal of discipline among workers in the pre-industrial economy. In a brilliant article entitled 'Time, work discipline and industrial capitalism', Thompson explored the relaxed discipline characteristic of the pre-industrial work force and the trauma of work intensification that came with the imposition of machine and factory methods of production.[39] Moreover, it was impossible fully to understand the response of the mass of the English population to the Industrial Revolution without taking account of the pre-industrial traditions of popular protest which reached far back into English history: religious non-conformity, notions of the rights of free-born Englishman, and the ideologies that helped to galvanize eighteenth-century popular protest.[40] In explaining the behaviour of the pre-industrial mob, Thompson, in a famous article published in *Past and Present*, singled out the existence of a popular ideology or moral economy of provision which rejected the unrestricted application of the laws of the market, of supply and demand, especially when it came to the availability of bread in times of dearth.[41] Since Thompson wrote, we note parenthetically, it has been demonstrated that pre-industrial protest shaped the character not only of the working class but of capitalism itself. The researches of historians like Berg and Andy Wood have shown that worker resistance or its absence helped determine the forms of industrial organization that emerged in different sectors of the economy.[42]

These currents of resistance resurfaced powerfully in the period of feverish revolutionary agitation in England which followed the taking of the Bastille in France in 1789. As part of this wave of protest which engulfed intellectuals, artisans and members of the radical-ized middle class, workers took an increasing part. Government repression during the Napoleonic Wars only strengthened demo-cratic resolve: 'while the [revolutionary] years 1791–5 provided the democratic impulse, it was in the repressive years that we can speak of a distinct "working class consciousness" maturing'.[43] Sympathy for revolutionary political change served as an impetus which helped to strengthen nascent working-class organizations.[44]

The new steam-driven factories struck contemporaries as embodying forces which were transforming nature itself: 'the mill appeared as symbol of social energies which were destroying the very "course of Nature"'.[45] Some commentators expressed alarm at the potential power not only of the new middle class of indus-trial capitalists, but also of the mass of workers who stood behind them.[46] To observers on the left and right, there seemed a direct correlation between steam power, the factory and the tumultuous emergence of the working class. According to such witnesses, the appearance of this new class was reflected in the waves of agitation that marked the years between the close of the Napoleonic wars and the mid-century, culminating in the Chartist movement.[47] Thompson disagreed. He insisted, on the contrary, that most of the unrest was focused in the ranks of the craftspeople and workers in the old crafts and industries rather than among the new mill hands. It was against the intrusion of familiar enemies like the master, the Tory magistrate and the parson that these craft workers protested in the first place.[48] In other words traditional complaints against the lack of democracy, the cost of living and political corruption continued to animate much of the social dissent.

Over time more and more protest came to include demands for the right to organize unions.[49] Such protest represented an outgrowth and amplification of the unrest of the eighteenth century and the French Revolutionary period. Indeed, the state and employers deliberately associated it with a detested revolutionary French Jacobinism.[50]

Despite echoes of the past, Thompson argues that the period between 1790 and 1830 saw the formation of the working class. This was reflected above all in the growth of class consciousness, the sense of an identity of interests between the diverse groups of working people as against the interests of other groups. It was manifest, likewise, in the eventual maturation of working-class political and industrial organization: 'by 1832 there were strongly based and self-conscious working-class institutions – trade unions, friendly societies, educational and religious movements, political organizations, periodicals – working class intellectual traditions, working-class community patterns and a working-class structure of feeling'.[51] But Thompson insisted that the formation of the working class was not the spontaneous product of the factory system. An external force – the Industrial Revolution – was not imposed on the undifferentiated mass of the population and did not single-handedly generate a working class. Rather, changing productive relations and working conditions associated with the Industrial Revolution interacted with the radical religious political and cultural traditions of the previous century and, in the hands of their heirs, resulted in the institutions, culture and social organization which became the English working class. According to Thompson, 'the making of the working class is a fact of political and cultural, as much as of economic history'.[52] At this point Thompson was not only invoking the agency of the working class in its own making, he was also insisting on the open-endedness and political nature of the historical process of class formation. For Thompson class is a political category. Thompson's project was not simply about recovering the history of the working class. It was about reasserting the agency of this class as the driving force of history against what he regarded as the attempt by Stalinism to repress such agency.

... BUT NOT IN CIRCUMSTANCES OF ITS OWN CHOOSING

This insistence on the centrality of working-class self-assertion was important in reintroducing the importance of culture and agency in Marxism. But they also proved very controversial. Thompson admitted that the development of capitalist industry had something to do with the emergence of the working class. But he put his emphasis upon the notion that the working class emerged through a history of its own making. It was above all the development of its collective consciousness that made it into a class, in his view. Thompson's stress on the importance of the cultural determinants

of class subsequently led some poststructuralist thinkers to a
questioning of the notion of class altogether. Scholars like Patrick
Joyce and Garth Stedman Jones took Thompson's emphasis on the
cultural aspect of class to the point of rejecting the Marxist notion
of class-in-itself, the insistence that the existence of a class must
reflect their common relations to the means of production as well
as 'class-for-itself', the consciousness of this common condition, the
political aims and projects and cultural trends that develop out of
it. For these poststructuralists, to tie economic and social location to
consciousness is to be economically determinist. Class has meaning
only in so far as its members recognize themselves to be members of
such a grouping, irrespective of any 'objective' or 'economic' determination. According to them, English workers demonstrably did
not recognize themselves as such. Those who insist on the existence
of class-in-itself in their eyes are guilty of class essentialism. On
this basis, these poststructuralists have questioned whether English
workers during the Industrial Revolution can be considered to have
belonged either to a class-in-itself or class-for-itself.[53]

Thompson disassociated himself from such a culturalist view,
which went with the suggestion that he had distanced himself from
the emphasis on economic and material factors characteristic of his
fellow British Marxist historians, particularly Dobb:

> I find actively unhelpful recent attempts to suggest a rupture in
> British Marxist historiography between the work of Maurice
> Dobb and the historiography of the 1960s (including the work of
> myself ...). I see on both sides of this supposed 'break' a common
> tradition of Marxist historiography submitted to an empirical
> discourse (albeit with differing emphases); and 'culturalism' is a
> term which I refuse.[54]

We would expect nothing else from someone who was not merely a
historian, but a committed historical materialist and political revolutionary. Indeed, Thompson's understanding of class as political
rather than something merely cultural should be underscored.

In *The Poverty of Theory*, Thompson's celebrated diatribe
against the structuralism of Louis Althusser (and Perry Anderson),
he sought to situate himself at some distance from others' attempts
to emphasize economic or social determinism. In his polemic
Thompson denounced what he thought of as Althusser's arbitrary
imposition of an unbefitting theoretical straitjacket on the concrete
facts of history. Nonetheless, it seems to us, as Perry Anderson has

suggested, that Thompson bent the branch too far – viewing class too much in terms of class-for-itself, its degree of consciousness and political organization.[55] Consequently he conceded too much to the poststructuralist critics of Marxism, who in the name of an empiricist or linguistic immanentism rejected what they called essentialism or the possibility of abstraction from the empirical, and in so doing discarded the Marxist view of history altogether.

Marx could never be accused of insisting on a one-to-one correspondence between thought and concrete historical facts. According to him, the two were separate in the sense that thought has its own specificity and the facts of history have an existence independent of thought. As a result, the order of exposition of the categories of thought differed from that which was manifest in the relations of real historical development. A process of abstraction was necessary to avoid limiting thought to the mere repetition of the concrete things that happened in history. Abstraction, which lay at core of Marx's method, allowed the interpretation of society in its complex manifestations. On the other hand, in order for this process of interpretation to be successful abstractions had to be constantly compared to historical realities so that the general logical determinations remained in accord with concrete history, while being distinguished from it.[56]

With regard to the existence or not of a working class during the Industrial Revolution, then, its existence as a class-in-itself would represent an abstraction from the relations of production existing in English society at that time. As such, it represents what may be described as a logical tendency which underlies the concrete historical circumstances. The existence or not of the working class as a class-for-itself then becomes a matter of interpreting the concrete historical realities of the period, which contrary to Stedman Jones and Joyce are still in dispute.[57] Richard Price, for one, believes that the period of the Industrial Revolution was a transitional age from the point of view of class relations. He interprets the late eighteenth and first part of the nineteenth century as a period in which paternalistic class relations decayed as well as the autonomy of wage workers characteristic of the seventeenth and eighteenth century. An industrial system of class relations in which the industrial proletariat became paramount crystallized toward the end of the nineteenth century.[58] In other terms older forms of class relations were decaying and new forms based on industrialization were being formed.

As is the way with poststructuralism, the culturalists arbitrarily and irrationally reject out of hand the method of abstraction. For

them the surface of things as revealed by its discourses is all that
matters. Reacting against the preconceived idea of some Marxists
that society can be thought of as made up of the interconnected
abstractions of a bounded system, they have replaced it with the
notion that it can be understood through a self-referential notion
of language or an all-encompassing concept of culture which subor-
dinates, dissipates or even excludes the categories of the social,
economic and political. Behind this cultural or idealist turn lies
a deep social pessimism, born of the revolutionary failures of the
1960s and the triumph of neoliberalism.

THE HUMAN COST

While Thompson's historiography of the working class, with
its brilliant evocation of popular subjectivity but lack of structural foundation, may have divided him from some Marxists, his
historiography of the Industrial Revolution, which reinstated the
catastrophic view of the Industrial Revolution, beat a path back to
traditional emphases. As studied first by Marx and Engels and then
amplified by historians like Arnold Toynbee, Beatrice and Sydney
Webb, and John Lawrence and Barbara Hammond, the period of
the Industrial Revolution was seen as one of economic instability,
poverty and exploitation. However, recent revisionist academics
have been interested less in the victims of industrialization than in
the rate of economic growth, less in the human cost of enclosure
than in improvements in agricultural output, less in exploitation and
ruthless competition than in dislocations, immature financial institutions and exchange, uncertain markets and the inevitable course of
the trade cycle.

These practitioners of what Thompson termed the anti-
catastrophic orthodoxy criticize the lack of precision of the older
catastrophic school. Thompson, in turn, challenged this new school
for its moral complacency, narrowness of frame of reference and
ignorance of the actual working-class movements of the time.[59] He
sought to gauge the historical meaning of the Industrial Revolution
from the perspective of a historian with a profound understanding
not merely of England in the throes of industrialization, but of the
social tempos of pre-industrial England. Thereby he put himself in
a position to measure the full human cost of industrial capitalism in
a way that escaped others.

Thompson's achievement is clearest in his contribution to the
so-called standard of living debate. The human cost of the Industrial

Revolution was an active issue for those who lived in the nineteenth century, and was much debated then. In the twentieth century it gave rise to the standard of living controversy among academic historians. It began with the publication of J. H. Clapham's *Economic History of Great Britain* (1926) and John Hammond's essay 'The Industrial Revolution and discontent' in the *Economic History Review* (1930). Using quantitative data, Clapham claimed that the average wage of industrial and agricultural workers increased by some 60 percent between 1790 and 1850. Hammond sought to raise doubts regarding Clapham's data by invoking the argument of previous critics like Toynbee, who stressed the deterioration in the quality of life but was largely ineffectual in dealing with the statistical evidence. And though Clapham's intellectual heir T. S. Ashton questioned his mentor's calculations in the 1950s, he agreed with Clapham that the Industrial Revolution had improved, rather than worsened, the lot of workers. It was not until 1957 that a more serious debate began when Hobsbawm entered into the fray. He began by criticizing the weakness of Hammond's reply to Clapham, while seeking to show that both the quality of life and the material standard of living of the working classes worsened during the Industrial Revolution. Like Ashton, he criticized Clapham's estimate of wages. He explored the question of mortality rates and unemployment, and while not being able to reach definitive conclusions, argued that the data suggested a worsening in the standard of living of workers. The main weight of his argument rested on evidence regarding levels of food consumption, which appeared to have declined. Hobsbawm was then answered by R. M. Hartwell who, in addition to disputing the points made by Hobsbawm, argued for an improvement in living standards based on the changing size and distribution of national income.[60]

As we would expect, Thompson placed himself squarely in the pessimists' camp without, however, allowing his underlying sense of moral indignation over this matter to cloud his scholarly judgement. On the question of the distribution of the national income, for example, he acknowledged the difficulties of determining the division of income between classes, and was prepared to concede that workers might even have seen a slight improvement in wages over the period 1790–1840. According to him, the meaning of any such hypothetical improvement was derisory in the face of the evidence that as a result of industrialization workers were more exploited, more insecure and more miserable than before. In his eyes what mattered most was the political and cultural trauma inflicted on workers by industrialization.[61] He conceded that the substitution of the potato for bread was nutritionally beneficial to workers, but he observed that no longer being able to afford the traditional white bread was taken as a mark of working-class humiliation. The consumption of meat, likewise, was a mark of status as well as having nutritional value. Meat consumption, he observed, declined between 1790 and 1850, but he admitted it was difficult to be definitive.[62]

On the other hand, his overall conclusion was scathing: 'his [the worker's] own share in the "benefits of economic progress" consisted in more potatoes, a few articles of cotton-clothing for his family, soap and candles, some tea and sugar, and a great many articles in the *Economic History Review*'.[63] On housing and the urban environment, he was even more bleak:

> this deterioration of the urban environment strikes us today, as it struck many contemporaries, as one of the most disastrous of the consequences of the Industrial Revolution, whether viewed in aesthetic terms, in terms of community amenities, or in terms of sanitation and density of population.[64]

The standard of living debate continued for the next half-century in article after article based on increasingly refined and sophisticated data. Its outcome has recently been summed up by Hans-Joachim Voth in the first volume of the academically authoritative *Cambridge Economic History of Modern Britain* (2004).[65] According to Voth, research since the 1980s lends increasing credence to the pessimist view. Real wages failed to increase by anywhere near the amount suggested by earlier calculations. Any gains made were likely the result of longer hours at more intensive work. Thompson's views on the horrors of life in the cities, furthermore, have been mainly sustained. Infant mortality remained quite high, life expectancy and average height at maturity disturbingly low as the Industrial Revolution unfolded through the first half of the nineteenth century.[66] On the question of lowered life expectancy, Thompson's view had already been anticipated by Hobsbawm.[67] Their common pessimism has been entirely vindicated by recent research.[68]

The debate over the consequences of the Industrial Revolution was not about the wisdom or not of economic growth. Marxists and non-Marxists both agreed that overcoming scarcity was important. The dispute centered around whether or not such growth came, and continues to come, at an acceptable human and environmental cost. Non-Marxists tended to ignore or deny that there were such costs in the past, and to minimize the possibility that there will be greater costs in the future. For them more or less unlimited capitalist growth is axiomatically positive, resolving the problems of the past and helping to resolve those of the future. On the contrary, Marxists do not regard economic growth as an end in itself. In their view it was important to recall the human and environmental price in order to fortify the working class politically with the memory and purpose of its historic struggle. The goal of growth in the past from a working-class perspective was to achieve economic sufficiency. Any back-of-the-envelope calculation of the relationship between current levels of world population and global GDP reveals that such material sufficiency is now possible. The justification for further human privation or environmental deterioration has disappeared. The issue for the twenty-first century is not further material growth, but redistribution of existing wealth on a world scale.

PROTO-INDUSTRIALIZATION

For Marx the modern factory was the most advanced form of industry and the birthplace of the industrial proletariat, which he believed would destroy capitalism. Hence he sought to identify the antecedents of such factories. He found them in the early modern 'manufacture' or large handicraft workshop and its workforce, which were the most advanced form of economic organization of the period preceding the Industrial Revolution. Rural industry in his view was merely an extension and dependency of such manufactures. But a recent historical school has identified the domestic manufacture or rural putting-out systems as a distinct historical phase which preceded and paved the way for industrialization proper. The point of this model is to direct historians to the regional and rural economy, not simply to agriculture, and to the country cottage rather than the urban workshop, as the crucial transitional site of economic development. This economic phase is now popularly known as 'proto-industrialization'.

The concept was first used by Franklin Mendels in an article published in the *Journal of Economic History* (1972), and the word and the concept soon became current in the writings of early modern economic historians.[69] A Marxist version of proto-industrialization was laid out by Peter Kriedte, Jürgen Schlumbohm and Hans Medick.[70] Economic historians have long recognized the existence and importance of the great increase in manufacturing production in the countryside between the seventeenth and nineteenth centuries. This rural industry, practised in conjunction with agriculture, has now been elevated into the crucible of early modern economic and social change. It is maintained that proto-industrialization paved the way for the factory system and wage labour, or in short industrialization. The development of proto-industrialization from the seventeenth to the nineteenth centuries was closely connected with the expansion of the market in Europe and overseas. The world market for mass-produced goods grew at such a pace from the later sixteenth century that traditional urban manufacturers could not efficiently respond, hampered as they were by guild restrictions and high labour costs. Complementary agricultural development entailed increasing regional differentiation between arable and pastoral regions. An inter-regional symbiosis based on comparative advantage came into being.

An underemployed peasantry in pastoral regions became the basis for a flexible and self-exploiting industrial labour force, and the industry it took up improved the seasonal employment of labour. The possibilities of alternative industrial employment broke through the traditional limits placed on population growth by the size of landholdings. Rural workers, living as they did in a world of traditional peasant culture and values, took less than the customary urban wage for their industrial work, and laboured more intensively in the face of falling wages. Access to small amounts of land enabled them to produce part of their own subsistence. Their dispersal across the countryside, furthermore, made it difficult for them to organize to prevent wage reductions by merchants. Access to this cheaper labour force, therefore, gave merchants a differential profit, one which was above the usual urban rates. This differential profit in turn provided a major source for capital accumulation.

Proto-industry is credited not just with being a source of labour and capital, but, in addition, with providing the entrepreneurship and the technical and organizational changes which led to the first major increases in productivity before the factory.[71] In the specifically Marxist version of proto-industrialization as conceived by Kriedte, Schlumbohm and Medick, proto-industrialization is seen as an intrinsic feature of the transition from feudalism to capitalism. In this version stress is laid on the contribution that proto-industrialization made to the growth of the labour supply necessary to the eventual Industrial Revolution. Proto-industry developed in regions where peasants exploited substandard agricultural land and were forced to seek employment to supplement their income. Alternately social differentiation and enclosure led to land shortage. The goal of those family households that became involved in proto-industry was, in the first instance, to preserve as much as possible of the norms of the subsistence peasant economy.

At the same time, merchant capital employed the inexpensive labour of such rural populations to supply growing foreign markets, bypassing guild restrictions in the towns. Over time involvement in proto-industry upset the traditional balance between land and population of feudal-peasant society in favour of expanding labour supplies resulting from early marriage. Proto-industrial rural households tended to be more egalitarian, without the rigid division of labour typical of patriarchal peasant families. Such families increasingly took on the characteristics of a proletariat. The demographic increase which resulted from the proliferation of such families set the stage, at least in England, for the mechanization and concentration of production.

While the latter might have happened in some regions of England, it should be pointed out that most regions of that country and the rest of Europe where proto-industry established itself over the course of centuries did not see a transition to mechanized and concentrated industries. On the contrary, most such areas eventually witnessed deindustrialization. Where industrialization eventually did develop, concentration and mechanization appeared to develop not out of the character of proto-industry but rather as a result of attempts to overcome its negative features: high inventories, high transaction costs, poor work intensity, theft, weak quality control and a lack of flexibility in adapting to market change.[72] Marx's view, which stressed that such rural industry was a mere adjunct to the large, hierarchically organized manufacturing urban workshop which he regarded as the true precursor of the modern factory, appears to me to be more convincing.[73] Furthermore for Marx the concentrated workforce at the site from within which the modern proletariat was spawned was a matter of not merely economic but also political significance.

But political commitment ought not to blind scholars to appreciating the full historical significance of a great economic change such as the Industrial Revolution. As an apologist for capitalism during the upheaval of the Industrial Revolution, Thomas Malthus complained that lack of sexual restraint on the part of the working class led inevitably to over-population and unalterable misery. The destitution of the emergent working class was its own fault. In response to this patently ideological argument, Marx in high dudgeon correctly pointed out that the true culprit was industrial capitalism, whose drive to accumulate was producing the relative surplus population or so-called reserve army of labour necessary to hold down wages. As a result of this dispute, Wally Seccombe argues that Marxists have wrongly shied away from including demographic factors in the analysis of capitalism and other modes of production. Without such an analysis no fully materialist analysis of capitalism is possible.

He bases his analysis on Marx's observation that 'every special historic mode of production has its own special laws of population, historically valid within its limits alone.'[74] Closely following Marx's own quite subtle analysis of the question of population, Seccombe urges that the specific fertility regime of major classes, including peasant and working-class producers, must figure in the analysis of a mode of production. Such a fertility regime should include cultural as well as social and economic factors.[75] In other words whereas Malthus treated population as an independent variable, it ought properly to be broken down and analyzed in terms of the evolution of a particular mode and its social relations of production. As to proto-industrialization Seccombe agrees that increases in fertility that attended proto-industrialization made possible part of the population growth which was necessary to the Industrial Revolution and the creation of a reserve army of labour. But drawing on recent research, he argues that higher fertility and increases in population after 1750 were the result of the more general and widespread phenomenon of West European proletarianization.[76] A fully materialist analysis of this critical period of capitalism requires that horizons be expanded beyond merely the production of an industrial labour force in England to the European development of capitalism overall.

THE INDUSTRIOUS REVOLUTION

Jan de Vries takes a sanguine view of proto-industrialization, seeing it as an element in what he labels as an industrious revolution. De Vries's concept of industrious revolution is meant to downgrade the historic significance of the Industrial Revolution proper. As a Continental historian focused on the early modern period in Holland, de Vries has been sceptical of an approach that is focused on the uniqueness of English capitalist development and its Industrial Revolution. The starting point of his analysis is a new academic perspective which downgrades the scale of economic change during that period.

Recent scholarship by quantitatively orientated economic

historians has given rise to a new consensus that the rate of economic growth in the Industrial Revolution was much less spectacular than originally believed. Earlier estimates of growth between 1760 and 1830 have been roughly halved. The long-term transformative effects of the new technology and modes of organization of this period are not denied, but it is argued that their weight in the overall economy was not substantial until the latter half of the nineteenth century.[77] Such a view at first glance diminishes the importance of technological innovation and other increased supply factors in initiating modern economic growth. This new perspective also lends some support to Marglin's contention that the initial purpose of industrialization was to increase capitalist control over the workforce, and that it was not driven by the requirements of a more productive new technology. But this might also suggest that we should look upon the coming of industrialization not as a once-and-for-all breakthrough of industrial machinery, but as a less sensational and much more prolonged history of cumulative technological progress. Indeed, Andy Wood has argued that early forms of industrial capitalism are to be found already in the seventeenth century in the metalware-producing regions of the West Midlands, the textile region of the West Riding, the lead fields of Derbyshire, the northern Pennines and Yorkshire and the Newcastle coal fields.[78] David Levine and Keith Wrightson take a similarly long view in their study of coal mining in Newcastle between 1560 and 1765.[79]

The implications of this research for Marxist scholarship are complex. On the one hand, it lends credence to the fundamental Marxist contention that the birth of capitalism in the sixteenth century was more historically decisive than the eventual Industrial Revolution. On the other hand, it also leads us to reconsider the historical significance of the distinction between the revolutionary and non-revolutionary paths to capitalism which was so important to Marx and Dobb. For them the revolutionary path was revolutionary because it entailed a reorganization or even a transformation of the means of production. The non-revolutionary path entailed a merely formal and external control of such means of production by merchant capital. As such, however, it could be connected with that other characteristic of early modern industry noted by Marx, the resistance of craft producers to industrial discipline. Resistance to such changes by producers and merchant capitalists was likely responsible for much of the delay in the onset of the Industrial Revolution.[80] Indeed, it is noteworthy that the first industry to undergo mechanization was the cotton industry, which was in fact a virtually new industry which came into being largely independent of the traditional textile trades. Older sectors of industry tended to resist such innovation.

To return to de Vries, his argument that the economic impact of the Industrial Revolution was not really felt until the second half of the nineteenth century implies that the most important economic changes came not in the Industrial Revolution but in the centuries prior to it. It was this early modern period that prepared the ground for the subsequent Industrial Revolution. It came about as a result of the so-called industrious revolution of the period from the sixteenth to eighteenth century, which affected not only England but the rest of Northwest Europe. According to de Vries, research has revealed the period preceding the technological breakthroughs of the Industrial Revolution to have been much more economically dynamic in England and on the Continent than previously believed. At the core of this dynamism lay changes in the relationship between the family-household economy and the market.[81] Such a view reminds of us of the fact that capitalism did not develop simply in England but in the whole northwest quadrant of Western Europe.

This research confirms that prior to the seventeenth century the number of hours worked and the intensity of work was much less than today. As a result society was leisure-rich for the great majority. In the seventeenth century the birth of a new urban and consumer society, based on an intensification of labour and greater specialization and division of labour, began to undermine this relaxed approach.[82] The amount of family labour per year oriented to the market increased, as did the purchase of commodities by family households. One way that such households increased money income available for the purchase of consumer goods was by increasing agricultural productivity, not through technological improvement, but by dint of reduced leisure and intensified work on the land.[83] The deepening of rural markets gradually led to the displacement of labour out of direct agricultural work toward rural transport, crafts and manufacture. Thus, whereas 75 percent of labour time in the countryside was devoted to agriculture in the early sixteenth century, this declined to approximately 50 percent by 1800.[84]

According to de Vries the chief implication of recent research is that proto-industry was about family-households redeploying female and child labour from subsistence agriculture toward money-producing commercial activity. While not doubting the involvement of family members in proto-industry, de Vries questions whether the

members of the household formed a single working unit, as proponents of the theory of proto-industrialization have argued.[85] From
the seventeenth century more and more female labour independent of
the family became engaged in the production of ready-made clothes.
Rising demand prompted the expansion of a retail clothing industry
which included tailors, dressmakers, seamstresses and second-hand
clothes dealers, many of whom were women. According to de Vries
over the course of the eighteenth and early nineteenth century 'one
can speak of a gradual feminization of retailing'.[86]

Over the period 1500–1800 both the intensity and duration of
work increased. De Vries observes that the Protestant Reformation
played a not insignificant part in facilitating this change by instilling
a work ethic and helping to suppress holy days.[87] That this period
of early modern capitalism saw a redeployment and some intensification of labour seems plausible. It fits well with the view that
while the exploitation of relative surplus value slowly increased, the
extraction of absolute surplus value remained centrally important
through the first three centuries of capitalism. It is suggestive as
well of a capitalist economy in which human labour as well as draft
animals and wind and water power played a much greater role than
in the capital and fossil-fuel intensive economy we inhabit.

There seems little to object to in de Vries's overall contention
that a more efficient use of labour helped to prepare the way for
the Industrial Revolution.[88] His further claim that the expansion of
internal demand played a role in the move to industrial capitalism
seems uncontroversial, at least on the surface.[89] On the other hand,
the second element of his 'industrious revolution', that increased
demand based on rising wage income in the family household was
what mobilized this more effective deployment of labour, appears
more questionable. De Vries provides evidence of a considerable
expansion of the market for consumer goods across a broad range
of commodities in the eighteenth century. He shows that parts of the
working class were able to increase purchases of coffee, tea, tobacco,
ready-made clothes and even watches in the same period.[90] On the
other hand, his evidence suggests that for workers the family-household was not an important site of either production or significant
market-based consumption.[91] Individual members of workers' families
found employment. But the actually quite limited number of relatively
cheap items bought in the market for consumption by workers were
consumed individually rather than by the family. In other words, the
working-class family did not act together as a productive unit, nor
did it practise collective consumption. As a result de Vries fails to

demonstrate that a rise of overall family-household income among workers was able significantly to compensate for stagnant real wages or per capita income during the Industrial Revolution. As we shall see, there is little evidence of a consumerist revolution among the working class.[92]

De Vries's industrious revolution is part of a current trend in historiography which seeks to shift the emphasis from supply to demand in explaining the Industrial Revolution. Basing itself on the somewhat exaggerated notion that the contemporary economy is built on consumption, it sees the origins of modernity, and indeed the Industrial Revolution, in the growth of this same consumption. Ben Fine and Ellen Leopold observe that this perspective on the Industrial Revolution is especially attractive to right-wing historians. Fine and Leopold argue that it is a perspective which stresses individual choice and consumer satisfaction, associates economic progress with the consuming rich both old and new, and draws attention from Marxist preoccupations with work, production and class.[93] Fine and Leopold have asserted with some exaggeration that the notion that demand can play a significant role in major economic change is quite weak. Rather, I would say that it could not play such a role until wages began to rise in the advanced capitalist countries after 1880. Demand certainly could not assume such a position under the conditions appertaining during the Industrial Revolution, which included declining real wages.[94] The purchase of new clothes which would have expanded demand was largely beyond the means of workers. Rather, it was through the acquisition of hand-me-downs from their betters or through the second-hand market that they acquired their apparel. Mass markets for manufactured clothes did not emerge until the second half of the nineteenth century.[95]

THE SCIENTIFIC REVOLUTION

Like de Vries, Margaret Jacob viewed the seventeenth and eighteenth centuries as decisive for the Industrial Revolution. But for her it was the contribution of the Scientific Revolution to creating a new scientific and technological culture that was critical to the breakthrough of the Industrial Revolution. Moreover she situated the roots of this movement in the context of the English Revolution. I have previously stressed the social and political importance of the English Revolution to the full institutionalization of capitalism. It

brought the state under the control of capitalist property owners
and abolished the political and social barriers in the way of further
capitalist development. According to Jacob, the essential context
for the emergence of the new science, likewise, was the English
Revolution:

> the English Revolution shaped both science and its [social] inte-
> gration, not only in England but, as English science spread, also
> in much of the Western world. ... By 1660 and the end of the first
> phase of the English Revolution, the prosperity of the English state
> came to be seen as linked – at first tentatively and then decisively –
> with the development of science and technology.[96]

The political and social upheaval which overthrew the established
order of society also established the new scientific culture. It shaped
the natural philosophical thought of Isaac Newton and Robert
Boyle, moving them towards a mathematical and experimental
method of inquiry and placing the question of the social uses of
the new knowledge in the forefront of serious discussion among
contemporaries. Scientific progress which could lead to human
improvement, as conceived originally by Francis Bacon, became an
intrinsic part of the revolutionary goals of the Puritan revolutionaries. The Puritan regime failed to realize these objectives, but in
failing it made science and natural philosophy an intrinsic feature of
a new social philosophy. By the time of the Restoration (1660), the
prosperity of the English state was seen to be linked with advancing
science and technology.

Jacob did not propose this in isolation. She acknowledges the
fundamental contribution of the left-wing English medical historian
Charles Webster and other researchers to the definitive establishment of this historiographical perspective.[97] By the late seventeenth
century a political economy crystallized which was committed to
the idea that the future of England lay with the development of an
economy based on manufacturing.[98] In the opening years of the
next century Newtonian ideas came to be disseminated widely, especially through pamphlets, public lectures, associations, dissenting
academies and textbooks, influencing engineers, practically minded
natural philosophers and merchants with industrial interests,[99]
and playing an important role in fostering innovation in manufacture. However, while she stresses its contribution to the Industrial
Revolution, Jacob makes it clear that the appearance of this new
culture should not be conceived of as an alternative to economic

explanations. Emphasis on culture should not be seen as supplanting the economic.[100]

Jacob's stress on the importance of the new scientific culture also resonates with our discussion of the relative role of capitalists and workers in technological change. While Jacob allows that skilled artisans were necessary to the Industrial Revolution, she underscores the importance of entrepreneurs imbued with Newtonian ideas to the mechanization of the cotton industry.[101] In contrast, the historian of technology Liliane Hilaire-Perez makes a strong case for the importance of the more tacit mechanical knowledge of skilled craftspeople.[102] The latter view echoes the perspective of Marx, who noted the importance of skilled artisans to the construction of the key machines of the Industrial Revolution. On the other hand, he also pointed out that once such scientific knowledge became embodied in machinery, it helped change the balance of power in the factory from the workers to the capitalist. Indeed, a fundamental objective of the leaders of the Scientific Revolution like Francis Bacon, Robert Boyle and William Petty was to appropriate the knowledge of craftspeople, reorganize it and deliver it into the hands of capitalists.[103]

Despite Jacob's efforts to root her analysis in economic and social reality, critics have falsely accused her of idealism, with William Ashworth seeing her work as a throwback to the views of Walter Rostow, who ascribed the Industrial Revolution to the ideas of the Scientific Revolution.[104] In fact, Jacob's scholarship, while not explicitly Marxist, nonetheless represents a courageous attempt to overcome an unfortunate legacy of anti-Marxism which hamstrung the development of the field of the history of science from the inception of the Cold War, if not earlier.[105] Others have followed Jacob's path. Gideon Freudenthal recently showed that the scientific ideas of the seventeenth century arose in the context of a rising interest in technological innovation coincident with the emergence of capitalism,[106] reviving the ideas of the Soviet scholar Boris Hessen and the great Marxist theoretician Henryk Grossman, who were subject to ferocious and derisive criticism by non-Marxist historians of science in the 1930s and 1940s.[107] Following up a suggestion in Marx's *Capital*, Grossman carefully analyzed the outstanding contribution of the French philosopher René Descartes in stressing the combination of theoretical and craft knowledge in transforming production.[108]

These works reveal how critical the ideas of the Scientific Revolution were to the triumph of industrial capitalism, that their roots lay in the skills of craftspeople and revolutionary intellectuals who flourished particularly during the English Revolution, and that later they came to be controlled by bourgeois intellectuals and entrepreneurs. This history has a significant bearing on the future. It should be recalled that the monopolization of knowledge of the whole process of production by capitalist management and the resulting ignorance of workers was basic to capitalist control of the industrial process. That was the conclusion that Marx drew from the development of nineteenth-century capitalist industry. The computer-driven capitalism of today, however, may be changing the balance of forces back in favour of producers, as internet optimists suggest. This may be reason for optimism on the part of socialists too. The essence of the socialist project, after all, is collective and increasingly rational control of the economy by the so-called collective worker. It points to a target toward which socialists should aim: that is, control over the intellectual heights of the economy in which knowledge brings control. Moreover, it should be added that this is a terrain which is highly favourable to those who aspire to socialism. Under socialism the sharing of ideas and information between socialist production and distribution collectives, and so the improvement of the standards of production, would be carried on as of a matter of course.

This transformation has been theorized by Carlo Vercellone and others who reflect the outlook of so-called autonomist Marxism.[109] According to Vercellone, industrial capitalism is being eclipsed by so-called cognitive capitalism, or a form of capitalism dependent on knowledge. Industrial capitalism still exists and is proliferating, particularly in the third world. But it is being overshadowed by the development of high-tech industries which prefigure, and will dominate, the future economy. Biotechnology, computer and other high-tech industries and university research parks, as well as corporate industrial campuses, are archetypes of such future knowledge-based industries. In the new cognitive stage of capitalism the hegemony of the older industrial capitalism with its mass production and hierarchical division of labour is eroded. In this new cognitive phase the relation of capital to labour is characterized by the decisive importance of knowledge, and the production of knowledge by means of knowledge connected to the increasingly immaterial, networked and cognitive character of labour, whose importance is vastly greater than in the phase of industrial capitalism. Under these conditions the balance of forces may have changed, and it might become progressively more difficult for capital to contain knowledge within the limits of the capitalist means of production and property rights which generate profits.

In this view the cognitive, interconnected and immaterial nature of labour erodes capital's ability to exploit it as wage labour, that is, to transform it into variable capital and thereby garner surplus value from it. For capital to continue to do so it has to fetter the development of the potentiality of labour. There is a striking similarity here with Marx's view. He argued that the further development of the forces of production, including scientific progress, is eventually stymied by the continued dependence of capital on wage labour:

> On the one side, then, it [capital] calls to life all the powers of science and of nature, as of social combination and of social intercourse, in order to make the creation of wealth independent (relatively) of the labour-time employed on it. On the other side, it wants to use labour time as the measuring rod for the giant social forces thereby created, and to confine them within the limits required to maintain the already created value as value.[110]

The difference in Marx's view and Vercellone's is eliminated if we assume that variable capital is a force of production whose further development is eventually constricted at the stage of cognitive capitalism by the need of capital to force labour into a form from which it can extract surplus value.

THE EFFACEMENT OF THE BOURGEOISIE

The reduction in the growth estimates for the period 1760–1830 has not only led to the view that the Industrial Revolution represented less of a dramatic break than had previously been supposed, it has also reinforced doubts that the period can be seen as one in which the industrial bourgeoisie achieved economic power, and political and cultural hegemony. A new orthodoxy has emerged which not only denies the revolutionary character of the Industrial Revolution from an economic perspective, but goes on to claim that the industrial middle class in England failed to gain the upper hand politically and economically. As a consequence, it is argued that the industrial bourgeoisie never came to determine state policy in ways favourable to industrial capitalism. The higher status attached to non-industrial forms of wealth alongside common cultural interests and sociability allowed the financial and landed elites to continue to dominate the English state. The industrial bourgeoisie subordinated itself to this elite and aspired to join it.

Such a 'gentlemanly capitalism' dominated nineteenth and

indeed twentieth-century Britain, causing a bias toward rentier and ultimately imperialist interests. This interpretation fits with a conservative revisionist view of British history which tends to minimize or dismiss the disruptive character of the seventeenth-century English Revolution.[111] Both views hold that the control of the landed and propertied classes was never seriously challenged. The modern history of Britain is one of ordered and gradual change without radical breaks.[112] The thesis of gentlemanly capitalism represented a new orthodoxy which emerged in the years of Thatcherism and neoliberalism. While both Thatcherism and neoliberalism ideologically were critical of the previously existing flabby and conciliatory postwar period of welfare-state capitalism, both have sought to present class rule and the rule of the market as part of a history that never really changes and is in fact part of the normal order of things. Thatcherism and neoliberalism were presented as an attempted restoration of this natural order. The reader will note the unfortunate congruence between the idea of the natural rule of the landed elite and the conception of Brenner, who insists that the landlords took the initiative in instituting capitalism from above.

Ironically the idea of gentlemanly capitalism emerged in the aftermath of a debate on English history between Thompson and Anderson, which grew out of their celebrated contretemps over class. In an article in *New Left Review* published in 1964, Anderson argued that the passage of the Reform Act (1832) and the repeal of the Corn Laws (1846), far from representing the triumph of the English bourgeoisie over the landed elite, marked its effacement in the face of the imminent threat of lower class radicalism:

> In the wake of the repeal of the Corn Laws a campaign was launched to do away with primogeniture the ultimate legal defense of the aristocracy: the call for 'free trade not only in corn but in land' aimed directly at the root power of the aristocracy. The bourgeoisie refused to follow the call. Its courage had gone. Henceforth it was bent exclusively on integrating itself into the aristocracy, not collectively as a class, but by individual vertical ascent. This treason not only perpetuated landlord control of political life, but was the source of the chronic problems of the incompletely modern English industrial capitalism faced with rising German and American competition.[113]

The aristocratic outlook which continued to dominate the British state and the mentality of the more successful layers of the bourgeoisie made it very difficult to address the declining competitiveness of British manufacturing. Britain drifted toward a rentier capitalism and a commitment to imperialism overseas as an alternative. The implication was that Britain missed its appointment with a necessary bourgeois revolution during the crises of 1832 and 1846. Anderson formulated this view in an effort to explain the apparent economic and social paralysis of Britain in the 1960s and 1970s. According to Anderson, the ongoing aristocratic ascendancy had blocked the further rational development of British capitalism.

Thompson responded to Anderson by insisting that the latter was intent on imposing a French model of revolutionary change on English history. According to Thompson, from 1688 the aristocracy as a class no longer dominated England. Aristocrats, gentry and merchants all were capitalists. Down to the Reform Bill of 1832 what he refers to as Old Corruption ruled over the English state – the state being relatively autonomous from the class system. As such, it included certain aristocratic magnates and great merchants as well as their hangers-on.[114] In the crisis of 1832 the industrial bourgeoisie played a role, but alongside the gentry who were also capitalist. Moreover, the industrial bourgeoisie left the heavy work of popular agitation and protest in the hands of plebeian radicals.[115] The Anderson view that the aristocracy emerged from the crisis as the masters of the state is seriously overstated in Thompson's opinion. According to Thompson, the aristocracy was useful in providing stability and order but the reality of political and even cultural power had passed into the hands of the bourgeoisie.[116]

In a subsequent article, Anderson made clear that, like Thompson, he considered England since 1688 a capitalist country. and that the aristocracy was already at that point a capitalist landed class. But he also reiterated his view that both before and after 1832 the landed elite as well as the financiers dominated British society and politics, with all the negative consequences that followed. In doing so, he argued that this was the consequence not simply of political and cultural privilege, but of their economic wealth, which was considerably greater than that of the industrial bourgeoisie.[117] It is Anderson's view that has, somewhat ironically, tended to prevail in conservative academic circles. This is due in part to the influence of a right-wing interpretation of the place of gentlemanly capitalism in the interpretation of British history. But I would also point out that Anderson's notion of persistent aristocratic power, which he extended to the entire European continent in *Lineages of the*

Absolutist State, became the foundation of a sweeping reinterpretation of European nineteenth century history by the Marxist historian
Arno J. Mayer. The situation in England figures largely in Mayer's
account: 'Although England's economy was dominated by manufacturing and merchant capitalism, the aristocracy continued to be
paramount. This was so because land remained the chief source of
wealth and income.'[118]

Anderson's view of continued aristocratic political dominance
represents an important corrective to the assumption of a triumphant
industrial bourgeoisie. It helps to explain a lot about the trajectory
of English capitalism in the late nineteenth century. But there is a
danger that such a view may obscure the determining character of
class conflict. As Thompson insisted and Anderson admitted, both
the industrial and aristocratic elite were members of the same capitalist class. Moreover, in the two great political conflicts between
these elites in the first part of the nineteenth century, it was the
interests of the industrial bourgeoisie that predominated. Finally
the ultimately conciliatory attitude of the industrial bourgeoisie
toward the nobility was dictated by their need to make common
cause against the political and economic threat of the emerging
working class. Their defensiveness in this respect parallels that of
the French bourgeoisie following the June Days and the Commune.
In my view the overall evolution of nineteenth-century England as
well as France was determined by class conflict rather than inter-elite
struggles. In both cases the state mediated an alliance between the
landed and manufacturing bourgeoisie against workers, and evolved
in the direction of favouring imperialism and high finance at the
expense of industrial modernization.

CONCLUSION

I conclude this discussion of the Industrial Revolution by insisting on
the ongoing importance of Marxist views. Not the least important
was Marx's own view of the historical meaning of the Industrial
Revolution, which remains fundamental to an understanding of
capital itself. Moreover, without derogating from the contributions of non-Marxist scholars it can be said that the contributions
of Hobsbawm, Thompson, Anderson and others working in this
tradition remain at the forefront of historiographical discussion of
the period. Hobsbawm's stress on the overseas and colonial market,
his and Thompson's emphasis on the turmoil and distress caused
by industrialization, and Thompson's and Anderson's discussion of

class relations constitute enduring contributions to understanding the transformations of the new industrial age.

I have also made a point of qualifying the importance of the Industrial Revolution, pointing to the greater significance of the sixteenth-century origins of capitalism and the trend to diminish the actual degree of economic transformation entailed in the initial phases of industrial capitalism. There is a danger that too much stress on the Industrial Revolution will only confirm what I have attempted to avoid in this narrative, a too Anglocentric view of capitalism. Industrialization began almost simultaneously in France and elsewhere on the Continent, although perhaps not to the same extent. Moreover, England's advantage proved short-lived, eroding significantly from the 1870s onwards. From then on industrial capitalism began to take hold in Germany, the United States and even Japan. It is important therefore in conclusion to try to place capitalism in global perspective, as I shall try to do in the final chapter of this account.

7

CAPITALISM AND WORLD HISTORY

The coming of the Industrial Revolution signalled the global triumph of capitalism. This economic revolution, coupled with imperialist rule, underpinned the subsequent two centuries of Western ascendancy. But what strikes me is how slow the arrival of the triumph was – it took three centuries – and how economically hard-pressed capitalism was up almost to the last moment before it finally prevailed. Up to the second half of the eighteenth century, the longstanding outflow of bullion from Europe toward Asia continued. This ongoing fiscal deficit reflected the competitive inferiority of Western products. This was particularly marked in the commercially decisive cotton industry. It was only toward the end of the eighteenth century that this commercial lag was overcome by technical innovation and machine production.[1] Far from the birth of the Industrial Revolution being seen as taking advantage of an enormous opportunity to capture an open world market, it can be interpreted as a defensive reaction faced with persistent and ongoing Asian commercial superiority. Moreover, this Eastern advantage was not merely a reflection of a positive balance of trade. As we shall learn, the internal economies of the most advanced regions of Asia were at least equal to those of the capitalist West until the beginning of the nineteenth century.

This last assertion points to the fact that in the last 20 years a revolution has taken place in our understanding of global history. This intellectual upheaval began with the advance of a wave of historical writing directed against Eurocentrism. This anti-Eurocentric trend in historiography formed part of the emergent postcolonial strain in poststructuralist thought. Dedicated to criticizing and eliminating the legacy of European colonialism, postcolonialism in the main was hostile to Marxism, which it regarded as a Eurocentric form of thinking. In reaction I shall show in the first place that Marxism in the twentieth century was actually in the vanguard in the fight against Eurocentric ideologies and their material roots in colonialism and imperialism. Furthermore, taken to its limit postcolonialism's rejection of Marxism and other kinds of Western thought falls into irrationalism, and is in fact a brand of conservatism strongly reminiscent of the romantic reaction to the Enlightenment. In this concluding chapter I shall turn the anti-Eurocentric historiography that this school has produced against itself by demonstrating that it actually reinforces our own Marxist interpretation of the history of capitalism.

It is worth recalling that the romantic movement of the early nine-teenth century which reacted against the French Revolution helped to create modern historiography. Similarly postcolonial thought has engendered a historiography of great importance to a proper global history of capitalism. Despite the anti-Marxist bias of much of it, the conclusions of postcolonial historiography underscore the basic argument of this narrative. Based largely on a reconsideration of the internal history of Western capitalism I have insisted that capitalism's global conquest proved to be a protracted process, requiring no less than three centuries. It will now be shown that looking at history from a global perspective, postcolonial historiography arrives at the same conclusion. It was only after 1800 that European capitalism came to dominate the globe.

As we saw in the earlier discussion of colonialism, Jim Blaut in the 1980s initiated the academic debate over capitalism and Eurocentrism. Reacting above all to the Eurocentric, not to say Anglocentric, views of Brenner, Blaut, who considered himself a Marxist, sought to defend Wallerstein and Frank by reasserting the importance of colonialism to the success of European capitalism. The first scholar systematically to challenge Eurocentric history, Blaut argued that protocapitalist currents were present in many places in Eurasia prior to the European discoveries. It was European colo-nialism that allowed Europe to dominate the rest of the world and block the development of capitalism elsewhere. In response I qualified Blaut's view by pointing out that the success of colonialism itself had to be understood as an outgrowth of a European capitalist dynamic.

Despite the drawbacks of Blaut's argument, important further attacks on Eurocentrism emerged in the work of John Hobson, Andre Gunder Frank and Jack Goody.[2] Insightful though these authors are in terms of the debate on Eurocentrism, their rejection of Marxist concepts like capitalism, mode of production and class relations, has tended to stifle discussion rather than enlarge it. In particular their refusal to engage with these categories makes it difficult for them to deal with the causes of the Industrial Revolution. The debate over the relationship between capitalism and Eurocentrism has recently come to a head in the dispute between Robert Brenner and Keith Pomeranz over the level of economic development in England compared with the lower Yangtze delta in the early modern period. Pomeranz's intervention may be seen as an attempt to bring the precision of neoclassical quantitative methods to the support of the postcolonial position.[3] In the course of the debate that followed it was shown that while Brenner is correct in asserting the ultimate advantage of the capitalist economy based on higher levels of productivity, this lead did not become manifest before 1800. This finding confirms a central thesis of this work, that the productive superiority of capitalism only became evident little by little, and then only under the aegis of the mercantilist state.

Indeed, as we shall see, Arrighi in *Adam Smith in Beijing* (2007) argues that the belated victory of Western capitalism has proven a Pyrrhic one given its capital and energy-intensive nature.[4] In Arrighi's view the more labour-intensive model of the market fostered by the contemporary Chinese state will prove more economically competitive and more ecologically sustainable in the twenty-first century. In conclusion we outline the premises of a non-Eurocentric approach to the history of capitalism. Among other elements we point to the importance of David Harvey's concept of spatial-temporal fix, Amiya Kumar Bagchi's vision of a common human fate under capitalism and Peter Linebaugh's account of the ecological ravages of the capitalist mode of production.[5]

THE ATTACK ON EUROCENTRISM

Blaut's was only the opening salvo in a barrage of attacks on Eurocentric history which were published from the 1990s onward. As these critics have explained, Eurocentrism has informed historical writing since the nineteenth century if not before. This was not only the case with European and American historiography, it affected the spatial and temporal conceptions of historical writing world-wide. Europeans and Americans conquered the world, renamed places and restructured economies, societies and politics. They destroyed or marginalized other ways of understanding basic concepts of space and time. History was universalized in their image, which was premised on the triumph of capitalist modernity.[6]

Eurocentrism first emerged as an early modern religious and cultural ethnocentrism, which intensified with the consolidation of territorial states in England, the Netherlands and France. It was further confirmed when the Enlightenment identified its rational human subject – the white European middle-class male – as the essential protagonist of a progressive history. But this would not have gone far without colonial conquest and the eventual take-over of the world by European capitalism. The Industrial Revolution provided a powerful confirmation of Eurocentric ideology. From this followed not merely European political and economic ascendancy, but a consciousness of cultural and even racial superiority. European scholarly disciplines, among others history, geography, anthropology, literary studies and philosophy, were deeply coloured by Eurocentric assumptions.

Postcolonial critics have argued that Marxism itself is contaminated by Eurocentrism, and for this reason is illegitimate in the struggle against it. I shall respond at two levels, by reviewing the actual historical development of the struggle against Eurocentrism and by exploring the theoretical foundations of this anti-Marxist stance. On the first level let me begin by asserting as undeniable that Marx and his disciple Lenin were committed to the idea of world socialist revolution. They stood opposed to capitalism and to the perpetuation of a world order dominated by the capitalist nations of Europe and North America. More to the point, the ideas of Marx and Lenin have been of immense importance to national liberation and socialist revolutionary struggles throughout the non-European world. As the postcolonial author Robert Young admits, 'with some exceptions, Marxism historically provided the theoretical inspiration and most effective political ideology for twentieth century anti-colonial resistance'.[7]

Eurocentrism developed in tandem with the expansion of the capitalist world market, reaching its climax in the period of capitalist imperialism and colonialism in the late nineteenth and early twentieth centuries. The material foundation of this ideology was shaken by the First World War and the 1930s Depression. It entered crisis as a result of the catastrophic political and economic consequences of the Second World War on the major colonial states: England, France, Holland and Belgium. The United States, the sole surviving capitalist great power, restructured both imperialism and the accompanying Eurocentric world view after 1945. It did so through its world-wide system of naval and air bases and its policy of open markets reinforced by new international financial institutions – the International Monetary Fund (IMF) and the World Bank – which it controlled. The hegemony of Eurocentric culture was strengthened by the invention of the American ideologies of mass consumerism and modernization on the model of postwar American society. The Point Four Aid Program (1949) facilitated the export of the modernization ideology to under-developed countries by linking educational and scientific institutions there to those in the United States.

Ideologically and politically Lenin's writings and the founding of
the Communist International (1919), the Congress of the Peoples of
the East (1920) and the creation in Brussels (1927) of the League
Against Imperialism laid the groundwork for resistance to imperialism and Western cultural hegemony.[8] Based on this political and
ideological groundwork, a major offensive against Eurocentrism
and imperialism was launched right after the Second World War
with the Chinese Revolution (1949) and the Korean War (1949–53).
It continued with the Cuban (1959–) and Vietnamese Revolutions
(1965–75). These uprisings inspired by Marxism were revolutionary struggles but also national liberation movements against
Western imperialism and colonialism. They were high points in a
great series of national liberation struggles in Iran, Algeria, Egypt,
Iraq, southern Africa, Ethiopia and Eritrea running from the 1950s
through the 1970s. Mao Zedong, Ho Chi Minh, Fidel Castro,
Ernesto Che Guevara, Kwame Nkrumah, Achmed Sukarono and
Abdal Nasser emerged as the most important political leaders of the
anti-imperialist movement.

In 1959 the newly decolonized states sought to give themselves a
degree of political cohesion by creating the non-aligned movement at
Bandung. Intellectually and politically Lenin's ideas on imperialism
and anticolonialism proved critically important. Mao's concept of
a people's war and Castro and Guevara's of guerrilla war played a
large part in the military strategy of anti-imperialist struggle. In terms
of economic development, Lenin's New Economic Policy, the Soviet
economist Evgenii Alexeyevich Preobrazhensky's theories of socialist
accumulation, Mao's conception of the Great Leap Forward and
Cultural Revolution, and the ideas of Latin American dependency
theorist Raúl Prebisch were important. Not to be overlooked especially in a discussion of Eurocentrism were the ideas of the Marxist
theoretician Frantz Fanon on the need to achieve a psychological
liberation from Eurocentric influence through struggling for national
liberation. Marxist ideas gained ascendancy throughout the under-
developed world but especially in Asia. This is obvious in the case of
China and Vietnam, but the ongoing political relevance of Marxist
ideology throughout the Indian subcontinent should also be noted.

By 1980 the combination of struggles in the under-developed
world, coupled with growing social and ideological protest in the
United States and the other advanced capitalist countries, had placed
Eurocentric ideas and imperialism on the defensive. But US counter-
insurgency campaigns, neoliberalism as well as ideological currents
like ethno-nationalism and postmodernism helped to take the wind

out of anti-imperialist resistance. It is in this context of attacks that
the hostility to Marxism in postcolonial studies should be placed.
For as Crystal Bartolovich has remarked: 'this field has been deeply
and constitutively informed by theoretical protocols and procedures
– Foucauldian discourse analysis, deconstruction, Lacanianism
– which are not merely indifferent, but in their dominant forms,
actively and explicitly hostile to Marxism'.[9] Capitalism since the
1980s has become thoroughly global, and nowhere is it more
dynamic than in Asia. It is likewise among the intellectual bourgeoisie of Asia that some of the strongest roots of postcolonialist
ideology are to be found. It is Marxism, of course, that continues to
be the most important critique of capitalism, continuing to inspire
active resistance notably in South Asia. Given the above historic
record and the global nature of contemporary capitalism, the postcolonial charge of Marxism being Eurocentric appears politically
suspect in its motivations.

As to the notion that Marxism is an intellectual construct
contaminated by its Western origins, Neil Lazarus points out that as
used by postcolonialists, the 'West' is invoked as an ideological trope
which serves to make it difficult to trace out the actual political and
economic roots of its historic power over the rest of the world.[10]
In this perspective, Eurocentrism including Marxism is seen not as
an ideology but as a world view, whose horizon cannot rationally
be transcended, only deconstructed and discounted. According to
the postcolonial view, Marxism is inscribed in the fabric of Western
disciplinarity and institutionalized knowledge production, and
hence is contaminated. Taken to its limit, postcolonialism falls into
complete irrationalism, considering all intellectual practices that
stake a claim to represent truth as inherently false.[11]

In my view, in so far as it is able to continue to grasp social
reality, Marxism must be regarded as applicable and useful outside
the European context. Indeed, Arif Dirlik claims that Mao produced
a specifically Chinese version of Marxism which became the foundation for a distinctive Chinese modernity.[12] As Mao Zedong
expressed it in 1938:

> Communists are Marxist internationalists, but Marxism must be
> realized through national forms. There is no such thing as abstract
> Marxism, there is only concrete Marxism. The so-called concrete
> Marxism is Marxism that has taken national form; we need to
> apply Marxism to concrete struggle in the concrete environment
> of China, we should not employ it in the abstract.[13]

In any event, given the place of Marxist thought and practice in twentieth-century China, the idea that Marxism is fundamentally Eurocentric appears absurd.

Academic arguments against Eurocentrism began when the radical political movements that had begun after 1945 subsided. Indeed, anti-Eurocentric scholarship began to flourish when Marxism and Communist movements and governments retreated. Like poststructuralism and cultural studies, postcolonialism or anti-Eurocentrism seems to have been a product of the reaction to the politics of national liberation and third world Marxism. Indeed, it arose coincidently with the full emergence on the world stage of East and South Asian capitalism in the 1980s, which helped to breathe new life into capitalism and the bourgeoisie. In this light I cannot help but feel that in the hands of some the debate over Eurocentrism, however important, represents an attempt to change the subject. Whereas in the 1960s and 1970s the future of the global capitalist system and imperialism was a political issue, from the 1980s the geographic centre and the cultural significance of the capitalist system became the question which vexed the minds of an increasingly depoliticized scholarship. That being said, like cultural studies and poststructuralism, postcolonial scholarship has had important impact on the discipline of history, and notably the question of the transition.

POSTCOLONIAL HISTORIES

As has been noted, attacks on Eurocentric historical conceptions multiplied from the 1990s onward. We shall consider three: John M. Hobson's *The Eastern Origins of Western Civilisation*, Jack Goody's *The Theft of History* and Andre Gunder Frank's *ReOrient*, which arguably are among the most important.[14] The most notable thing about Hobson's work is its demonstration of the astonishing technological dependence of the West on Asia up to the very eve of the Industrial Revolution. Meanwhile, in a thorough-going and convincing fashion Goody shows how deeply Eurocentric geographic and historiographical conceptions have shaped and distorted the consciousness of both Europeans and non-Europeans. Finally Frank argues that Asia rather than Europe dominated the world system until the Industrial Revolution.

Professionally Hobson is interested in international relations theory and globalization from a postcolonial perspective. His work 'argues that the East (which was more advanced than the West between 500 and 1800) provided a crucial role in enabling the rise of modern Western civilization' and seeks 'to replace the notion of the autonomous or pristine West with that of the oriental West'.[15] More specifically, he asserts that the peoples of Asia after 500 AD created a global communications and economic network which allowed the diffusion of Eastern ideas, institutions and technology which were assimilated by the West, and that the development of Western imperialism after 1500 enabled the West to appropriate all manner of economic resources, enabling it to develop at the expense of the East and the rest of the world.[16] Hobson shows that the West's technological reliance on Asia did not end abruptly with the opening of the age of colonialism at the beginning of the sixteenth century, but went on throughout the early modern period. He demonstrates that such key inventions of the eighteenth-century agricultural revolution as the iron moldboard plough, rotary winnowing machine, seed-drills and horse-harrowing husbandry and crop rotation schemes originated in China.[17]

Hobson's argument that the West's triumph was due to a sequence of fortuitous accidents, that the rise of the West could be explained almost wholly through contingency, is less convincing. According to Hobson, 'the Europeans needed a great deal of luck given that they had been neither sufficiently rational, liberal-democratic nor ingenious to independently pioneer their own development'.[18] Hobson even explains the British Industrial Revolution by pointing to the fact that the latter were good copycats of other people's ideas, as used to be said disparagingly of the Japanese.[19]

Beyond the notion of the West as lucky or good copycats, Hobson does not offer any explanation for the emergence of Western capitalism. As I pointed out in the Introduction, the rise of capitalism cannot be explained as a merely aleatory matter. Otherwise history as a discipline has no rational foundation. The task of the historian is rather to elicit the factors that if they did not determine, nonetheless shaped events: in this case, the emergence of capitalism. As to the matter of copying, what Hobson fails to acknowledge is that being open to foreign techniques and ideas might reflect a positive feature of a society, whose internal social and political structures consequently are worth analyzing. Many societies of course borrow techniques and ideas from elsewhere. But there were a number of structural features of emergent capitalism that made such borrowings fall on particularly fertile economic ground. Marx's insistence on capitalism's distinctive social relations of production, in which capitalists fully control the means of production and are able to innovate at will, is of most significance. But also notable is Hobsbawm's stress on the West's historic backwardness and marginality, which tended to make it open to exogenous influences. Likewise Wallerstein's emphasis on the failure to consolidate an overarching imperial political order, as well as Harman's underlining of the internal weakness of the early modern territorial states, need to be taken into consideration. Together these structural features of capitalism point to the existence in Europe of a space for the market and the productive classes which was not evident elsewhere. In short, in his eagerness to combat Eurocentrism Hobson turns a blind eye to any internal characteristics of Western society that may have enabled it to achieve political and economic supremacy. It is not surprising therefore that Hobson concludes that Marx, the student of capitalism, was nothing but a Eurocentric orientalist.[20]

Perhaps the most sweeping critique of Eurocentrism thus far has come from the British anthropologist Jack Goody. As a social anthropologist with a deep interest in the study of kinship and family systems, he has in recent years devoted his attention to a comparative analysis of complex societies and their interactions. Goody regards economic surplus, towns and trade and communication as key to the analysis of such societies. Over long periods of time there has been ongoing interaction between the developed areas of the world, with no region able to claim an inherent superiority.

He is not always but is mainly respectful of Marx, and in the pages of *New Left Review* has been highly laudatory of the work of the French Marxist anthropologist Maurice Godelier, for whom, he notes in passing, the last instance never arrives.[21] On the other hand, he is impatient with what he regards as the simplistic formulations of Marxists who harp on about class and the social relations of production. But his objections are mainly directed against Eurocentrism, of which Marxism forms a part in his view.

His recent work *The Theft of History* (2006), reveals just how deeply entrenched Eurocentric conceptions have been: 'Europe has not simply neglected or underplayed the rest of the world, as a consequence of which it has misinterpreted its own history, but ... it has imposed historical concepts and periods that have aggravated our understanding of Asia'.[22] On the one hand, Goody attempts to challenge the grand Eurocentric narrative which teleologically links Antiquity, the Renaissance, Reformation, Scientific Revolution, Enlightenment and the Industrial Revolution. On the other hand, he aims to begin to reintegrate the history of Africa and Eurasia into the narrative of world history.[23] In this regard Goody acknowledges his debt to the work of Martin Bernal, the Marxist scholar who frontally challenged the received conception of the Aryan origins of Greek civilization.[24] Bernal underlined the affiliation of Greek culture with Egypt, Africa and the Levant. He stressed the racist character of the Aryan myth, which he argued developed in nineteenth-century Europe. Goody agrees, but asserts that the roots of this myth lie much deeper in European thought.[25]

Goody demonstrates the degree to which African and Asian cultural and technological achievement has gone unacknowledged by Eurocentric thinkers and historians. At the same time, he points out that these same scholars have arbitrarily annexed whole periods of history to the European narrative. Indeed, he underlines that fundamental European conceptions of space, time and periodization have been imposed on the rest of the world.[26] According to Goody, Eurocentricity permeates the work of even the most non-Eurocentric of Europeans, like the Marxist scientist and sinologist Joseph Needham. Goody recognizes that the latter's monumental history of ancient Chinese science pioneered in demonstrating the achievements of non-European civilizations. Yet Needham's unfortunate commitment to Marxism (in Goody's eyes at least) led him to the mistaken view that bureaucratic feudalism impeded Chinese development and blocked the emergence of a capitalist class.[27] Goody meanwhile offers no critique of Needham's extremely positive assessment of Chinese science, nor does he find Needham's assessment Eurocentric, which after all are the main points.

The non-Marxist historian Braudel is likewise chastised by Goody for insisting on the uniquely progressive nature of Western merchant capitalism. Goody himself insists on the equally vibrant character of Chinese, South Asian and Middle Eastern merchants and financial institutions.[28] His critique of Braudel leads him to ask:

> whether we really need the concept of capitalism, which always seems to push the analysis in a Eurocentric direction. ... Can we not therefore dispense with this pejorative term drawn from nineteenth century Britain and recognize the element of continuity in the market and bourgeois activities from the Bronze Age until modern times.[29]

Goody argues that a proper historical perspective would be a Eurasian and African one, in which there was a steady progress in urbanization, increases in the production of goods and ideas, and expansion of mercantile capital over a 5,000-year period. He agrees that the process of industrialization in Britain that began in the eighteenth century was of utmost significance for the future. But he concludes that:

> all that process can be described without adopting the nineteenth-century notion of the emergence of capitalism as a specific stage in the development of world society, and we can dispense with the supposed sequence of periods of production leading to it that are confined to Europe. Such an account avoids European periodization and its assumption of long-term superiority.[30]

In effect Goody calls for the rejection of the transition from feudalism to capitalism as a problem. How then to account for British industrialization, so important to the future, as Goody admits? While recognizing the significance of the enormous expansion of the forces of production which follow from industrialization, he fails to acknowledge that it was based on changes in the relations of production. However important Goody's challenge to Eurocentricity is, in rejecting the question of the transition he takes things too far. Indeed, by singling out the transition problem for attack, Goody underscores its continuing significance.

A ground-breaking historical work in the struggle against Eurocentrism has been Andre Gunder Frank's *ReOrient*.[31] Unlike the works of Hobson and Goody which are rooted in social anthropology and postcolonialism, Frank's account is solidly anchored in comparative study of early modern Asian and European history. Frank was a founder of dependency theory, and helped inspire Wallerstein's and Arrighi's research. Deeply committed to third world Marxism, he contributed as best he could to national liberation struggles in the 1950s and 1960s. In his later years, he drifted away from these Marxist commitments, questioning Wallerstein's ideas about the onset of the capitalist world system in the sixteenth century in a work published in 1993.[32] Then in *ReOrient* he took his distance from Marx himself by first of all castigating his supposed orientalism and mistaken ideas about the Asiatic mode of production.[33] Taking a step further, he explicitly rejected the theoretical notion of a capitalist mode of production, preferring instead to discuss the world economy. He regards as:

> questionable to say the least the very concept of a 'capitalist mode of production' and the supposed significance of its alleged spread from Europe to the rest of the world ... [and the] very significance imputed to different modes of production of course

including 'feudalism' and 'capitalism', not to mention any alleged 'transition' between them.[34]

Frank's perspective on global history deserves our attention because it embodies an important corrective to a too Eurocentric view. As Frank saw it, Europe was hardly a factor in the world economy prior to the sixteenth century. It was the East that created a world market which it controlled until as late as 1800. Contrary to the Eurocentric conception, Europe was not in the global economic vanguard after 1492. In terms of population growth, gains in productivity, technological innovation and per capita income, China and India preserved their lead over Europe until the eighteenth century. It was bullion from the New World that allowed Europe to increase its economic role for the first time in the sixteenth century. But its trade deficit with the East remained in place for centuries. The Scientific Revolution did not provide Europe with a higher level of scientific and technological capacity than Asia. The ideas of the Scientific Revolution did not influence European technology until the nineteenth century. China and other places in Asia had a level of technological facility in guns, ships, textiles, metallurgy and agriculture which was as high as or higher than that of Europe in the early modern period. Many technological and scientific ideas which appeared in Europe were borrowed from the rest of Eurasia in the medieval and early modern period. The financial and economic institutions of Asia were no less rational and no more despotic than those of the West.

The ascendancy of the West which dates from the eighteenth century was based in the first place on the cyclical nature of the world economy. Europe advanced as a result of a cyclical oscillation downward of the Asian economy. Meanwhile, colonialism and slavery provided the Europeans with the capital to invest in industrial technology. But such resources were not enough at first to induce them to invest in labour-saving technology. It was the high cost of wages and other resources that finally caused Europeans to invest in new means of production which reduced the cost of labour. Meanwhile, the low-wage structure of the Chinese economy brought about by a rising population precluded such investment.

Frank's work elicited an important riposte from his erstwhile colleagues in dependency theory, Samir Amin, Arrighi and Wallerstein, in the pages of the latter's journal *Review*.[35] In his refusal to recognize the importance of changes in modes of production, and specifically the importance of the advent of capitalism, Frank was accused by them of denying the significance of historic breaks and turning points, and more importantly their causes. Amin went so far as to claim he was even practising a kind of history based on eternal cycles. Indeed, according to these former colleagues Frank's obsession with economic flows was nothing less than an economism which amounted to a paean to economic efficiency in the neoliberal mode. Frank ignored the importance of the development of the law of value and the decisive importance of political and military power in history, and particularly the history of global capitalism. He wrongly denied the world-wide character of capitalism, and its polarizing effects in terms of the development of core and periphery. In his eagerness to deny a dialectical relationship between the two phenomena, Frank asserts, but fails to provide evidence for, the overall decline of Asia prior to the rise of the West. Amin, Arrighi and Wallerstein argue, I believe correctly, that the way to look at the early modern period is not merely on its own terms, but also in terms of the development of the underlying forces determining the future, which was to be a capitalist one. Frank deliberately ignores the future by practising a kind of empiricism uninterested in what lies ahead.

Despite their criticisms, Amin, Arrighi and Wallerstein do not deny the economic superiority of Asia in the early modern period, lasting into the eighteenth century, which Frank insisted on. It was left to a Canadian scholar, Ricardo Duchesne, to try to do so in an article which was published in 2003 in *Science and Society*.[36] In opposition to Frank, Duchesne argued that there was not one world economy at the beginning of the eighteenth century, but two – an Asian and a European one – and that of the two it was Europe that had the better part.[37] Europe's economy, based on emerging capitalist relations of production, was on the rise while Asia's was in decline. Based on a paper published by Patrick O'Brien in 1991, Duchesne even claimed that overseas trade and colonialism had little to do with the Industrial Revolution. In that piece O'Brien asserted that the 'connexions from the world economy to the industrial revolution are not nearly strong enough to seriously weaken the present "Eurocentric consensus" that its mainsprings are to be found within and not beyond the continent'.[38] O'Brien's view, if true, would confound not merely Frank, but also Blackburn, who we saw demonstrated the intimate tie between colonial slavery and the origins of the Industrial Revolution. In fact O'Brien has been quite inconsistent on this matter, and not on just one occasion. In any case, in a relatively recent piece published in *New Left Review* in

1999 he reversed his position again, and allowed the manifold and close links between the Industrial Revolution and overseas trade.[39]

Frank claimed that England was spurred toward industrialization as a result of its relatively high wages. Duchesne complains that Frank does not supply proof. Moreover, he asserts that, according to the consensus, wages remained stationary in the early stages of the Industrial Revolution and rose between 1820 and 1850. In fact Frank is correct on the matter of high wages as a catalyst to industrialization, as pointed out by Dobb and more recent authorities.[40] Moreover, the new consensus on the direction of wages during the heyday of the Industrial Revolution, as noted by Voth, is opposite to what Duchesne has asserted. On the other hand, Duchesne rightly points out that although Frank admits that prolonged economic expansion in Asia did eventually lead to polarization and a lack of effective demand, Frank in his post-Marxist phase chooses to ignore the important point that such a situation arose from the over-exploitation of the mass of the population by the ruling bureaucratic and landed elites. Internally these regimes were weakening economically and politically, and as a result preparing the way for a takeover by Western imperialism. Duchesne concludes that it seems evident that Chinese economic expansion in the early modern period was based on extensive growth, in which population and total economic output grew at about the same rate, with no increases in output per capita. On the other hand, England experienced a prolonged process of steady if gradual increase in agricultural productivity.[41] True China was able to increase the productivity of the land, but such increases came at the expense of greater and greater inputs of labour – in other words, there was declining labour productivity. In the eighteenth century England experienced significant increases in the productivity of both land and labour.[42]

THE GREAT DIVERGENCE

It is this argument about differential rates of productivity in China and England which constitutes Duchesne's strong suit against Frank. From at least the early eighteenth century England was outpacing China economically, Duchesne concludes. Indeed, the latter was on the threshold of an economic crisis. But Duchesne's view on this matter had already been challenged by the appearance of Kenneth Pomeranz's *The Great Divergence* (2000).[43] Pomeranz is a historian of China who studies the past from the point of view of neoclassical economics. He is part of a network of California economic historians who came to prominence in the age of neoliberalism, it is fair to say, while rewriting economic history from this perspective. Pomeranz was not directly answering Duchesne. If he was challenging anyone it was the bigger fish Robert Brenner. Reviewing Brenner's social property approach at the beginning of his work, he looks down his nose at it, noting that in the final analysis it corresponds to the institutional approach of Douglas North, especially in its stress on individual property rights. Such private property rights imply alienated labour, in other words producers, earning wages and unable to enjoy the full fruits of their labour. Both North and Brenner assume as a result that the most productive economy is one where land and labour are completely separated.[44]

Pomeranz starts his quantitative analysis by insisting that a proper discussion of the respective economic performance of Europe and Asia should narrow the focus to the most advanced areas of development. Accordingly, he focuses on England and the lower Yangtze delta. He then attempts to show that these regions were quite similar in the character of their economies, the nature of their respective patterns of growth and the effects of such growth up to 1800. In both cases the institutional structures and population patterns reinforced economic growth. Growth of fixed capital and levels of productivity and gross domestic product per capita were approximately similar. It was only after 1800 that England and the rest of Western Europe embarked on a growth path different from and superior to that of the lower delta.

But England was not able to move to a higher growth path as a result of an advantage inherent in its internal economy. Given his neoclassical approach Pomeranz is not prepared to consider the relationship between England's mercantile state and trading companies, and its internal capitalist relations of production. Nor is he interested in the internal social relations of the Yangtze valley which might account for its economic dynamism. Consideration of productive relations of a given mode of production is irrelevant. Rather, England's accelerated growth was the a result of the unique form of its mercantile state and merchant companies, which made possible access to the land, raw materials and slave labour of the American colonies.

For Pomeranz growth is the result of population increase, a subsequent increase in demand, followed by the growth of supply as result of specialization and an increasing division of labour. This sequence follows in the absence of institutional or demographic constraints. Meeting these conditions, England and the lower Yangtze both experienced impressive growth and increases in standard of living. Land, labour and commodity markets in both cases were equally free, while the rules governing private property were likewise favourable to growth. In both China and England the erosion of family wealth through excessive childbirth was excluded by birth control measures including late marriage and infanticide. Whatever advantages England possessed in industrial technology were offset by China's superiority in agricultural technology. Levels of capital accumulation, productivity and well-being were entirely comparable.

Nonetheless, towards the end of the eighteenth century the population increase in both societies began to create the possibility of shortages of land, raw materials and animal fibres. If allowed to continue such trends would have required a resort to increasingly labour-intensive methods to compensate for the shortage of land. Such resources were potentially available in Eastern Europe as well as in Western China, where millions of peasants migrated in the eighteenth century. Potentially raw materials from these regions could have been exchanged for English or Chinese manufactures. In both cases poverty and remoteness ruled out such plans. In other words the imperial expansion of China in the eighteenth century and the growth of the East European commerce proved incapable of generating sufficient demand to absorb English or Chinese manufactures. Accordingly, these outlying regions were not able to become reliable suppliers of food and raw materials.

What opened the path for England's exit from this cul de sac was Atlantic expansion. This allowed the establishment of the distinctive overseas food and raw-material-producing economies using slave labour that allowed England and later Europe to escape the Malthusian trap. This kind of unequal exchange was not established between the core and periphery in China. The result was that after 1800 China moved toward Malthusian crisis. In the meantime, Europe was able to exchange an expanding volume of manufactured exports for sugar, grain, cotton and timber, while avoiding committing the massive amount of land and labour which would have been necessary to produce them at home. The development of this trade, meanwhile, made it feasible to develop the coal resources and steam power attendant on the Industrial Revolution. In arguing for the notion of equal levels of economic development between England and China in the early modern period, Pomeranz joins Blaut and Frank in challenging Eurocentrism. But from our perspective, that of the transition debate, Pomeranz's perspective offers important support to the idea that colonialism and slavery played a critical role in the triumph of industrial capitalism.

Reacting to the threat that Pomeranz's sophisticated analysis poses to his own view, Brenner, assisted by the China specialist Christopher Isett, soon entered the lists against him.[45] As with Pomeranz, the focus of Brenner's and Isett's response is on a comparison of England and the delta of the Yangzte. But with Brenner there is a welcome return to a social relations of production, or what he calls a social relations of property approach. According to him, there is a complete contrast between these relations in England in the early modern period and the Yangtze delta in the Qing period (1644–1912). The contrasting economic strategies of the upper and lower classes in these regions led to decisively different outcomes, manifest already in the period prior to the Industrial Revolution.

In the Yangtze delta peasants and landlords possessed direct access to the means of social reproduction: land and rent, the latter based on extra-economic coercion. They were accordingly shielded from the need to utilize resources in the most productive way possible in the face of market competition. As a result, they had no need to allocate resources in ways that would promote economic development. The region experienced a Malthusian trajectory, which by the eighteenth and nineteenth centuries turned into a demographic and ecological crisis. In England the situation was reversed. Most peasants did not have direct control of land, and landlords were unable to garner rent based on extra-economic coercion. They were both free and compelled by market competition to use resources so as to maximize their rate of return. As a result England experienced economic growth which led to the Industrial Revolution. The obvious conclusion from this analysis, and one with which I agree, is that the contrasting relations of production in bureaucratic and feudal China and capitalist England explain the radically different outcomes. In my view there is no question that the divergent course of class struggle between peasant producers and landlords in China and England determined this different result. The bureaucratic feudal state in China was repeatedly rescued from peasant revolt by foreign invasion, as in the Mongol invasion of the thirteenth century and again in the Manchu invasion of the seventeenth century. In England, to the contrary, late-medieval peasant revolt began to move England away from feudalism and toward capitalism. The only modern invasion of England in 1688, rather than reinforcing bureaucratic and feudal control, destroyed the vestiges of the bureaucratic feudal order with the political support of English and Dutch capital. Brenner goes on to reiterate, not very convincingly, that colonialism and slavery had nothing to do with English economic growth and the origins of the Industrial Revolution.

But this was not the last word. In 2009 Robert C. Allen published a paper which challenged the views of Brenner and Isett.[46] Allen is known as a brilliant and iconoclastic econometric historian. Among his remarkable works is an analysis of Soviet industrialization in the 1930s which surprisingly concluded that it represented a noteworthy example of the efficient use of economic resources.[47] Allen criticized both Brenner and Pomeranz for basing their work on a comparison of a few crops: rice and wheat in the Yangtze, and wheat in England. Allen points out that agriculture in both cases was about much more than grains. Meat, butter and wool were produced by farmers in England, while Chinese farmers raised pigs and chickens, and cultivated cotton and mulberry trees. A full analysis requires that all these products be factored in, especially since animal and vegetable production reinforced each other. On this basis Allen reanalyzed the data. His conclusions reinforced Pomeranz: that productivity and incomes in China were on a par with those in England. The Great Divergence came after 1800.

Do Allen's conclusions put Brenner's relations of production approach into question? They do not, in my view. What they do is to postpone its full impact to the nineteenth century. It took centuries for capitalist relations of production, and especially the extraction of relative surplus value, to manifest their economic superiority. Allen's data on the development of English agricultural productivity which Brenner himself cites makes this clear.[48] Between 1500 and 1750 labour productivity in English agriculture rose by slightly more than 50 percent. Yet in its first hundred years (1500–1600), when capitalist relations were first starting up, there was a net decline in productivity. The next century saw moderate cumulative gains, which were enough to overcome the previous threat of Malthusian crisis. But the major rate of gain over the whole period came between 1700 and 1750, with continuing increases into the nineteenth century. At a certain point, quantitative economic gains turned into a qualitative economic transformation. But looking back it is important to reiterate that primitive accumulation and the extraction of absolute surplus value were intrinsic to the early development of capitalism, including the gradual rise of the importance of the extraction of relative surplus value. The importance of the extraction of relative surplus value in increasing the rate of growth only became evident over the long run. The prevalence of capitalist relations of production in the West was thus a gradual process.

Yet in conclusion it is important to recall that the West's colonial conquests, to which Pomeranz attributes so much, already reflected the internal dynamism of capitalist relations of production in the early modern period.

THE ASIAN INDUSTRIOUS REVOLUTION

Brenner and others who have insisted on the importance of the extraction of relative as against absolute value have viewed China and Asia as the prime examples of where continued reliance on the latter can lead. Given ongoing Malthusian constraints, more and more labour must be invested in maintaining an existing per capita level of output. Rather than development, the result is what is referred to as involutionary growth, diminishing returns on increasing inputs of labour. Eventually even this expedient is exhausted and society falls into demographic crisis. Pomeranz and Allen fundamentally agree with this assessment, contesting only the date at which China moved toward such a crisis. But in a recent work, *Adam Smith in Beijing* (2007), Giovanni Arrighi questioned the whole concept of Asian involutionary growth as a Eurocentric presumption. Indeed, he argues that it is precisely labour-intensive growth that in the longest run is the only sustainable form of economic growth. Capital-intensive and resource and energy-consuming forms of expansion, characteristic of the West, are necessarily transitory and have a declining prospect.[49]

We encountered Arrighi previously through his study of the history of the cycles of capitalist accumulation. In *The Long Twentieth Century* Arrighi postulated four great phases of capital accumulation – Spanish/Genoese, Dutch, English and American – each functioning on a larger scale than the preceding one. In each hegemonic cycle, elites combined financial and economic power with state political power in order to impose control over the world market while reaping a maximum of profits. Within each cycle, capital moved through an initial period of investment in the commodity form of capital, towards a withdrawal to the safer realm of financial circulation as opportunities for profitable investment in the real economy dried up. The onset of financialization represents a signal of the eventual decline of a given historical phase of capital accumulation and the passage of capital via the international credit system into the hands of a new hegemonic power.

According to Arrighi, the decline of the American phase of capital accumulation in the late twentieth century was signalled by the financialization of the American economy beginning in the 1970s. This presaged the decline of its economic and political hegemony, and the emergence of a new hegemon in East Asia. At the time he wrote *The Long Twentieth Century* in the 1990s, Arrighi forecast that Japan would become the new hegemon. In his new work he claims that China rather than Japan has emerged as the leading East Asian economic power. But whether it can play, or is willing to play, the role of hegemonic power is debatable.

The unending accumulation of capital and power is what defines the European developmental path as capitalist. In contrast, the absence of such an unlimited quest characterized the developmental path of East Asia prior to the Great Divergence. East Asia was a market economy but not a capitalist one.[50] In this light it is Adam Smith, the champion of the market, rather than Marx, the analyst of the capitalist mode of production, who inspires Arrighi. According to Arrighi, it was Smith, towards the end of the eighteenth century, who extolled China as a market economy superior to Europe.[51] At the same time it was Smith who insisted that the social division of labour was the basis of economic development.[52] Parenthetically, we should recall that Marx chastised Smith for not taking the social division of labour seriously into account. Instead, he based his claims of the virtues of the market division of labour on the analytically inappropriate technical division of labour (the pin factory).[53] Indeed this is a crucial point, for Marx believed that Smith not only side-stepped discussing the pitfalls of the market division of labour, but in so doing obscured the fact that a socialist economy could create a superior social division of labour. Arrighi admits that Smith mistakenly used the pin factory as his example of the virtues of the market division of labour. He furthermore acknowledges that Smith decried even the technical division of labour within the pin factory as soul-destroying. But even so Arrighi endorses Smith's correlation of rising labour productivity with the development of specialized units and branches of production arising from an expanding market.[54]

Based on his positive view of the market, Smith considered China as the ultimate exemplar of what he called the 'natural' path of development. Such a natural path uses exchange to develop the home market to promote agriculture and retail trade rather than to expand foreign trade. Coupled with Smith's critique of the technical division of labour and of the negative effects of large-scale capital (the joint-stock company), Arrighi notes that Smith believed that the European path to development which emphasized the capture of foreign markets was 'unnatural' and ultimately unsustainable.[55]

Smith's recognition of China's inward rather than outward-directed economic path is undoubtedly historically correct. Yet he does not sufficiently acknowledge Smith's simultaneous disparagement of China's low wages and lack of economic dynamism. Furthermore, Arrighi should acknowledge that Smith actually had little real knowledge of the vastness and complexity of the Chinese economy.[56] In any event Arrighi argues that China's more 'natural' or Smithian path not only was the basis of China's development in the past, but is the key to the growing emergence of China as the world's future economic powerhouse.

The source of his view lies in the theory of the industrious revolution developed by the Japanese economic historian Kaoru Sugihara, who according to Arrighi has put Smith's view into modern context.[57] As we have seen, de Vries took up Sughira's term 'industrious revolution' and applied it to the development of the early modern European economy. But in de Vries's conception the Western form of industrious revolution entailed the increasing pull of market demand and consumption in a way which was not true of Sughira's Asia.[58] Whereas Brenner and Pomeranz see China sooner or later falling into a Malthusian crisis, Sugihara instead posits an early modern Chinese industrious revolution which enabled it to avoid such a fate. In the early modern period (1500–1800), the development of labour-absorbing institutions and labour-intensive technologies in response to shortages of land and natural resources enabled China and East Asia to dramatically increase their populations, while experiencing not a deterioration, but a modest increase in their standard of living. Japan in fact followed a similar course to China with an even more impressive gain in standard of living.

The concept of industrious revolution was first set forth by Hayami Akira with reference to Tokugawa, or early modern Japan. According to Akira, the liberation of the peasants from outright servitude in the seventeenth century, the entrenchment of family-based farming, an increase in population and a growing scarcity of arable land contributed to a mode of production that depended on the investment of labour. Peasants worked longer and harder but their incomes also grew. They accordingly came to value work, developing a strong work ethic. In applying Akira's concept of industrious revolution to China, Sugihara does not see it as a prelude to a home-grown industrial revolution. In contrast to Europe, the industrious revolution in Asia was a market-based development which did not have the capacity to generate the capital and energy-intensive development characteristic of Britain and later the United States. On the contrary, based on the family household and to a certain extent the village community, it represented a technological and institutional path which was distinct from that of the West, and one which would eventually enable it to challenge the latter's dominance.

Workers in the West were progressively deprived of the opportunity to use their skills and initiative on account of the increasing dominance of capital. In contrast, in East Asia workers were encouraged to share the concerns of employers and to develop the interpersonal skills necessary for flexible specialization. In the countryside stress was placed on being able to perform not one, but a multiplicity of tasks, while cooperation rather than individual achievement was inculcated. The management and prospects of the family farm were a matter of common concern to all members of the household. Overall know-how and management skills were prized among family members.

Within this context the development of labour-intensive technologies led to small improvements in living standards based on full employment. Such development mobilized human rather than non-human resources. Sugihara argues that this tendency to mobilize human as against non-human resources in the course of development continued to mark East Asia even as states there began to absorb Western technologies into their economies. In Japan, China and elsewhere in the region, a hybrid style of development or labour-intensive industrialization took hold, which in the relative absence of industrial capital, cheap energy and abundant raw materials substituted flexible, cooperative and skilled forms of labour. After the Second World War this form of development fully merged with that of Western capital-intensive and energy-consuming forms of development, in Japan first of all, but later in post-revolutionary China and elsewhere in East Asia.

The rise of East Asia, and notably China, has thus been due not to a convergence with the Western capital and energy-intensive path, but to a fusion between the latter and the East Asian labour-intensive approach. This synthesis has great importance in terms of the future of the world economy. The Western economic development path was an extraordinary achievement, greatly expanding the productive capacity of a small proportion of the world's population. The Eastern path, on the other hand, was a miracle of distribution holding out the prospect of a diffusion of the benefits of the miracle of production, originally a monopoly of the West, to the great majority of the world's population through labour-intensive and energy-saving forms of industrialization. Indeed, in the light of the growing ecological crisis associated with industrialization, the miracle of distribution can only continue if the Western path converges with that of the East.[59]

It is Sugihara's thesis, which he claims descends from the views of Smith, that Arrighi applies to China. Indeed, he maintains that there are tentative signs that the current political leadership of this emerging economic power has lately committed itself to this combined path as the only means of achieving an economic development which is environmentally sustainable.[60] While the focal point of world economic power is moving to East Asia, Arrighi does not believe that this heralds the emergence of a new Chinese hegemony. Rather, it suggests the necessity of a multilateral world order. Indeed, his conception of a convergence between the Eastern and Western paths of development points not to socialism in the classic sense, but to some sort of transcendence of capitalism based on the market.

China evolved as a market society dominated by a paternalistic bureaucratic state. Its preoccupation with internal development was largely responsible for its mainly peaceful and non-aggressive relation with its neighbours. No doubt, too, its great size also allowed it to intimidate its neighbours without resort to war. But the exclusion of aggressive bourgeois influence from government further helped to limit its involvement in wars of expansion. In contrast to Frank, Arrighi does not believe the Chinese and European economies were closely linked together until the intrusion of Western imperialism in the nineteenth century. The Chinese Revolution created the conditions under which this kind of market society could re-emerge once Mao exited the scene. Capitalism has made great inroads in China, but continued peasant access to the land blocks the process of primitive accumulation necessary to capitalism.[61]

Reaction to Arrighi's notion of the importance of the industrious revolution to Chinese past and future development is epitomized by Mark Elvin. Invoking various authorities, Elvin insists that China's attempt to substitute labour for capital is a classic example of the dead end of involutionary growth. Moreover, whatever economic progress China made in the twentieth century was through the application of capital-intensive techniques stemming from the West.[62]

Arrighi stresses the importance of the Chinese Revolution, which was based on the peasantry. That upheaval cleared the ground for reviving and empowering its traditional market economy based on small-scale producers.[63] On the other hand, in my opinion he ignores or dismisses the key link between the overthrow of the feudal landlords by the Revolution and the emergence in China of an American path to capitalism, as defined by Lenin and Byres. The overthrow of the landlords and of feudal rent by Mao's revolution placed power in the hands of the Communist party and state while empowering the petty producers. Once Deng Tsao Ping decided to liberalize the market, an explosion of market exchange took place which has been encouraging social differentiation and tremendous accumulation of capital, especially by a bourgeoisie closely tied to the party-state. It is only the reticence of the state in the face of rising levels of rural protest that blocks this process of social differentiation accompanied by primitive accumulation from moving toward a complete capitalist transition. How long these restrictions on capitalist development will continue remains to be seen.[64]

A NON-EUROCENTRIC HISTORY

In the light of these postcolonial historical accounts, in this concluding section we consider what a non-Eurocentric but Marxist history of capitalism would look like. Such a history would pay due regard to the fact of the European birth of capitalism and the economic potential of the capitalist mode of production. But it would also recognize that what gives capitalism importance today is not its past association with the culture or politics of the West, but rather its transcendence of its European origins. Capitalism is sweeping the globe while finding new centres of accumulation, and at the same time is in the midst of a crisis whose outcome is uncertain. It has proved to be both a revolutionary mode of production and an intrinsically unstable and unsustainable one. From this perspective Eurocentrism, including attempts to link capitalism to some intrinsically European essence, must be rejected. Accordingly a non-Eurocentric view of the origins of capitalism eschews a culturalist explanation of its beginnings. Instead it recognizes the relative backwardness of Europe and the existence of proto-capitalist elements in non-European societies. It analyzes the objective social, economic and political conditions which favoured capitalism in some places and blocked its path in others. It acknowledges the critical role of state-backed colonialism and imperialism in fostering the success of Western capitalism and blocking its development elsewhere.

As much as possible a non-Eurocentric history of capitalism pursues a comparative perspective, examining the development of capitalism in both European and non-European contexts. Finally a non-Eurocentric history of capitalism acknowledges that the centre of capital has been displaced repeatedly, and that it is being displaced again. In this connection Harvey's work on spatial fixes is of great importance because it points to the intrinsically uneven character of capitalist development and the shifting location of its historical epicentre. Finally a non-Eurocentric history ought to be based on the assumption that whatever its economic benefits may have been, capitalism has operated against the interests of the mass of a common humanity, and threatens the natural foundations of human society.

HARVEY'S SPATIAL FIX

A scholar who has been particular aware of the effects of the historical and geographic unevenness of the capitalist accumulation process and the importance of the current shift of its global epicentre to China is David Harvey. We can recall that Harvey's insistence on the notion of accumulation by dispossession helped to deepen our understanding of primitive accumulation as an ongoing process that is intrinsic to capitalism not merely in the early modern period, but right up to the present. But his notion of accumulation by dispossession is but part of his overall conception of the renewal of the process of capital accumulation by means of what he terms spatial fix. Harvey argues that one of the ways that capitalism has repeatedly attempted to overcome its crises of over-accumulation is through the abandonment of older centres of accumulation which have exhausted their profit potential, and movement toward new poles of accumulation. In the contemporary context, the movement of investment capital from the United States toward China is a key instance.[65] Such displacement can provoke severe social and political turbulence, in what Harvey calls a switching crisis. Arrighi has lately applied Harvey's ideas of spatial fix and a switching crisis, to illuminate his own conception of the outbreak of signal crises and the initiation of a financial or declining phase of power in the historical cycles of successive Genoese/Spanish, Dutch, British and American hegemonies.[66] In each instance, it is the displacement of capital from a place where over-accumulation has led to stagnation toward a fresh centre of accumulation that provokes crisis and conflict.

It was Marx himself, of course, who first pointed out how capital had successively moved from Venice to Holland to England and finally to the United States, from one pole of accumulation to the next through the mechanism of the international banking and financial system.[67] While we have limited hard or quantitative data on such capital movements, the sequence has been more or less confirmed by Braudel and Richard Goldthwaite.[68] It is to Harvey's credit that he has brought this geographical dimension of the historical movement of capital to the fore. Nonetheless, this spatial displacement of capital should be seen in light of Marx's more fundamental notion of uneven development, which he considered a characteristic feature of capitalism.

We can recall that it was uneven development that marked the genesis of capitalism in backward Western Europe emerging out of the more civilized parts of Eurasia, as pointed out by Hobsbawm. But we have also observed the characteristic geographic unevenness of capitalist development making itself felt through the concentration of wealth, initially created by widely scattered petty producers, into the hands of early capitalists, whose relatively dispersed points of economic activity ultimately became concentrated in cities like Milan, Paris and London. Moreover, from capitalism's early spread over Italy, Germany and France we have seen its step-by-step geographical concentration in Holland and England. Spatial fix appears to be one feature of this overall tendency toward uneven development, which seems to be related to opportunities to make and sustain profits, or the lack thereof.

CAPITALISM VERSUS HUMANITY AND NATURE

Amiya Kumar Bagchi's *Perilous Passage: Mankind and the Global Ascendancy of Capital* looks at the global impact of the development of capitalism from the perspective of global human development.[69] As such it helps to transcend the divide between Eurocentric and non-Eurocentric conceptions of history. Bagchi, an eminent historian and political economist, rose from humble circumstances to become one of India's most distinguished social scientists and head of the Institute of Development Studies in Kolkata. Like Frank and Arrighi he denies that Europeans gained any decisive advantage in technology and standard of living over Asia prior to the Industrial Revolution. Until the nineteenth century European manufactures could not compete on equal terms with those of China and India.[70] Unlike other critics of Eurocentrism, Bagchi remains committed to a Marxist view of history.

Marx's theoretical works lay out the basic dynamics of capitalist accumulation on a world scale.[71] Capitalism is not simply about free trade and free markets. Competition among capitalists and the states that backed them was an integral part of the rise of capitalism in

Europe and its spread to the rest of the world. The social relations of production are fundamental to an understanding of the nature of capitalism. Ongoing conflicts between labour and capital continually challenged the uninterrupted accumulation of capital. There is a fundamental difference between a state like Qing China, which reined in the unrestricted accumulation of capital, and one like eighteenth-century England, which promoted the unchecked accumulation of economic power, thereby facilitating the development of factory production.[72]

But what is truly unique among anti-Eurocentric historians, and indeed all the scholars considered to this point, is Bagchi's analysis of capitalism from the perspective of human development. Human development he defines as progress toward the achievement of decent levels of health, literacy, political and social freedom and environmental sustainability.[73] Economic growth in the form of an expansion of goods and services is positive, but only if leads to global human improvement: 'I argue that economic growth in the sense of production of more goods and services can be said to be a good thing only if it leads to greater human development.'[74] By that measure the development of capitalism was negative even for most Europeans until nearly the end of the nineteenth century. The advantages reaped by the European elites came at the expense of the suffering of millions of people in Europe, the Americas, Africa and Asia.

Bagchi properly emphasizes the exploitation and ravages of European imperialism and colonialism on non-Europeans, and their role in barring the way to economic development outside of Europe. But his narrative also documents the dispossession and exploitation of the peasant and working-class producers of Europe by emergent capitalism.[75] His survey of global demography demonstrates that the development of capitalism has over most of its history been associated with high infant mortality and death rates. Indeed, he shows that Holland's decline as a leading capitalist power was related to population loss as a result of the unhealthy and dangerous conditions in which workers, including large number of merchant sailors, were forced to live.[76] In other words, capitalism has oppressed human beings, whether they were European or non-European. Despite his anti-Eurocentric perspective, Bagchi understands that capitalism has been a system that has inflicted harm on most of humankind including European peasants and workers. Indeed, he makes the important point that if hypothetically the capitalist breakthrough had occurred in India or China, the result would have been the same.[77] The political lesson of such a perspective could not be clearer.

Bagchi admits that damage to the environment occurred prior to the onset of capitalism and colonialism.[78] But he demonstrates that Western colonialism inflicted enormous damage to the ecology of China and India. Recently a former student of E. P. Thompson, Peter Linebaugh, has attempted to document the terrible harm inflicted on the natural environment by the destruction of the commons worldwide by capitalism. In his *Magna Carta Manifesto* (2008) Linebaugh lays stress not so much on the internal dynamics of capitalism, but on its devastation of the commons, which historically has been fundamental to the subsistence economy of the mass of humankind.[79] Enclosure of the land entailed the expropriation and privatization not merely of the subsistence holdings of peasant producers, but also of the woodlands, meadowlands and marshlands which were customarily exploited in common. The privatization of such common resources was a key factor in forcing producers to sell their labour for a wage, which as we have seen was in turn critical to the accumulation of capital. But the transformation of the land and its products into commodities meant an economy based on use values was made impossible. More to the point, such expropriation of the commons and conversion of it into private property intensified the exploitation of the natural environment.

Over time the exploitation of the environment by capital developed into what Marx called a metabolic rift between capitalist society and nature. Linebaugh convincingly demonstrates the beginnings of this process in the Tudor and Stuart period.[80] Deforestation, pollution of the air from coal burning and of the water from industrial and human waste were already problematic in the sixteenth century. But especially impressive is his panoramic description of the step-by-step extension of this process into Africa, India and the Americas until it has engulfed the whole world. Nature has always been a free good for capitalism to dispose of as it saw fit. This was a precondition for the existence of capitalism, and an enormous boon to its operations across five centuries. But at the beginning of the twenty-first century we are approaching the limit of such a framework. The existence of humanity and the planet itself is imperilled if such exploitation of nature continues.

CONCLUSION

In bringing this discussion of the transition problem to a close, I can offer a number of observations. With respect to the nature of the debate, virtually all of its participants claimed to have been inspired by Marx's texts. Yet as the initial exchange between Dobb and Sweezy and the subsequent one between Brenner and Wallerstein suggest, they have drawn different conclusions from Marx's writings. It is my view that in these instances Dobb and Brenner have the better part, in being closer to Marx's view and the historical evidence. Yet even in this respect Brenner fails to appreciate Marx's dialectical method. It would have allowed him to appreciate the unity of the process of capitalist accumulation, which entails both the extraction of surplus value through the development of capitalist relations of production(capitalists and workers) and the realization of profit through the development of the market. The latter is posited by the former.

In part divergent interpretations of Marx arise from the fact that Marxist scholars bring different political and intellectual agendas to the texts in the first place. Furthermore, the enormous and sometimes contradictory corpus of Marx's writings fosters the development of opposing viewpoints. The authoritative standing of Marx's texts, moreover, lends them to different interpretations, as authoritative texts tend to do. Indeed, I would go further in suggesting that the promethean nature of the content and style of Marx's writings is apt to provoke creative reinterpretations of it in the light of changing circumstances. The intellectual vibrancy of the controversies in the transition debate confirms this point. But rather than lamenting this state of affairs, it should be celebrated as affirming the ongoing intellectual strength of Marxist thought.

With respect to the basic themes of this work, I should first insist once more on the protracted nature of the transition which took place over three or more centuries, confirming its gradual nature. There were revolutionary moments – the fourteenth-century class conflicts, the Renaissance, the English and French Revolutions, the Industrial Revolution – when, as a result of long-term underlying changes, quantity became quality and sudden and even violent change took place. Rather than insisting on unending historical continuity or inexplicable revolution, it is important to comprehend the relation or rhythm that exists between slow and long-term change and sudden leaps and transformations. The movement from feudalism to capitalism in any case unfolded over many centuries. Although we cannot be specific, it is likely that any transition to socialism, likewise, will take a long time, with many sudden changes, surprises and reversals – the collapse of the Soviet Union being a case in point.

In the second place, the late seventeenth and eighteenth centuries appear to be the period when the basic commodity categories of capitalism – private property, money, exchange in the competitive market, the concept of labour as the basis of value – consolidated into a new mode of production. Private property – the legal form of the commodity – crystallized into a legal concept in the late seventeenth century. A basic framework for the circulation of money capital and a credit market was created in the same period, with the creation of the Bank of England, a national debt and a stock exchange. A competitive market for land and labour came into existence in the seventeenth and early eighteenth centuries. The notion of wage labour as the source of value, in contradistinction to other forms of value, made its appearance in economic treatises in the late seventeenth century. Indeed, the birth of an increasingly sophisticated capitalist political economy from the late seventeenth century onward was an important symptom of capitalism's maturation. It is important to note that this process of consolidation followed the English Revolution, confirming the importance of revolution at the level of the state as an integral feature of capitalism's genesis.

Just as the English capitalist state consolidated the new mode of production at home, it played an equally decisive role in orchestrating overseas expansion and colonialism. The Industrial Revolution was decisive in European capitalism's conquest of the rest of the world. The Industrial Revolution and colonialism opened the way for the Great Divergence at the beginning of the nineteenth century which saw the economic triumph of the West over the rest of the world. This triumph was reinforced and extended by the political and military intervention of European imperialism, which crippled non-European economic progress.

But the moment of the Great Divergence was also the period of the French Revolution, a capitalist revolution with European and global impact. Among its reverberations was the Haitian Revolution, which dealt a body blow to the emergent capitalism of the French *Ancien Régime*. The revolution in Haiti, coupled with the Tupac Amaru revolt in the Andes and the Pontiac Revolt in

North America, marked the beginning of the long resistance of third world countries to Western colonialism and imperialism.

In this account of the transition, it is the petty producers – peasants and urban craftspeople – who figure as central agents of the transition. They were the underclass of the feudal system, whose ambitions were kept in check by heavy rent and other legal and personal restrictions maintained by the upper class. Their combativeness revealed itself during the late medieval crisis and played a key role in the decline of feudalism. At the same time, the removal of feudal constraints allowed the economic ambitions of the better-off small-scale producers to assert themselves. The social splitting of this group was apparent as early as the late fifteenth century, and in the next century led to the birth of two new classes, capitalist farmers and agricultural wage workers. The development of these two largely rural classes was visible in Italy, France and Holland, but above all in sixteenth-century England where it proved critical to the emergence of capitalism. Capitalist farmers, a group whose economic ambitions were evident in the late medieval period, together with well-to-do craftspeople followed a revolutionary path by reorganizing production in both agriculture and industry from the sixteenth century onward. Led by these same proto-capitalist elements, petty producers and wage workers provided the shock troops of the early modern social and political revolutions.

Early more or less successful variants of capitalism were manifest in Italy, Germany, France and Holland. The new mode of production finally consolidated itself in England in the course of the seventeenth century. From the beginning the development of the global market played an essential role in both helping to dissolve the vestiges of the feudal system and providing a market for capitalist manufactured commodities. The distinguishing feature of the new mode of production was the use of wage labour, and its employment as variable capital in both agriculture and industry. The new social relations of production made possible capital accumulation on the basis of the extraction of relative as against absolute value. While these advantages were already evident from the sixteenth century, their superiority did not become evident until the eighteenth century. It was only towards the end of the eighteenth century and the onset of the Industrial Revolution that the Great Divergence between this mode of production and those in place elsewhere became clear.

Having discussed the origins of capitalism at length and carried his sketch of the history of capitalism down to the twentieth century, Dobb ventured to discuss its future prospects at the conclusion of his *Studies in the Development of Capitalism*. Based on this long perspective, he cautiously took the view that the role of state monopoly capitalism, evident since the beginning of the twentieth century, was bound to increase. The Great Depression of the 1930s and the two World Wars had permanently increased the role of the state in the economy. He also asserted that the influence of the socialist states led by the Soviet Union, and of the countries of the third world, would likely grow. As Dobb presented them, these developments seemed to be the more or less inevitable outcome of a long historical process. The first of these forecasts has been more or less sustained. The role of the state as an instrument of big capital looms larger than ever, especially in the light of the collapse of the recent experiment in global neoliberalism. On the other hand, Dobb's further prediction about the future influence of the Soviet Union and its allies as well as the under-developed countries represents a cautionary tale of the dangers of historical prediction. The Soviet Union is no more, while with the exception of China and possibly India and Brazil, the economic gap between the developed and under-developed countries has increased rather than diminished.[1]

Forecasting the future in the wake of the Second World War, the basis of Dobb's predictions was that the development of state monopoly capitalism, the growing power of the Soviet bloc and the third world states would hem capitalism in and eventually lead to its collapse. The neoliberal experiment that began in the 1980s represented a temporarily successful reaction to these trends. This neoliberal endeavour has collapsed, and the global capitalist system has entered a period of the doldrums if not outright decline. If there is no immediate remedy this period of decay could prove indeterminately prolonged and dark. In my more pessimistic moments I recall Dobb's own characterization of the decline of feudalism as stretching out over centuries.

Writing in 2000 while the neoliberal experiment was still going strong, Guy Bois saw neoliberalism as a symptom of deepening capitalist crisis. Toward the conclusion of his account of the late medieval feudal crisis, Bois offered a qualified comparison between that crisis and the contemporary crisis of capitalism.[2] In doing so, Bois was able to suggest the gravity of the current situation from a historical perspective. Like the late medieval crisis, the current state of affairs is marked by ongoing large-scale unemployment, growing insecurity, violence and social marginalization. The two eras are likewise characterized by outbursts of the irrational in the realm of culture in which the existing elites are fully complicit. At the same time, Bois hastened to distinguish the sources of crisis in each case: the one engendered by an insufficiency of production in an economy based on petty production, the other rooted in a crisis of over-production in an economy based on industrial capitalism.

According to Bois, the response to this contemporary crisis of over-production at the heart of the economy has been the emergence of a powerful financial capitalism. This financial capitalist regime freed itself from state regulation while subordinating the spheres of commercial and industrial capitalism to itself. In its pursuit of higher and higher rates of return it forced down wages and induced a fall of demand which has exacerbated the problems of the global economy. Meanwhile ongoing unbalanced consumption in the American economy, based on massive debts and commercial deficits, is the linchpin of the system. Financial speculation has propped up the system so far. Published eight years before the bursting of the great financial bubble, Bois's analysis must be regarded as prescient. Set off by his discussion of the late medieval crisis, it suggests the seriousness of the current situation.

Arrighi too offered an analysis of the contemporary crisis. In *The Long Twentieth Century*, published in 1994, he portrayed the crisis as one of American capitalism but not of capitalism as a whole. Analyzing capitalism's history, he divided it into four successive hegemonic periods over five centuries, the last of which was the American. Like Bois, Arrighi saw the onset of the recent financial phase of capitalism as a symptom of decline preliminary to the ultimate emergence of a new hegemonic power. In this context, he predicted the rise of a new hegemon in the form of the East Asian powerhouse Japan. By the time he came to publish *Adam Smith in Beijing* in 2007, he was still convinced that the rising centre of world economic power lay in the East. His bet was now not on Japan but on China. More importantly his new forecast for the first time acknowledged that the capitalist system itself and not simply American capitalism was in crisis. China would lead the way not because it was the embodiment of a new and superior form of capitalist hegemony, but because it offered a form of economic activity that was not only more competitive in the market, but sustainable, in contrast to the energy and capital-intensive economies of the West. The ecological crisis had made such economies into dinosaurs. A global market economy of a sort could continue, but no longer based on capitalism and a regime of political hegemony.

Arrighi's prediction of a non-capitalist future for China should be taken with a grain of salt. On the other hand, it does reflect an awareness that the current crisis is not merely a short-term crisis of profits and demand, but a more long-term one involving a crisis of energy shortage and environmental sustainability as well as global governability. In the latter context, no one can rule out the possibility that the current hegemon, the United States, will attempt to hold onto its status by resorting to war against its rivals, and notably against China. It has already demonstrated its willingness to fight for control of the energy resources of the Middle East, and its determination to defend the hegemonic position of the dollar at almost any cost. In the face of its industrial decline and massive international indebtedness, the continuation of the global dollar standard is essential to holding on to its remaining power. While the situation has obviously evolved from that described so clearly and brilliantly by Lenin in *Imperialism the Highest Stage of Capitalism*, the possibility of conflicts over energy and the control of financial markets between unequal and rival centres of capitalist accumulation cannot be dismissed. Contrariwise, a new global system of financial and political regulation may itself fetter the possible emergence of a stable new phase of capitalist accumulation. In any case, the future governability of the global financial and political system remains an intractable structural feature of the current crisis.

Indeed, the political order has been central to my account of capitalism's history. I have underscored the role of the state in nurturing capitalism at its beginnings, overseeing its development through mercantilism and through combined and uneven development, and then being itself transformed by revolution. Throughout I have insisted on its role in totalizing capitalist relations: generalizing, maintaining and integrating capitalist relations right through society. At the same time I have underscored the fact that capitalism internationally has developed historically through a system of rival and competitive states. I have harped on the role of the state in part because of the need to reject what has been an overly economistic understanding of capitalism. But I have also focused on the role of the state because I believe it to have been no less an essential feature of capitalism than the market and capitalist relations of production themselves, and its future role is today among the most important contradictory aspects of the current crisis. For one of the essential elements of the present situation is that the state and its territorial base continues to be essential to the continued operation of capitalism, and yet has become an obstacle to the further development of capitalism as a global system with an appropriately global means of regulating itself. Indeed, the development of such a world-wide institutional mechanism, necessarily limiting the power of the territorial state, might well constitute a barrier to further capital accumulation. In the light of this crisis of the capitalist state, the objective of the working class should be to organize itself politically in order to advance the democratization of the political order, locally, nationally and internationally, as an alternative to capitalism.

Let me conclude this discussion of the limits confronting capitalism by referring to the problem of sustaining value, the central concept of Marxist political economy. Marx observed that the accumulation of capital itself becomes a barrier to future accumulation. In the first instance, he was referring to the short-term and recurrent difficulty of maintaining profit margins on the basis of a growing mass of capital. But in a wider and longer perspective, he was pointing to the problem of the continued accumulation of surplus in the form of capital becoming a barrier to the further development of the forces of production.

In order to understand why this is the case, it is important to recall that the application of scientific culture to economic life was of great importance to Marx's understanding of capitalism, and more importantly, its eventual transformation into socialism. According to Marx's *Capital*, the introduction of machinery into production in the Industrial Revolution, rather than lightening labour, had the effect of enlarging the pool of proletarians, increasing the workday, intensifying the character of work, and enslaving the worker to the machine.[3] Under capitalist conditions the quest for surplus value increases the exploitation of workers while deskilling them.

On the other hand, writing in the *Grundrisse*, Marx argued that beyond a certain point the colossal development of capitalist industry undermines value or abstract labour as a measure of social wealth. He contrasts value – a form of wealth bound to the expenditure of human labour-time – with the gigantic wealth-producing potential of modern science and technology. Value, which is intrinsic to the initial period of industrialization, becomes increasingly anachronistic in terms of the potential of the mature system of production to which it gives rise:

> but to the degree that large industry develops, the creation of real wealth comes to depend less on labour time and on the amount of labour employed than on the power of the agencies set in motion during labour time, whose 'powerful effectiveness' is itself ... out of all proportion to the direct labour time spent on their

production, but depends rather on the general state of science and on the progress of technology.[4]

Under such circumstances the full realization of the potential of the mature productive system would entail the withering away of value. But capitalism cannot permit such an abolition of value because it lives off of it: 'the theft of alien labour time, on which the present wealth is based, appears a miserable foundation in face of this new one, created by large-scale industry itself'.[5] The overthrow of value is only possible through the overthrow of capitalism by socialism. Otherwise, the further transformation and development of the forces of production in the direction of the full application of science and new technologies, including those that are more ecologically sound, is crippled by the persistence of the indispensable quest by capital for value, and especially surplus value.[6]

We have seen how step-by-step a regime of capital was constituted in the early modern period based on the development of private property, the exchange of commodities based on competitive markets and the realization of profit. At the heart of this profit-based system lies the creation of value from the sale of labour power, and especially, the ultimate extraction of surplus value from the process. The existence of capital is tied to the creation of value, off which it lives and without which it cannot exist. On this basis, there has been historically a tremendous development of the forces of production. Included in these forces of production are all the scientific, technical and cultural resources, including the ecological sciences, necessary to further human development and the preservation of humanity's relationship with nature. Yet these resources are being increasingly commodified, because they are proving vital to the development of the most technically advanced forms of productive capital. Indeed, in order to produce profits the production of such knowledge must necessarily be tied to a labour process that produces value.

But the further creation of such knowledge is being inhibited in so far as such resources are commodified. Turned into intellectual property, such resources cannot be developed further if they do not fit within the increasingly narrow limits prescribed by capital accumulation. In other words, the production of knowledge itself is being privatized and tied down on the Procrustean bed of value creation. On the contrary, the effective production of knowledge is based on the free exchange and sharing of information. Such a constricted set-up is not viable even on its own terms. Meanwhile, it is proving difficult for capital to garner surplus from the intellectual and cultural products so produced, or to keep control of the workers who produce them. In other words, the relations of production necessary to the production and safeguarding of profits fetter innovation, on which the competitive marketplace is based. Marx argued that the freeing of the forces of production from the necessity of value creation would make possible their unrestricted development and application to human development.

NOTES

INTRODUCTION: PROBLEMS AND METHODS

1   Dobb (1946).
2   Perry Anderson sketched the outlines of a transition from antiquity to feudalism in *Passages from Antiquity to Feudalism* (1974a). See Chris Wickham's study of the transition from the slave mode of production to feudalism, *Framing the Early Middle Ages* (2005).
3   Dobb (1946). A third edition appeared in 1972.
4   Rodney Hilton, *The Transition from Feudalism to Capitalism* (1976a); Immanuel Wallerstein, *The Modern World System: Vol. I, Capitalist Agriculture and the Origins of the European World-Economy* (1974); Anderson (1974a) and *Lineages of the Absolutist State* (1974b); Robert Brenner, 'Agrarian class structure and economic development in pre-industrial Europe' (1976) and 'The origins of capitalist development: a critique of neo-Smithian Marxism' (1977).
5   Wallerstein, 'US weakness and the struggle for hegemony' (2003).
6   Amiva Kumar Bagchi, *Perilous Passages: Mankind and the Global Ascendancy of Capital* (2005); Neil Davidson, 'How revolutionary were the bourgeois revolutions?' (2005); Chris Harman, 'An age of transition?' (2008).
7   Guy Bois, *La grande dépression médiévale: XIVe–XVe siecles* (2000), pp. 207–11.
8   Alex Callinicos, *Imperialism and Global Political Economy* (2009), pp. 80–1.
9   T. J. Byres, *Capitalism from Above and Capitalism from Below* (1996), p. 12.
10 Holton (1985), p. 35.
11 Douglas North and Robert Paul Thomas, *The Rise of the Western World* (1973).
12 Holton (1985), p. 55.
13 Holton (1985), pp. 110–13.
14 Karl Marx, *Grundrisse* (1973), p. 232.
15 Friedrich Engels, 'Introduction' to the English edition of *Socialism: Utopian and Scientific* (Marx and Engels, 1975–, Vol. 27), p. 292.
16 R. H. Tawney, *Religion and the Rise of Capitalism* (1926).
17 Marx, *Capital*, Vol. 3 ((Marx and Engels, 1975–, Vol. 37), pp. 777–8.
18 Engels, 'Review of Karl Marx, *A Contibution to the Critique of Political Economy*' (1859).
19 Moishe Postone, 'Rethinking *Capital* in the light of the *Grundrisse*' (2008), pp. 129–30.
20 Perry Anderson, *Arguments Within English Marxism* (1980); E. P. Thompson, *The Poverty of Theory and Other Essays* (1978).

21 Ellen Meiskins Wood points out that Thompson was arguing against those in particular who turned a blind eye to the traumatic consequences of the industrialization process on workers: *Democracy Against Capitalism* (1995), p. 86.
22 Ellen Meiskins Wood and John Bellamy Foster (eds), *In Defense of History* (1997).
23 Wood (1995), p. 55.
24 Jack Goody, *The Theft of History* (2006); John M. Hobson, *The Eastern Origins of Western Civilisation* (2004).
25 Chris Harman, 'The rise of capitalism' (2004).
26 Giovanni Arrighi, *Adam Smith in Beijing* (2007) and *The Long Twentieth Century* (1994).
27 Minqi Li, 'An age of transition: the United States, China, peak oil, and the demise of neo-liberalism' (2008).

1 THE DECLINE OF FEUDALISM

1 Amartya Sen, 'Dobb' (2008).
2 Dobb (1946), p. viii.
3 Dobb (1946), p. 7. See Brenner, 'Dobb on the transition from feudalism to capitalism' (1978).
4 Dobb (1946), p. 11.
5 Dobb (1946), pp. 18–19.
6 Dobb (1946), p. 18.
7 Brenner, 'Feudalism' (2008).
8 Dobb (1946), pp. 35–7.
9 Dobb (1946), pp. 65, 70, 81–2.
10 Dobb (1946), pp. 63, 65–6.
11 Dobb (1946), pp. 19–21.
12 Dobb (1946), pp. 35–41.
13 Dobb (1946), p. 42.
14 Dobb (1946), p. 45.
15 Dobb (1946), pp. 43–6.
16 Dobb (1946), pp. 60, 62, 65.
17 Dobb (1946), p. 70.
18 Dobb (1946), p. 42.
19 Paul M. Sweezy et al., *The Transition from Feudalism to Capitalism: A Symposium* (1954).
20 Dobb and Paul M. Sweezy, *Du féodalisme au capitalisme: problèmes de la transition*, Vol. 1 (1977), pp. 5–6.
21 Sweezy et al. (1954).
22 John Bellamy Foster, 'Sweezy in perspective' (2008).
23 Sweezy, 'Critique', in Rodney Hilton, *The Transition from Feudalism to Capitalism* (1976a), pp. 36–8.
24 Sweezy, 'Critique', in Hilton (1976a), p. 40.
25 Dobb, 'Reply', in Hilton (1976a), p. 59.
26 Dobb, 'Reply', in Hilton (1976a), p. 60.

27 Dobb, 'Reply', in Hilton (1976a), p. 60.
28 Dobb, 'Reply', in Hilton (1976a), pp. 60–1.
29 Sweezy, 'Critique', in Hilton (1976a), pp. 49–51.
30 Sweezy, 'Critique', in Hilton (1976a), pp. 62–3.
31 On Kohachiro Takahashi see Y. Komatu, 'The study of economic history in Japan' (1961), and Germaine A. Hoston, *Marxism and the Crisis of Development in Prewar Japan* (1986), pp. 287–8.
32 Takahashi, 'A contribution to the discussion' (1976), p. 68.
33 Takahashi (1976), pp. 70–1.
34 Takahashi (1976), pp. 72–3.
35 Hilton, 'A crisis of feudalism' (1985), p. 135.
36 See the *festschrift* 'Rodney Hilton's Middle Ages' (Dyer, Coss, and Wickham, eds, 2007).
37 Hilton, 'A comment' (1976b).
38 S. R. Epstein, 'Rodney Hilton, Marxism and the transition from feudalism to capitalism (2007).
39 Epstein (2007).
40 Hilton (1976b), pp. 113–16.
41 Hilton (1976b), pp. 116–17.
42 Hilton (1976b), p. 117.
43 Hilton, 'Capitalism – what's in a name' (1976c), p. 150.
44 Hilton (1976c), p. 150.
45 Hilton (1976c), p. 154.
46 Hilton (1976c), p. 155.
47 Hilton, 'Feudalism in Europe' (1984).
48 John Merrington, 'Town and country in the transition to capitalism' (1975).
49 Merrington (1975), pp. 177–8.
50 Merrington (1975), p. 191.
51 Eric C. Hobsbawm, 'From feudalism to capitalism' (1976), p. 160.
52 Patrick Bond, 'Uneven development' (1999); Neil Smith, 'The geography of uneven development' (2006) and *Uneven Development: Nature, Capital and the Production of Space* (2008).
53 Hobsbawm (1976), p. 160.
54 Hobsbawm (1976), p. 164.
55 Hobsbawm (1976), p. 163.
56 Anderson (1974a), pp. 16–19 and (1974b), p. 149.
57 Takahashi, 'La place de la révolution de Meiji dans l'histoire agraire du Japon' (1977).
58 Bagchi (2005), pp. 179–90; Herbert P. Bix, *Peasant Protest in Japan, 1590–1884* (1986), pp. 149–73.
59 Anderson (1974b), pp. 435–71.
60 This point is forcefully made for the feudal mode of production generally by Wickham in 'Productive forces and the economic logic of the feudal mode of production' (2008).
61 Anderson (1974a), p. 147.
62 Anderson (1974a), p. 190.
63 Anderson (1974a), pp. 198–9.

64 Anderson (1974a), pp. 205–6.
65 In his comparative study *The Origins of Capitalism and the 'Rise of the West'* (2007), Edward Mielant stresses the political power and city-state rivalries of medieval urban merchants in Western Europe compared with the merely economic power of merchants in China, India and the Maghreb.
66 Anderson (1974b), p. 21, n. 10.
67 Anderson (1974b), p. 21.
68 Anderson (1974b), p. 18.
69 Anderson (1974b), p. 17.
70 Anderson (1974b), p. 23.
71 Anderson (1974b), pp. 23–4.
72 Brenner, 'Agrarian class structure' (1985a) and 'The agrarian roots of European capitalism' (1985b).
73 Brenner, *The Boom and the Bubble* (2002).
74 Brenner, *Merchants and Revolution* (1993).
75 George A. Reisch, *How the Cold War Transformed Philosophy of Science* (2005), p. 384.
76 For a critique of the methodology of analytical Marxism and Brenner, see Michael A. Lebowitz, *Following Marx* (2009), pp. 39–61. The continuing intellectual and philosophical significance of Marxian dialectics is made evident in David Harvey, *Cosmopolitanism and the Geographies of Freedom* (2009), pp. 230–36.
77 Brenner (1985a), p. 36.
78 Brenner (1985a), pp. 38–40.
79 Brenner (1985a), pp. 40–1.
80 Brenner (1985a), pp. 54–5.
81 Brenner (1985a), p. 49.
82 Brenner (1985a), pp. 46–52, and (1985b), pp. 214–15.
83 Brenner sets out the competing logics of non-capitalist and capitalist modes of production in 'The social basis of economic development' (1986).
84 Brenner (1977), pp. 25–93.
85 Brenner (1985b), pp. 217–27.
86 Bois, 'Against the neo-Malthusian orthodoxy' (1985), p. 115.
87 Bois (2000), pp. 41–2.
88 Bois (2000), pp. 25–8, 42, 47–53.
89 Bois (1985), p. 111, and (2000), pp. 21, 50.
90 Bois (2000), pp. 143–76.
91 See E. M. Wood (1999); George Comninel, *Rethinking the French Revolution* (1987); Benno Teschke, *The Myth of 1648* (2003).
92 Chris Harman, *Marxism and History* (1998) and 'An age of transition?' (2008).
93 Harman, *A People's History of the World* (1999/2008).
94 Harman (1998), p. 68.
95 Harman (2008), p. 187. See the further debate between Harman and Brenner, 'Origins of capitalism (2006).
96 Byres, 'Differentiation of the peasantry under feudalism and the transition to capitalism' (2006).

97 Byres (1996).
98 Byres (2006), p. 27.
99 Callinicos, *Making History* (2004).
100 Ernesto Laclau, 'Feudalism and capitalism in Latin America' (1971).
101 Jairus Banaji, 'Modes of production in a materialist conception of history' (1977).

2 EXPERIMENTS IN CAPITALISM: ITALY, GERMANY, FRANCE

1 Marx, *Capital*, Vol. 1 (Marx and Engels, 1975–, Vol. 35), p. 723.
2 Marx, *Capital*, Vol. 1, p. 707. See Henry Kamen, *The Iron Century* (1971), pp. 386–403; Catharina Lis, *Poverty and Capitalism in Pre-Industrial Europe* (1979), pp. 71–82.
3 Marx, *Capital*, Vol. 1 (Marx and Engels, 1975–, Vol. 35), p. 707.
4 Marx, *Capital*, Vol. 1 (Marx and Engels, 1975–, Vol. 35), p. 739.
5 Anderson, *Spectrum* (2005), p. 251.
6 Krantz and Hohenberg (1975).
7 Giuliano Procacci, 'Italy: commentary' (1975), pp. 27–8.
8 Maurice Aymard, 'From feudalism to capitalism in Italy' (1982).
9 Maurice Aymard (ed.), *Lire Braudel* (1988).
10 Emilio Sereni, *History of the Italian Agricultural Landscape* (1997), p. 143.
11 Renato Zangheri, 'Agricoltura e sviluppo del capitalismo' (1968).
12 Aymard (1982), pp. 163–4, 186,
13 Aymard (1982), p. 167.
14 Ruggerio Romano, 'La Storia Economica dal secolo XIV al Settecento' (1972–76).
15 Renato Zangheri, 'I rapporti storici tra progresso agricolo e svillupo economico in Italia' (1979).
16 Wallerstein (1974), pp. 216–21.
17 Aymard (1982), pp. 185–96.
18 Sereni (1977), pp. 158, 187; Faruk Tabak, *The Waning of the Mediterranean, 1550–1870* (2008), p. 192.
19 Fernand Braudel, 'L'Italia Fuori d'Italia' (1972–6), p. 2114.
20 Anderson (1974a), p. 192.
21 Anderson (1974b), pp. 152, 156.
22 Anderson (1974a), p.162
23 Herman van de Wee, *The Growth of the Antwerp Market and the European Economy (Fourteenth–Sixteenth Centuries)* (1963).
24 On the role of silver in the expansion of the world economy see Ronald Findlay and Kevin H. O'Rourke, *Power and Plenty* (2007), pp. 224–5.
25 Engels, *The Peasant War in Germany* (Marx and Engels, 1975–, Vol. 10), pp. 397–482. For appreciations of Engels's work from a Marxist point of view see the remarks of Ernst Engelber and Günter Vogler, 'The Peasant War in Germany – 125 years later' (1976).
26 Engels, *Peasant War*, p. 399.
27 Engels, *Peasant War*, p. 401.

28 Engels, *Peasant War*, p. 402.
29 Engels, *Peasant War*, pp. 406–7.
30 Engels, *Peasant War*, p. 411.
31 Engels, *Peasant War*, pp. 412–13.
32 Engels, *Peasant War*, pp. 413–14.
33 Engels, *Peasant War*, p. 415.
34 Engels, *Peasant War*, pp. 415–16.
35 Engels, *Peasant War*, pp. 421–2.
36 Engels, *Peasant War*, p. 443.
37 Engels, *Peasant War*, p. 461.
38 Engels, *Peasant War*, p. 410.
39 Cited in Engelber (1976), pp. 105–6.
40 Adolf Laube, Max Steinmetz and Günter Vogler, *Illustrierte Geschichte der deutschen frühbürgerlichen Revolution* (1974).
41 Laube et al. (1974), pp. 9, 16–17.
42 Laube et al. (1974), pp. 14–15.
43 Laube et al. (1974), pp. 18–22. See also Tom Scott, *Society and Economy in Germany 1300–1600* (2003), pp. 90–112; Wieland Held, *Zwischen Marktplatz und Anger* (1988), pp. 143, 160, 173, 178–80, 182; Günter Vogler, 'Thüringens Wirtschaft und Sozialstruktur zur Bauernkriegszeit' (2008), pp. 63–4.
44 Laube et al. (1974), pp. 51, 53.
45 Laube et al. (1974), pp. 68, 70–2, 87–9, 91, 96–102, 104.
46 Laube et al. (1974), p. 102.
47 Laube et al. (1974), p. 206.
48 Laube et al. (1974), p. 233.
49 Laube et al. (1974), pp. 192–3, 290.
50 Marcel van der Linden, 'Marx and Engels, Dutch Marxism and the "model capitalist nation of the seventeenth century"' (1997).
51 See, for example, Abraham Friesen, *Reformation and Utopia* (1974) and Andreas Dorpalen, *German History in Marxist Perspective* (1985), pp. 99–112.
52 Peter Blickle, *Die Revolution von 1525* (2004).
53 Tom Scott, 'The German Peasants' War and the "crisis of feudalism"' (2002).
54 Scott (2002).
55 Scott (2003), pp. 90–152.
56 Scott (2002), p. 292.
57 Scott (2002), pp. 254–85.
58 Scott (2002), p. 289.
59 Scott (2003), p. 5.
60 Scott (2002), p. 289.
61 Anderson (1974b), pp. 15–17.
62 Anderson (1974b), p. 40.
63 Brenner (1976), p. 61.
64 Brenner, 'The Low Countries in the transition to capitalism' (2001).
65 Michel Vovelle, 'Reflections on the revisionist interpretation of the French Revolution' (1990), pp. 749–55.

66   George Comninel, *Rethinking the French Revolution* (1987).
67   Comninel (1987), pp. 190–1, 200.
68   Wood, *The Origins of Capitalism: A Longer View* (2002), pp. 50–63.
69   Heller, 'The longue duréee of the French bourgeoisie' (2009).
70   Heller, *Iron and Blood* (1991), pp. 60–1.
71   Emmanuel Le Roy Ladurie, *Carnival in Romans* (1989), pp. 108, 122,
      127–8, 339–70; Heller (1991), pp. 60–3, 86–101, 111–15, 120–3, Jean-
      Marie Constant, *La Ligue* (1996), pp. 259–312.
72   Heller (1991), pp. 142–8.
73   Heller, *Labour, Science and Technology in France 1500–1620* (1996),
      pp. 28–32; Jean-Marc Moriceau, *Les fermiers de l'Ile-de-France* (1994),
      pp. 145–341, and 'Le laboureur et ses enfants' (1993).
74   Heller (1996), pp. 65–84.
75   Heller (2009), p. 51; Moriceau (1994), pp. 611–23, 631–42.

3 ENGLISH CAPITALISM

1   Maurice Dobb *Studies in the Development of Capitalism* (1946), pp.
      19–20.
2   Sweezy, 'A critique', in Rodney Howard Hilton (ed.), *The Transition
      from Feudalism to Capitalism* (1976a), pp. 51–2.
3   Dobb, 'A reply', in Hilton (1976a), pp. 62–3.
4   Perry Anderson, *Lineages of the Absolutist State* (1974b), p. 122.
5   Dobb (1946), p. 18.
6   Dobb (1946), pp. 237–8.
7   Dobb (1946), pp. 242, 244, 253.
8   Dobb (1946), p. 196.
9   Dobb (1946), p. 178.
10   Dobb (1946), pp. 185–6.
11   Dobb (1946), pp. 222–3.
12   Dobb (1946), pp. 223–8.
13   Marx, *Capital*, Vol. 3, pp. 332–3.
14   Dobb (1946), pp. 161–2, 164, 170–2.
15   Dobb (1946), pp. 125–6.
16   Sweezy, 'A critique', in Hilton (1976a), pp. 52–4.
17   Dobb (1946), p. 172.
18   Henry Heller, 'The transition debate in historical perspective' (1985).
19   Dobb (1946), pp. 157, 160.
20   Immanuel Wallerstein, *The Modern World-System* (1974).
21   Wallerstein, *World Systems Analysis: An Introduction* (2004), p. 14.
22   Wallerstein (1974), pp. 24, 51.
23   Wallerstein (1974), pp. 37–8, 77, 127.
24   Wallerstein (1974), Vol. 1, pp. 127, 165–221, and 'The rise and future
      demise of the world capitalist system: concepts for comparative analysis'
      (1979), pp. 5–6.
25   Wallerstein (1974), p. 68.
26   Wallerstein (1974), pp. 86–7, 95, 103, 104–7, 112, 116.

27 Wallerstein (1974), p. 127.
28 Wallerstein (1974), p. 122.
29 Wallerstein (1974), pp. 308–12, 355.
30 Wallerstein (1974), pp. 119, 124, 162, 237, 256.
31 Wallerstein (1974), pp. 95–6, 100.
32 Wallerstein (1974), p. 350.
33 Wallerstein (1974), p. 350.
34 Wallerstein (1974), p. 350.
35 Wallerstein (1974), p. 350.
36 Robert C. Allen, 'Economic structure and agricultural productivity in Europe, 1300–1800' (2000).
37 Robert Brenner, 'The origins of capitalist development' (1977), p. 72.
37 Brenner (1977), p. 72.
38 Jan de Vries, *The Industrious Revolution* (2008), pp. 82–3.
39 De Vries (2008), pp. 85–6.
40 Marx, *Capital,* Vol. 1 (Marx and Engels, 1975–, Vol. 35), pp. 395–6.
41 Brenner (1977), p. 92.
42 James Morris Blaut, *The Colonizer's Model of the World* (1993), p. 189.
43 Brenner, 'Bourgeois revolution and transition to capitalism' (1989), pp. 271–305.
44 Brenner (1989), pp. 273, 293–4, 302–3.
45 Marx, *Capital,* Vol. 1 (Marx and Engels, 1975–, Vol. 35), p. 739.
46 Marx, *Capital,* Vol. 1 (Marx and Engels, 1975–, Vol. 35), pp. 740–1. See Javier Cuenca-Estaban, 'India's Contribution to the British balance of payments, 1757–1812' (2007); Irfan Habib, 'Introduction: Marx's perception of India' (2006), p. xli; Utsa Patnaik, 'The free lunch' (2006), pp. 36–9.
47 Rosa Luxemburg, *The Accumulation of Capital* (2003), p. 434.
48 Massimo de Angelis, 'Marx and primitive accumulation' (2001).
49 David Harvey, *The New Imperialism* (2003), pp. 142–52.
50 Marx, *Capital,* Vol. 1, (Marx and Engels, 1975–, Vol. 35), p. 707, cited in Brenner (1989), p. 293.
51 Brenner (1989), p. 294.
52 James Galloway, 'One market or many?' (2000), pp. 23–42; J. A. Chartres, 'Market integration and agricultural output in seventeenth, eighteenth and early nineteenth century England' (1995), p. 27; Robert Goldthwaite, *The Economy of Renaissance Florence* (2009), pp. 588–9.
53 C. G. A. Clay, *Economic Expansion and Social Change: England 1500–1700, Vol. 1* (1984), pp. 78–9, 80, 83–5, 302–5.
54 Dobb (1946), pp. 114–22.
55 Gregory Clark, 'Land rental values and the agrarian economy in England and Wales: 1500–1914' (2002).
56 Keith Wrightson, *Earthly Necessities* (2000), pp. 72–5, 133–5, 136–7, 183–90.
57 Mark Overton, *Agricultural Revolution in England* (1996), p. 44.
58 Robert J. Steinfeld, *The Invention of Free Labor* (1991), pp. 60, 63–5;

Peter Clark, 'Migration in England during the late seventeenth and early eighteenth centuries' (1987), pp. 236–42.

59 W. E. Minchinton (ed.), *Wage Regulation in Pre-Industrial England* (1972), p. 22; Christopher Frank, *Master and Servant Law* (2010), pp. 4–5; Marc Steinberg, 'Capitalist development, labour process and the law' (2003), p. 456.

60 Marx, *Grundrisse*, p. 770.

61 István Mészáros, *Beyond Capital* (1995), pp. 110–33.

62 Jane Whittle, *The Development of Agrarian Capitalism: Land and Labour in Norfolk 1440–1580* (2000).

63 Whittle (2000), pp. 307–8.

64 Overton (1996), p. 205.

65 Robert C. Allen, *Enclosure and the Yeoman* (1992), pp. 14–15, 18–19, 21, 208.

66 H. J. Habakkuk, 'Economic functions of English landowners in the seventeenth and eighteenth centuries' (1968).

67 P. K. O'Brien and D. Heath, 'English and French landowners 1688–1789' (1994), p. 43.

68 Ellen Meiskins Wood, *The Origin of Capitalism* (1999).

69 E. M. Wood (1999), pp. 137–9.

70 E. M. Wood (1999), pp. 130–1.

71 Gregory King, *Two Tracts: (a) Natural and Political Observations and Conclusions upon the State and Condition of England; (b) Of the Naval Trade of England and the National Profit then Arising Thereby* (1936).

72 De Vries (2008), p. 82. For a European-wide survey of the place of wage and other forms of labour see Jan Lucassen, 'Mobilization of Labour in Early Modern Europe' (2001).

73 E. M. Wood (1999), pp. 52–3, 58–60.

74 E. M. Wood (1999), pp. 21–6.

75 Bob Kiernan, *Blood and Soil* (2007), pp. 169–212; Theodore W. Allen, *The Invention of the White Race*, Vol. 1 (1994), pp. 44–6, 48–9.

76 E. M. Wood (1999), pp. 110–15, 152–65.

77 Ronald L. Meek, *Studies in the Labor Theory of Value* (1975), pp. 20–1; Neal Wood, *John Locke and Agrarian Capitalism* (1984), p. 37.

78 Joachim Bischoff and Christoph Lieber, 'The concept of value in modern economy (2008), p. 36.

79 Marx, *Capital*, Vol. 1 (Marx and Engels, 1975–, Vol. 35), p. 70.

4 BOURGEOIS REVOLUTION

1 Brenner conveniently recapitulates Marx's theory of transition to capitalism in 'Bourgeois revolution' (1989), pp. 278–9.

2 Marcel van der Linden, 'Marx and Engels, Dutch Marxism' (1997), p. 163.

3 Jonathan Irvine Israel, *Dutch Primacy in World Trade, 1585–1740* (1989), pp. 10, 25, 27; Jan de Vries, *The First Modern Economy* (1997), pp. 198–210, 279–83.

4   Van der Linden (1997), pp. 168–70.
5   Van der Linden (1997), pp. 177–8.
6   For a recent updating see Pepijn Brandon, 'The Dutch revolt' (2007).
7   Giovanni Arrighi, *The Long Twentieth Century* (1994), pp. 44–7, 155–7.
8   Marx, *Capital*, Vol. 3 (Marx and Engels, 1975–, Vol. 37), pp. 326–7.
9   Marx, *Capital*, Vol. 3 (Marx and Engels, 1975–, Vol. 37), pp. 329–30.
10 Hobsbawm, 'The crisis of the seventeenth century' (1965), pp. 5–58.
11 Hobsbawm's view as well as that of others can be found in Aston (1965). See also Jonathan Dewald, Geoffey Parker et al., 'AHR Forum' (2008).
12 Hobsbawm (1965), p. 42.
13 Hobsbawm (1965), p. 42.
14 Ellen Meiskins Wood, *The Origin of Capitalism* (1999), pp. 87–90.
15 Benno Teschke, *The Myth of 1648* (2003), p. 136.
16 Teschke (2003), p. 207.
17 Marx, *Capital*, Vol. 1 (Marx and Engels, 1975–, Vol. 35), pp. 742–4.
18 Jan Lucassen, 'Labour and early modern economic development' (1995).
19 Marx, *Capital*, Vol. 3(Marx and Engels, 1975–, Vol. 37), p. 597.
20 Karel Davids, 'Shifts of technological leadership in early modern Europe' (1995), pp. 347–8.
21 Brenner, 'The Low Countries in the transition to capitalism' (2001).
22 Brenner (2001), p. 311.
23 Wood, 'The question of market dependence' (2002b).
24 Wood (2002b).
25 Marjolein 'T Hart, Pepijn Brandon and Thomas Goosens, 'The commercialization of warfare as a strategy for hegemonial powers' (2008).
26 George Comninel, *Rethinking the French Revolution* (1987).
27 Paul Blackledge, 'Political Marxism' (2008).
28 Marx, *The Eighteenth Brumaire of Louis Napoleon* (Marx and Engels, 1975–, Vol. 11), pp. 103–4.
29 English and French revisionism is critically reviewed in Brian Manning, 'The English Revolution' (1999) and Michel Vovelle, 'Reflections on the revisionist interpretation of the French Revolution' (1990).
30 Benno Teschke, 'Bourgeois revolution, state formation and the absence of the international' (2005), p. 11.
31 Teschke (2005), p. 12.
32 Ellen Meiskins Wood and John Bellamy Foster (eds), *In Defense of History* (1997).
33 Brenner (1989), pp. 278–9.
34 Brenner (1989), p. 286.
35 Brenner (1989), pp. 293–4.
36 Brenner (1989), p. 295.
37 Hill's views were sharpened by his participation in the debates of the British Communist historians group. See now David Parker, *Ideology, Absolutism and the English Revolution* (2009), p. 9.
38 Lawrence Stone, *The Crisis of the Aristocracy 1558–1641* (1965).

262 NOTES

39 Brenner (1989), pp. 297–8.
40 Brenner (1989), p. 302.
41 Brenner, *Merchants and Revolution* (1993), pp. 647–8.
42 Brenner (1993), pp. 651–8.
43 Anderson, 'Robert Brenner' (2005), p, 250. On the difficulties involved in defining the nature of the English monarchy see Parker (2009), pp. 34–5, 40–5.
44 E. M. Wood (1999), p. 20.
45 Lawrence Stone, 'The bourgeois revolution in seventeenth-century England revisited' (1985).
46 Norah Carlin, *The Causes of the English Civil War* (1999), pp. 157–8.
47 John Merrill, *The Nature of the English Revolution* (1993), p. 163.
48 Andrew Bell Appleby, 'Agrarian capitalism or seigneurial reaction' (1975).
49 Roger B. Manning, *Village Revolts* (1988), p. 36.
50 Marx, *Capital*, Vol. 1 (Marx and Engels, 1975–, Vol. 35), pp. 731–2.
51 Marx, *Capital*, Vol. 3 (Marx and Engels, 1975–, Vol. 37), p. 786.
52 Dobb (1946), pp. 125–6.
53 An appreciation of his approach and a complete bibliography can be found in Paul Blackledge, 'Editorial introduction: Brian Manning, 21 May 1927–24 April 2004, historian of the people and the English Revolution' (2003).
54 This account is largely drawn from Manning (1991), *Aristocrats, Plebians and Revolution in England 1640–1660* (1996), and *Revolution and Counter-Revolution in England, Ireland and Scotland 1658–60* (2003).
55 Andrew Hopper, *'Black Tom'* (2007), pp. 33–53, 130–51; John Walter, *Understanding Popular Violence in the English Revolution* (1999), pp. 278–9; I. J. Gentles, *The English Revolution and the War in the Three Kingdoms, 1638–1652* (2007), p. 130.
56 Tony Smith, *Globalisation* (2006), pp. 232–3.
57 Christopher Hill, 'A bourgeois revolution?' (1980), pp. 134–5.
58 Manning (1991), p. 139.
59 Alex Callinicos, 'Bourgeois revolutions and historical materialism' (1989).
60 See above pp. 71–2.
61 Comninel (1987), p. 200.
62 Comninel (1987), pp. 190–1.
63 E. M. Wood (1999), pp. 56, 111, 119–21.
64 Henry Heller, 'The longue durée of the French bourgeoisie' (2009).
65 Anatoli Ado, *Paysans en révolution* (1996), p. 51.
66 Jean-Marc Moriceau, *Les fermiers de l'Ile-de-France* (1994a), pp. 703–69; 'Les gros fermiers en 1789: vice-rois de la plain de France' (1989), pp. 46–7.
67 Ado (1996), p. 53.
68 Jean-Marc Moriceau, 'Au rendez-vous de la "revolution agricole" dans la France du XVIIIe siècle: à propos des regions de grande culture' (1994b).
69 Henry Heller, *The Bourgeois Revolution in France 1789–1815* (2006), pp. 27–41.

70 John Shovlin, *The Political Economy of Virtue* (2006), p. 2.
71 Heller (2006), pp. 4–5, 48; Christian Gehrke and Heinz D. Kurz, 'Marx on physiocracy' (1995).
72 Giani Vaggi, 'The role of profits in physiocratic economics' (1985).
73 Nicolaus Baudeau, *Première introduction à la philosophie économique, ou analyse des états policés* (1767/1910), pp. 41–67.
74 Claude Morilhat, *La prise de conscience du capitalisme* (1988), pp. 157–8.
75 Morilhat, (1988), pp. 158–9, 164, 168–9, 171.
76 Morilhat (1988), pp. 156, 173–4.
77 Anne-Robert-Jacques Turgot, *Reflections on the Formation and Distribution of Riches* (1898), p. 24.
78 Morilhat (1988), pp. 167–8.
79 Jean-Joseph-Louis Graslin, *Essai analytique sur la richesse et sur l'impôt* (1767/1911), pp. 59–60; Marcel Dorigny, 'La formation de la pensée économiques de Sieyès d'après ses manuscrits (1770–1789)' (1988).
80 Comninel (1987), p.190.
81 J. M. Nesson, *Commoners, Common Right, Enclosures and Social Change in England, 1700–1820* (1993), pp. 297–330.
82 See Kenneth E. Carpenter, *The Dissemination of the Wealth of Nations in French and in France 1776–1843* (2002), pp. xxii–xxiii, xxix, xlii; Richard Whatmore, 'Adam Smith's role in the French Revolution' (2002).
83 Whatmore (2002); Dorigny, 'Les courants du libéralisme français à la fin de l'Ancien Régime et aux débuts de la Révolution' (1989), p. 26.
84 Heller (2006), pp. 54–60.
85 Peter McPhee, 'Revolution or Jacquerie?' (2008), pp. 46–67.
86 Samuel Guicheteau, *Révolution des ouvriers nantais* (2008).

5 POLITICAL CAPITALISM

1   Barrington Moore Jr., *Social Origins of Dictatorship and Democracy* (1966).
2   Peter D. Thomas, *The Gramscian Moment* (2009), pp. 75–6, 148–50.
3   Terence J. Byres, *Capitalism from Above and Capitalism from Below* (1996), p. 20.
4   Engels, *The Peasant Question in France and Germany* (Marx and Engels, *Collected Works*, Vol. 27), p. 500.
5   Byres (1996), pp. 22–3, Jairus Banaji, 'Illusions about the peasantry' (1990).
6   V. I. Lenin, *The Development of Capitalism in Russia* (1964a), pp. 32–3.
7   Lenin, *The Agrarian Programme of Social-Democracy in the First Russian Revolution, 1905–1907* (1964b), p. 347.
8   Lenin (1964b), p. 238.
9   Lenin (1964b), p. 423.
10 Kevin B. Anderson, 'The rediscovery and persistence of the dialectic in philosophy and world politics' (2007), p. 131.

11 Byres (1996).
12 Marx, *Capital*, Vol. 1 (Marx and Engels, 1975–, Vol. 35), p. 739.
13 Marx, *Capital*, Vol. 1 (Marx and Engels, 1975–, Vol. 35), p. 741.
14 Quoted in Byres (1996), p. 31.
15 Byres (1996), pp. 31–2.
16 Byres (1996), p. 28.
17 Byres (1996), pp. 27–9.
18 Byres (1996), p. 151.
19 Byres (1996), pp. 393–406.
20 Byres (1996), p. 397.
21 Susan A. Mann and James A. Dickinson, 'State and agriculture in two eras of American capitalism' (1980).
22 Byres (1996), p. 419.
23 Byres (1996), p. 421.
24 Byres (1996), pp. 422, 425–6.
25 Byres (1996), p. 432.
26 Byres, 'The agrarian question, forms of capitalist agrarian transition and the state' (1986), 'The agrarian question and differing forms of capitalist agrarian transition' (1991).
27 Neil Davidson, 'The Scottish path to capitalist agriculture 1' (2004b), pp. 232–5.
28 Davidson (2004b), pp. 246–8.
29 Davidson, *Discovering the Scottish Revolution 1792–1746* (2003), pp. 94–101.
30 Davidson (2004b), pp. 253–4.
31 Davidson, 'The Scottish path to capitalist agriculture 2' (2004c), pp. 417–18.
32 Davidson, *The Origins of Scottish Nationhood* (2000), p. 182.
33 Davidson (2000), p.168.
34 Davidson (2000), p.168.
35 Davidson, 'Putting the nation back into "the international"' (2009).
36 Davidson (2000), p.168.
37 Davidson (2000), p.168.
38 Leon Trotsky, 'For the internationalist perspective' (1972), p. 199, quoted in Davidson (2009), p. 15.
39 Trotsky, *History of the Russian Revolution* (1961), pp. 4–5.
40 Davidson (2000), pp. 168–9.
41 Trotsky (1961), p. 6.
42 Eric Hobsbawm, 'Scottish reformers of the eighteenth century and capitalist agriculture' (1980), p. 5.
43 Davidson, 'The Scottish path to capitalist agriculture 3' (2005b), pp. 22–3.
44 Davidson (2005b), p. 53.
45 Davidson (2005b), p. 23.
46 Quoted in Byres (1986), p. 42.
47 Byres (1986), pp. 42–3.
48 Byres (1986), pp. 49–50.
49 Wolf Ladejinsky, 'Agrarian revolution in Japan' (1959); Teruoka Shuzo,

'Land reform and postwar Japanese capitalism' (1989); Shigeto Tsuru, *Japan's Capitalism* (1993), pp. 20–2.

50 Byres (1986), pp. 58–9.

51 Byres (1986), p. 60. For further discussion of the development of capitalism in under-developed states see Henry Bernstein, 'Agrarian classes in capitalist development' (1994).

52 Amiya Kumar Bagchi, 'The past and future of the developmental state' (2000).

53 John Gallagher and Ronald Robinson, 'The imperialism of free trade (1953).

54 Adam Smith, *The Wealth of Nations* (1937), p. 391.

55 William Petty, *Political Arithmetik* (1899/1963), Vol. 1, p. 295.

56 Michael Perelman, *The Invention of Capitalism* (2000), pp. 127–8.

57 Eli F. Heckscher, *Mercantilism* (1935); Jacob Viner, *Studies in the Theory of International Trade* (1937).

58 John Maynard Keynes, *The General Theory of Employment, Interest and Money* (1936), pp. 333–71. See also Elize S. Brezis, 'Mercantilism' (2003), Vol. 3, pp. 481–5.

59 Ronald Findlay, and Kevin H. O'Rourke, *Power and Plenty* (2007), pp. 228–9.

60 Marx, *Capital*, Vol. 1 (Marx and Engels, 1975–, Vol. 35), p. 739.

61 Perelman (2000), p. 218.

62 Marx, *Capital*, Vol. 1 (Marx and Engels, 1975–, Vol. 35), p. 745.

63 Marx, *Capital*, Vol. 3 (Marx and Engels, 1975–, Vol. 37), p. 335.

64 Marx, *Capital*, Vol. 3 (Marx and Engels, 1975–, Vol. 37), p. 335.

65 Marx, *Capital*, Vol. 3 (Marx and Engels, 1975–, Vol. 37), p. 771.

66 Marx, *Grundrisse*, p. 328.

67 Dobb (1946), p. 199. As Richard Grassby, 'English merchant capitalism' (1970), pp. 95, 100, 105–6 has suggested, the best profits were to be found in speculation and overseas trade.

68 Dobb (1946), pp. 199–200.

69 Dobb (1946), pp. 202, 204–5.

70 Dobb (1946), p. 209.

71 Dobb (1946), pp. 213–14.

72 Dobb (1946), pp. 206, 217–19.

73 Dobb (1946), p. 219.

74 Anderson (1974b), pp. 35–9.

75 Arrighi (1994), pp. 49–51.

76 Benno Teschke, *The Myth of 1648* (2003), p. 208.

77 Teschke (2003), pp. 204–7.

78 David Ormrod, *The Rise of Commercial Empires* (2003); François Crouzet, 'Mercantilism, war and the rise of British power' (2002); Kenneth Morgan, 'Mercantilism and the British Empire' (2002).

79 Robin Blackburn, *The Making of New World Slavery* (1997), p. 515.

80 Philippe Minard, *La fortune du colbertisme* (1998).

81 Marx, *Capital*, Vol. 1, p. 742.

82 Kevin Anderson, *Marx at the Margins* (2010), pp. 9–11, 17–20, 22–3, 31–33.

83 Anderson (2010), p. 244.
84 Pranav Jani, 'Karl Marx, Eurocentrism and the 1857 Revolt in British India' (2002).
85 Marx's writings on India are collected in *Karl Marx on India* (2006).
86 Habib, 'Marx's perception of India', in Marx (2006), pp. xix–liv.
87 While it praises Marx's materialist approach to Indian history, his views are subject to a brilliant critique in Adith, 'Re-reading Marx on India' (2009).
88 Eamonn Slater and Terrence McDonough, 'Marx on 19th century colonial Ireland' (2009).
89 Ellen Meiskins Wood, *The Origin of Capitalism* (1999), pp. 110–11, 152–65.
90 Marx, 'The Indian question–Irish tenant right' (in Marx and Engels, 1972), pp. 59–61.
91 Theodore W. Allen, *The Invention of the White Race* (1994), Vol. 1, p. 51.
92 Samir Amin, *Unequal Development* (1976), pp. 143–4.
93 Marx, *Grundrisse*, p. 872.
94 Marx, *Grundrisse*, p. 872.
95 James Morris Blaut, 'Political geography debates no. 3' (1992). See also his *The Colonizer's Model of the World* (1993) and *Eight Eurocentric Historians* (2000), pp. 45–72.
96 Blaut (1992), p. 355.
97 Chris Harman (2004), 'The rise of capitalism' (2004).
98 Andre Gunder Frank, 'Fourteen ninety-two again' (1992).
99 Blackburn (1997), p. 524; Joseph E. Inikori, *Africans and the Industrial Revolution in England* (2002), p. 118.
100 Blackburn (1997), p. 542.
101 Blackburn (1997), p. 377.
102 Eric Eustace Williams, *Capitalism and Slavery* (1944).
103 The debate over the Williams thesis is surveyed in Richard B. Sheridan, 'Eric Williams and capitalism and slavery' (1987).
104 Geoffrey E. M. de Ste Croix, *The Class Struggle in the Ancient Greek World* (1981).
105 Ste Croix (1981), p. 58.
106 Paul Blackledge, *Reflections on the Marxist Theory of History* (2006), p. 105.
107 Robert William Fogel and Stanley L. Engerman, *Time on the Cross* (1974), pp. 203–4.
108 Paul A. David and Peter Temin, 'Slavery: the progressive institution?' (1976).
109 Byres (1996), pp. 238–9.
110 Rakesh Bhandari, 'The disguises of wage labour' (2008).
111 Robin Blackburn, *The Overthrow of Colonial Slavery, 1776–1848* (1988) and (1997).
112 Blackburn (1997), pp. 375–6.
113 Blackburn (1997), p. 515.
114 Blackburn (1997), p. 554; Marx, *Capital*, Vol. 1, p. 244.

115 Inikori (2002), p. 91.
116 Eric Hobsbawm, *Industry and Empire* (1969); Christopher Hill, *Reformation to Industrial Revolution* (1967).
116 Hobsbawm (1969).
117 Inikori (2002), pp. 116–17.
118 Cedric J. Robinson, 'Capitalism, slavery and bourgeois historiography' (1987).
119 Inikori (2002), pp. 105–6; Blackburn, (1997), p. 531.
120 Patrick K. O'Brien and Stanley L. Engerman, 'Exports and the growth of the British economy from the Glorious Revolution to the Peace of Amiens' (1994). Despite the importance he attributes to exports in stimulating manufacturing, O'Brien confuses by claiming that the capital needed for the Industrial Revolution was overwhelmingly generated internally. See O'Brien, 'Global economic history as the accumulation of capital through a process of combined and uneven development' (2007).
121 Utsa Patnaik, 'The free lunch' (2006).
122 Blackburn (1997), pp. 541–2.
123 Blackburn (1997), p. 543.
124 Blackburn (1997), pp. 547–8.
125 Blackburn (1997), pp. 554–6.
126 Byres (1996), pp. 263–73

6 THE INDUSTRIAL REVOLUTION: MARXIST PERSPECTIVES

1 It is surveyed in Joseph E. Inikori, *Africans and the Industrial Revolution* (2002), pp. 89–155.
2 Peter Gaskell, *The Manufacturing Population of England* (1833/1972), p. 52; Raymond Williams, *Keywords* (1976), p. 136.
3 Engels, *The Condition of the Working Class in England* (1844), *Collected Works*, Vol. 4, p. 307.
4 Eric Hobsbawm, *Industry and Empire* (1969).
5 Hobsbawm (1969), p. 32.
6 Hobsbawm (1969), p. 37.
7 Hobsbawm (1969), p. 34.
8 Richard Price, *British Society* (1999), p. 65.
9 David Cannadine, 'The present and the past in the English Industrial Revolution: 1880–1980' (1984).
10 Hobsbawm (1969), pp. 32, 35.
11 Marx, *Capital,* Vol. 1, *Collected Works*, Vol. 35, pp. 733–4, 736. On the relationship between agricultural improvement and industrialization cf. Inikori (2002), pp. 103–5; Pat Hudson, *The Industrial Revolution* (1992), pp. 71, 75, 90, 91, 95.
12 Marx, *Capital*, Vol. 1 (Marx and Engels, 1975–, Vol. 35), p. 341.
13 Marx, *Capital*, Vol. 1 (Marx and Engels, 1975–, Vol. 35), p. 373.
14 Marx, *Capital*, Vol. 1 (Marx and Engels, 1975–, Vol. 35), p. 372.
15 Marx, *Capital*, Vol. 1 (Marx and Engels, 1975–, Vol. 35), p. 343.

16 Marx, *Capital,* Vol. 1 (Marx and Engels, 1975–, Vol. 35), p. 367.
17 Marx, *Capital*, Vol. 1 (Marx and Engels, 1975–, Vol. 35), p. 373.
18 Maxine Berg, *The Age of Manufactures, 1700–1820* (1994), pp. 63–6.
19 Marx, *Capital*, Vol. 1, p. 385.
20 Marx, *Capital*, Vol. 1, p. 374.
21 Marx, *Capital*, Vol. 1, p. 378.
22 Marx, *Capital*, Vol. 1, p. 622.
23 Marx, *Capital*, Vol. 1, p. 425.
24 Marx, Appendix to *Capital*, Vol. 1 (1977–81), pp. 1034–5.
25 Marx, *Capital*, Vol. 1 (Marx and Engels, 1975–, Vol. 35), pp. 302, 314–15.
26 Maurice Dobb, *Studies in the Development of Capitalism* (1946), p. 257.
27 Dobb (1946), p. 265.
28 Dobb (1946), p. 277.
29 Dobb (1946), p. 273.
30 Dobb (1946), pp. 277–8.
31 Stephen Marglin, 'What do bosses do?' (1974).
32 Harry Braverman, *Labor and Monopoly Capital* (1974).
33 Marglin (1974); Berg (1994), pp. 182–3; Pat Hudson, *The Industrial Revolution* (1992), p. 3.
34 Berg (1994), pp. 166–7.
35 Marx, *Capital*, Vol. 1 (Marx and Engels, 1975–, Vol. 35), p. 303.
36 Marx and Engels, *The Communist Manifesto* (Marx and Engels, 1975–, Vol. 6), p. 491.
37 Ralph Samuel, 'Workshop of the world' (1977).
38 Hobsbawm (1969), p. 77.
39 E. P. Thompson, 'Time, work discipline and industrial capitalism' (1967).
40 E. P. Thompson, *The Making of the English Working Class* (1968), p. 27.
41 E. P. Thompson, 'The moral economy of the English crowd in the eighteenth century' (1971).
42 Maxine Berg, 'Workers and machinery in eighteenth century Britain' (1988); Andy Wood, *The Politics of Social Conflict* (1999), p. 124.
43 Thompson (1968), p. 199.
44 Thompson (1968), pp. 199–203.
45 Thompson (1968), p. 207.
46 Thompson (1968), pp. 207–8.
47 Thompson (1968), p. 209.
48 Thompson (1968), p. 487.
49 Thompson (1968), pp. 500–4.
50 Thompson (1968), p. 211.
51 Thompson (1968), p. 213.
52 Thompson (1968), p. 213.
53 Geoff Eley and Keith Nierd, *The Future of Class in History* (2007), pp. 81–137; Paul Blackledge, *Reflections on the Marxist Theory of History* (2006), pp. 6–8.

54 E. P. Thompson, *The Poverty of Theory and Other Essays* (1978), p. 204, n. 168.
55 Perry Anderson, *Arguments Within English Marxism* (1980), pp. 29–50.
56 Marcello Musto, 'History, production and method in the 1857 "Introduction"' (2008), p. 21.
57 Richard Price, 'Conflict and co-operation' (1984); Marc W. Steinberg, 'Culturally speaking' (1996).
58 Richard Price, *British Society: 1680–1880* (1999), pp. 330–1.
59 Thompson (1968), pp. 213–14.
60 Arthur J. Taylor (ed.), *The Standard of Living in Britain in the Industrial Revolution* (1975), pp. xi–xiii.
61 Thompson (1968), pp. 212.
62 Thompson (1968), pp. 347–51.
63 Thompson (1968), p. 351.
64 Thompson (1968), p. 352.
65 Hans-Joachim Voth, 'Living standards and urban disamenities', in *Cambridge Economic History of Modern Britain, Vol. 1: Industrialization, 1700–1860* (2004), pp. 268–94.
66 Voth (2004), p. 293.
67 Taylor (1975), pp. 67–8.
68 Simon R. S. Szreter and Graham Mooney, 'Urbanisation, mortality and the standard of living debate' (1998).
69 Franklin Mendels, 'Proto-industrialization' (1972).
70 Peter Kriedte, Jürgen Schlumbohm and Hans Medick, *Industrialization Before Industrialization* (1981).
71 Berg (1994), pp. 68–9.
72 Berg (1994), pp. 70, 73.
73 Berg (1994), p. 74.
74 Marx, *Capital,* Vol. 1, (Marx and Engels, 1975–, Vol. 35), p. 626.
75 Wally Seccombe, 'Marxism and demography' (1983), pp. 29, 31.
76 Seccombe (1983), pp. 34–6, 42.
77 Jan de Vries, *The Industrious Revolution* (2008), p. 85; Berg (1994), pp. 18, 21.
78 Andy Wood (1999), p. 116.
79 David Levine and Keith Wrightson, *The Making of an Industrial Society* (1991), pp. vii, 788–9.
80 On worker resistance organized and unorganized and overall attitudes to machinery see Berg (1988); Keith Wrightson, *Earthly Necessities* (2000), pp. 325–30; Peter Linebaugh, *The London Hanged* (1991), pp. 23–4, 68, 222, 271, 286.
81 De Vries (2008), pp. 7–8, 10, 85–6.
82 De Vries (2008), pp. 41–3.
83 De Vries (2008), p. 93.
84 De Vries (2008), p. 94.
85 De Vries (2008), pp. 101–2.
86 De Vries (2008), p. 107.
87 De Vries (2008), pp. 87–92, 112.

88 De Vries (2008), p. 94.
89 De Vries (2008), p. 138.
90 De Vries (2008), pp. 154–77.
91 De Vries (2008), pp. 101–2, 178–9.
92 De Vries (2008), p. 85.
93 Ben Fine and Ellen Leopold, 'Consumerism and the Industrial Revolution' (1990).
94 Fine and Leopold (1990), p. 161.
95 Fine and Leopold (1990), pp. 168–71.
96 Margaret Jacob, *Scientific Culture and the Making of the Industrial West* (1997), pp. 51–2.
97 Charles Webster, *The Great Instauration* (1975); Christopher Hill, 'Review: *A New Kind of Clergy*' (1986).
98 Steven Pincus, 'Whigs, political economy and the revolution of 1688–89' (2005), p. 74.
99 Larry Stewart and Paul Weindling, 'Philosophical threads: natural philosophy and public experiment among the weavers of Spitalfields' (1995).
100 Jacob (1997), pp. 107–8.
101 Margaret Jacob, 'Mechanical science on the factory floor' (2007).
102 Liliane Hilaire-Perez, 'Technology as a public culture in the eighteenth century' (2007).
103 Walter E. Houghton, 'The history of trades: its relation to seventeenth-century thought', (1941); Kathleen H. Ochs, 'The Royal Society of London's History of Trades Programme' (1985).
104 William J. Ashworth, 'The ghost of Rostow' (2008).
105 Anna K. Mayer, 'Setting up a discipline II' (2004).
106 Gideon Freudenthal, 'The Hessen–Grossman thesis' (2005).
107 Boris Hessen and Henryk Grossman, *The Social and Economic Roots of the Scientific Revolution* (2009).
108 Marx, *Capital*, Vol. 1, p. 393.
109 Carlo Vercellone, 'From formal subsumption to general intellect' (2007).
110 Marx, *Grundrisse*, p. 706.
111 See, for example, J. C. D. Clark, *Revolution and Rebellion* (1986).
112 Berg (1994), pp. 21–2; Hudson (1992), pp. 218–19.
113 Perry Anderson, 'Origins of the present crisis' (1964).
114 E. P. Thompson, 'The peculiarities of the English', in *The Poverty of Theory and Other Essays* (1978), pp. 258–9.
115 Thompson, 'Peculiarities' (1978), pp. 260–1.
116 Thompson, 'Peculiarities' (1978), pp. 262–4.
117 Perry Anderson, 'The figures of descent' (1987).
118 Arno J. Mayer, *The Persistence of the Old Regime* (1981), p. 10.

7 CAPITALISM AND WORLD HISTORY

1   Giorgio Riello, 'Asian knowledge and the development of calico printing in Europe in the seventeenth and eighteenth centuries' (2010).

2 John M. Hobson, *The Eastern Origins of Western Civilisation* (2004); Jack Goody, *The Theft of History* (2006); Andre Gunder Frank, *ReOrient* (1998).
3 Keith Pomeranz, *The Great Divergence* (2000).
4 Giovanni Arrighi, *Adam Smith in Beijing* (2007).
5 Amiya Kumar Bagchi, *Perilous Passage* (2005); Peter Linebaugh, *The Magna Carta Manifesto* (2008).
6 Arif Dirlik, 'Is there history after Eurocentrism? (2000), p. 27.
7 Robert J. C. Young, *Postcolonialism* (2001), p. 169.
8 Timothy Brennan, 'Postcolonial studies between the European wars' (2002); Vijay Prashad, *The Darker Nations* (2007), pp. 19–21.
9 Crystal Bartolovitch, 'Introduction: Marxism, modernity and postcolonial studies' (2002), p. 3.
10 Neil Lazarus, 'The fetish of "the West" in post-colonial theory', (2002), pp. 44–5.
11 Neil Lazarus and Rashmi Varma, 'Marxism and postcolonial studies' (2008), pp. 315–16.
12 Arif Dirlik, *Marxism in the Chinese Revolution* (2005), p. 114.
13 Mao Zedong, *Collected Works* (1976), Vol. 6, pp. 260–1 quoted in Dirlik (2005), p. 82.
14 Hobson (2004); Goody (2006); Frank (1998).
15 Hobson (2004), p. 2.
16 Hobson (2004), p. 2.
17 Hobson (2004), pp. 201–7.
18 Hobson (2004), p. 313.
19 Hobson (2004), p. 192.
20 Hobson (2004), pp. 12–14.
21 Jack Goody, 'The labyrinth of kinship' (2005), p. 134.
22 Goody (2006), p. 8.
23 Goody (2006), p. 8.
24 Martin Bernal, *Black Athena* (1987–91).
25 Goody (2006), pp. 60–3.
26 Goody (2006), pp. 13–25.
27 Goody (2006), p. 143.
28 Goody (2006), pp. 187, 192–3.
29 Goody (2006), p. 211.
30 Goody (2006), p. 211.
31 Frank (1998).
32 Andre Gunder Frank and Barry K. Gills (eds), *The World System* (1993).
33 Frank (1998), pp. 13–17. For a sophisticated defense of this concept see Neil Davidson, 'Asiatic, tributary or absolutist' (2004a).
34 Frank (1998), p. 330.
35 Under the title 'ReOrientalism?' the critiques of Amin, Arrighi and Wallerstein were published together in *Review*: Amin, 'History conceived as an eternal cycle' (1999); Arrighi, 'The world according to Andre Gunder Frank' (1999); Wallerstein, ' Frank proves the European miracle' (1999).

36 Ricardo Duchesne, 'Between sinocentrism and Eurocentrism' (2001–02). I am indebted to Professor Duchesne's summary of Frank's work.
37 Duchesne (2001–02).
38 Patrick K. O'Brien, 'The foundations of European industrialization' (1991).
39 Patrick K. O'Brien, 'Imperialism and the rise and decline of the British economy, 1688–1999' (1999).
40 Robert C. Allen, *The British Industrial Revolution in Global Perspective* (2009b), pp. 25–56.
41 Duchesne (2001–2), p. 444.
42 Duchesne (2001–2), p. 453.
43 Pomeranz (2000).
44 Pomeranz (2000), pp. 14–15.
45 Robert Brenner and Christopher Isett, 'England's divergence from China's Yangzi delta' (2002). I am indebted to Brenner and Isett for their summation of Pomeranz's views.
46 Robert C. Allen, 'Agricultural productivity and rural incomes in England and the Yangtze delta, c. 1620–1820' (2009a).
47 Robert C. Allen, *Farm to Factory* (2003).
48 Robert C. Allen, 'Economic structure and agricultural productivity in Europe, 1300–1800' (2000).
49 Arrighi (2007).
50 Arrighi (2007), p. 93.
51 Arrighi (2007), pp. 25–6.
52 Arrighi (2007), p. 51.
53 See ch. 4, p. 23, n.1.
54 Arrighi (2007), p. 54.
55 Arrighi (2007), pp. 55–63.
56 Flemming Christiansen, 'Arrighi's *Adam Smith in Beijing*' (2010), p. 112.
57 Arrighi (2007), p. 72.
58 Jan De Vries, *The Industrious Revolution* (2008), p. 80.
59 Arrighi (2007), pp. 32–7.
60 Arrighi (2007), pp. 388–9.
61 Arrighi (2007), pp. 16, 369.
62 Mark Elvin, 'The historian as haruspex' (2008).
63 Arrighi (2007), pp. 369–70, 374.
64 Dale Jiajun Wen, 'The debate about land privatization and real democracy' (2009).
65 David Harvey, *The New Imperialism* (2005), pp. 122–3.
66 Giovanni Arrighi, 'Spatial and other "fixes" of historical capitalism' (2003).
67 Marx, *Capital,* Vol. 1, in *Collected Works,* Vol. 35, pp. 743–4.
68 Richard Goldthwaite, *The Economy of Renaissance Florence* (2009), pp. 135–6; Fernand Braudel, *Civilisation matérielle, économie et capitalisme, XVe–XVIIIe siècle* (1979), pp. 118, 202–7, 228, 252–3.
69 Bagchi (2005).
70 Bagchi (2005), p. xv.

71 Bagchi (2005), p. 38.
72 Bagchi (2005), pp. xiv–xv.
73 Bagchi (2005), pp. 6–9.
74 Bagchi (2005), p. xiv.
75 Bagchi (2005), pp. xiv–xv.
76 Bagchi (2005), pp. 74–84, 94–6.
77 Bagchi (2005), p. xv.
79 Linebaugh (2008).
80 Linebaugh (2008), pp. 46–93.

CONCLUSION

1 Giovanni Arrighi, 'World income inequalities and the future of socialism' (1991).
2 Guy Bois, *La grande dépression médiévale* (2000), pp. 207–11.
3 Marx, *Grundrisse*, pp. 704–5.
4 Marx, *Grundrisse*, p. 705.
5 Marx, *Grundrisse*, p. 705.
6 Moishe Postone, 'Rethinking *Capital* in the light of the *Grundrisse*' (2008), pp. 124–8.

BIBLIOGRAPHY

Adam, Thomas (2003) 'Saxony', pp. 453–4, Vol. 4 in Joel Mokyr (ed.), *The Oxford Encyclopedia of Economic History*, 5 vols. Oxford, New York: Oxford University Press.

Adith (2008) 'Re-reading Marx on India', < http://parisar.wordpress.com> (accessed July 1, 2009).

Ado, Anatoli (1996) *Paysans en révolution: terre, pouvoir et jacquerie, 1789–1794*. Paris: Société des études robespierristes.

Allen, Robert C. (1992) *Enclosure and the Yeoman*. Oxford: Clarendon.

Allen, Robert C. (2000) 'Economic structure and agricultural productivity in Europe, 1300–1800', *European Review of Economic History*, Vol. 4, No. 1, pp. 1–25.

Allen, Robert C. (2003) *Farm to Factory: A Reinterpretation of the Soviet Industrial Revolution*. Princeton, N.J.: Princeton University Press.

Allen, Robert C. (2009a) 'Agricultural productivity and rural incomes in England and the Yangtze Delta, c. 1620–1820', *Economic History Review*, Vol. 62, No. 3, pp. 525–50.

Allen, Robert C. (2009b) *The British Industrial Revolution in Global Perspective*. Cambridge/New York: Cambridge University Press.

Allen, Theodore W. (1994) *The Invention of the White Race: Racial Oppression and Social Control*, 2 vols. London/New York: Verso.

Amin, Samir (1976) *Unequal Development: An Essay on the Social Formation of Peripheral Capitalism*. New York: Monthly Review Press.

Amin, Samir (1999) 'History conceived as an eternal cycle', *Review*, Vol. 22, No. 3, pp. 291–326.

Amin, Shahid and Marcel van der Linden (1996) 'Introduction' to "Peripheral Labour? Studies in the History of Partial Proletarianization"', *International Review of Social History*, Vol. 41, Suppl. 4.

Anderson, Kevin B. (2007) 'The rediscovery and persistence of the dialectic in philosophy and world politics', pp. 120–47 in Sebastian Budgen, Stathiis Kouvelakis and Slavoj Sizek (eds), *Lenin Reloaded: Toward a Politics of Truth*. Durham, N.C./London: Duke University Press.

Anderson, Kevin B. (2010) *Marx at the Margins: On Nationalism, Ethnicity and the Non-Western Societies*. Chicago, Ill./London: University of Chicago Press.

Anderson, Perry (1964) 'Origins of the present crisis', *New Left Review*, Vol. 23, pp. 26–53.

Anderson, Perry (1974a) *Passages from Antiquity to Feudalism*. London: Verso.

Anderson, Perry (1974b) *Lineages of the Absolutist State*. London: Verso.

Anderson, Perry (1980) *Arguments Within English Marxism*. London: New Left Books.

Anderson, Perry (1987) 'The figures of descent', *New Left Review*, Vol. 161, pp. 20–77.

Anderson, Perry (2005) 'Robert Brenner', pp. 232–56 in *Spectrum*. London/ New York: Verso.

Appleby, Andrew Bell (1975) 'Agrarian capitalism or seigneurial reaction', *American Historical Review*, Vol. 80, No. 3, pp. 574–94.

Arrighi, Giovanni (1991) 'World income inequalities and the future of socialism', *New Left Review*, Vol. 189, pp. 39–64.

Arrighi, Giovanni (1994) *The Long Twentieth Century: Money, Power and the Origins of Our Times*. London/New York: Verso.

Arrighi, Giovanni (1999) 'The world according to Andre Gunder Frank', *Review*, Vol. 22, No. 3, pp. 327–54,

Arrighi, Giovanni (2003) 'Spatial and other "fixes" of historical capitalism', Conference on Globalization in the World-System: Mapping Change over Time. University of California, Riverside, <http://www.irows.ucr. edu/conferences/globgis/papers/Arrighi.htm> (accessed July 1, 2009).

Arrighi, Giovanni (2007) *Adam Smith in Beijing: Lineages of the Twenty-First Century*. London/New York: Verso.

Ashworth, William J. (2008) 'The ghost of Rostow: science, culture and the British Industrial Revolution', *History of Science*, Vol. 46, No. 3, pp. 249–74.

Ashton, Thomas S. (1948) *The Industrial Revolution: 1760–1830*. London: Oxford University Press.

Aston, Trevor H. (ed.) (1965) *Crisis in Europe, 1560–1660: Essays from 'Past and Present'*. London: Routledge & Kegan Paul.

Aston, Trevor H. and C. H. E. Philpin (eds) (1985) *The Brenner Debate: Agrarian Class Structure and Economic Development in Pre–Industrial Europe*. Cambridge/London: Cambridge University Press.

Aymard, Maurice (1982) 'From feudalism to capitalism in Italy: the case that doesn't fit', *Review*, Vol. 6, No. 2, pp. 131–208.

Aymard, Maurice (1988) *Lire Braudel*. Paris: La Découverte.

Bagchi, Amiya Kumar (2000) 'The past and future of the developmental state', *Journal of World-Systems Research*, Vol. 11, No. 2 (Summer–Fall).

Bagchi, Amiya Kumar (2005) *Perilous Passage: Mankind and the Global Ascendancy of Capital*. New Delhi/ Oxford/New York: Oxford University Press.

Banaji, Jairus (1977) 'Modes of production in a materialist conception of history', *Capital and Class*, No. 3, pp. 1–44.

Banaji, Jairus (1990) 'Illusions about the peasantry: Karl Kautsky and the agrarian question', *Journal of Peasant Studies*, Vol. 17, No. 2, pp. 288–96.

Bartolovitch, Crystal (2002) 'Introduction: Marxism, modernity and post-colonial studies', pp. 1–20 in C. Bartolovitch and Neil Lazarus (eds), *Marxism, Modernity and Postcolonial Studies*. Cambridge/New York: Cambridge University Press.

Baudeau, Nicolaus (1767, 1910) *Première introduction à la philosophie économique, ou analyse des états policés*, ed. Auguste Dubois. Paris: Didot, reprint Paris: P. Geuthner.

Béaur, Gérard (2000) *Histoire agraire de la France au XVIIIe siècle: inerties et changements dans les campagnes françaises entre 1715 et 1815*. Paris: SEDES.

Berg, Maxine (1988) 'Workers and machinery in eighteenth century England', pp. 52–73 in John Rule (ed.), *British Trade Unionism 1750–1850: The Formative Years*. London/New York: Longman.

Berg, Maxine (1994) *The Age of Manufactures, 1700–1820: Industry, Innovation, and Work in Britain*. London/New York: Routledge. Bergier, Jean-François (1983) *Histoire économique de la Suisse*. Paris: A. Colin.

Bernal, Martin (1987–91) *Black Athena: The Afroasiatic Roots of Classical Civilization*, 3 vols. New Brunswick, N.J.: Rutgers University Press.

Bernstein, Henry (1994) 'Agrarian classes in capitalist development', pp. 40–71 in Leslie Sklar (ed.), *Capitalism and Development*. London/New York: Routledge.

Bhandari, Rakesh (2008) 'The disguises of wage labour: juridical illusions, unfree conditions and novel extensions', *Historical Materialism*, Vol. 16, No. 1, pp. 77–99.

Bischoff, Joachim and Christoph Lieber (2008) 'The concept of value in modern economy: on the relationship between money and capital in the *Grundrisse*', pp. 33–47 in Marcello Musto (ed.), *Karl Marx's Grundrisse*. London/New York: Routledge.

Bix, Herbert P. (1986) *Peasant Protest in Japan, 1590–1884*. New Haven, Conn. and London: Yale University Press.

Blackburn, Robin (1988) *The Overthrow of Colonial Slavery, 1776–1848*. London/New York: Verso.

Blackburn, Robin (1997) *The Making of New World Slavery: From the Baroque to the Modern 1492–1800*. London/New York: Verso.

Blackledge, Paul (2003) 'Editorial introduction: Brian Manning, 21 May 1927–24 April 2004, historian of the people and the English Revolution', *Historical Materialism*, Vol. 13, No. 3, pp. 107–18.

Blackledge, Paul (2006) *Reflections on the Marxist Theory of History*. Manchester: Manchester University Press.

Blackledge, Paul (2008) 'Political Marxism', pp. 267–84 in Jacques Bidet and Stathis Kouvelakis (eds), *Critical Companion to Contemporary Marxism*. Leiden/Boston, Mass.: Brill.

Blaut, James Morris (1992) 'Political geography debates no. 3: On the significance of 1492', *Political Geography*, Vol. 11, No. 4, pp. 355–85.

Blaut, James Morris (1993) *The Colonizer's Model of the World: Geographical Diffusionism and Eurocentric History*. New York: Guilford Press.

Blaut, James Morris (2000) *Eight Eurocentric Historians*. New York: Guilford Press.

Blickle, Peter (2004) *Die Revolution von 1525*. Munich: Oldenbourg Verlag.

Bois, Guy (1985) 'Against the neo-Malthusian orthodoxy', pp. 107–18 in T. H. Aston and C. H. E. Philpin (eds), *The Brenner Debate: Agrarian Class Structure and Economic Devlopment in Pre-Industrial Europe*. Cambridge/London: Cambridge University Press.

Bois, Guy (2000) *La grande dépression médiévale: XIVe–XVe siecles: le précédent d'une crise systémique*. Paris: PUF.

Bond, Patrick (1999) 'Uneven development', pp. 1198–2000, Vol. 2, in P. A. O'Hara (ed.), *Encyclopedia of Political Economy*, 2 vols. New York/London: Routledge.

Brandon, Pepijn (2007) 'The Dutch revolt: a social analysis', *International Socialism*, Vol. 116 <http://www.isj.org.uk/index.php4?s=back> (accessed June 21, 2009).

Braudel, Fernand (ed.) (1972–76) 'L'Italia Fuori d'Italia: Due Secoli e Tre Italie', pp. 2088–248, Vol. 2, Part 2 in Ruggerio Romano and Corrado Vivanti (eds), *Storia d' Italia, Dall caduta dell'Impero romano al secolo XVIII*, 10 vols. Turin: Giulia Einaudi.

Braudel, Fernand (1979) *Civilisation matérielle, économie et capitalisme, XVe–XVIIIe siècle*. Paris: A. Colin.

Braudel, Fernand and Ernst Labrousse (eds) (1970) *Des derniers temps de l'âge seigneurial aux préludes de l'âge industriel (1660–1789)*, Vol. 2 of *Histoire économique et sociale de la France*, 4 vols. Paris: PUF.

Braverman, Harry (1974) *Labor and Monopoly Capital: The Degradation of Work in the Twentieth Century*. New York: Monthly Review Press.

Brennan, Timothy (2002) 'Postcolonial studies between the European wars: an intellectual history', pp. 185–203 in Neil Lazarus and Crystal Bartolovitch (eds), *Marxism, Modernity and Postcolonial Studies*. Cambridge/New York: Cambridge University Press.

Brenner, Robert (1976) 'Agrarian class structure and economic development in pre-industrial Europe', *Past and Present*, Vol. 70. No. 170. Repr. as pp. 30–75 in T. H. Aston and C. H. E. Philpin (eds), *The Brenner Debate: Agrarian Class Structure and Economic Devlopment in Pre-Industrial Europe*. Cambridge/London: Cambridge University Press.

Brenner, Robert (1977) 'The origins of capitalist development: a critique of neo-Smithian Marxism', *New Left Review*, Vol. 104, pp. 25–93.

Brenner, Robert (1978) 'Dobb on the transition from feudalism to capitalism', *Cambridge Journal of Economics*, Vol. 2, No. 2, pp. 121–40.

Brenner, Robert (1985a) 'Agrarian class structure', in T. H. Aston and C. H. E. Philpin (eds), *The Brenner Debate: Agrarian Class Structure and Economic Development in Pre-Industrial Europe*. Cambridge/London: Cambridge University Press.

Brenner, Robert (1985b) 'The agrarian roots of European capitalism', pp. 213–327 in T. H. Aston and C. H. E. Philpin (eds), *The Brenner Debate: Agrarian Class Structure and Economic Development in Pre-Industrial Europe*. Cambridge/London: Cambridge University Press.

Brenner, Robert (1986) 'The social basis of economic development', pp. 275–338 in John Roemer (ed.), *Analytical Marxism*. Cambridge/New Rochelle: Cambridge University Press.

Brenner, Robert (1989) 'Bourgeois revolution and transition to capitalism', pp. 271–305 in A. L. Beier, David Cannadine and James M. Rosenheim (eds), *The First Modern Society: Essays in English History in Honour of Lawrence Stone*. Cambridge/New York: Cambridge University Press.

Brenner, Robert (1993) *Merchants and Revolution: Commercial Change, Political Conflict, and London's Overseas Traders, 1550–1653*. Princeton, N.J.: Princeton University Press.

Brenner, Robert (2001) 'The Low Countries in the transition to capitalism', pp. 275–338 in Peter Hoppenbrouwers and Jan Luiten van Zanden (eds), *Peasants into Farmers? The Transformation of Rural Economy and Society in the Low Countries (Middle Ages–19th Century) in Light of the Brenner Debate*. Turnhout, Belgium: Brepols.

Brenner, Robert (2002) *The Boom and the Bubble: The U.S. in the World Economy*. London/New York: Verso.

Brenner, Robert (2008) 'Feudalism', in Steven N. Durlauf and Lawrence E. Blume (eds), *The New Palgrave Dictionary of Economics*, 2nd edn. Basingstoke: Palgrave Macmillan. <http://www.dictionaryofeconomics. com.proxy.lib> (accessed September 15, 2009.

Brenner, Robert and Christopher Isett (2002) 'England's divergence from China's Yangzi delta: property relations, microeconomics, and patterns of development', *Journal of Asian Studies*, Vol. 61, No. 2, pp. 609–62.

Brezis, Elize S. (2003) 'Mercantilism', pp. 481–5, Vol. 3 in Joel Mokyr (ed.), *Oxford Encyclopedia of Economic History*. Oxford: Oxford University Press.

Burgin, Alfred (1988) *Aspekte der frühkapitalistischen Entwicklung in Italien in der Renaissancezeit*. Basel: Wirtschaftswissenschaftliches Zentrum der Universität Basel.

Byres, Terence J. (1985) 'Modes of production and non-European pre-colonial societies: the nature and significance of the debate', *Journal of Peasant Studies*, Vol. 12, No. 2–3, pp. 1–18.

Byres, Terence J. (1986) 'The agrarian question, forms of capitalist agrarian transition and the state: an essay with reference to Asia', *Social Scientist*, Vol. 14, No. 11, pp. 3–67.

Byres, Terence J. (1991) 'The agrarian question and differing forms of capitalist agrarian transition: an essay with reference to Asia', pp. 3–76 in Jan Breman and Sudipto Mundle (eds), *Rural Transformation in Asia*. Delhi/Oxford/New York: Oxford University Press.

Byres, Terence J. (1996) *Capitalism from Above and Capitalism from Below: An Essay in Comparative Political Economy*. London: Macmillan/New York: St. Martin's Press.

Byres, Terence J. (2006) 'Differentiation of the peasantry under feudalism and the transition to capitalism: in defence of Rodney Hilton', *Journal of Agrarian Change*, Vol. 6, No. 1, pp. 17–68.

Byres, Terence J. (2009) 'The landlord class, peasant differentiation, class struggle and the transition to capitalism: England, France and Prussia Compared', *Journal of Peasant Studies*, Vol. 36, No. 1, pp. 33–54.

Byres, Terence J. and Harbans Mukhia (eds) (1985) 'Feudalism and non-European societies', *Journal of Peasant Studies*, Special Issue, Vol. 12, No. 2–3.

Callinicos, Alex (1989) 'Bourgeois revolutions and historical materialism', *International Socialism*, Vol. 43, No. 2, pp. 113–71.

Callinicos, Alex (2004) *Making History: Agency, Structure and Change in Social Theory*. Leiden/Boston, Mass.: Brill.

Callinicos, Alex (2009) *Imperialism and Global Political Economy*. Cambridge/Malden, Mass.: Polity Press.

Cannadine, David (1984) 'The present and the past in the English Industrial Revolution: 1880–1980', *Past and Present*, Vol. 103, No. 1, pp. 131–72.

Carlin, Norah (1999) *The Causes of the English Civil War.* Oxford/Malden, Mass: Blackwell.

Carpenter, Kenneth E. (2002) *The Dissemination of the Wealth of Nations in French and in France 1776–1843.* New York: Bibliographical Society of America.

Casalilla, Bartolome Yun (1986) *Sobre la transicion al captialismo en Castilla: Economia y sociedad en Tierra de Campos (1500–1830).* Salamanaca, Spain: Junta de Castila y Leon, Consejeria de Educacion y Cultura.

Chang, Ha-Joon (2002) *Kicking Away the Ladder: Development Strategy in Historical Perspective.* London: Anthem Press.

Chartres, J. A. (1977) *Internal Trade in England 1500–1700.* London/Basingstoke: Macmillan.

Chartres, J. A. (1995) 'Market integration and agricultural output in seventeenth, eighteenth and early nineteenth century England', *Agricultural History Review*, Vol. 43, No. 1, pp. 117–38.

Christiansen, Flemming (2010) 'Arrighi's *Adam Smith in Beijing*: engaging China', *Historical Materialism*, Vol. 18, No. 1, pp. 110–29.

Cipolla, Carlo M. (1970) 'The economic decline of Italy', pp. 196–214 in Carlo M. Cipolla (ed.), *The Economic Decline of Empires.* London: Methuen.

Clapham, J. H. (1926) *An Economic History of Modern Britain*, 3 vols. Cambridge: Cambridge University Press.

Clark, Gregory (2002) 'Land rental values and the agrarian economy in England and Wales: 1500–1914', *European Review of Economic History*, Vol. 6, No. 3, pp. 281–308.

Clark, Gregory (2007) *A Farewell to Alms: A Brief Economic History of the World.* Princeton, N.J./Oxford: Princeton University Press.

Clark, J. C. D. (1986) *Revolution and Rebellion: State and Society in England in the Seventeenth and Eighteenth Centuries.* Cambridge/New York: Cambridge University Press.

Clark, Peter (1987) 'Migration in England during the late seventeenth and early eighteenth centuries', pp. 213–52 in Peter Clark and David Souden (eds), *Migration and Society In Early Modern England.* Totowa, N.J.: Barnes & Noble.

Clay, C. G. A. (1984) *Economic Expansion and Social Change: England 1500–1700,* 2 vols. Cambridge/New York: Cambridge University Press.

Comninel, George (1987) *Rethinking the French Revolution: Marxism and the Revisionist Challenge.* London: Verso.

Constant, Jean-Marie (1996) *La Ligue.* Paris: PUF.

Crouzet, François (2002) 'Mercantilism, war and the rise of British power', pp. 67–85 in Patrick Karl O'Brien and Armand Cleese (eds), *Two Hegemonies; Britain 1846–1914 and the United States 1941–2001.* Aldershot/Burlington, Vt: Ashgate.

Cuenca-Estaban, Javier (2007) 'India's contribution to the British balance of payments, 1757–1812', *Explorations in Economic History*, Vol. 44, No. 1, pp. 154–76.

David, Paul A. and Peter Temin (1976) 'Slavery: the progressive institution?', pp. 165–230 in Paul A. David, Hebert G. Gutman, Richard Sutch et al. (eds), *Reckoning With Slavery: A Critical Study in the Quantitative History of American Negro Slavery.* New York: Oxford University Press.

Davids, Karel (1995) 'Shifts of technological leadership in early modern Europe', pp. 338–66 in Karel Davids and Jan Lucassen (eds), *A Miracle Mirrored: The Dutch Republic in European Perspective.* Cambridge/New York: Cambridge University Press.

Davidson, Neil (2000) *The Origin of Scottish Nationhood.* London: Pluto Press.

Davidson, Neil (2003) *Discovering the Scottish Revolution 1792–1746.* London: Pluto Press.

Davidson, Neil (2004a) 'Asiatic, tributary or absolutist: a comment on Chris Harman's "The rise of capitalism"', *International Socialism*, November. <www.isj.org.uk/?s=resources> (accessed July 1, 2009).

Davidson, Neil (2004b), 'The Scottish path to capitalist agriculture 1: From the crisis of feudalism to the origins of agrarian transformation (1688–1746)', *Journal of Agrarian Change*, Vol. 4, No. 3, pp. 227–68.

Davidson, Neil (2004c) 'The Scottish path to capitalist agriculture 2: The capitalist offensive (1747–1815)', *Journal of Agrarian Change*, Vol. 4, No. 4, pp. 411–60.

Davidson, Neil (2005a) 'How revolutionary were the bourgeois revolutions?' *Historical Materialism*, Vol. 13, No. 3, pp. 3–33.

Davidson, Neil (2005b) 'The Scottish path to capitalist agriculture 3: The Enlightenment as the theory and practice of improvement', *Journal of Agrarian Change*, Vol. 5, No. 1, pp. 1–72.

Davidson, Neil (2009) 'Putting the nation back into "the international"', *Cambridge Review of International Affairs*, Vol. 22, No. 1, pp. 9–28.

De Angelis, Massimo (2001) 'Marx and primitive accumulation: the continuous character of capital's enclosure', *The Commoner*, Vol. 2, No. 2, pp. 1–22. <www.commoner.org.uk/02deangelis.pdf> (accessed June 1, 2009).

De Vries, Jan (1997) *The First Modern Economy: Success, Failure and Perseverance of the Dutch Economy, 1500–1815.* Cambridge: Cambridge University Press.

De Vries, Jan (2001) 'The transition to capitalism in a land without feudalism', pp. 67–84 in Peter Hoppenbrouwers and Jan Luiten van Zanden (eds), *Peasants into Farmers? The Transformation of Rural Economy and Society in the Low Countries (Middle Ages–19th century) in Light of the Brenner Debate.* Turnhout, Belgium: Brepols.

De Vries, Jan (2008) *The Industrious Revolution: Consumer Behaviour and the Household Economy, 1650 to the Present.* Cambridge/New York: Cambridge University Press.

Dewald, Jonathan, Geoffrey Parker et al. (2008) 'AHR forum: the general crisis of the seventeenth century revisited', *American Historical Review*, Vol. 113, No. 4, pp. 1029–99.

Dirlik, Arif (1985) 'The universalisation of a concept', *Journal of Peasant Studies*, Vol. 12, No. 2–3, pp.197–227.

Dirlik, Arif (2000) 'Is there history after eurocentrism? Globalism, post-colonialism, and the disavowal of history', pp. 25–47 in Arif Dirlik, Vinay Bahl and Peter Gran (eds), *History After the Three Worlds: Post-Eurocentric Historiographies*. London/Boulder, Colo./New York: Rowman & Littlefield.

Dirlik, Arif (2005) *Marxism in the Chinese Revolution*. London/Boulder, Colo./New York: Rowman & Littlefield.

Dobb, Maurice (1946/1963) *Studies in the Development of Capitalism*. New York: International Publishers/London: Routledge & Kegan Paul.

Dobb, Maurice and Paul M. Sweezy (eds) (1977) *Du féodalisme au capitalisme: problèmes de la transition*, trans. Florence Gauthier and Françoise Murray, 2 vols. Paris: Maspero.

Dorigny, Marcel (1988) 'La formation de la pensée économique de Sieyès d'après ses manuscrits (1770–1789)', *Annales historiques de la Révolution française*, Vol. 271, No. 1, pp. 17–34.

Dorigny, Marcel (1989) 'Les courants du libéralisme français à la fin de l'Ancien Régime et aux débuts de la Révolution: Quesnay ou Smith?' pp. 26–36 in Maxine Berg (ed.), *Französiche Revolution und Politische Ökonomie*. Trier, Germany: Karl Marx Haus.

Dorpalen, Andreas (1985) *German History in Marxist Perspective: The East German Approach*. Detroit, Mich.: Wayne State University Press.

Duchesne, Ricardo (2003) 'Between Sinocentrism and Eurocentrism: debating Andre Gunder Frank's *ReOrient: Global Economy in the Asian Age*', *Science and Society*, Vol. 65, No. 4, pp. 428–63.

Dyer, Christopher, Peter Coss and Chris Wickham (eds) (2007) 'Rodney Hilton's Middle Ages: an exploration of historical themes', *Past and Present*, Vol. 195, Supplement No. 2.

Eley, Geoff and Keith Nierd (2007) *The Future of Class in History: What's Left of the Social*. Ann Arbor, Mich.: University of Michigan Press.

Elliot, J. H. (2002) *Imperial Spain 1469–1716*. London/New York: Penguin.

Elvin, Mark (2008) 'The historian as haruspex', *New Left Review*, Vol. 52, pp. 83–109.

Emigh, Rebecca Jean (2003) 'Economic interests and sectoral relations: the undevelopment of capitalism in fifteenth-century Tuscany', *American Journal of Sociology*, Vol. 108, No. 5, pp. 1075–112.

Engelber, Ernst and Günter Vogler (1976) 'The Peasant War in Germany –125 years later', pp. 103–16 in Janos Bak (ed.), *The German Peasant War of 1525*. London: Frank Cass.

Engels, Friedrich (1844) *The Condition of the Working Class in England*, pp. 295–661, Vol. 4 in *Marx and Engels, Collected Works*.

Engels, Friedrich (1850) 'The Peasant War in Germany', in Marx and Engels, pp. 397–482, Vol. 10 in *Marx and Engels, Collected Works*, trans. Richard Dixon et al. London: Lawrence & Wishart/ New York: International Publishers/Moscow: Progress Books.

Engels, Friedrich (1859) 'Review of Karl Marx, *A Contibution to the Critique of Political Economy*', *Das Volk*, April. Marxist Internet Archive, <www.marxistsfr.org/archive/marx/works/1859/critique-pol-economy/appx2.htm> (accessed June 1, 2009).

Epstein, S. R. (2007) 'Rodney Hilton, Marxism and the transition from feudalism to capitalism', *Past and Present*, Vol. 95, Suppl. 2, pp. 248–69.

Findlay, Ronald and Kevin H. O'Rourke (2007) *Power and Plenty: Trade, War, and the World Economy in the Second Millennium*. Princeton, N.J./Woodstock, UK: Princeton University Press.

Fine, Ben and Ellen Leopold (1990) 'Consumerism and the Industrial Revolution', *Social History*, Vol. 15, No. 1, pp. 151–79.

Fogel, Robert William and Stanley L. Engerman (1974) *Time on the Cross: The Economics of American Negro Slavery*. New York: Little, Brown.

Foster, John Bellamy (2008) 'Sweezy in perspective', *Monthly Review*, Vol. 60, No. 1, pp. 45–9.

Frank, Andre Gunder (1998) *Re-Orient: Global Economy in the Asian Age*. Berkeley, Calif.: University of California Press.

Frank, Andre Gunder (1992) 'Fourteen ninety-two again', *Political Geography*, Vol. 11, No. 4, pp. 386–93.

Frank, Andre Gunder and Barry K. Gills (eds) (1993) *The World System: Five Hundred Years or Five Thousand?* London: Routledge.

Frank, Christopher (2010) *Master and Servant Law: Chartists, Trade Unions, Radical Lawyers and the Magistracy in England, 1840–1865*. Farnham, Surrey/Burlington, Vt: Ashgate.

Freudenthal, Gideon (2005) 'The Hessen–Grossman thesis. An attempt at rehabilitation', *Perspectives on Science*, Vol. 13, No. 2, pp. 166–93.

Friesen, Abraham (1974) *Reformation and Utopia: The Marxist Interpretation of the Reformation and its Antecedents*. Wiesbaden, Germany: F. Steiner.

Furniss, Edgar (1920) *The Position of the Laborer in a System of Nationalism: A Study of the Labor Theories of the Later English Mercantilists*. Boston, Mass./New York: Houghton Mifflin.

Gallagher, John and Ronald Robinson (1953) 'The imperialism of free trade', *Economic History Review*, New Series, Vol. 6, No. 1, pp. 1–15.

Galloway, James (2000) 'One market or many? London and the grain trade of England', pp. 23–42 in James Galloway (ed.), *Trade, Urban Integration and Market Integration c.1300–1600*. Centre for Metropolitan History Working Papers Series No. 3.

Gaskell, Peter (1833/1972) *The Manufacturing Population of England*. London: Baldwin & Cradock/New York: Arno Press.

Gehrke, Christian and Heinz D. Kurz (1995) 'Marx on physiocracy', *European Journal of the History of Economic Thought*, Vol. 2, No. 1, pp. 53–90.

Gentles, I. J. (2007) *The English Revolution and the War in the Three Kingdoms, 1638–1652*. Harlow, UK/New York: Pearson Longman.

Goldthwaite, Richard (2009) *The Economy of Renaissance Florence*. Baltimore, Md.: Johns Hopkins University Press.

Goody, Jack (2005) 'The labyrinth of kinship', *New Left Review*, Vol. 36, pp. 127–38.

Goody, Jack (2006) *The Theft of History*. Cambridge/New York: Cambridge University Press.

Graslin, Jean-Joseph-Louis (1767/1911) *Essai analytique sur la richesse et sur l'impôt*, ed. A. Dubois. Paris: P. Geuthner.

Grassby, Richard (1970) 'English merchant capitalism in the late seventeenth century: the composition of business fortunes', *Past and Present*, Vol. 46, No. 1, pp. 87–107.

Guicheteau, Samuel (2008) *Révolution des ouvriers nantais: Mutation économique, identité sociale et dynamique révolutionnaire (1740–1815)*. Rennes, France: Presse de l'université de Rennes.

Habakkuk, H. J. (1968) 'Economic functions of English landowners in the seventeenth and eighteenth centuries', pp. 24–62 in W. E. Minchinton (ed.), *Essays in Agrarian History*. Newton Abbot: David & Charles.

Habib, Irfan (1985) 'Classifying pre-colonial India', *Journal of Peasant Studies*, Vol. 12, No. 2–3, pp. 44–53.

Habib, Irfan (2006) 'Introduction: Marx's perception of India', pp. xix–liv in Iqbal Husain (ed.), *Karl Marx on India*. New Delhi: Tulika Books.

Hammond, J.L.(1930) 'The Industrial Revolution and discontent', *Economic History Review*, Vol. a2, No. 2, pp. 215–28.

Harman, Chris (1998) *Marxism and History: Two Essays*. London: Bookmarks.

Harman, Chris (1999, 2008) *A People's History of the World*. London: Bookmarks, Verso.

Harman, Chris (2004) 'The rise of capitalism', *International Socialism*, Vol. 102. <www.isj.org.uk/?id=21> (accessed June 1, 2009).

Harman, Chris (2006) 'Origins of capitalism', *International Socialism*, Vol. 111. <www.isj.org.uk/index.php4?id=219&issue=111> (accessed June 2, 2009).

Harman, Chris (2008) 'An age of transition? Economy and society in England in the later Middle Ages', *Historical Materialism*, Vol. 16, No. 1, pp. 185–99.

Hartwell, R. M. (1961) 'The rising standard of living in England, 1800–1850', *Economic History Review*, New Series, Vol. 13, No. 3, pp. 397–416.

Harvey, David (2003) *The New Imperialism*. Oxford: Oxford University Press.

Harvey, David (2009) *Cosmopolitanism and the Geographies of Freedom*. New York: Columbia University Press.

Heckscher, Eli F. (1935) *Mercantilism,* 2 vols. London: Allen & Unwin.

Held, Wieland (1988) *Zwischen Marktplatz und Anger: Stadt-Land Beziehungen im 16. Jahrhundert in Thüringen*. Weimar, Germany: Herman Böhlau Nachfolger.

Heller, Henry (1985) 'The transition debate in historical perspective', *Science and Society*, Vol. 49, No. 2, pp. 208–15.

Heller, Henry (1991) *Iron and Blood: Civil Wars in Sixteenth Century France*. Montreal/Kingston: McGill-Queens University Press.

Heller, Henry (1996) *Labour, Science and Technology in France 1500–1620*. Cambridge: Cambridge University Press.

Heller, Henry (2003) *Anti-Italianism in Sixteenth Century France*. Toronto: University of Toronto Press.

Heller, Henry (2006) *The Bourgeois Revolution in France 1789–1815*. New York: Berghahn.

Heller, Henry (2009) 'The longue durée of the French bourgeoisie', *Historical Materialism*, Vol. 17, No. 1, pp. 31–59.

Hessen, Boris and Henryk Grossman (2009) *The Social and Economic Roots of the Scientific Revolution: Texts*, ed. Freudenthal and Peter McLaughlin. Dordrecht, Netherlands: Springer.

Hilaire-Perez, Liliane (2007) 'Technology as a public culture in the eighteenth century: the artisan's legacy', *History of Science*, Vol. 45, No. 2, pp. 135–53.

Hill, Christopher (1967) *Reformation to Industrial Revolution: A Social and Economic History of Britain, 1530–1780*. London: Weidenfeld & Nicholson.

Hill, Christopher (1980) 'A bourgeois revolution?', pp. 109–39 in J. G. A. Pocock (ed.), *Three British Revolutions: 1641, 1688, 1776*. Princeton, N.J.: Princeton University Press.

Hill, Christopher (1986) 'Review: *A New Kind of Clergy: Ideology and the Experimental Method*', *Social Studies of Science*, Vol. 16, No. 4, pp. 726–35.

Hilton, Rodney Howard (ed.) (1976a) *The Transition from Feudalism to Capitalism*. London: New Left Books.

Hilton, Rodney Howard (1976b) 'A comment', pp. 109–111 in R. H. Hilton (ed.), *The Transition from Feudalism to Capitalism*. London: New Left Books.

Hilton, Rodney Howard (1976c) 'Capitalism – what's in a name?', pp. 145–58 in R. H. Hilton (ed.), *The Transition from Feudalism to Capitalism*. London: New Left Books.

Hilton, Rodney Howard (1984) 'Feudalism in Europe: problems for historical materialists', *New Left Review*, Vol. 147, pp. 84–93.

Hilton, Rodney Howard (1985) 'A crisis of feudalism', in Aston and Philpin (eds), *The Brenner Debate*, pp. 119–37.

Howbsbawm, Eric C. (1957), 'The British standard of living 1790–1850' *Economic History Review*, New Series, Vol. 10, No. 1, pp. 46–68.

Hobsbawm, Eric C. (1965) 'The crisis of the seventeenth century', pp. 5–58 in Trevor Aston (ed.), *Crisis in Europe 1560–1660: Essays from Past and Present*. London: Routledge & Kegan Paul.

Hobsbawm, Eric C. (1969) *Industry and Empire: From 1750 to the Present Day: The Penguin Economic History of Britain*, Vol. 3. Harmondsworth, UK/New York: Penguin.

Hobsbawm, Eric C. (1976) 'From feudalism to capitalism', in R. H. Hilton (ed.), *The Transition from Feudalism to Capitalism*. London: New Left Books.

Hobsbawm, Eric C. (1980) 'Scottish reformers of the eighteenth century and capitalist agriculture', pp. 3–29 in Eric C. Hobsbawm (ed.), *Peasants in History*. Calcutta: Oxford University Press.

Hobson, John M. (2004) *The Eastern Origins of Western Civliisation*. Cambridge/New York: Cambridge University Press.

Holton, R. J. (1985) *The Transition from Feudalism to Capitalism*. New York: St. Martin's Press.

Hopper, Andrew (2007) *'Black Tom': Sir Thomas Fairfax and the English Revolution*. Manchester: Manchester University Press.

Hoston, Germaine A. (1986) *Marxism and the Crisis of Development in Prewar Japan*. Berkeley, Calif.: University of California Press.

Houghton, Walter E. (1941) 'The history of trades: its relation to seventeenth-century thought: as seen in Bacon, Petty, Evelyn, and Boyle', *Journal of the History of Ideas*, Vol. 2, No. 1, pp. 33–60.

Hudson, Pat (1981) 'Proto-industrialization: the case of the West Riding wool textile industry in the 18th and early 19th centuries', *History Workshop*, Vol. 12, No. 1, pp. 34–61.

Hudson, Pat (1992) *The Industrial Revolution*. London: Edward Arnold.

Inikori, Joseph E. (2002) *Africans and the Industrial Revolution in England: A Study in International Trade and Economic Development*. Cambridge/New York: Cambridge University Press.

Israel, Jonathan Irvine (1989) *Dutch Primacy in World Trade, 1585–1740*. Oxford: Clarendon/New York: Oxford University Press.

Jacob, Margaret (1997) *Scientific Culture and the Making of the Industrial West*. Oxford, New York: Oxford University Press.

Jacob, Margaret (2007) 'Mechanical science on the factory floor: the early Industrial Revolution in Leeds', *History of Science*, Vol. 45, No. 2, pp. 197–221.

Jameson, Frederic (2008) 'Marxism and historicism', pp. 451–82 in *The Ideologies of Theory*. London/New York: Verso.

Jani, Pranav (2002) 'Karl Marx, Eurocentrism and the 1857 revolt in British India', pp. 81–100 in Crystal Bartolovich and Neil Lazarus (eds), *Marxism, Modernity and Postcolonial Studies*. Cambridge/New York: Cambridge University Press.

Jones, Eric Lionel (1988) *Growth Recurring: Economic Change in World History*. Oxford: Clarendon Press, New York: Oxford University Press.

Kamen, Henry (1971) *The Iron Century: Social Change in Europe, 1550–1660*. New York: Praeger.

Kerridge, Eric (1953) 'The movement of rent', *Economic History Review*, New Series, Vol. 6, No. 1, pp. 16–34.

Keynes, John Maynard (1936) *The General Theory of Employment, Interest and Money*. London: Macmillan.

Kiernan, Bob (2007) *Blood and Soil: A World History of Genocide and Extermination from Sparta to Darfur*. New Haven, Conn.: Yale University Press.

King, Gregory (1936) *Two Tracts: (a) Natural and Political Observations and Conclusions upon the State and Condition of England; (b) Of the Naval Trade of England and the National Profit then Arising Thereby*, ed. George E. Barnett. Baltimore, Md.: Johns Hopkins University Press.

Komatu, Y. (1961) 'The study of economic history in Japan', *Economic History Review*, New Series, Vol. 14, No. 1, pp. 115–21.

Krantz, Frederick and Paul M. Hohenberg (eds) (1975) *Failed Transitions to Modern Industrial Society: Renaissance Italy and Seventeenth Century Holland: Proceedings of the First International Colloquium, April 18–20, 1974*. Montreal: Interuniversity Centre for European Studies.

Kriedte, Peter, Jürgen Schlumbohm and Hans Medick (1981) *Industrialization Before Industrialization*. Cambridge/New York: Cambridge University Press.

Laclau, Ernesto (1971) 'Feudalism and capitalism in Latin America', *New Left Review*, Vol. 67, pp. 19–38.

Ladejinsky, Wolf (1959) 'Agrarian revolution in Japan', *Foreign Affairs*, Vol. 38, No. 1 (October), pp. 95–109.

Laube, Adolf, Max Steinmetz and Günter Vogler (1974) *Illustrierte Geschichte der deutschen frühbürgerlichen Revolution*. Berlin: Dietz.

Lazarus, Neil (2002) 'The fetish of "the West" in post-colonial theory', pp. 43–65 in Neil Lazarus and Crystal Bartolovitch (eds), *Marxism, Modernity and Postcolonial Studies*. Cambridge/New York: Cambridge University Press.

Lazarus, Neil and Rashmi Varma (2008) 'Marxism and postcolonial studies', pp. 309–31 in Jacques Bidet and Stathis Kouvelakis (eds), *Critical Companion to Contemporary Marxism*. Boston, Mass./Leiden, Netherlands: Brill.

Le Roy Ladurie, Emmanuel (1989) *Carnival in Romans*, trans. Mary Feeney. New York: G. Brazillier.

Lebowitz, Michael A. (2009) *Following Marx: Method, Critique and Crisis*. London, Boston: Brill.

Lemarchand, Guy (2008) *L'économie en France de 1770 à 1830: de la crise de l'Ancien Régime à la révolution industrielle*. Paris: A. Michel.

Lenin, V. I. (1964a) *The Development of Capitalism in Russia*. Collected Works, Vol. 3. Moscow: Progress.

Lenin, V. I. (1964b) *The Agrarian Programme of Social–Democracy in the First Russian Revolution, 1905–1907*. Collected Works, Vol. 13. Moscow: Progress.

Léon, Pierre (1974) 'Structure du commerce extérieur et évolution industrielle de la France à la fin du XVIIIe siècle', pp. 407–32 in F. Braudel (ed.), *Conjoncture économique, structures sociales. Hommage à Ernest Labrousse*. Paris: PUF.

Levine, David and Keith Wrightson (1991) *The Making of an Industrial Society: Whickham 1560–1765*. Oxford: Clarendon.

Li, Minqi (2008) 'An age of transition: the United States, China, peak oil, and the demise of neo-liberalism', *Monthly Review*, Vol. 59, No. 4 (April), pp. 20–34.

Linebaugh, Peter (1991) *The London Hanged: Crime and Civil Society in the Eighteenth Century*. London: Penguin.

Linebaugh, Peter (2008) *The Magna Carta Manifesto: Liberties and Commons for All*. Berkeley, Calif.: University of California Press.

Lis, Catharina (1979) *Poverty and Capitalism in Pre-Industrial Europe*. Atlantic Highlands, N.J.: Humanities Press.

Lucassen, Jan (1995) 'Labour and early modern economic development', pp. 367–410 in Karel Davids and Jan Lucassen (eds), *A Miracle Mirrored*. Cambridge/New York: Cambridge University Press.

Lucassen, Jan (2001) 'Mobilization of labour in early modern Europe', pp. 161–73 in Maarten Prak (ed.), *Early Modern Capitalism: Economic and Social Change in Europe, 1400–1800*. London: Routledge.

Luxemburg, Rosa (2003) *The Accumulation of Capital.* London and New York: Routledge.

Mann, Susan A. and James A. Dickinson (1980) 'State and agriculture in two eras of American capitalism', pp. 283–325 in Frederick H. Buttel and Howard Newby (eds), *The Rural Sociology of the Advanced Societies: Critical Perspectives.* Montclair/Allanheld/Osmun/London: Croom Helm.

Manning, Brian (1991) *The English People and the English Revolution.* London: Bookmarks.

Manning, Brian (1996) *Aristocrats, Plebeians and Revolution in England 1640–1660.* London/Easthaven, Conn.: Pluto.

Manning, Brian (1999) 'The English Revolution: the decline and fall of revisionism', *Socialist History Journal,* Vol. 14, No. 1, pp. 40–53.

Manning, Brian (2003) *Revolution and Counter-Revolution in England, Ireland and Scotland 1658–60.* London/Sydney: Bookmarks.

Manning, Roger B. (1988) *Village Revolts: Social Protest and Popular Disturbances in England, 1509–1640.* Oxford: Clarendon Press/New York: Oxford University Press.

Marglin, Stephen (1974) 'What do bosses do? The origins and functions of hierarchy in capitalist production. Part I', *Review of Radical Economics,* Vol. 6, No. 2, pp. 60–112.

Marx, Karl (1973) *Grundrisse: Foundations of the Critique of Political Economy,* trans. Martin Nicolaus. Harmondsworth, U.K., Baltimore, Md.: Penguin.

Marx, Karl (1977–81) *Capital,* 3 vols, trans. Ben Fowkes. New York: Vintage.

Marx, Karl (2006) *Karl Marx on India,* ed. Iqbal Husain. New Delhi: Tulika Books.

Marx, Karl and Friedrich Engels (1972) *Ireland and the Irish Question: A Collection of Writings.* New York: International Publishers.

Marx, Karl and Friedrich Engels (1975–) *Collected Works,* trans. Richard Dixon et al. London: Lawrence & Wishart/New York: International Publishers/Moscow: Progress Books.

Mayer, Anna K. (2004) 'Setting up a discipline II: British history of science and the "end of ideology", 1931–1948', *Studies in History and Philosophy of Science,* Vol. 35, No. 1, pp. 41–72.

Mayer, Arno J. (1981) *The Persistence of the Old Regime: Europe to the Great War.* New York: Pantheon.

McPhee, Peter (1989) 'The French Revolution, peasants and capitalism', *American Historical Review,* Vol. 94, No. 5, pp. 1265–80.

McPhee, Peter (2008) 'Revolution or Jacquerie? Rethinking peasant insurrection in 1789', *Socialist History,* Vol. 33, No. 1, pp. 46–67.

Meek, Ronald L. (1975) *Studies in the Labor Theory of Value,* 2nd edn. New York: Monthly Review Press.

Mendels, Franklin (1972) 'Proto-industrialization: the first phase of the industrialization process', *Journal of Economic History,* Vol. 32, No. 1, pp. 241–61.

Mendoza, Jaime García (1998) 'Dos innovaciones al beneficio de plate por azogue en el siglo XVI', *Estudios de Historia Novohispana*, Vol. 19, No. 2, pp. 133–143.

Merrill, John (1993) *The Nature of the English Revolution*. London: Longman.

Merrington, John (1975), 'Town and country in the transition to capitalism', *New Left Review*, Vol. 93, pp. 71–92. Repr. as pp. 171–95 in R. H. Hilton (ed.), *The Transition from Feudalism to Capitalism*. London: New Left Books (1976).

Mészáros, István (1995) *Beyond Capital: Toward a Theory of Transition*. New York: Monthly Review Press.

Mielant, Edward (2007) *The Origins of Capitalism and the 'Rise of the West'*. Philadelphia, Pa.: Temple University Press.

Minard, Philippe (1998) *La fortune du colbertisme. État et industrie dans la France des Lumières*. Paris: Fayard.

Minchinton, W. E. (ed.) (1972) *Wage Regulation in Pre-Industrial England*. Newton Abbot: David & Charles.

Mokyr, Joel (1976) *Industrialization in the Low Countries, 1795–1850*. New Haven, Conn.: Yale University Press.

Mokyr, Joel (ed.) (2003) *Oxford Encyclopedia of Economic History*, 5 vols. New York/London: Oxford University Press.

Moore, Barrington Jr. (1966) *Social Origins of Dictatorship and Democracy: Lord and Peasant in the Making of the Modern World*. Boston, Mass.: Beacon Press.

Morgan, Kenneth (2002) 'Mercantilism and the British Empire', pp. 165–92 in Patrick K. O'Brien and Donald Winch (eds), *The Political Economy of British Historical Experience 1688–1914*. Oxford: Oxford University Press.

Moriceau, Jean-Marc (1989) 'Les gros fermiers en 1789: vice-rois de la plain de France', pp. 35–63 in *Les paysans et la révolution en pays de France: actes du Colloque de Tremblay-lès-Gonesse: 15–16 octobre 1988*. Paris: L'Association Tremblay-lès-Gonesse.

Moriceau, Jean-Marc (1993) 'Le laboureur et ses enfants. Formation professionnelle et mobilité sociale en Ile-de-France (second moitié du XVIe siècle)', *Revue d'histoire moderne et contemporaine*, Vol. 50, No. 2, pp. 353–86.

Moriceau, Jean-Marc (1994a) *Les fermiers de l'Ile-de-France: l'ascension d'un patronat agricole, XVe–XVIIIe siècle*. Paris: Fayard.

Moriceau, Jean-Marc (1994b) 'Au rendez–vous de la « revolution agricole » dans la France du XVIIIe siècle: à propos des regions de grande culture', *Annales: Economies, Sociétés*, Vol. 49, No. 1, pp. 27–63.

Moriceau, Jean-Marc (2002) *Terres mouvantes: les campagnes françaises du féodalisme à la mondialisation: XIIe–XIXe siècle*. Paris: Fayard.

Morilhat, Claude (1988), *La prise de conscience du capitalisme: économie et philosophie chez Turgot*. Paris: Méridiens Klincksieck.

Musto, Marcello (2008) 'History, production and method in the 1857 "Introduction"', pp. 3–32 in Marcello Musto (ed.), *Karl Marx's Grundrisse: Foundations of the Critique of Political Economy 159 Years Later*. London/New York: Routledge.

Nef, J. U. (1932) *The Rise of the British Coal Industry*, 2 vols. London: Routledge.

Nesson, J. M. (1993) *Commoners, Common Right, Enclosures and Social Change in England, 1700–1820*. Cambridge/New York: Cambridge University Press.

North, Douglas and Robert Paul Thomas (1973) *The Rise of the Western World: A New Economic History*. Cambridge/New York: Cambridge University Press.

O'Brien, Patrick K. (1991) 'The foundations of European industrialization: from the perspective of the world', *Journal of Historical Sociology*, Vol. 4, No. 3, pp. 288–317.

O'Brien, Patrick K. (1997) 'The Britishness of the first Industrial Revolution and the British contribution to the industrialization of "follower countries" on the mainland, 1756–1914', *Diplomacy and Statecraft*, Vol. 8, No. 3, pp. 48–67.

O'Brien, Patrick K. (1999) 'Imperialism and the rise and decline of the British economy, 1688–1999', *New Left Review*, Vol. 239, pp. 48–80.

O'Brien, Patrick K. (2000) 'The reconstruction, rehabilitation and reconfiguration of the British Industrial Revolution as a conjuncture in global history', *Itinerario*, Vol. 24, No. 3–4, pp. 117–32.

O'Brien, Patrick K. (2007) 'Global economic history as the accumulation of capital through a process of combined and uneven development', *Historical Materialism*, Vol. 15, No. 1, pp. 75–108.

O'Brien, Patrick K. and Stanley L. Engerman (1994) 'Exports and the growth of the British economy from the Glorious Revolution to the Peace of Amiens', pp. 177–209 in Barbara L. Solow (ed.), *Slavery and the Rise of the Atlantic System*. Cambridge/New York: Cambridge University Press.

O'Brien, Patrick K. and D. Heath (1994) 'English and French landowners 1688–1789', pp. 24–62 in F. M. L. Thompson (ed.) *Landowners, Capitalists and Entrepreneurs: Essays for Sir John Habakkuk*. Oxford: Clarendon Press.

O'Brien, Patrick K. and Caglar Keyder (1978) *Economic Growth in Britain and France 1780–1914: Two Paths to the Twentieth Century*. London/Boston, Mass.: G. Allen & Unwin.

O'Brien, Patrick K. and Peter Mathias (1976) 'Taxation in Britain and France 1715–1810: a comparison of the social and economic consequences of taxes collected for the central governments', *Journal of Economic History*, Vol. 5, No. 3, pp. 601–50.

Ochs, Kathleen H. (1985) 'The Royal Society of London's History of Trades Programme: an early episode in applied science', *Notes and Records of the Royal Society of London*, Vol. 39, No. 2, pp. 129–58.

Ormrod, David (2003) *The Rise of Commercial Empires: England and the Netherlands in the Age of Mercantilism, 1650–1770*. Cambridge/New York: Cambridge University Press.

Overton, Mark (1996) *Agricultural Revolution in England: The Transformation of the Agrarian Economy 1500–1850*. Cambridge/New York: Cambridge University Press.

Parker, David (2009) *Ideology, Absolutism and the English Revolution: Debates of the British Communist Historians, 1940–1956*. London: Lawrence & Wishart.

Patniak, Utsa (2006) 'The free lunch: transfers from tropical countries and their role in capital formation in Britain during the Industrial Revolution', pp. 30–70 in K. S. Jomo (ed.), *Globalization Under Hegemony: The Changing World Economy*. Oxford: Oxford University Press.

Perelman, Michael (2000) *The Invention of Capitalism: Classical Political Economy and the Secret History of Primitive Accumulation*. Durham, N.C. and London: Duke University Press.

Perez, Joseph (1981) *La revolucion de los communidades*, 4th edn. Madrid: Siglo XX de Espana.

Petty, William (1899/1963) *Political Arithmetik*, pp. 233–313, Vol. 1 in *The Writings of William Petty*, 2 vols, ed. C. H. Hull. Cambridge: Cambridge University Press/New York: Augustus M. Kelley.

Pincus, Steven (2000) 'The making of a great power? Universal monarchy, political economy, and the transformation of English political culture', *The European Legacy*, Vol. 5, No. 4, pp. 531–45.

Pincus, Steven (2005) 'Whigs, political economy and the revolution of 1688–89', pp. 62–85 in David Womersley (ed.), *Cultures of Whiggism*. Newark, Del.: University of Delaware Press.

Pomeranz, Keith (2000) *The Great Divergence: China, Europe, and the Making of the Modern World Economy*. Princeton, N.J.: Princeton University Press.

Postone, Moishe (2008) 'Rethinking *Capital* in the light of the *Grundrisse*', pp. 120–35 in Marcello Musto (ed.), *Karl Marx's Grundrisse: Foundations of the Critique of Political Economy 159 Years Later*. London/New York: Routledge.

Prashad, Vijay (2007) *The Darker Nations: A People's History of the Third World*. New York: New Press.

Price, Richard (1984) 'Conflict and co-operation: a reply to Patrick Joyce', *Social History*, Vol. 9, No. 2, pp. 217–24.

Price, Richard (1999) *British Society: 1680–1880: Dynamism, Containment and Change*. Cambridge/New York: Cambridge University Press.

Procacci, Giuliano (1975) 'Italy: commentary', pp. 27–8 in Frederick Krantz and Paul M. Hohenberg (eds), *Failed Transitions to Modern Industrial Society: Renaissance Italy and Seventeenth Century Holland: Proceedings of the First International Colloquium, April 18–20, 1974*. Montreal: Interuniversity Centre for European Studies.

Reisch, George A. (2005) *How the Cold War Transformed Philosophy of Science: To the Icy Slopes of Logic*. Cambridge/New York: Cambridge University Press.

Resende, Hernâni (1976) *Socialisme utopique et question agraire dans la transition du féodalisme au capitalisme*. Paris: Centre d'études et de recherches marxistes.

Riello, Giorgio (2010) 'Asian knowledge and the development of calico printing in Europe in the seventeenth and eighteenth centuries', *Journal of Global History*, Vol. 5, No. 1, pp. 1–28.

Robinson, Cedric J. (1987) 'Capitalism, slavery and bourgeois historiography', *History Workshop*, Vol. 23, No. 1, pp. 122–40.

Romano, Ruggerio (1972–76) 'La Storia Economica dal secolo XIV al Settecento', pp. 1811–1931, Vol. 2, Part 2, in Ruggerio Romano and Corrado Vivanti (eds), *Storia d' Italia, Dall caduta dell'Impero romano al secolo XVIII*, 10 vols. Turin, Italy: Giulia Einaudi.

Samuel, Ralph (1977) 'Workshop of the world: steam power and hand technology in mid-Victorian Britain', *History Workshop Journal*, Vol. 3, No. 1, pp. 6–72.

Scott, Tom (2002) 'The German Peasants' War and the "crisis of feudalism": reflections on a neglected theme', *Journal of Early Modern History*, Vol. 6, No. 3, pp. 265–95.

Scott, Tom (2003) *Society and Economy in Germany 1300–1600*. London: Routledge.

Seccombe, Wally (1983) 'Marxism and demography', *New Left Review*, Vol. 137, pp. 22–47.

Sella, Domenico (1997) *Italy in the Seventeenth Century*. New York: Longmans.

Sen, Amartya (2008) 'Dobb, Maurice Herbert (1900–1976)', in *The New Palgrave Dictionary of Economics Online*, Palgrave Macmillan, <www.dictionaryofeconomics.com> (accessed June 11, 2008).

Sereni, Emilio (1997) *History of the Italian Agricultural Landscape,* trans. R. Burr Litchfield. Princeton, N.J.: Princeton University Press.

Sheridan, Richard B. (1987) 'Eric Williams and capitalism and slavery: a bibliographical and historiographical essay', pp. 317–45 in Barbara L. Solow and Stanley L. Engerman (eds), *British Capitalism and Caribbean Slavery: The Legacy of Eric Williams*. Cambridge/New York: Cambridge University Press.

Shovlin, John (2006) *The Political Economy of Virtue: Luxury, Patriotism and the Origins of the French Revolution*. Ithaca, N.Y. and London: Cornell University Press.

Shuzo, Teruoka (1989) 'Land reform and postwar Japanese capitalism', pp. 85–92 in T. Morris-Suzuki and T. Seiyama (eds), *Japanese Capitalism Since 1945: Critical Perspectives*. Armonk, N.Y./London: M. E. Sharpe.

Slack, Paul (1999) *From Reformation to Improvement: Public Welfare in Early Modern England*. Oxford: Clarendon Press/New York: Oxford University Press.

Slater, Eamonn and Terrence McDonough (2008) 'Marx on 19th century colonial Ireland: analyzing colonialism beyond dependency', NIRSA Working Papers, National University of Ireland, Maynooth, Ireland <http://eprints.nuim.ie/1151/1/cover36slater_V2.pdf> (accessed July 1, 2009).

Smith, Adam (1776, 1937) *The Wealth of Nations*. New York: Random House.

Smith, Neil (2006) 'The geography of uneven development', pp. 180–95 in Bill Dunn and Hugo Radice (eds), *100 Years of Permanent Revolution: Results and Prospects*. London/Ann Arbor, Mich.: Pluto Press.

Smith, Neil (2008) *Uneven Development: Nature, Capital and the Production of Space*. Athens, Ga./London: University of Georgia Press.

Smith, Tony (2006) *Globalisation: A Systematic Marxian Account*. Leiden, Netherlands/Boston, Mass.: Brill.

Solow, Barbara L. and Stanley L. Engerman (1987) 'Introduction', pp. 1–10 in Barbara L. Solow and Stanley L. Engerman (eds), *British Capitalism and Caribbean Slavery: The Legacy of Eric Williams*. Cambridge/New York: Cambridge University Press.

Ste Croix, Geoffrey E. M. de (1981) *The Class Struggle in the Ancient Greek World: From the Archaic Age to the Arab Conquests*. Ithaca, N.Y.: Cornell University Press.

Steinberg, Marc (1996) 'Culturally speaking: finding a commons between post-structuralism and the Thompsonian perspective', *Social History*, Vol. 21, No. 2, pp. 193–214.

Steinberg, Marc (2003) 'Capitalist development, labour process and the law', *American Journal of Sociology*, Vol. 109, No. 2, pp. 445–95.

Steinfeld, Robert J. (1991) *The Invention of Free Labor: The Employment Relation in English and American Law and Culture, 1350–1870*. Chapel Hill, N.C. and London: University of North Carolina Press.

Stewart, Larry and Paul Weindling (1995) 'Philosophical threads: natural philosophy and public experiment among the weavers of Spitalfields', *British Journal for the History of Science*, Vol. 28, No. 1, pp. 37–62.

Stone, Lawrence (1965) *The Crisis of the Aristocracy 1558–1641*. Oxford: Clarendon Press.

Stone, Lawrence (1985) 'The bourgeois revolution in seventeenth-century England revisited', *Past and Present*, Vol. 109, No. 1, pp. 44–54.

Sweezy, Paul M. (1938) *Monopoly and Competition in the English Coal Trade, 1550–1850*. Cambridge, Mass: Harvard University Press.

Sweezy, Paul M. et al. (1954) *The Transition from Feudalism to Capitalism: A Symposium* (articles by various writers from *Science and Society*). London: Fore.

Szreter, Simon R. S. and Graham Mooney (1998) 'Urbanisation, mortality and the standard of living debate: new estimates of the expectation of life at birth in nineteenth-century British cities', *Economic History Review*, Vol. 40, No. 1, pp. 84–112.

T'Hart, Marjolein, Pepijn Brandon and Thomas Goosens (2008) 'The commercialization of warfare as a strategy for hegemonial powers: the Dutch case compared', Second European Conference of World and Global History, Dresden, 3–5 July 2008 <www.unileipzig.de/~eniugh/congress/documents/paper%20marjolein%20t'hart.pdf> (accessed on July 1, 2009).

Tabak, Faruk (2008) *The Waning of the Mediterranean, 1550–1870: A Geohistorical Approach*. Baltimore, Md.: Johns Hopkins University Press.

Takahashi, Kohachiro (1976) 'A contribution to the discussion',p. 68–97 in R. H. Hilton (ed.), *The Transition from Feudalism to Capitalism*. London: New Left Books.

Takahashi, Kohachiro (1977) 'La place de la révolution de Meiji dans l'histoire agraire du Japon', pp. 23–79, Vol. 2 in M. Dobb and P. M. Sweezy (eds), *Du feodalisme au capitalisme: problèmes de la transition*, 2 vols. Paris: Maspero.

Tawney, R. H. (1926) *Religion and the Rise of Capitalism: A Historical Study*. London: J. Murray.

Taylor, Arthur J. (ed.) (1975) *The Standard of Living in Britain in the Industrial Revolution*. London: Methuen.

Teschke, Benno (2003) *The Myth of 1648: Class, Geopolitics and the Making of Modern International Relations*. London/New York: Verso.

Teschke, Benno (2005) 'Bourgeois revolution, state formation and the absence of the international', *Historical Materialism*, Vol. 13, No. 2, pp. 3–26.

Thomas, Peter D. (2009) *The Gramscian Moment: Philosophy, Hegemony and Marxism*. London/Boston: Brill.

Thompson, E. P. (1967) 'Time, work discipline and industrial capitalism', *Past and Present*, Vol. 38, No. 1, pp. 57–97.

Thompson, E. P. (1968) *The Making of the English Working Class*. Harmondsworth, UK: Penguin.

Thompson, E. P. (1971) 'The moral economy of the English crowd in the eighteenth century', *Past and Present*, Vol. 50, No. 1, pp. 76–136.

Thompson, E. P. (1978) *The Poverty of Theory and Other Essays*. London: Merlin Press.

Trotsky, Leon (1961) *History of the Russian Revolution*, trans. Max Eastman. Ann Arbor, Mich.: University of Michigan Press.

Trotsky, Leon (1972) 'For the internationalist perspective', in *Leon Trotsky Speaks*. New York: Pathfinder Press.

Tsuru, Shigeto (1993) *Japan's Capitalism: Creative Defeat and Beyond*. Cambridge/New York: Cambridge University Press.

Turgot, Anne-Robert-Jacques (1898) *Reflections on the Formation and Distribution of Riches*. London/New York: Macmillan.

Vaggi, Gianni (1985) 'The role of profits in physiocratic economics', *History of Political Economy*, Vol. 17, No. 3, pp. 367–84.

Van de Wee, Herman (1963) *The Growth of the Antwerp Market and the European Economy (Fourteenth–Sixteenth Centuries)*, 3 vols. The Hague, Netherlands: Nijhoff.

Van der Linden, Marcel (1997) 'Marx and Engels, Dutch Marxism and the "Model capitalist nation of the seventeenth century"', *Science and Society*, Vol. 61, No. 2, pp. 161–92.

Vercellone, Carlo (2007) 'From formal subsumption to general intellect: elements for a Marxist reading of the thesis of cognitive capitalism', *Historical Materialism*, Vol. 15, No. 1, pp. 13–36.

Viner, Jacob (1937) *Studies in the Theory of International Trade*. London/New York: Harpers.

Vogler, Günter (2008) 'Thüringens Wirtschaft und Sozialstruktur zur Bauernkriegszeit', pp. 43–64 in Günter Vogler (ed.), *Bauernkrieg zwischen Harz und Thüringer Wald*. Stuttgart, Germany: Franz Steiner.

Voth, Hans-Joachim (2004) 'Living standards and urban disamenities', pp. 268–94 in Roderick Floud and Paul Johnson (eds), *Cambridge Economic History of Modern Britain, Vol. 1: Industrialization, 1700–1860*. Cambridge/New York: Cambridge University Press.

Vovelle, Michel (1990) 'Reflections on the revisionist interpretation of the French Revolution', *French Historical Studies*, Vol. 16, No. 4, pp. 749–55.

Wallerstein, Immanuel (1974) *The Modern World-System, Vol. 1: Capitalist*

Agriculture and the Origins of the European World-Economy. New York: Academic Press.

Wallerstein, Immanuel (1979) 'The rise and future demise of the world capitalist system: concepts for comparative analysis', pp. 1–36 in *The Capitalist World-Economy: Essays.* Cambridge: Cambridge University Press/Paris: Maison des Sciences de l'Homme.

Wallerstein, Immanuel (1980) *The Modern World-System, Vol. 2: Mercantilism and the Consolidation of the European World-Economy.* New York: Academic Press.

Wallerstein, Immanuel (1999) 'Frank proves the European miracle', *Review*, Vol. 22, No. 3, pp. 355–72.

Wallerstein, Immanuel (2003) 'US weakness and the struggle for hegemony', *Monthly Review*, Vol. 55, No. 3, pp. 23–9.

Wallerstein, Immanuel (2004) *World Systems Analysis: An Introduction.* Durham, N.C.: Duke University Press.

Walter, John (1999) *Understanding Popular Violence in the English Revolution: The Colchester Plunderers.* Cambridge/New York: Cambridge University Press.

Webster, Charles (1975) *The Great Instauration: Science, Medicine and Reform: 1626–1660.* London: Duckworth.

Wen, Dale Jiajun (2009) 'The debate about land privatization and real democracy', *China Left Review*, Vol. 1, No. 19, <www.chinaleftreview.org> (accessed July 27, 2010).

Whatmore, Richard (2002) 'Adam Smith's role in the French Revolution', *Past and Present*, Vol. 17, No. 15, pp. 65–89.

Whittle, Jane (2000) *The Development of Agrarian Capitalism: Land and Labour in Norfolk 1440–1580.* Oxford: Oxford University Press.

Wickham, Chris (1985) 'The uniqueness of the East', *Journal of Peasant Studies*, Vol. 12, No. 2–3, pp. 166–96.

Wickham, Chris (2005) *Framing the Early Middle Ages: Europe and the Mediterranean.* Oxford, New York: Oxford University Press.

Wickham, Chris (2008) 'Productive forces and the economic logic of the feudal mode of production', *Historical Materialism*, Vol. 16, No. 2, pp. 3–22.

Williams, Eric Eustace (1944) *Capitalism and Slavery.* Chapel Hill, N.C.: University of North Carolina Press.

Williams, Raymond (1976) *Keywords: A Vocabulary of Culture and Society.* New York: Oxford University Press.

Wood, Andy (1999) *The Politics of Social Conflict: The Peak Country, 1520–1770.* Cambridge/New York: Cambridge University Press.

Wood, Ellen Meiksins (1995) *Democracy Against Capitalism: Renewing Historical Materialism.* Cambridge/New York: Cambridge University Press.

Wood, Ellen Meiksins (1999) *The Origin of Capitalism.* New York: Monthly Review Press.

Wood, Ellen Meiksins (2002a) *The Origin of Capitalism: A Longer View.* London/New York: Verso.

Wood, Ellen Meiksins (2002b) 'The question of market dependence', *Journal of Agrarian Change*, Vol. 2, No. 1, pp. 50–87.

Wood, Ellen Meiskins and John Bellamy Foster (eds) (1997) *In Defense of History: Marxism and the Postmodern Agenda*. New York: Monthly Review Press.

Wood, Neal (1984) *John Locke and Agrarian Capitalism*. Berkeley, Calif.: University of California Press.

Wrightson, Keith (1990) *English Society 1580–1680*. London: Routledge.

Wrightson, Keith (2000) *Earthly Necessities: Economic Lives in Early Modern Britain*. New Haven, Conn.: Yale University Press.

Young, Robert J. C. (2001) *Postcolonialism: An Historical Introduction*. Oxford/Malden, Mass.: Blackwells.

Zangheri, Renato (1968) 'Agricoltura e sviluppo del capitalismo. Problemi storiografici', *Studi Storici*, Vol. 9, No. 3–4, pp. 35–95.

Zangheri, Renato (1979) 'I rapporti storici tra progresso agricolo e svillupo economico in Italia', pp. 35–55 in E. L. Jones and Stuart J. Woolf (eds), *Agricoltura e svillupo economico: Gli aspetti storici*. Turin, Italy: Einaudi.

Zedong, Mao (1976) *Collected Works*, ed. Takeuchi Minoru, 10 vols. Hong Kong: Po Wen.

INDEX

Webb, Beatrice and Sidney 196
Weber, Max 14, 12
Webster, Charles 207
Williams, Eric Eustace 168–9, 172
Wittle, Jane 98
Wood, Andy 192, 203
Wood, Ellen 2, 18, 72, 100, 102,
    104, 110, 111, 114–15, 117,
    120–1, 123, 160, 164
working class 132, 133, 178, 179,
    190, 191–4, 249
world empire 81–2

world history 215–42
world systems theory 76, 77, 81–3,
    108, 169–70, 225
Wrightson, Keith 96, 203

Y
Yangtze 216, 229–33

Z
Zangheri, Renato 58
Zimmerman, William 62